'The Gospels and the rest of the New Testame[nt] ... [were not written] in a vacuum, but as part of the continuing stor[y] ... it had been expounded in the Old Testament. R[ead]... ...p...s who pay close attention to how their allusions to the Old Testament are expected to inform our understanding are reading as the authors intended and find rich rewards in a fuller understanding of each text. Nick Lunn has spent years doing that kind of careful reading and now shares his insightful observations with all who want to learn to do the same. Be prepared to have your understanding enriched and your own reading transformed!'
Roy E. Ciampa, S. Louis and Ann W. Armstrong Chair of Religion, Department of Biblical and Religious Studies, Samford University, Alabama

'Another brilliant work by a lucid and clear teacher of Scripture. Using his vast knowledge and skills in Hebrew and Greek and his many years of experience in meticulous reading and exegesis of both the Old and New Testaments in their original languages as a translation consultant, Nick Lunn opens before our eyes a completely new dimension of the meaning of the Gospels. Case after case and passage after passage, we see Christ shining from behind the same familiar passages in new and amazing ways. At a time when the discipline of biblical exegesis is freeing itself more and more from the limitations imposed on it by the old naturalist and historicist presuppositions often lurking beneath and behind the old grammatical-historical method, reading Lunn's book, *The Gospels through Old Testament Eyes*, is like enjoying a cool breeze of fresh air in a very hot summer.'
The Revd Dr Mehrdad Fatehi, Executive Director, Pars Theological Centre, London

'This book alerts us to new possibilities when it comes to understanding the meaning, significance and artistry of New Testament texts. Starting from the premise that the Bible has a unity that springs from the divine author's hand behind the human authors' hands, Nick Lunn investigates how indirect extended allusions to Old Testament texts are used in the New Testament not just as literary devices but with theological intent, especially the intent to establish Christological truths.

'Lunn seeks to uncover new and illuminating points of contact between the testaments. For example, connections are made between Mary and the ark of the covenant; Herod and Pharaoh; Zacchaeus and Rahab; Gethsemane and the Day of Atonement; the two thieves on the cross and the baker and cupbearer (Genesis 40). Lunn writes with clarity and conviction. He confidently appraises

the New Testament text, drawing on scholarly insight, showing respect for details such as literary design and linguistic choices. He hopes that his writing will be faith-building – and indeed this aim is reflected in the tone and emphases throughout. I was not convinced by every premise or conclusion, but I was stimulated by the journey . . . I am very glad I pushed beyond my own approach to the biblical text to listen to the voice of a different approach that opens up a new world of interpretative possibilities.'
Debra Reid, Director of Undergraduate Studies and Tutor in Old Testament, Spurgeon's College, London

'The Gospel narratives continue to exercise great power as the authoritative record of Jesus' life, works and words, his death, resurrection and ascension. Simply in the history they recount they remain life-transforming. And yet there also lurk depths within them which can be uncovered by the patient reader who recognizes that they are the climax of a grander story still – the story of God and his purposes from the dawn of time, whose earlier stages are told in the Old Testament.

'Nicholas Lunn is such a reader, and he helps us to dig behind familiar passages from the Gospels and discover a wealth of allusion to those earlier texts. A sense of the wonder and mystery of Jesus' nature as the human embodiment of the God of Israel is enhanced, as we see how these allusions illumine the events of his life with fresh theological meaning. Drawing on a wealth of scholarship from a wide range of Christian as well as Jewish sources, this fascinating study will also help us to appreciate the unity of Scripture as the gift of a single divine Author. Divided into concise, clearly written chapters focusing on Gospel episodes, it offers plentiful new insights for preachers and will enrich the devotion of Christian believers to their Lord.'
Stephen I. Wright, Vice Principal and Academic Director, Spurgeon's College, London

THE GOSPELS THROUGH OLD TESTAMENT EYES

THE GOSPELS THROUGH OLD TESTAMENT EYES

Exploring extended allusions

Nicholas P. Lunn

APOLLOS (an imprint of Inter-Varsity Press)
Studio 101, The Record Hall, 16–16A Baldwins Gardens, London, EC1N 7RJ, UK
Email: ivp@ivpbooks.com
Website: www.ivpbooks.com

Unless otherwise noted, Scripture quotations are the author's own translation.

First published 2023

British Library Cataloguing-in-Publication Data
A catalogue record for this book is available from the British Library.

ISBN: 978–1–78974–410–1
eBook ISBN: 978–1–78974–411–8

Set in Minion Pro 10.75/13.75pt
Typeset in Great Britain by CRB Associates, Potterhanworth, Lincolnshire
Printed in Great Britain by Ashford Colour Press Ltd, Gosport, Hampshire

Produced on paper from sustainable sources

*Inter-Varsity Press publishes Christian books that are true to the Bible and that communicate
the gospel, develop discipleship and strengthen the church for its mission in the world.*

*IVP originated within the Inter-Varsity Fellowship, now the Universities and Colleges Christian
Fellowship, a student movement connecting Christian Unions in universities and colleges throughout
Great Britain, and a member movement of the International Fellowship of Evangelical Students.
Website: www.uccf.org.uk. That historic association is maintained, and all senior IVP staff and
committee members subscribe to the UCCF Basis of Faith.*

Contents

List of abbreviations   ix

1 Introduction   1
2 Mary the mother of Christ   16
3 The decree of Caesar Augustus   24
4 The birth of Christ   30
5 The baby in a manger   36
6 The flight into Egypt   44
7 The baptism and temptation   51
8 The Sermon on the Mount   61
9 Calming the storm   67
10 The feeding of the multitude   72
11 Walking on the water   87
12 The Syro-Phoenician woman   97
13 The transfiguration   106
14 The parable of the rich fool   123
15 The woman taken in adultery   127
16 The conversion of Zacchaeus   140
17 Jesus comes to Jerusalem   144
18 The parable of the wicked tenants   151
19 The last supper   156
20 Gethsemane 1   161
21 Gethsemane 2   170
22 Peter's denials   184
23 The trial and crucifixion 1   189
24 The trial and crucifixion 2   205
25 The two thieves   211
26 Resurrection appearances in the synoptic Gospels   214
27 The burial and the empty tomb   229
28 Jesus appears to Mary   240

Contents

29 Jesus appears on the eighth day   247

30 Jesus appears by the Sea of Galilee   255

31 Conclusion   261

Bibliography   263

Scripture acknowledgments   275

Index of Scripture references   277

Abbreviations

AB	Anchor Bible
ASV	American Standard Version
AV	Authorized Version (King James Version)
BBR	*Bulletin for Biblical Research*
BECNT	Baker Exegetical Commentary on the New Testament
CBQ	*Catholic Biblical Quarterly*
CEB	Common English Bible
CEV	Contemporary English Version
CSB	Christian Standard Bible
ESV	English Standard Version
GNT	Good News Translation
HCSB	Holman Christian Standard Bible
HTR	*Harvard Theological Review*
ICC	International Critical Commentary
ISV	International Standard Version
JBL	*Journal of Biblical Literature*
JETS	*Journal of the Evangelical Theological Society*
JSNT	*Journal for the Study of the New Testament*
LNTS	Library of New Testament Studies
LXX	Septuagint (Greek Old Testament)
MT	Masoretic Text (Hebrew Old Testament)
NAC	New American Commentary
NASB	New American Standard Bible
NCV	New Century Version
NET	New English Translation
NICNT	New International Commentary on the New Testament
NICOT	New International Commentary on the Old Testament
NIGTC	New International Greek Testament Commentary
NIV	New International Version
NJB	New Jerusalem Bible
NJPS	New Jerusalem Publication Society (Tanakh)
NKJV	New King James Version

NLT	New Living Translation
NovT	*Novum Testamentum*
NRSV	New Revised Standard Version
NSBT	New Studies in Biblical Theology
NTL	New Testament Library
PNTC	Pillar New Testament Commentary
REB	Revised English Bible
WBC	Word Biblical Commentary
ZECNT	Zondervan Exegetical Commentary on the New Testament

1

Introduction

This is a book about the Gospels and their use of the Old Testament. Underpinning this whole study is a firm belief in the essential unity of the Bible, a unity that ultimately springs from the oneness of its prime author, namely God. Of course, human authors were inspired to compose the biblical documents, with the result that these writings include their own perceptions and sentiments, and bear the impression of their own characters. Yet overarching all this human compositional activity lies the divine mind, which can, and indeed sometimes does, transcend the ordinary mental abilities of human beings. Many readers, probably the large majority, will have no problem with such a view of Scripture. In fact some may respond with a loud 'Amen!' However, all might not agree, especially those holding the view promoted to a large extent by biblical studies departments within the contemporary academy, a view that gives greater emphasis to the human authorship of the biblical writings, even to the extent of diminishing the divine. I myself am obviously convinced that the approach adopted here, together with the interpretations resulting from its application to specific texts, is a legitimate way to read the Gospel accounts. But in view of the possible scepticism on the part of some, this introductory chapter will offer a description of the method adopted and some rationale for it. In keeping with the broader goals of this book, the discussion will be kept fairly accessible and concise. The chapter also contains important background information that might not be familiar to some readers.

The aims

To give a brief orientation to the contents at the very outset, it would be good to state two particular aims. First, it was not my intention to write an academic volume. The following chapters are directed primarily at those engaged in preaching, teaching and studying the word of God in a church context. The book is directed at pastors and lay people alike who simply wish to learn more about the Bible, and especially about Jesus and the Gospels. That does not mean to say that there is nothing in it that might be enlightening for the professional theologian or biblical scholar. I hope that these latter too might derive some benefit. Second, although the work is almost exclusively concerned with the way in which the New Testament makes use of the Old, it deals only with one specific manner in which this is done. This is not a general treatment of how the Gospels draw upon the earlier Hebrew Scriptures. I basically take a single literary technique, defined below, and apply it throughout the whole volume to various passages in Matthew, Mark, Luke and John. And my reason for doing this, as will soon become apparent, is the fact that in all the numerous and diverse studies of the use of the Old Testament in the New the particular technique I apply here is one that is largely overlooked, and perhaps in many cases not even acknowledged. It is this feature of the present work that sets it apart from a number of others that at first sight seem to deal with a similar area of biblical investigation.

The approach

Without doubt the writings of the New Testament direct their readers' attention to the ancient Scriptures of Israel on numerous occasions and in several different ways. The most obvious of these is through direct citation. One only has to start flipping through the pages of the New Testament for a matter of seconds before one's eyes alight upon a place where a Gospel-writer or apostle includes a text from the Law, the Prophets or other sacred books. These are often marked by some particular introductory formula, such as 'As it is written' (e.g. John 12:14) or 'As Isaiah foretold' (Rom. 9:29). Such quotations are frequently made even more conspicuous in modern versions through the practice of indenting the words being cited. There are also many instances of short citation, which is neither introduced nor indented (e.g. 1 Cor. 15:27; Gal. 3:11). Careful examination of such passages can be found in the relevant commentaries, and other volumes that deal more specifically with Old Testament quotations in the New.[1]

To look at such citations in the Gospels, whether full or partial, is not the purpose of this volume. Our intention is more refined. In the following chapters we shall only concern ourselves with the literary device of *allusion*. It is possible, and indeed common in much of literature, that a piece of writing may refer to an earlier work other than by quotation. The later document can also allude to what came before. Allusion is a universally recognized form of

---

[1] See especially G. K. Beale and D. A. Carson (eds.), *Commentary on the New Testament Use of the Old Testament* (Grand Rapids, MI: Baker Academic, 2007). See also the new series of commentaries on New Testament books *Through Old Testament Eyes*, published by Kregel.

establishing a connection between two texts, or what scholars refer to as 'intertextuality'. But it has to be said that there is some difference in the precise way in which the characteristics of allusion are understood. Here I will be using the term in a more restricted sense, while some may allow it a broader definition.

One brief dictionary entry presents the meaning of allusion as 'a passing or casual reference to something, either directly or implied'.[2] Such an understanding includes the idea of *direct* reference. For the purposes of this book, this is not how the term is being used. Other dictionary and encyclopedic definitions in fact exclude the element of directness. Note the following from three reputable sources:

> Allusion, in literature, an implied or indirect reference to a person, event, or thing or to a part of another text.[3]

> [A]n implied or indirect reference especially in literature.[4]

> An allusion is an indirect reference to someone or something.[5]

Though from distinct sources, their definitions all agree in a certain respect. All three define allusion as potentially consisting of an *indirect* manner of reference. Indirectness indicates that the act of reference does not lie on the surface of the text. As another definition puts it, an allusion is 'an expression designed to call something to mind without mentioning it explicitly'.[6] The lack of any explicit mention is a major component in the kind of allusion that is applied throughout this book.

The question naturally comes to mind how it is that the allusion is detected if direct and open reference to the earlier text forms no part. The *Encyclopaedia Britannica*, cited in part above, offers a fuller explanation in the following terms:

> Allusion, in literature, an implied or indirect reference to a person, event, or thing or to a part of another text. Most allusions are based on the assumption that there is a body of knowledge that is shared by the author

---

2 See <www.thefreedictionary.com/allusion> (accessed 23 Jan. 2023).
3 See <www.britannica.com/art/allusion> (accessed 23 Jan. 2023).
4 See <www.merriam-webster.com/dictionary/allusion> (accessed 23 Jan. 2023).
5 See <www.collinsdictionary.com/dictionary/english/allusion> (accessed 23 Jan. 2023).
6 See <www.grammar.com/allusion_vs._illusion> (accessed 23 Jan. 2023).

and the reader and that therefore the reader will understand the author's referent . . . An allusion can be used as a straightforward device to enhance a text by providing further meaning, but it can also be used in a more complex sense to make an ironic comment on one thing by comparing it to something that is dissimilar.[7]

The foregoing serves well as the basic understanding of allusion that we will operate with. Both the author and his audience have in common a familiarity with a certain body of knowledge, which in this instance is the contents of the Old Testament. It is our contention that the Gospels contain oblique references to the Scriptures of Israel which may readily be detected by readers acquainted with those writings. As far as the Gospels are concerned, these readers would at first have been early Jewish believers in Christ, most of whom would have possessed an intimate knowledge of those Scriptures, in either their Hebrew or Greek version, and then later Gentile Christians, who with the passing of time would have become increasingly conversant with the Old Testament, primarily in its Greek form, known as the Septuagint.

These ancient Scriptures, then, were a readily available and reasonably familiar body of literature for the New Testament writers to draw upon. This being so, what indicators need to be present in the later text in order to establish that allusion to the earlier text is at work? Such a question has been discussed in detail by others,[8] so a brief summary of the principal elements must suffice us here. What we look for in the textual data itself is basically correspondences in matters of setting, language and concept. Setting denotes the time or the place in which the events recorded in the passage are located. This could be, for example, on a mountain or by a body of water, in the middle of the night or during a particular religious festival. Correspondences of language could entail individual words that appear in both texts, possibly in identical or closely related form. Or sometimes a whole phrase or clause consisting of several identical or similar words might occur. Obviously, the rarer the vocabulary, the more involved the grammar and the more specific the forms, then the more probable it is that the earlier wording is being deliberately echoed. A conceptual relationship between the two texts is based on a similarity of the subject matter, or theme, and of the actions that take place. Each passage might, for instance, relate to eating and drinking, or to childbirth. If data of all the foregoing

---

[7] See <www.britannica.com/art/allusion> (accessed 23 Jan. 2023).

[8] A good discussion may be found in Jeffery M. Leonard, 'Identifying Inner-Biblical Allusions: Psalm 78 as a Test Case', *JBL* 127.2 (2008): 241–265; also Christopher A. Beetham, *Echoes of Scripture in the Letter of Paul to the Colossians* (Leiden: Brill, 2008), 17–20.

varieties is in evidence, then there is very good reason to believe that allusion is intentionally present.[9]

Yet one other important component that can be added to the foregoing is whether or not the allusion is meaningful in the context in which it appears. What we are looking for, as the above definition states, is an understanding of the allusion that enhances the surface meaning of the text in question. Often in allusions drawn from the Old Testament by the New a deeper meaning is provided, typically in terms of lesser to greater, from partial to complete, from physical to spiritual, or from temporal to eternal. This alerts us to the fact that allusions are not generally based on total identity and similarity. We are not looking at mere repetition. Again the foregoing definition is helpful here when it says that allusion 'can also be used in a more complex sense to make an ironic comment on one thing by comparing it to something that is dissimilar'. Therefore, in certain instances we ought not to be surprised if we discover dissimilarity, or contrast, in the allusive relationship. This is all part of the artistry that may be exhibited in the application of this particular literary device.[10] Several examples of contrastive allusion are treated in the following chapters.

A further corollary of the foregoing is the fact that allusions in themselves do not function as a means of communicating new doctrines. There are no teachings of the new-covenant revelation that are secreted away in allusive interpretations of texts and only discoverable by identifying such. Rather, this literary device serves to 'enhance' what is already there. Detecting the presence of allusion may indeed cause us to see a particular passage in a new light, but it will only do so by relating that text to some matter taught plainly elsewhere.[11]

So far I have said nothing new, nor anything especially controversial. There have, of course, been quite a number of recent treatments of allusion, including the indirect kind, within the discipline of biblical studies. Certain of these have

---

[9] When considering the validity of an extended allusion, which forms the main focus of our study, besides correspondences in setting, language and concepts, we find a further corroboration to exist in the fact that the allusions are bounded. By this I mean that the allusions are contained within the parameters of a definable literary unit. The Old Testament text in question is not alluded to in the text before the Gospel passage, and the allusions cease at an identifiable point in the narrative.

[10] This is all part of a deliberate hermeneutical ploy noted by some scholars and classed as a form of 'motif inversion'. See, e.g., Mary Ann Beavis, 'The Resurrection of Jephthah's Daughter: Judges 11:34–40 and Mark 5:21–24, 35–42', *CBQ* 72.1 (2010): 46–62.

[11] This can be illustrated with reference to the Jewish festival of the Day of Atonement. As we shall see, the sufferings of Christ as recorded in the Gospels make distinct allusions to what took place on that occasion (see especially chapters 20 and 23). However, to relate Christ to the Day of Atonement does not depend on such allusions, since the writer to the Hebrews brings out the same connection in plain speech.

even focused especially on allusions in the Gospels, as we do in this volume.[12] However, this present work does differ in a significant respect from previous studies. The majority of these latter deal in the main with fairly localized uses of allusion, often in a single verse. This book, however, has as one of its chief features the fact that it deals exclusively in *extended* allusions. By this I mean that running through a particular Gospel text there exists, not just one, or two, allusions but a series of several allusions which all point to one and the same Old Testament passage.[13] Biblical scholars have indeed identified instances of such a phenomenon occurring in the Gospels. Commentators have long recognized, for example, that the latter half of Matthew 2, concerning the infancy of Jesus, contains a number of allusions to the life of Moses as recorded in the early chapters of Exodus.[14] This present study affirms the presence of such, yet in a manner that goes beyond what most commentators have noted. Not only is extended allusion far more common than writers of commentaries would suggest, especially in the narrative passages of the Gospels, but also we here go beyond the usual set boundaries within which such longer applications of allusion are believed to occur.

I would maintain that this extended manner of allusive reference is also to be witnessed beyond the confines of a single Gospel-writer's composition. I would contend that the allusions to a particular Old Testament passage might be found distributed among two or more of the four canonical Gospels where they contain parallel accounts, as they often do. It may be the case that one of the four provides the essential recognizable outline of the allusive connection, while one or more of the others gives an extra element or two pointing to the same connection. Alternatively, it could be that two or more parallel Gospel accounts have to be pieced together before the Old Testament source of the allusion can be identified. A significant number of modern Gospel scholars, it has to be said, tend not to move in this direction. They are open to seeing consistent allusion to a specific Old Testament text in a single Gospel, and would accept that in parallel passages more than one Gospel-writer may make the same allusions. But the prevailing contemporary scholarly understanding of biblical inspiration and authorship would probably have reservations in allowing that an extended allusion to a portion of the Jewish Scriptures might

---

[12] We mention here particularly the insightful work of Richard Hays on the Gospels: *Echoes of Scripture in the Gospels* (Waco, TX: Baylor University Press, 2016); *Reading Backwards: Figural Christology and the Fourfold Gospel Witness* (London: SPCK, 2015).

[13] Or at least to the same event, which may be recorded in more than a single Old Testament passage.

[14] This is dealt with in chapter 6.

only be discerned once parallel passages are studied in unison, which is what I am advocating here.

The cause for such a situation lies in the fact that much of modern biblical scholarship, even that segment classed as evangelical and conservative, views the matter of authorship largely in terms of the human author. This contrasts with the traditional view, prevailing throughout the centuries and still widely held among ordinary believers today, that God is the primary author, through the Holy Spirit, and that the men who actually penned the documents were, more precisely, secondary authors.[15] This does not mean to say that the prophets and apostles were mere automatons, but they were nevertheless 'moved by the Holy Spirit', as Scripture tells us (2 Pet. 1:21). This latter fact allows for the possibility that what these men wrote, though not in all instances by any means, could contain information beyond natural human knowledge. Matters were revealed to them that no amount of merely human thought or searching would be able to discover. Prophecy is a case in point. Prophetic oracles make up a substantial portion of the Old Testament, and a good deal of these contain forecasts of the future, both near and distant. To write of such events in advance is plainly a revelation of supernatural knowledge. It is probably true that the authors were aware of occasions when they were writing of future things beyond the ordinary human ability to know. Yet there is also the matter of typology. This is where some event, person or object in the Old Testament acts in such a way as to prefigure something fulfilled much later in the New Testament.[16] Well-known examples of such include the person of Melchizedek (Gen. 14:17–24), the Passover lamb (Exod. 12) and the bronze serpent raised in the wilderness (Num. 21:4–9).[17] When recording things of this nature, it is doubtful whether the human author, or authors, involved would have had any inkling of the infinitely greater reality to which they pointed. In other words, they wrote of historical happenings within the horizons of their own knowledge, or that of earlier sources they employed, while not seeing beyond the historical limitations to future and more significant matters. It may therefore be concluded that the prefigural nature of what they wrote could only be attributed to the Holy Spirit at work within them.

---

[15] Cf. Desmond T. Alexander and Brian S. Rosner (eds.), *New Dictionary of Biblical Theology: Exploring the Unity and Diversity of Scripture* (Leicester: Inter-Varsity Press, 2000), 34–35, where the traditional view is summarized followed by a presentation of the academic criticism of it.

[16] See Nicholas P. Lunn, *Jesus in the Jewish Scriptures: How the Old Testament Bears Witness to Christ* (London: Faithbuilders, 2020), ch. 7, 'Prefiguration'.

[17] All of these are explicitly treated as types in the New Testament. See, e.g., John 3:14–15; 19:36; Heb. 7:1–22; 1 Pet. 1:18–19; Rev. 5:6, 9.

It has to be said that the view that has dominated academic biblical studies since the late nineteenth century which restricts meaning to human authorial intent has come under considerable criticism from within the scholarly community in recent decades. This is not the place to present the various arguments. It will have to suffice to list some significant works in a lengthy footnote.[18] Here I simply wish it to be noted that the prevailing academic view has not gone unchallenged within the scholarly community itself.

Much of the allusion discussed in this book exists beyond the boundaries of the writing of a single human author. Since there is no evidence, nor any reason to believe, that the Gospel-writers were in league with one another in this matter, it is necessary to look to the inspiring Spirit himself as the author of these elements. Ultimately, however, whether found in a single Gospel, or consisting of elements taken from more than one Gospel, the feature of literary allusion is, I believe, there by divine intent. This should occasion no great surprise. If human authors can resort to the literary device of making subtle allusions, as they frequently do, then how much more can God!

I recognize that the approach here might be a point of contention for readers steeped in modern higher-critical methods of interpretation, but in its defence it does look as though what I am advocating actually appears in the Gospels. What I mean is that the results that we obtain from the extended allusions claimed to be present in the parallel passages of two or more Gospels differ in no way in their delineation and character from those that scholars are happy to discern within a single Gospel. We find the same correspondences of setting, language and concept, and together with these the same meaningful interpretation of the allusions in context. At the end of the day, the proof of the pudding is in the eating. I myself would maintain that all the extended allusions presented here are actual rather than imaginary, and are there intentionally,

---

[18] See, e.g., William M. Wright IV, and Francis Martin, *Encountering the Living God in Scripture: Theological and Philosophical Principles for Interpretation* (Grand Rapids, MI: Baker Academic, 2019). In the foreword to this volume Professor Robert Sokolowski opens his remarks with the statement: 'This book is written to show how we can read the Scriptures as being addressed to us, not only by their particular authors, such as the psalmist or Saint Paul, but also by their primary author, God himself, whose words the Scriptures ultimately are.' For several other fairly recent works that emphasize the nature of Scripture as divine revelation having God as its author, see Vern S. Poythress, 'Dispensing with Merely Human Meaning: Gains and Losses from Focusing on the Human Author, Illustrated by Zephaniah 1:2–3', *JETS* 57 (2014): 481–499; John Webster, *The Domain of the Word: Scripture and Theological Reason* (London: Bloomsbury, 2012); and Matthew Levering, *Participatory Biblical Exegesis: A Theology of Biblical Interpretation* (Notre Dame, IN: University of Notre Dame Press, 2008); Jared M. Compton, 'Shared Intentions? Reflections on Inspiration and Interpretation in Light of Scripture's Dual Authorship', *Themelios* 33 (2008): 23–33; Vern S. Poythress, 'The Presence of God Qualifying Our Notions of Grammatical-Historical Interpretation: Genesis 3:15 as a Test Case', *JETS* 50 (2007): 87–103. See also Philip B. Payne, 'The Fallacy of Equating Meaning with the Human Author's Intention', *JETS* 20 (1977): 243–252.

with a meaning to communicate to the discerning reader.[19] In the final analysis, therefore, it is for the reader to assess the textual evidence and determine for himself or herself whether or not each allusion being proposed is a bona fide constituent of inspired Scripture. I hope that in each instance, or at least in the majority, it will be concluded that the allusion put forward is real, and that it has been placed there moreover for the express purpose of edifying the believer.

Extended allusions: distribution and complexity

Allusions of the kind which concern us in this volume are primarily located within the narrative portions of the Gospels rather than in sections of speech. For this reason, a good deal of this book is taken up with the passages that begin and end the Gospels, since these sections are largely in narrative form. Here we find, as most readers will be aware, the accounts of Christ's birth and infancy, his baptism and temptation that marked the commencement of his ministry, then later the climactic events of Passion Week and his subsequent resurrection appearances. In the central portions that record Christ's actual ministry there is a good deal of teaching and less narration. Even so, certain miracle stories are seen to contain Old Testament allusions, and this is likewise true of a number of parables. These latter draw upon a wide variety of sources for their imagery, and are often expressed in narrative format. For the most part, parabolic images relate to nature (e.g. trees, yeast, the weather) or to common social, religious and cultural practices of the time (e.g. farming, marriage, hospitality, judgeship, prayer, belief in the afterlife). One or two perhaps make allusion to recent or current affairs (e.g. to the appointment of Archelaus as Herod's successor).[20] Then a handful of others allude to Old Testament persons and events, certain of which will be examined in due course. It should also be pointed out that some Gospel allusions are actually to passages earlier within the same Gospel.[21] I say this only to stress that not all allusions in the Gospels

---

[19] In this regard, I would point out a fact which lends some support to the intentional nature of these extended allusions, which is that in a good many cases the Gospels allude to a particular Old Testament event or character more than once. This is so, for example, with respect to Isaac, Moses, the Passover, the exodus and the Day of Atonement. In other words, a particular instance of allusion, which for whatever reason might be doubted by some, finds a certain corroboration from allusion being made to that selfsame Old Testament passage elsewhere in the Gospel corpus.

[20] Here thinking of the parable in Luke 19:11–27; cf. Brad H. Young, *The Parables: Jewish Tradition and Christian Interpretation* (Grand Rapids, MI: Baker Academic, 2012), 86–87.

[21] E.g. the young man in Mark 16:5 would seem to relate back to the young man of 14:51–52; cf. Pieter G. R. de Villiers, 'The Powerful Transformation of the Young Man in Mark 14:51–52 and 16:5', *HTS Theological Studies* 66.1 (2010): article 893, seven pages.

direct their readers to the Old Testament. Nevertheless, I would say that since these ancient Scriptures occupied such a central position in the devotion of the Jews, we find that the large majority of Gospel allusions do indeed refer back to them.

We further note that one discovery emerging from the investigation of allusion in the Bible is the fact that it is often multilayered. This means that the same passage in the New Testament may in fact allude to diverse events and persons in the Old. Accordingly, we shall sometimes find that the allusions discernible in a Gospel episode might hearken back to more than one Old Testament source. This is an indicator, I believe, of the wonderful richness of the Gospel accounts. The basis of the Gospel-writers' drawing upon such a multiplicity of figures and events within Israel's Scriptures has, at its heart, the essential fact that ultimately all these Scriptures find their fulfilment in Jesus Christ. Without the coming of the Messiah, their meaning is reduced to mere religious history. He is *the* king of Israel, *the* great high priest, *the* prophet like Moses; he is the greater David, the greater Solomon, the one greater than the temple; he is the Lamb of God, the better sacrifice, and more besides.[22]

Such a multiplex use of allusion especially, though not exclusively, occurs in connection with the more paramount events relating to the first advent of Jesus, namely, his birth, death and resurrection. To take his death on the cross as an example, so many Old Testament figures and themes find their fulfilment here that it is impossible for them all to be expressed within a single layer of meaning. Besides the ordinary surface level of communication, the Gospels also resort to a range of allusions that point the reader to a variety of Old Testament themes and images. We shall find that such diversity becomes in fact a necessity in order, for example, to convey the idea that Jesus is as much the ultimate fulfilment of the Day of Atonement as he is of the feast of the Passover.

Not infrequently, it should be noted, when the Gospels draw upon two or more Old Testament persons or events by way of allusion, we discover that these latter do in fact already bear a relationship to one another within the older

---

[22] This phenomenon has been noted by certain modern biblical scholars. Pertaining to Matthew, but applicable to any biblical human author, Patrick Schreiner remarks that the writer may intermix figures of Jesus, one moment depicting him as a new Moses, and as a new David in the next. This, Schreiner explains, is 'because all of Israel's history is unified in Jesus. All of these figures connect not only because they are part of Israel's history but also because they are unified in Christ . . . Multiple analyses can stand side by side rather than our needing to argue that only one character or theme predominates . . . Readers don't need to choose teams but can end up seeing the varied layers of meaning presented in the text' (Patrick Schreiner, *Matthew, Disciple and Scribe: The First Gospel and Its Portrait of Jesus* [Grand Rapids, MI: Baker Academic, 2019], 209). Schreiner goes on to give the examples of the temptation narrative, in which Jesus acts as both the new Adam and the new Israel (cf. chapter 7 below), and the feeding of the multitude, where Jesus is depicted as the new Moses and the new Elisha (cf. chapter 10 below). Cf. also Hays, *Echoes of Scripture in the Gospels*, 117.

Scriptures. This shows, among other things, that there is not a complete and utter freedom in the object of the allusions. The entities referenced exhibit a previous association, and that connection is utilized in the Gospel allusions. So we find, for example, that in the Old Testament there is some correlation between the two figures of Moses and Elijah, and certain individual Gospel passages therefore allude not just to one of these but to both, even within the same context.

In what follows, where two or more persons or events are alluded to which are already related in the Old Testament itself, these will be treated within the confines of a single chapter. However, where no such connection is evident, each will be assigned a chapter of its own.

Source texts

For the most part, the Old Testament text that will be referenced during the course of this study will be the Greek translation commonly known as the Septuagint (LXX).[23] This project began with the five books of Moses in the middle of the third century BC and was gradually followed by the translation of the remaining books over the next century or so.

The reason for our use of the Septuagint is simple. When the apostles and Gospel-writers cite the Old Testament, as they often do in their writings, the Septuagint is by far the most common version they resort to. On a few occasions they do seem to be adhering to a literal Greek rendering of the Hebrew, but that is exceptional. In what they wrote, as a testimony to Christ and to the Christian faith, their objective was evidently for the message to be cast abroad as widely as possible, in keeping with their commission, and to be understood by as many as possible. To such an end the Septuagint was readily available, and they put it to good use. We follow their lead therefore in giving citations predominantly from this Greek version, though we may sometimes have occasion to consult the Hebrew text also.

While the Old Testament is obviously the principal source of Gospel allusions, occasionally in this volume reference will be made in the text or in footnotes to other Jewish writings. I do this for one reason only, which is that these writings might give us some insight into how the Jews interpreted and applied the Old Testament in the first century AD, when the events recorded in the Gospels occurred. The compositions that I will refer to most are the Mishnah

---

[23] The name derives from the tradition that seventy translators were involved in the original translation of the Pentateuch, the first portion of the Old Testament to be rendered into Greek. This is regularly abbreviated by means of the Latin numeral for '70', which is LXX.

11

and the Targums. There will also be some mention of the Talmud and the Midrash. None would deny that all of these were written down long after the time of Christ. Yet it is also recognized that the Jews had a strong and effective oral tradition and that it is highly possible, if not probable, that these writings have preserved interpretations and practices from a much earlier period.[24] Here I will give the briefest orientation to this body of literature for the benefit of the reader unacquainted with it.[25]

Of all these writings, it is the Mishnah that most likely provides us with information relating to the time of Christ and the apostles. As is well known, the whole system of temple worship came to an end when the Jews unsuccessfully staged a rebellion against the Romans, who came and besieged Jerusalem and destroyed the temple in response. This happened in AD 70, several decades after the ministry of Jesus. We know that the Jews had long observed not only the written law of Moses but also an oral law alongside it. This fact is reflected in the Gospels (e.g. Matt. 15:9; Mark 7:11; cf. Gal. 1:14). The oral law contained numerous rules and regulations with regard to how the written law was to be understood and applied – for example, how far one could walk on the sabbath, and how thorough a search had to be made for fragments of yeast in readiness for the feast of Unleavened Bread. This oral tradition had been passed on from one generation of Torah scholars to another long before the time of Jesus. It was strongly felt that it should not be written down in order to keep it distinct from the written law. But after the fall of Jerusalem to the Romans and the destruction of the temple, that attitude seemed to relax somewhat. In the latter part of the second century the whole body of earlier oral law was codified in a composition, recorded in rabbinic Hebrew, known as the Mishnah. For scholars of the New Testament this is a useful resource for discovering how certain passages of the written Torah were understood and practised during the time of the ministry of Jesus and the apostles. The Mishnah was divided into six volumes, called *sedarim*, or 'orders', and each order contained several tractates, subdivided into chapters and paragraphs.[26] The whole Mishnah is readily available in a good English translation, both in book form and online.[27]

---

[24] See, e.g., David Instone-Brewer, *Traditions of the Rabbis from the Era of the New Testament, vol. 1: Prayer and Agriculture* (Grand Rapids, MI: Eerdmans, 2004), 28–40.

[25] For a much more detailed introduction to Jewish sources of this era, see Jacob Neusner, *Introduction to Rabbinic Literature* (New York, NY: Doubleday, 1994).

[26] The orders and tractates are given names reflecting their contents (e.g. *Nedarim*, 'Vows'), while the chapters and paragraphs are numbered.

[27] The classic translation is that by Herbert Danby, *The Mishnah, Translated from the Hebrew with Introduction and Brief Explanatory Notes* (Oxford: Oxford University Press, 1933). The Mishnah in English may be accessed online at <www.sefaria.org/texts/Mishnah>.

Over the following centuries the Mishnah was much discussed and commented upon by the rabbis, giving rise to another body of tradition, quite vast in scale. Much of it consisted of quotations, sayings and aphorisms, from literally thousands of different rabbis. All of this eventually came to be written down alongside the text of the Mishnah, and in this way the work known as the Talmud was conceived. Its text of the Mishnah remained in Hebrew, while the rabbinic comment, called the Gemara, was largely in Aramaic. The work was compiled over a lengthy period of time, mainly between the third and fifth centuries. The Talmud came to exist in two forms, the Jerusalem Talmud and the Babylonian Talmud.[28] The latter is by far the more influential. Dating the various rabbinic sayings is not an easy task. Some may be quite ancient and reflect the second-temple situation. The Talmud is referenced sparingly in the present volume.

After the Mishnah the most interesting items of Jewish literature from this period are undoubtedly the Targums. A Targum (meaning 'interpretation, translation') was originally an oral translation of the Hebrew Old Testament into Aramaic that was delivered to the congregation within the context of worship. The usual explanation for its cause was the poor understanding of Hebrew on the part of many Jews following their exile in Babylonia. Whether this was the case or not we cannot be absolutely certain, but the Targums came to play an important role in transmitting traditional interpretations of the Hebrew Scriptures. This is largely because during the rendition of the Hebrew text into Aramaic explanations and interpretations were sometimes included. These could amount to as little as a single word or phrase, or as much as several sentences. With the passing of time the Targums were written down, and there were two in particular which gained authority among the Jewish communities. The first of these is Targum Onkelos, an Aramaic rendering of the five books of the law. This for the most part is a fairly literal translation with the occasional brief addition. The second is generally known as Targum Jonathan, traditionally ascribed to one Jonathan ben Uzziel.[29] This covers the prophetic books of the Old Testament, which for the Jews embrace the historical books (Joshua to 2 Kings). Other less authoritative works of this kind include Targum Neofiti and the Jerusalem Targum, both of the Torah.[30]

Then, lastly, there is that manner of composition known as Midrash. The term itself means 'study', and the various midrashic works come closest to what

---

[28] Portions of the Talmud appear in English at <www.sefaria.org/texts/Talmud>.

[29] Since the attribution to this Jonathan remains unproven, some refer to this work as Targum Pseudo-Jonathan.

[30] English translations of the standard Targums may be viewed at <http://targum.info/targumic-texts>.

might be called a commentary. Yet they are commentaries that extensively employ the specifically rabbinic mode of exegesis. This involved interpretative devices such as word association, the forms of letters, and the numerical values of letters and words. The earliest of these writings dates from the third century of our era, and they continued to be composed well into the medieval period. The most influential works of this genre are known as the Midrash Rabbah ('The Great Midrash'). In a number of places such works will be cited in what follows.[31]

Since the primary text that the Gospels interact with is the canonical Old Testament, the number of references to this later Jewish literature is not extensive. In a few instances we find that the extra information or insight derived from these sources appears to be quite pertinent to the matter in hand.

Additionally, on a small number of occasions reference will be made to the works of Philo (c. 20 BC – AD 50) and Josephus (AD 37–100). These were two Jewish writers who lived in the first century itself. Philo was a Jewish scholar from Alexandria in Egypt who left many commentaries and treatises, for the most part relating to the Old Testament. His writings may appear strange to modern readers since he adopted a philosophical approach to biblical interpretation, but they do nevertheless yield interesting insights at times. The works of Josephus ben Matthias are more relevant, as Josephus was a noted Jewish historian, originating from Jerusalem. His volumes are still consulted as a valuable source of background information for the New Testament period.

Primacy of plain meaning

While in what follows our interpretation focuses predominantly on the allusory content of Gospel texts, it should not be concluded from this that this allusive sense is the primary intent of what the texts communicate. Though I do not discuss in any great depth the surface-level meaning of the passages included, this by no means indicates that I believe the latter to be inconsequential or of secondary importance. The historical-grammatical sense of the text is the absolutely essential starting point for other levels of interpretation, whether prophetic, typological or allusive. Since the plain sense of the text is that with which the efforts of most modern commentators are concerned, it was not felt necessary to duplicate such investigations here. As stated earlier, our approach is quite specific in its aims, but is naturally not intended to be in the least bit exclusive. It rather complements, and hopefully adds more depth to, what we read on the surface.

---

[31] Portions of the Midrash can be seen in English translation at <www.sefaria.org/texts/Midrash>.

Originality

In identifying Gospel allusions to the Old Testament, I do not pretend to claim originality throughout. A handful of chapters contain allusions that are not at all original but may be found in the more detailed commentaries and other treatments that are attentive to such matters. These have been included largely for the sake of completeness. Other allusions have been noted elsewhere before, but in these cases the present volume expands on what has been previously written, with respect either to the connections or to the meaning, or perhaps to both. Then there are chapters where I have come across a hint at an Old Testament allusion in some ancient or relatively unknown exposition of a Gospel passage. Taking this as my cue, I have developed it and taken it much further. Finally, a reasonable number of instances are included in which the suggested allusions are, as far as I am aware, completely original to the present volume.[32]

---

[32] Unless otherwise stated, biblical citations in the book are my own translations. As far as I am aware, there is nothing controversial present in any of them. The renderings are fairly literal, in the tradition of versions such as the NASB, NRSV and ESV. This is deliberately so, since an appreciation of the original wording is fundamental for the detection of allusions.

2
Mary the mother of Christ
Luke 1:26–56

To any moderately well-informed reader it is evident that the Gospels open with passages and scenes that either directly refer back to the Scriptures of Israel or are at least highly evocative of them. Matthew's opening line employs a formula that is straight out of the book of Genesis (e.g. 2:4; 5:1 LXX), and the following genealogy is largely a list of Old Testament characters which serves to identify the Davidic descent of Jesus, the Messiah (Matt. 1:1–17). Luke's first chapter presents an infertile couple whose prayers are miraculously answered by God and whose son is to play a significant role in the divine purpose (1:5–25), a scene that is strongly reminiscent of several similar episodes in the Jewish Scriptures, such as those featuring Abraham and Sarah and the birth of Isaac (Gen. 18:1–15; 21:1–7), Manoah and his wife who became the parents of Samson (Judg. 13), as well as Elkanah and Hannah and the birth of Samuel (1 Sam. 1). And then John the evangelist launches his work, the fourth Gospel, with those immortal words, 'In the beginning . . .' (1:1), that plainly echo the opening verse of the first book of the Bible (Gen. 1:1), suggesting that a new act of creation is now under way. But the first narrative we shall consider that draws upon something specific in the Old Testament by way of sustained allusion concerns the mother of Jesus.

This chapter will consider the passages in the first chapter of Luke's Gospel regarding Mary. Here is described the annunciation by the angel Gabriel of Christ's coming birth (vv. 26–38) and Mary's visit to her relative Elizabeth (vv. 39–56). The matter to be discussed lies primarily in the latter of these two portions, but the first will also briefly be treated as it prepares the way for the second.

When Gabriel comes to Mary in Bethlehem, six months have passed since the divine promise that the elderly and childless Zechariah and Elizabeth would give birth to a son, John the Baptist, to be the forerunner of the Messiah (Luke 1:5–25). Now the Messiah's own birth is foretold to the one who would bear him, Mary of Nazareth in Galilee. As his herald is miraculously to be born to an aged couple,[1] so the Christ himself is to be born supernaturally to one who is a virgin (vv. 27, 34). After he has allayed her fears at his sudden and extraordinary appearance (vv. 28–30), the angel enunciates to Mary the fact of the coming birth and certain of the attendant details (vv. 31–35). He then informs her about the pregnancy of Elizabeth (vv. 36–37), and makes his departure (v. 38). A short while later Mary undertakes the journey from Galilee in the north to Judah in the south to visit Elizabeth (v. 39), to whom she is related. Upon the meeting and greeting of the two expectant mothers, the child in Elizabeth's womb leaps for joy (vv. 41–44). The older woman pronounces a blessing on the younger (v. 45), at which point the latter utters the wonderful song of praise commonly called the Magnificat (vv. 46–55).[2] Mary then stays with Elizabeth for a period of time before returning home (v. 56).

The passages in question contain a number of allusions to one particular item in the history of Israel as found in the Jewish Scriptures. There is no mistaking the fact that Mary is being portrayed in some way as the sacred object known as the 'ark of the covenant'. This was that wooden box overlaid and decorated with gold (cf. Exod. 25:10–22) which was uniquely situated in the most holy place of the ancient Israelite sanctuary. It therefore occupied an important place at the very heart of the levitical ceremonies which were then enacted.

Looking initially at the first passage of Luke 1:26–38, we read of the angel Gabriel coming to Mary to announce the birth of her child. There are two especially relevant matters that interest us here. First, there is the obvious fact that the angel's words are couched in terms of the promises God made to David, otherwise known as the Davidic covenant.[3] This is found in 2 Samuel 7, with a parallel text in 1 Chronicles 17. Mary, as well as Joseph to whom she was betrothed, were descended from David of Bethlehem (cf. Luke 1:27, 32; 2:4–5).[4] The angel makes it clear that the child to be born is the long-awaited son of David, in fulfilment of the divine promise. Prominent ideas in both the angel's announcement and the ancient promises include the idea that the one to be born would also be God's Son (Luke 1:32b; cf. 2 Sam. 7:14), and that he would reign on the throne of David over an everlasting kingdom (Luke 1:32c–33; cf. 2 Sam. 7:13, 16). Consequently, upon reading this passage our minds are

---

[1] The statement that 'nothing is impossible with God' (Luke 1:37) shows that Zechariah and Elizabeth were aged beyond the possibility of normal childbirth.

[2] The name comes from the first word of the song in the Latin Vulgate version: *Magnificat anima mea Dominum* ('My soul magnifies the Lord').

[3] Modern commentators indicate this fact. See, e.g., Joel B. Green, *The Gospel of Luke* (NICNT; Grand Rapids, MI: Eerdmans, 1997), 88. Green states that '[t]he connection of [Luke 1] vv 32–33 with a restored Davidic monarchy is unmistakable'. Similarly, David E. Garland, *Luke* (ZECNT 3; Grand Rapids, MI: Zondervan, 2011), 80.

[4] Cf. also Rom. 1:3; 2 Tim. 2:8; Rev. 22:16.

firmly fixed on David the king and the words of God to him in 2 Samuel 7 concerning a future descendant.

The second significant feature of Gabriel's message appears in Luke 1:35. When Mary enquires about how the foretold birth could happen, as she was involved in no sexual relations with a man (v. 34), the angel replies, 'The Holy Spirit will come upon you, and the power of the Most High will over-shadow [*episkiasei*] you' (v. 35). Here the verb 'overshadow' correlates with an important Old Testament event recorded in Exodus. When the tabernacle was finally completed and set up, we read that 'Moses was not able to enter the tent of meeting because the cloud overshadowed [*epeskiazen*] it and the glory of the LORD filled the tabernacle' (Exod. 40:35). This verb is not at all common in the Greek Old Testament; in fact this is its sole usage in the Pentateuch and historical books, and the only one that relates to a theophany, that is, a manifestation of the divine presence.[5] In the New Testament it is a verb par-ticularly associated elsewhere with the occurrence of theophany.[6] The Exodus text tells us that it was specifically the 'tent of meeting' that was so over-shadowed. An examination of the usage of this phrase suggests that here it is an alternative description of that compartment of the tabernacle where God met Moses, and later Aaron, the high priest (cf. Num. 7:89).[7] In other words, the overshadowing that then took place more particularly related to that inner chamber known as 'the most holy place' (or, more literally according to the Hebrew, 'the holy of holies'). Here was the very location within the larger tabernacle in which the ark of the covenant, and this object only, was situated. It was here, rather than in the larger outer compartment, that the divine presence, symbolized by the cloud of glory, was believed to dwell. And now in Luke 1 this same term is being applied to Mary, the mother-to-be, intimating that she too is set to be the locus for a significant manifestation of the divine.

In the angelic annunciation, then, there is an indication of the all-important role that Mary is going to play. Biologically, she will be the mother of the child. When to this is added the theophanic term 'overshadow', the connotation is evidently much more than the mere fact of ordinary human motherhood, even if through a virgin conception. It is a theologically charged term, as we shall go on to see.

---

[5] The same verb in Pss 91:4 and 139:8 concerns the matter of divine protection rather than presence.

[6] In the New Testament the verb is prominent in the theophany of the transfiguration, occurring in all three versions (Matt. 17:5; Mark 9:7; Luke 9:34). See chapter 13.

[7] This is not to be confused with that earlier temporary 'tent of meeting' that was used before the taber-nacle came into operation (Exod. 33:7).

Soon after the departure of the angel, Mary went to visit her relative Elizabeth, since the angel had informed her that she too was pregnant (Luke 1:36). There now begins a series of allusions to the Old Testament narrative recounting the moving of the ark up to Jerusalem, particularly centring on the account in 2 Samuel 6.[8] It is relevant to point out that these allusions take us to the same portion of the Jewish Scriptures as the references to the Davidic covenant in Gabriel's annunciation. There we noted that mention was being made of the promised son of David in 2 Samuel 7. This latter passage is not entirely independent from the ark narrative, which immediately precedes it. Indeed, the inciting circumstance in the introduction to that chapter is the fact that David is now settled in his palace, while 'the ark of God remains in a tent' (vv. 1–2). A major consideration in David's mind that forms an important element in the underlying theme of this chapter is the building of a house for God, in the form of the ark, to dwell in (cf. vv. 5–6). The two chapters, 2 Samuel 6 and 7, are therefore interrelated.[9] The Davidic kingship and an earthly dwelling-place for God are here inextricably connected.

As Luke commences his narrative concerning Mary's visitation, the first detail of interest is the introductory construction consisting of two consecutive verbs of motion. The narrative tells us that 'having arisen [*anastasa*] . . . Mary went [*eporeuthē*]' (Luke 1:39). Precisely the same two verbs appear in relation to David as the ark narrative begins: 'David . . . arose [*anestē*] and went [*eporeuthē*]' (2 Sam. 6:2).

Mary leaves Nazareth in Galilee[10] and makes the journey 'to a town in the hill country of Judah' (Luke 1:39). In the Old Testament account of the ark, after a period when it was exiled among the Philistines, it was transported to Judah and kept there (2 Sam. 6:2), specifically 'on a hill' (v. 3). David's first aborted attempt to bring the ark up to Jerusalem meant that the ark was brought into the home of Obed-Edom, a Levite (cf. 1 Chr. 15:17–18, 21, 24).[11] The home that Mary comes to is that of Zechariah and Elizabeth, both of priestly descent and therefore of the tribe of Levi (Luke 1:5).

---

[8] Due no doubt to their particular devotion to Mary, Catholic biblical scholars have widely recognized the parallels between Mary and the ark that are now described. See, e.g., William M. Wright IV, *The Bible and Catholic Ressourcement: Essays on Scripture and Theology* (Steubenville, OH: Emmaus Academic, 2019), 23–24; Joseph Ratzinger, *Jesus of Nazareth: The Infancy Narratives* (London: Bloomsbury, 2012), 28; John Saward, *Redeemer in the Womb: Jesus Living in Mary* (San Francisco, CA: Ignatius Press, 1993), 27; Yves M. J. Congar, *The Mystery of the Temple, Or the Manner of God's Presence to His Creatures from Genesis to the Apocalypse* (London: Burns & Oates, 1962), 257–260.

[9] The same relationship holds true for the parallel narrative in 1 Chr. 15–17.

[10] A region described in Isa. 9:1 as 'Galilee of the Gentiles'.

[11] Although Obed-Edom is also called a 'Gittite', his levitical role precludes him from being a native-born Philistine from Gath. Perhaps he is so described because it was his clan name, or perhaps he or his forebears once resided in that place before the Philistines took it over.

When Mary enters the house, the baby in Elizabeth's womb, later to become known as John the Baptist, 'leaped' (Luke 1:41, 44). This reminds us of the fact that in the ark narrative David was to be seen 'leaping' in the presence of the ark (2 Sam. 6:16). John was a son conceived within a priestly family; his father Zechariah was a priest and so he himself was a priest, since it was a hereditary office. Mary and her unborn child are therefore greeted, in effect, by a leaping priest. David was not a priest but a king, of the tribe of Judah. For this particular occasion, however, he donned an ephod (2 Sam. 6:14). The ephod was a special garment worn by those of priestly office (Exod. 28:4). David was additionally clothed in a 'robe [*mĕ'îl*] of fine linen' (1 Chr. 15:27) such as was worn by all the ministers of the sanctuary (also Exod. 28:4). Evidently, then, for this special event David had, to all intents and purposes, assumed the identity of a priest.

We are next informed that Elizabeth 'sounded forth [*anephōnēsen*] with a loud voice' (Luke 1:42). At first sight this may appear to be of little consequence. Yet the verb translated 'sound forth' is extremely rare in Scripture. In fact this is the sole place in the whole New Testament where it occurs. Why here? In the Greek Old Testament the verb only occurs five times, all in the books of Chronicles, and all with the levitical ministers of worship as the ones performing the action (1 Chr. 15:28; 16:4, 5, 42; 2 Chr. 5:13). More than this, it is surely remarkable that every single one of the five instances is found either directly associated with the ark of the covenant, or in a narrative in which the ark is a central component. This can hardly be mere coincidence. As the ark was brought up the Levites 'sounded forth', and so did the Levite Elizabeth as Mary, bearing the divine child, came to her. Also note that Elizabeth here gives voice 'with a shout' (Luke 1:42), as indeed the people did at the bringing up of the ark (2 Sam. 6:15).[12]

Another notable parallel exists between the words of Elizabeth with regard to Mary and those of David in the ark narrative regarding the ark. In the earlier passage David asked, 'How can the ark of the LORD come to me [*eiseleusetai pros me*]?' (2 Sam. 6:9). In the Gospel Elizabeth asks, 'Why has this happened to me, that the mother of my Lord should come to me [*elthē . . . pros eme*]?' (Luke 1:43). In each instance we find a question of an obviously rhetorical nature, containing an identical verbal phrase ('come to me').[13]

---

[12] The noun 'shout' is in both instances *kraugē*. Of lesser importance, but also present in each narrative, is the phrase 'with joy' (2 Sam. 6:12; cf. Luke 1:44). The nouns this time differ, but the phrases are similarly constructed (*en euphrosynē* and *en agalliasei* respectively) and the nouns are virtual synonyms.

[13] The non-Greek reader should be aware that *eiseleusetai* and *elthē* are two forms derived from the same verb (*erchomai*).

Then there is the particular duration of stay. In the ark narrative we read that: 'The ark of the Lord stayed in the house of Obed-Edom the Gittite for three months [mēnas treis]' (2 Sam. 6:11). In the case of Jesus' mother we discover that 'Mary stayed with Elizabeth for about three months [mēnas treis]' (Luke 1:56).

Lastly, we point out the place given to praise, expressed in direct speech, towards the end of each account. The Old Testament ark narrative builds up to the psalmic praise of 1 Chronicles 16:7–36,[14] while the visitation of Mary leads to her aforementioned Magnificat in Luke 1:46–55. Links may be detected between the two, minor and major. Of particular interest is the correspondence between 1 Chronicles 16:13–17 and Luke 1:54–55. Here, each passage refers to Israel as 'his [God's] servant' (1 Chr. 16:13 [Heb. 'abdô]; cf. Luke 1:54),[15] and more importantly each speaks of God remembering his covenant with Abraham, a covenant that was to stand for ever (1 Chr. 16:15, 17; cf. Luke 1:55).

The foregoing, then, is the textual evidence that warrants the reader making a connection between Mary and the ark of the covenant.

In order to appreciate why the mother of Jesus is being associated with this sacred object of the old-covenant era, we need to have a basic understanding of the purpose the ark served as the principal item within the Hebrew sanctuary in Old Testament times.

First, the ark was a representation of God's presence among his people. The shape of the object and its design, a low flat box layered with gold, having an ornate golden lid with figures of cherubim at each end, obviously made it appear like a seat, or more precisely a throne. God was described as the 'one who dwells between the cherubim' (e.g. 2 Sam. 6:2; Pss 80:1; 99:1). Upon the ark, as a token of his presence, a divine theophany appeared to those permitted to enter the most holy place (cf. Lev. 16:2, 'I will appear in the cloud upon the mercy-seat'). Accordingly, the ark was conceived to be, in symbolic form, the very dwelling-place of God within Israel.[16] It indicated God living on earth. And in the miraculous conception experienced by Mary God did indeed come down to earth. In Mary, however, it was not the divine presence in a mere theophanic representation, but astoundingly the divine essence itself descended to take up residence, for a period of months at least, within her virginal womb. In her, therefore, God was truly present in every sense of the word.[17]

---

[14] The verses here are reproduced from Ps. 105.

[15] Note the closeness of the LXX text (Israēl paides autou) to that of the phrase in the Gospel (Israēl paidos autou).

[16] Biblical Hebrew possesses a single verb (yāšab) meaning both 'sit' and 'dwell'.

[17] Cf. Ratzinger (Jesus of Nazareth: The Infancy Narratives, 28): 'Mary becomes the Ark of the Covenant, the place where the Lord truly dwells.'

Second, since God's earthly presence was centred on the ark, it was understood to be a meeting-place of the highest importance. This was where God met the people of Israel (cf. Exod. 25:22, 'There I will meet with you . . . between the two cherubim that are on the ark'). In other words this was the place where the divine and the human had contact with each other. How this act of meeting becomes even more true in Mary! It was within her womb that God and humanity met in the closest possible union. For there, divine nature and human nature were conjoined in the single person of her son Jesus. He was, as defined in the creeds, one Person in two natures.[18] As such, the one so uniting in himself both deity and humanity could become the perfect mediator between God and humankind.

Then, third, the ark was a receptacle. It was basically a box that contained a number of significant items that featured in the immediate post-exodus experience of the Israelites. These were the two stone tablets of the law, a golden pot of manna – this being the food that God had miraculously provided to sustain the people in the desert – and Aaron's rod that budded (Exod. 16:33–34; 25:16, 21; Num. 17:10; Deut. 10:2; cf. Heb. 9:4). Each of these literal objects had an evident symbolic value. At the most basic level, the stone tablets indicated God's law, the manna was a life-giving food that came down from heaven, and the rod represented the true priesthood, since it belonged to the high priest. As Christian expositors have explained throughout the ages, each item has a patently Christological interpretation. Mary was the receptacle, or bearer, of the Christ who would become the ultimate reality of what all these objects in the ark portrayed. Jesus was one who alone had the law of God firmly laid up within his heart, a law which he fully obeyed (Ps. 40:8; cf. Heb. 10:5–7). He was uniquely, according to his own description, the living bread that came down from heaven, namely the bread of life, the true manna (John 6:41, 48, 51).[19] And he was indeed, as the writer to the Hebrews tells us, a great high priest for ever, our mediator (Heb. 4:14; 7:26; 9:15; etc.).[20] As the ark of old bore

---

[18] Cf. the Chalcedonian Creed: 'our Lord Jesus Christ, the same perfect in Godhead and also perfect in manhood; truly God and truly man . . . consubstantial with the Father according to the Godhead, and consubstantial with us according to the Manhood . . . begotten before all ages of the Father according to the Godhead, and in these latter days, for us and for our salvation, born of the Virgin Mary, the Mother of God according to the Manhood; one and the same Christ, Son, Lord, only-begotten, to be acknowledged in two natures . . . concurring in one Person and one Subsistence . . . one and the same Son, and only-begotten, God the Word, the Lord Jesus Christ'.

[19] Cf. Saward (*Redeemer in the Womb*, 49): 'She carries in her womb him who is the Bread of Life, the heavenly Manna.'

[20] The fact that buds and blossoms appeared on the rod, which was in essence a dead stick, and that it even produced almonds (Num. 17:8) is probably an indication that the priesthood would be an everlasting priesthood, based on a resurrected life; cf. Heb. 7:16, which speaks of Jesus as 'one who has become a priest, not through a legal requirement concerning physical descent, but through the power of an indestructible life' (NRSV).

the figural representations of these things, Mary was privileged to carry within her own flesh the one who would embody and enact in the fullest sense what each of these intimated. In that sense, therefore, Mary could justly be said to be not only the true ark but indeed greater than the ark.[21]

---

[21] This is an appropriate high note to end on, but a word of qualification does need to be added. In what has been discussed in this chapter it should be evident that Mary has a highly honoured position in view of her motherhood of the Son of God. For this reason she ought to be properly revered within the church. Reverence is one thing, but adoration and invocation in prayer, as practised by our Catholic and Orthodox brothers and sisters, are of an altogether different nature. I do not believe that there is anything in what we have seen regarding Mary to justify such a status and role for her within Christian piety and practice. We further observe that the association between Mary and the ark only pertains to the time in which she was bearing Christ (see chapter 5).

3

The decree of Caesar Augustus

Luke 2:1–5

Since it forms a prominent part of the background to the Christmas story, the occurrence of an imperial edict that the population of the Roman Empire should be submitted to a census is familiar to many. Luke records, 'Now in those days a decree went forth from Caesar Augustus that all the world should be registered' (2:1). And so it was that in obedience to this decree Joseph and Mary, the expectant mother, made their way from Nazareth to Bethlehem (vv. 4–5), where Jesus was subsequently born.[1]

It is here claimed that this episode in the third Gospel contains echoes of a similar happening found in the Old Testament, and that an appreciation of the connection between the two adds significantly to our understanding of the later occurrence. The place where the earlier event is recorded is in the opening section of the book of Ezra. The very first words of that book are:

In the first year of Cyrus king of Persia, in order to fulfil the word of the LORD by the mouth of Jeremiah, the LORD stirred up the spirit of Cyrus king of Persia, so that he would issue a proclamation throughout all his kingdom, and also put it in writing, saying: 'Thus says Cyrus king of Persia, "The LORD, the God of heaven, has given me all the kingdoms of the earth and has appointed me to build a house for him in Jerusalem, which is in Judah. Whoever there is among you of all his people, may his God be with him! Let him go up to Jerusalem which is in Judah and build the house of the LORD, the God of Israel, the God who is in Jerusalem"'. (Ezra 1:1–3)

---

[1] The historicity of this decree has often been doubted. It is not at all my intention to discuss the genuineness of the event. This has been ably done by others. See, e.g., Gerard Gertoux's convincing presentation, 'Dating the Two Censuses of P. Sulpicius Quirinius', located at <www.academia.edu/3184175/Dating_the_two_Censuses_of_Quirinius> (accessed 23 Jan. 2023); also Harold W. Hoehner, *Chronological Aspects of the Life of Christ* (Grand Rapids, MI: Zondervan, 1978), 13–23.

This is describing that momentous occasion, usually dated at 538 BC, when the Persian ruler Cyrus, conqueror of Babylon and founder of the Achaemenid Empire, issued an edict authorizing people groups previously transported into exile by the Babylonians to return home. As a result of this, as we read in the books of Ezra and Nehemiah, thousands of exiled Jews returned to their homeland and set about reconstructing the temple and the city of Jerusalem.

First, Ezra 1 – 2 and Luke 2:1–5 relate thematically in that each describes a decree issued by the ruler of the current world empire (Persia, Rome). More specifically, both decrees entail the movement of large numbers of subjects, and in the entirety of the canonical writings it is solely these two texts that speak of a decree involving such an action.[2] Both accounts of the imperial edict, we observe, include a phrase descriptive of the totality of its extent, Ezra 1:1 having 'all his kingdom', and Luke 2:1, 'all the world'.

In response to the Persian decree the verb employed to express the return of the exiles to Judah is 'go up', represented by forms of *anabainō* in the LXX (Ezra 1:3 [*anabēsetai*], 5 [*anabēnai*], 11 [*anabainonto*]; 2:1 [*anabainontes*], 59 [*anabantes*]). This same verb of ascending motion is also used to describe Joseph's particular journey in Luke: 'Joseph also went up [*anebē*]' (2:4). There is a closer similarity than appears at first sight in that one of the instances in Ezra (1:11), in its Greek version, contains the verb 'go up' accompanied by a series of three distinct prepositional phrases. Two of these indicate the point of origin and the third the destination, literally 'from [*apo*] the settlement out of [*ek*] Babylon to [*eis*] Jerusalem'. The same three prepositions appear, in the same order, of the going up of Joseph with Mary, 'from [*apo*] Galilee out of [*ek*] the town of Nazareth to [*eis*] Judah'. Such a precise correspondence is quite remarkable. We note too that in Ezra, as well as in Luke, the broader goal of the journey is Judah (Ezra 1:2; 2:1).

In each case the sentence relating to the ultimate destination of the respective journeys is qualified by a distributive phrase meaning 'each to his own town'. At the end of Ezra 2:1 LXX we find the words *anēr eis polin autou*. This is matched by the Lukan phrase *hekastos eis tēn heautou polin* in 2:3. The differences are minimal.[3] Semantically, the two phrases are virtually identical.[4]

---

[2] Luke (2:1) styles this decree as a *dogma*. While this term does not appear in Ezra, the same noun and its verbal cognate do occur in other texts in connection with Persian imperial decrees (Esth. 3:9; Dan. 6:12).

[3] The Hebrew noun *'îš* literally means 'man', but is also commonly used as the distributive 'each' (E. Kautzsch and A. E. Cowley, *Gesenius' Hebrew Grammar* [Oxford: Clarendon, 2nd English edn., 1910], §39b). The LXX frequently renders *'îš* by the Greek *hekastos*, 'each' (e.g. Gen. 10:5; Deut. 3:20), as in Luke 2:3, though 'man' is not uncommon in such contexts (e.g. Judg. 7:8; 1 Kgs 1:49).

[4] Both phrases consist of a distributive, the same preposition, and an accusative noun phrase with the selfsame noun (*polis*) qualified by a possessive pronoun.

Both texts make reference to Bethlehem, and prominently so. In Ezra (2:21) it is a town of Judah from which certain of the exiles originated and to which they now return. In Luke, of course, it is the place to which Joseph and Mary, whose ancestors hailed from there, travel according to the terms of the imperial decree (2:4). Two things are worth highlighting regarding Bethlehem in Ezra 2. First, this particular town, it should be noted, is hardly spoken of in the Old Testament in a post-exilic context. In fact this verse in Ezra and its exact parallel in the list of Nehemiah 7:26 are the only instances. Second, among the twenty-one place names in Ezra 2:21–35, Bethlehem receives prominence in that it is positioned first. The author may have done this because of the Davidic (and possibly messianic) association of the town (cf. Mic. 5:2).

In both Ezra and Luke, mention is made of the act of registering at the place of arrival. While this is a dominant component of the Gospel text (Luke 2:1 [*apographesthai*], 2 [*apographē*]), the idea also features in the Old Testament passage. In Ezra 2:62 in connection with certain priests among the returnees we read: 'These sought their registration [*graphēn*] among those enrolled in the genealogies; but they were not found there, and so they were excluded from the priesthood as unclean'. Relevant in this context is the later but closely related text of Nehemiah 7:5:

> Then my God put it into my heart to assemble the nobles, the officials and the people, that they might be registered by genealogy. I found the book of the genealogy of those who came up first and found the following written in it.

Here Nehemiah is undoubtedly referring back to the events of Ezra 1 – 2,[5] noting that at that time a genealogical register was made in fact of all those who returned.

Certain specific lexical items relating to familial lineage are also common to both texts. In each we find *oikos*, indicating 'house' in its familial sense (Ezra 2:36, 59; Luke 2:4). Closely connected with this is the noun *patria*, 'family' or 'lineage' (Ezra 1:5; 2:59, 68; Luke 2:4). In Ezra 2:59 both nouns occur together, as they do in Luke 2:4.

In Ezra we find, apart from the prominent place given to Bethlehem, a further detail with a Davidic connection. The Jewish returnees were headed up by Zerubbabel (2:2). As Bethlehem is first of the place names, so Zerubbabel is the first of the many personal names listed in this chapter. This individual, as

---

[5] Cf. H. G. M. Williamson, *Ezra, Nehemiah* (WBC 16; Waco, TX: Word, 1985), 271.

we are informed by the genealogies of Chronicles, was of the royal line of David (1 Chr. 3:19). Joseph, Mary's betrothed, was also of that very same Davidic descent (Luke 2:4; cf. 1:32; 2:11). Each man was the current heir to the throne in his own generation, yet neither occupied it. So we find a royal but non-reigning descendant of David of Bethlehem to be the leading male in each passage.[6]

There is one last curious fact about Ezra 2 to which attention should be drawn. Placed immediately after the name Zerubbabel in 2:2 is a certain Jeshua. It was these two men together, one the royal descendant of David, the other the high priest, who gave civil and spiritual leadership to the post-exilic Jewish community (cf. 3:2, 8; 4:3). As leaders, they also initiated the reconstruction of the Jewish temple: 'Zerubbabel son of Shealtiel and Jeshua son of Jozadak rose up to build the house of God in Jerusalem' (Ezra 5:2). Elsewhere this Jeshua, or *yēšûaʿ* in Hebrew, is named 'Joshua' (Hag. 1:1; Zech. 6:11), for the two are simply variations of the same name. When the Hebrew Scriptures were translated into Greek, both these names were rendered as *Iēsous* in the Septuagint, the identical form that occurs for 'Jesus' in the New Testament (cf. Acts 7:45; Heb. 4:8). Consequently, in the two Jewish leaders at that time of restoration, Zerubbabel and Jeshua, we see one who is the son of David, the rightful heir to the throne, and the other a priestly figure named Jesus. There is an obvious connection with Luke 2, where we read of the birth of the royal son of David who is given the name Jesus, thus bringing the two leaders of post-exilic Judah into one person. We may further note the fact that in the list of names of Jewish people that follows Ezra 2:2, there is one name in particular that stands out. The passage contains well over a hundred proper names, most of which are personal. Some names appear twice (Bigvai, Elam, Ater, Akkub, Giddel, Nekoda, Barzillai), since it is not unusual for two different characters to bear the same name. No name occurs three times. There is just one that has four instances, and that is precisely the name Jeshua, or Jesus, referring to four distinct characters (2:2, 6, 36, 40). Thus, aside from the prominence given through initial position to Bethlehem, the town of David, and to Zerubbabel, the son of David, the name 'Jesus' is also here made salient through repetition. From the perspective of divine design in Scripture, it would seem that the relationship between the two texts in question is not simply one of Luke alluding back to Ezra, but that the earlier text was actually pre-empting what was yet to come. Such a perspective would maintain that in view of the coming Jesus, son of David, to be born in Bethlehem, the passage in Ezra gave deliberate prominence to terms relating to the name, lineage and birthplace of the one to come.

---

[6] The same Zerubbabel appears in the genealogy of Jesus that comes in the third chapter of Luke (v. 27).

Once the allusions made by Luke to the opening section of Ezra are discerned, the reason for their presence is not difficult to ascertain. The event recorded in Ezra is of momentous significance. Several decades earlier, the people of Judah and Jerusalem had suffered a calamitous defeat at the hands of their enemy, the Babylonians. Their king had been removed from his throne, thousands of Jews had been taken into exile, and more importantly, the temple of God, which had stood since the time of Solomon, was completely destroyed and the divinely prescribed sacrifices ceased. The decree of Cyrus in Ezra 1 marked the end of this captivity. Following that decree, the Jews who had been deported were able to return to Judah, and upon their arrival steps were taken to rebuild the house of the Lord and to resume the sacrificial worship.

However, when the Jews came back to their land, despite the positive elements to this event, there was one enormous downside. This was the fact that the Jews were no longer under their own rule. The person of Zerubbabel, though the legitimate descendant in the royal line, never became king. Rather, Cyrus himself, despite allowing the return and the rebuilding, remained ultimate ruler of Judah, which was a mere province of the Persian Empire.

From the foregoing it could be said that in a very real sense, although the return from exile had taken place, the people nevertheless remained in essence captive to Persia. This indeed is how Ezra himself viewed the situation. In his lengthy prayer of confession he admitted that 'we are slaves' (Ezra 9:9), and this was later reiterated when the people declared, 'Behold, we are slaves today' (Neh. 9:36). In effect, then, while the Jews were under a foreign ruler and the Davidic heir continued without a throne, the exile could in no way be described as fully ended.

Another noteworthy feature of the return from Babylon is the place given to the temple. It is highly significant that when the first temple was built, many years earlier in the time of Solomon, upon its completion and dedication the glory of the Lord had visibly come in the form of a cloud and entered it (1 Kgs 8:10–11), thus symbolizing God's presence in the holy place. The same had happened earlier still at the dedication of the tabernacle, the portable sanctuary of Israel constructed several centuries before the more permanent temple (Exod. 40:34–35). But when the second temple was built by the returned exiles, nothing at all happened of this nature (Ezra 6:16–18). The people had come back to Jerusalem, but the Lord had not come into his temple in the way he had before.

It may be concluded, therefore, that the wonderful Old Testament prophecies uttered by Isaiah, Ezekiel and others regarding a glorious restoration following the people's return from exile were not actually fulfilled in the events recorded in Ezra. After the collapse of the Persian Empire, the Jewish plight continued unabated under Greek rule and later when Judea was made a Roman province. The fulfilment of the prophecies had still not happened.[7]

And then Jesus was born. At the time of another imperial edict, Jews returned to their familial homes, and the scene was set for the true restoration of the people of God in all its fullness. Jesus was the genuine Davidic offspring, a descendant of Zerubbabel (Matt. 1:13; Luke 3:27), who, unlike this ancestor, would rule on the throne of David, and do so for ever (Luke 1:32–33). And he was also the greater Jeshua, that is, Jesus, the true high priest of his people,[8] who would not simply restore sacrifices of animals, but offer up the one true ultimate sacrifice once and for all.

The literary allusions, therefore, that can be discerned in Luke 2 tell the perceptive reader that, with the birth that occurred at the time of this second imperial decree, the exile of the people of God is now finally over.[9] Everything that failed to happen at the time of that earlier decree, or that only happened in part, is now come in its perfection and fullness – release from all captivity, an everlasting king and an equally everlasting kingdom, a spiritual temple and worship – for both Jew and Gentile alike.

---

[7] The views of New Testament scholar N. T. Wright are well known on this subject. He writes: 'Babylon had taken the people into captivity; Babylon fell, and the people returned. But in Jesus' day many, if not most, Jews regarded the exile as still continuing. The people had returned in a geographical sense, but the great prophecies of restoration had not yet come true' (N. T. Wright, *Jesus and the Victory of God* [London: SPCK, 1996], 126).

[8] Another consideration here is the element of the registration. It was seen that in Ezra those priests who failed to register were excluded from the priesthood (2:62). The ability to find one's name in the appropriate genealogical records demonstrated genuine lineage. Thus the fact that Joseph and Mary did so register in Bethlehem, being 'of the house and lineage of David', as Luke records (2:4), verified their descent from the royal line. Their son therefore implicitly qualified to receive the throne of his father David and to rule over the house of Jacob (1:32–33).

[9] Cf. Wright (*Jesus and the Victory of God*, 127): 'The real return from exile, including the real resurrection from the dead, is taking place, in an extremely paradoxical fashion, in Jesus' own ministry.'

4

The birth of Christ

Matthew 1:18–25; Luke 1:26–38

In this chapter we primarily consider the birth narrative as it appears in Matthew, but we will also be taking a sideways glance at the corresponding account in Luke. These, we remember, are the only two Gospels that deal with Christ's birth.

The first section of Matthew's Gospel (1:1–17) is particularly concerned with presenting the Messiah as one descended from Abraham, in the lineage of David the king. Immediately following this genealogical introduction comes the account of Christ's birth, which begins with 'Now the birth of Jesus Christ was as follows . . .' (vv. 18–25). The passage first speaks of Joseph and Mary, their betrothal, the fact of Mary's pregnancy, and Joseph's intention to end the relationship (vv. 18–19). Before he can do this, however, an angel appears to him and tells him to proceed with the marriage for the child was conceived by the Holy Spirit. The angel explains that Mary will bear a son who will be a Saviour from sin, as reflected in the name he is to be given, Jesus (vv. 20–21).[1] Matthew, the narrator, then points out that this conception and birth happens in fulfilment of a prophecy from the Old Testament, found in Isaiah, a prophecy which identifies the mother as a 'virgin' (vv. 22–23). Lastly, we are informed as to how Joseph complies with the angel's words. He goes ahead and marries Mary, though they have no sexual relations before the child's birth. The son is then born and named Jesus (vv. 24–25). From this we see that the verses do not concern the physical act of giving birth so much as matters that occurred beforehand.

Before examining allusions within the passage, one particular element of its surface-level meaning should be stressed. As was emphasized in the introduction, the investigation of allusions should never detract from the importance of the text as plainly understood. Here our passage presents a crucial fact with regard to the identity of Jesus Christ. Direct citation is made of the Old

---

[1] The Hebrew for 'Jesus' means either 'The LORD saves' or 'The salvation of the LORD'.

Testament prophecy of Isaiah 7:14, which concerns the virgin birth and the child to be born: 'Behold, the virgin shall be with child and bear a son, and they shall call his name Immanuel' (Matt. 1:23). To this Matthew adds the explanation that the name Immanuel means 'God with us'. The context, that is, the twofold statement that Joseph had no relations with Mary (vv. 18, 25), as well as the precise meaning of the Greek noun *parthenos*, 'virgin',[2] demands that we interpret this event as a truly miraculous virginal conception.[3] A human father played no part in it. Consequently, according to traditional exegesis of these verses,[4] with which I wholly concur, the one born as a human being was also in very nature 'God', hence the title 'Immanuel'. While Matthew's opening genealogy and what we proceed to discuss will focus on Christ's human lineage, this ought not in any way to detract from the fact that, in the human being in question, the divine was also present.[5]

Regarding the allusory component of the text, we first point out that the two opening passages of Matthew (vv. 1–17 and vv. 18–25) are evidently very closely interlinked. Both begin (1:1, 18) with an echo of Genesis, as each contains the Greek noun *genesis*, meaning 'genealogy, origin, birth', this being the same word of course from which the first book of the Bible receives its title. Furthermore, as the genealogy draws to its end we are introduced to the names of Joseph and Mary (v. 16), who then continue as the main characters of the following section (v. 18). It is obvious, then, that verses 1–17 lead directly into verses 18–25. As the former lay out the genealogical descent of the Messiah, so the latter present the circumstances of his actual coming into the world. The first section has set the context for what happens in the following, and that context, we should observe, is one in which the patriarchal figure of Abraham looms large. He is mentioned in the title of verse 1, he is the starting point for the genealogy itself in verse 2, and his name appears again at the conclusion in verse 17.

Matthew, then, gives special prominence to Abraham, but also to David (1:1, 6, 17). In Luke's corresponding narratives the Davidic lineage is more in view (1:27, 32, 69; 2:4, 11), though the patriarchs are still present. According to Luke's

---

[2] To which may be added the parallel testimony in Luke (1:34).

[3] For a discussion of how this Isaianic prophecy is to be interpreted and of the meaning of the Hebrew term traditionally translated 'virgin', see Nicholas P. Lunn, *Jesus in the Jewish Scriptures: How the Old Testament Bears Witness to Christ* (London: Faithbuilders, 2020), 103–109.

[4] Cf. Thomas Aquinas, *Catena Aurea*, on Matt. 1:23. Much more recently, Stanley Hauerwas comments: 'Mary had to be a virgin, because Jesus is the Son of God . . . Mary's virginity is simply required by the way the story runs. The one to whom she gave birth is none other than Emmanuel, "God with us," and such a one can have no other father than the Father who is the first person of the Trinity . . . Jesus is very God and very man' (*Matthew* [Brazos Theological Commentary on the Bible; Grand Rapids, MI: Brazos, 2006], 36).

[5] This momentous truth, already seen implicitly in chapter 2, will be encountered several times more in the studies that follow.

record, the one to be born will reign over 'the house of Jacob' for ever (1:33). Both Mary's song (the Magnificat) and that of Zechariah (the Benedictus) make mention of Abraham (1:55, 73), in words that echo the ancient divine promise. So, while it is more evident in Matthew, each of these two Gospels infuses its account of Christ's origins with references back to the great forefather of Israel. As the entrance of Messiah into the world is announced, the name of Abraham is also being hailed, a feature which takes the mind of the reader back to the pertinent portions of Genesis. What we read in the Gospels, therefore, is to be understood against the background of the Old Testament passages concerning Abraham that are being evoked.

As Matthew's introduction specifies that the Messiah is the son of Abraham, it is not unreasonable to expect that any literary allusions present in the account of his birth should be drawn from the record of the birth of Abraham's first son, Isaac. And when the contents of Matthew 1:18–25 are examined, this is precisely what we discover. In the persons, events and language, allusions are being made to the announcement of the birth of a son to Abraham (or Abram) and Sarah (or Sarai), as appears in Genesis chapters 15–18 (the promise and announcement) and chapter 21 (the birth).[6]

Viewed most generally, we see that both the patriarchal and Matthean scenarios concern the birth of a male child, a descendant of Abraham, whose arrival in the world was foretold and long awaited. More than this, as one scholar puts it: 'In both stories a heavenly person (the angel and God) announces to the fathers (Joseph and Abraham) that their respective wives (Mary and Sarah) will conceive promised children (Jesus and Isaac)'.[7] So, as regards the role of the characters and the general subject matter involved, there is a distinct correlation.

Looking in closer detail, we find that the announcement to Abraham regarding a natural heir and the annunciation of Christ's birth to Joseph occur in revelations of a special kind, in the former case 'in a vision' (Gen. 15:1), and in the latter 'in a dream' (Matt. 1:20).

The principal male characters are each described as having the same attribute. Abraham, Sarah's husband, is one to whom God 'accounted righteousness [*dikaiosynē*]' (Gen. 15:6), while Joseph, Mary's 'husband',[8] is described as 'being righteous [*dikaios*]' (Matt. 1:19).

---

6 This chapter, at least as far as Matthew's Gospel is concerned, leans heavily on the writings of two scholars: Leroy A. Huizenga, *Behold the Christ: Proclaiming the Gospel of Matthew* (Steubenville, OH: Emmaus Road, 2019), and also by the same author, *The New Isaac: Tradition and Intertextuality in the Gospel of Matthew* (Leiden: Brill, 2009); and Richard J. Erickson, 'Joseph and the Birth of Isaac in Matthew 1', *BBR* 10 (2000): 35–51.

7 Huizenga, *Behold the Christ*, 93.

8 Matt. 1:19 refers to Joseph as 'her husband' even before their betrothal is consummated.

The opening words of the Lord to Abraham in his vision are 'Do not be afraid [*mē phobou*], Abram' (Gen. 15:1), and the angel of the Lord says to Joseph, 'Joseph, son of David, do not be afraid [*mē phobēthēs*]' (Matt. 1:20).

For the male offspring to be born he first has to be conceived. In both cases the conception is supernatural. In the earlier case, Abraham and Sarah were very aged, well beyond the age of childbearing, and Sarah had been infertile all her life in any case (cf. Gen. 11:30; 16:1; 18:11). For their child to be conceived, therefore, required divine intervention. In the Gospel Mary is a virgin, a young woman who has not had sexual relations with a man (Matt. 1:23, 25), so the baby is directly conceived through the miraculous working of the Holy Spirit (vv. 18, 20).[9]

We read that God told Abraham regarding 'Sarah your wife' that 'she will bear you a son [*texetai . . . hyion*], and you shall call his name [*kai kaleseis to onoma autou*] Isaac' (Gen. 17:19). In Joseph's dream, the Lord's angel similarly spoke to him concerning 'Mary your wife', whom he should not be afraid to marry. The angel announced that 'she will bear a son [*texetai . . . hyion*], and you shall call his name [*kai kaleseis to onoma autou*] Jesus' (Matt. 1:21). Both these utterances actually give a name to the child before he is born. The correspondences here are too close to be coincidental. The earlier text is most clearly being echoed in the later.[10]

Then later, when the child is born, it is the husband who gives the name, as commanded in the preceding revelation. We read 'and Abraham called the name [*kai ekalesen . . . to onoma*] of his son . . . Isaac' (Gen. 21:3), while the Gospel text says: 'and he [Joseph] called his name [*kai ekalesen to onoma*] Jesus' (Matt. 1:25). We understand why the absence of the phrase 'of his son' from Matthew's statement is necessary, for whereas Abraham was the actual biological father, Joseph was not.[11]

I said above that Abraham does not figure so prominently in Luke's birth narrative as in Matthew's, though he is still mentioned twice. Additionally, Luke includes an interesting parallel between Sarah and Mary, the two mothers-to-be. When Sarah overheard the angel's announcement of the birth, she questioned it, saying, 'Am I really going to bear a child, now I am old?' (Gen. 18:13). To this the Lord responded (literally according to the LXX), 'Shall any

---

9 We note too that the apostle Paul describes the birth of Isaac as 'according to the Spirit' (Gal. 4:29).

10 On the strength of the allusion, see Huizenga, *The New Isaac*, 150–151. Huizenga here defends the proposed allusion against the charge that the language is merely that of any Old Testament character's birth. The number and form of the particular elements involved, alongside the several other allusions to Abraham, Sarah and Isaac, demonstrate that this is patently not the case.

11 The same may be said for the words 'whom she bore to him [Abraham]' also occurring in Gen. 21:3. These again are obviously not applicable to Joseph.

matter be impossible with God?' (v. 14). In the third Gospel, upon hearing the annunciation, Mary poses the question 'How can this be, since I am a virgin?' (Luke 1:34). In his answer the angel declares that 'no matter will be impossible with God' (v. 37). The two utterances bear an obvious close relationship. The former, in its Greek version, reads *mē adynatei para tō theō rēma*, and the latter *ouk adynatēsei para tō theō pan rēma*.[12] Each has the same noun for the grammatical subject, the selfsame verb, negated in both cases, and an identical prepositional phrase. The additional fact that the order of the clause components is identical[13] very strongly suggests an intentional recalling of the earlier passage.

It would seem, then, that Luke's Gospel is likewise deliberately evoking the patriarchal narrative with regard to the coming birth of Isaac. If this is so, then we might expect other allusions in Luke's work. While there is nothing else that is especially outstanding, we note the occurrence of the phrase 'find favour', referring to Abraham (Gen. 18:3, *heuron charin*) and to Mary (Luke 1:30, *heures charin*). This might be taken as mere coincidence, though each does occur at the onset of a passage relating to the future birth, and Luke's is the only usage of this particularly Hebraic idiom in the Gospels. As a matter of fact, its sole other New Testament usage is Acts 7:46, which also relates back to the Old Testament. The passage in Luke sees a double appearance of the verb 'visited' (1:68, 78, *epeskepsato*),[14] in its special sense of divine visitation. The same verb occurs at the beginning of the account of Isaac's birth (Gen. 21:1, *epeskepsato*). Following the birth in each account there comes the statement 'and the child grew' (Gen. 21:8; Luke 2:40).

We find, then, that through their literary allusions the Gospel records of Christ's birth point the reader back to Abraham, Sarah and their son Isaac. The reason for doing so may be readily discerned. God had promised Abraham, the forefather of what was to become the nation of Israel, that through him all nations of the world would be blessed (Gen. 12:3). As the promise is later reiterated, God made it clear that the way this promise would come to pass was not through Abraham personally, but through his 'offspring' (22:18),[15] the first of which was Isaac.[16] Yet once Isaac was born it becomes evident to the reader

---

[12] We here follow the Greek text as it appears in the vast majority of manuscripts. Fewer copies read *para tou theou*, which shows slightly different grammar but bears the same basic sense, 'with God'.

[13] The order in each is: negative + verb + prepositional phrase + subject. Word order can be quite fluid in Greek, yet here both statements are expressed in exactly the same order.

[14] In 1:78 a variant reading in a small number of manuscripts puts the same verb in a different tense (*episkepsetai*).

[15] The Hebrew word *zera'* means 'seed' or 'descendant'. It can also indicate 'offspring' in either its individual or collective sense.

[16] Ishmael is excluded since he was not born to both Abraham and Sarah, according to the terms of the divine promise (cf. Gen. 17:18–21).

of Genesis that the blessing foretold was not to come to the nations through him. Rather, the very same promise, 'in your offspring all nations of the earth will be blessed', was repeated to Isaac (26:4), and then to Isaac's son Jacob (28:14). It becomes clear that the promise would be fulfilled in some future descendant of Abraham. And it is the eventual arrival of this one that the opening sections of Matthew's Gospel portray. Through the allusions in 1:18–25, reinforced by those in Luke 1:28–38, the momentous fact is being underlined that the ultimate son of Abraham, the one in whom the blessing would come to the nations of the world, has now finally been born. Isaac had been the first son of Abraham and Sarah, a son born in a humanly impossible manner. That birth and that son betokened the coming, many centuries later, of the greater offspring, *the* son of Abraham. With the birth of Jesus the time of waiting has passed and the time of divine blessing for all peoples has now arrived.

We would lastly point out that any reader familiar with the story of Isaac will realize that these allusions to the birth of Jesus as the coming of the true son of Abraham also presage the fact that God instructed Abraham to offer up Isaac as a sacrifice (Gen. 22). This did not, of course, literally happen, for Isaac was not the ultimate son of the promise. Intimated here, therefore, is the fact that as *the* son of Abraham, Jesus will one day be called upon to present himself as *the* sacrifice, of which Isaac's experience was a mere shadow. But this is a topic for later.[17]

---

[17] See chapters 21 and 24.

5
The baby in a manger
Matthew 2:18–25; Luke 2:8–20

Now that the long-awaited Christ has been born in Bethlehem, we come to consider what is traditionally called the 'nativity scene', the details of which are variously recorded by Matthew and Luke. The latter of these gives an account of the earlier events immediately following the child's birth, which includes the visit of the shepherds, while the former focuses on the coming of the wise men, also known as the Magi, some time later.

The scene that is portrayed to us conjointly in these passages, it seems to me, has the deliberate design of once again evoking the Old Testament passages concerning the ark of the covenant in the sanctuary where God was believed to dwell, presenting a picture that includes both the sacred object itself and those who came to minister and worship there. The manner in which the ark is evoked on this occasion is notably distinct from the previous set of allusions relating to Mary. Attention will be given to the importance of this fact in due course.

Every reader will no doubt be familiar with the typical nativity scene: the stable, the baby in a manger, Mary and Joseph, a gathering of animals, the shepherds and the wise men, not forgetting the star and perhaps a few angels overhead. Most, though not all, of these elements are found in the biblical descriptions of what transpired following Christ's birth. We do not know for sure that the event took place in a stable. This deduction is made on the basis that, wherever it was, a manger was present. We do, then, seem to have a setting of some enclosed space containing a feeding trough. This latter was most probably made of wood or possibly of stone, and would almost certainly have been rectangular in shape. In this structure lay the focal point of the whole scene, namely the newly born Jesus, previously identified as 'God with us' (Matt. 1:23). In constant attendance on him, no doubt spending much of the time bending over peering into the manger, were the two figures of Mary and Joseph (cf. Luke 2:16).

I would submit that already, in the primary elements of the scene before us, the reader attuned to worship under the old covenant, as all Jewish readers of the Gospels were, would be led to think of the rectangular receptacle which was the ark of the covenant, located at the centre of the inner sanctum known as the holy of holies. As noted in our earlier chapter,[1] this rectangular object, made of wood and gold, was the most sacred item in the whole of Hebrew religion. It represented the very presence of God himself, come to dwell among his people, symbolically speaking at least. Overarching this chest-like structure were the two cherubim, with the face of each looking down on the top of the ark (Exod. 25:18–20). All this, we saw, was but a foreshadowing of the greater truth to come, that of God coming to live among us in our own nature, the incarnation of Deity as the human being Jesus. The details of the nativity scene, therefore, since they record the reality prefigured in the ancient sanctuary, would appear to deliberately call to mind that earlier scene to highlight that what the figures of old foreshadowed had now finally come to pass.

Besides the general outline of the scene, a number of other features in the two Gospel passages point in the same direction. The specific occasion when God came to abide in the sanctuary was marked by the appearance of the 'glory of the LORD' (Exod. 40:34–35; 1 Kgs 8:11; cf. Ezek. 43:5). Similarly, the 'glory of the LORD' was seen the night Christ was born and laid in the manger (Luke 2:9). Together with this glory was the phenomenon of the cloud over the tabernacle. Originally coming down on Mount Sinai (Exod. 19:16; 24:15), this cloud moved to cover the sanctuary as God descended on it (40:34), and the cloud 'looked like fire' (Num. 9:15). The birth narrative includes the star that moved and 'stood over the place' where Jesus was (Matt. 2:9). Both the cloud and the star were natural phenomena that behaved supernaturally and served a theophanic purpose, that is, to indicate the presence of the divine in the place below where they stood.[2]

The descriptions of the shepherds and Magi in themselves give strong support to what we are suggesting. These are two groups of people who come into the presence of the infant. Sacerdotal overtones may be detected in the activities of both. Each account relating to these two sets of visitors includes an expression that is quite neutral in its Gospel setting, yet in the Old Testament forms an idiomatic phrase that specifically concerns the service of ministers in the sanctuary. With regard to the shepherds, we read: 'Now in that region there were shepherds staying out in the fields, keeping watch [*phylassontes phylakas*] over their flock at night' (Luke 2:8). The phrase in question consists of what is known

---

[1] Chapter 2.

[2] We note too that this cloud was 'going before' the Israelites (Exod. 13:21) to lead them to Sinai, just as the star 'went before' the wise men (Matt. 2:9) to guide them to Bethlehem, the places where those being led would encounter God.

as a cognate accusative, where the object noun is formed from the same root as the governing verb. It literally means 'guard the guard' or 'watch the watch'. Here in Luke it has quite an ordinary application, concerning the tending of animals, yet in the Old Testament it has a very significant usage. In these older Scriptures this particular phrase, *šāmar mišmeret* in the original Hebrew, frequently occurs in specific relation to the work performed by various designated ministers in connection with the sanctuary, that is, the tabernacle or temple. English versions generally translate it as 'keep charge' or 'have charge'. Here are a few examples, with their Greek renderings, by way of illustration:

> They [the Levites] shall keep charge [*phylaxousin tas phylakas*] for him [Aaron] and for the whole congregation before the tent of meeting, doing the work of the tabernacle.
> (Num. 3:7)

> Now those who were to camp before the tabernacle on the east, in front of the tent of meeting towards the sunrise, were Moses, Aaron, and his sons [the priests], keeping charge [*phylassontes tas phylakas*] of the sanctuary on behalf of the Israelites.
> (Num. 3:38)

> They [the older Levites] may minister with their brothers in the tent of meeting, to keep charge [*phylassein phylakas*], but they themselves shall do no work.
> (Num. 8:26)

> They [the Levites] are to keep charge [*phylaxousin tas phylakas*] of the tent of meeting and charge of the holy place
> (1 Chr. 23:32)

> You appointed others to keep charge [*phylassein phylakas*] of my sanctuary for you.
> (Ezek. 44:8)

Almost without exception,[3] the expression describes the function of priests or Levites in the old-covenant sanctuary. In applying it to the shepherds, therefore,

---

[3] It should be noted, for the sake of completeness, that when the Hebrew noun *mišmeret* is qualified by a personal possessive, such as '*his* charge', this creates an altogether different idiom relating to the observance of God's commandments (e.g. Gen. 26:5). This latter phrase is therefore distinct from the expression under discussion.

it is introducing a distinct connotation into the Gospel text, one that brings to mind the temple service.

More may be said concerning these shepherds. First, there is the fact that the terms used in both Old and New Testaments which find their way into English as 'shepherd' have a broader meaning in the original languages. As far as their biblical usage is concerned, neither the Hebrew *rō'eh* nor the Greek *poimēn* need be limited to the tending of sheep. The same words, and their respective verbal forms, may indicate the care of other domestic animals besides sheep, especially goats (cf. Song 1:8; Ezek. 34:17). Second, we find a statement in the Mishnah (*Shekalim* 7.4) which informs us implicitly that the animals pastured in the region of Bethlehem, along with other places near to Jerusalem, were used especially for sacrifices in the temple.[4] Lambs, ewes, rams, goats and kids formed the staple for the regular sacrificial offerings,[5] and the shepherds of Luke 2 would have been responsible for the provision of these. Here, therefore, is a further linkage, this time one that is actual and not merely linguistic, between the shepherds and the Jewish sanctuary. These shepherds provided the animals essential for the sacrificial worship, while the Levites and priests carried out the necessary rituals with those animals in the temple.

Luke's shepherds, then, are closely identified with the temple service, both by the allusive use of the phrase *phylassontes phylakas* and by the fact that the location of their pasturing meant their involvement with sacrificial animals, something that was in all probability common knowledge among the Jews at the time. For these reasons the shepherds present a suitable depiction of those who performed offerings in the sanctuary. And in the Gospel they do in fact draw near and enter that allusory holy place, more of which shortly.

Coming to the Magi, it may be that their original office within their own culture was a priestly one, as some scholars propose.[6] If so, this fact of itself would confer connotations of priesthood on their role within the present Gospel scenario. Were the Magi actual priests or not, we discover that, through the technique of allusion, these men too are depicted in sacerdotal terms. In describing what they do when they come into the presence of the child, we again notice, among other things, another idiomatic expression

---

[4] The place name that appears in this Mishnah text, 'Migdal Eder', is known to have been in the vicinity of Bethlehem (cf. Gen. 35:21).

[5] The sacrifice of larger animals, such as bulls, cows, calves and heifers, was much more exceptional (e.g. for rulers and the rich, and for special ceremonies, such as the burning of the red heifer). For the common mass of the population the animals pastured by shepherds would have sufficed for offerings on their behalf and for the regular daily sacrifices also.

[6] E.g. Joseph Ratzinger, *Jesus of Nazareth: The Infancy Narratives* (London: Bloomsbury, 2012), 90: 'Magi are understood to be members of the Persian priestly caste'; also R. T. France, *The Gospel of Matthew* (NICNT; Grand Rapids, MI: Eerdmans, 2007), 66.

which has a specific Old Testament connotation. The first Gospel tells us that, in the context of their worship, 'they presented gifts [*prosēnenkan . . . dōra*] to him of gold, frankincense, and myrrh' (Matt. 2:11). This sentence is laden with terms relating to the priestly service and the sanctuary. The seemingly ordinary phrase 'present gifts' in the context of temple worship has the sense of 'present an offering', as in:

If he presents a lamb as his offering [*prosenenkē to dōron*] for sin . . .
(Lev. 4:32)

Since he has a defect, he shall not come near to present the offerings [*ta dōra . . . prosenenkein*] to his God.
(Lev. 21:21)

Until you have presented the offerings [*prosenenkēte . . . ta dōra*] to your God, you shall eat no bread nor roasted grain nor new grain.
(Lev. 23:14)

Why are we kept from presenting the offering [*prosenenkai to dōron*] to the LORD at its appointed time among the children of Israel?
(Num. 9:7)[7]

We find, therefore, specialized terminology relating to the temple ministry applied to the wise men as it was to the shepherds.

Nouns appearing in the same verse, 'gold, frankincense, and myrrh' (Matt. 2:11), also indicate elements used in connection with the priesthood and sanctuary. Gold was a prominent metal in the construction of both the tabernacle (e.g. Exod. 25:11, 18, 24; 26:6, 29) and the Jerusalem temple (e.g. 1 Kgs 6:20, 21, 22, 28, 30), as well as in the manufacturing of the high-priestly garments ('gold' appears sixteen times in Exod. 28). Frankincense was a key ingredient in the sacred incense employed in the various ceremonies of the sanctuary (Exod. 30:34), and frankincense was added to the grain-offering (Lev. 2:1) and the bread of the presence (24:7). Nehemiah 13:5 and 9 tell us that this frankincense was stored in the temple.[8] Myrrh was the primary component of the holy anointing oil (Exod. 30:23), the oil used to anoint the tabernacle at its dedication

---

[7] Exactly the same expression appears in the New Testament for the priestly task: 'every high priest taken from among men is appointed for men in matters pertaining to God, in order to *offer gifts*' (Heb. 5:1).

[8] NIV, NET and NJB all render the Hebrew term *lĕbônâ* here by 'incense', though it is unambiguously 'frankincense', translated into Greek as *libanos* in the Septuagint, the same word as in Matt. 2:11.

(40:9) and the priests upon their ordination (Lev. 8:10). These three items, therefore, have similar connotations to the verbal phrase 'present gifts', all pointing to the temple and its ministration.[9]

Another detail about the wise men is that they come 'from the east' (Matt. 2:1). In the context of the sanctuary this is noteworthy information since both tabernacle and temple had their entrance on the eastern side (Exod. 27:13–15; cf. Ezek. 40:6), entailing that all entering would approach from the east.

Also, the specific building the wise men enter is termed 'the house' (Matt. 2:11).[10] In its Gospel context this, of course, plainly means a house of the usual kind, a human habitation. Yet this could also be a further connection with the Old Testament sanctuary. On numerous occasions the temple itself was simply called 'the house'. The temple is referred to as 'the house' no fewer than twenty-nine times in 1 Kings 6, the chapter that deals with the construction of Solomon's temple. It states, for instance, that 'he [Solomon] prepared an inner sanctuary within the house, to set there the ark of the covenant of the LORD' (v. 19). It is in this 'house' that the Magi perform an act of worship: 'falling down [pesontes] they worshipped [prosekynēsan] him' (Matt. 2:11), an act very suited to being in a sacred place such as the temple. This is precisely what the Israelites did when the glory of the Lord descended on God's 'house' in Jerusalem: 'they fell [epeson] face down on the ground and worshipped [prosekynēsan] . . . the LORD' (2 Chr. 7:3).

We have a picture then of these Magi, men trained in certain esoteric or priestly arts, coming from the east, entering the 'house' with gold and precious spices, the focal point of which is the rectangular box-like object and its special contents, where they bow in worship and offer gifts. These elements of the narrative, taken together with what was stated with regard to the shepherds, create a compelling case for deliberate allusion to the ancient form of approach to God by the ministers in the tabernacle and temple.

This brings us now to consider the import of the allusions. I believe that two essential truths are being taught. First and foremost, since the infant Jesus occupies the central position as the object of adoration in this allusory temple scene, it can be concluded that the presence of God is now to be found in him. As the ark in the sanctuary once represented that presence, as an inanimate object functioning symbolically, now that presence is embodied, or rather incarnated, in a human being in whom God dwells as an actual reality,

---

[9] We further note, for good measure, that the term 'treasures' (thēsaurous) in 'opening their treasures, they presented gifts to him of gold, frankincense, and myrrh' (Matt. 2:11) also occurs in both a tabernacle (e.g. Josh. 6:24; 1 Chr. 9:26) and a temple context (e.g. 1 Kgs 7:51; 2 Chr. 8:15).

[10] Note that the noun 'house', though previously unmentioned, is grammatically definite ('the house').

and not merely in a representative way. Jesus, even as the baby in a manger, is the Lord of glory in whom 'the whole fullness of the Godhead dwells bodily' (Col. 2:9).

At this point we remind ourselves of what we saw earlier concerning the allusions to the ark that had surrounded Mary, the mother of Jesus.[11] As a holy vessel who bore the Christ-child, such literary features were entirely appropriate with respect to her. But now that Jesus has exited the virgin womb and been born into the world as an independent being, such allusions now pertain to him alone.[12] Mary's crucial purpose in this particular regard has ceased. This fact is also conveyed through the scene before us. It is evident that Mary now takes on a subsidiary role, both here and hereafter in the Gospel narratives.

The second truth concerns the nature of those who approach the baby in his allusory sanctum, themselves as allusory priestly figures. That this is done by shepherds and wise men speaks volumes about the accessibility of the God made flesh. Under the old-covenant form of worship only specifically desig-nated ministers could serve in the sanctuary, and of them only one, the high priest, could actually enter into the divine presence. All others were excluded. Even the Levites, who made up the larger number of attendants in the holy precincts, were not allowed to go into the inner recesses of the structure to view the sacred objects inside. They would pay the ultimate penalty if they did: 'they shall not go in [*ou mē eiselthōsin*] to see [*idein*] the holy things, or they will die' (Num. 4:20). With respect to both the shepherds and the Magi, they actually did go into where the child was and saw him. Note the words: 'When they [the shepherds] had seen [*idontes*] him . . .' (Luke 2:17), and 'When they [the Magi] had entered [*elthontes eis*] the house they saw [*eidon*] the child' (Matt. 2:11).[13] What was expressly denied to the Levites in the symbolic old-covenant sanctuary was freely granted to the shepherds and wise men in the allusory scene portrayed. This is surely communicating the fact that ministerial restric-tions of any kind no longer apply now that the symbol (the ark in a temple) has given way to the reality (God in Christ). In the new era those not especially ordained to sacred service may freely enter into the divine presence and see. This is true of Jews of low rank, such as the shepherds, and more than this, of

---

[11] See chapter 2.

[12] As one notable Catholic scholar, Yves Congar, remarked: 'The new ark of the new and definitive covenant is indeed Mary during the period in which she bears Jesus in her womb' (Yves M. J. Congar, *The Mystery of the Temple, Or the Manner of God's Presence to His Creatures from Genesis to the Apocalypse* [London: Burns & Oates, 1962], 257). Consequently, once the birth of her child has taken place, the Gospels show no more allusions that present Mary in such a manner. Rather, it is Jesus himself who occupies the place of the Old Testament ark.

[13] We shall find the same truth revealed once again in the allusions explored in chapter 27.

the Magi, who most certainly were Gentiles.[14] It is not just that non-priests and non-Levites may enter, but also non-Jews. In such a way, with the coming of the new covenant, centring on the incarnate Son, God has made his presence accessible to all.

---

[14] On the Persian origin of the Magi, see Edwin M. Yamauchi, *Persia and the Bible* (Grand Rapids, MI: Baker, 1990), 467.

6
The flight into Egypt
Matthew 2:13–23

We now take a look at two closely related events that occurred in the time of Christ's infancy. At that time Herod the Great was king of Judea. From all accounts Herod was an evil man who would brook no rival, even within his own family.[1] The events we consider here immediately follow the departure of the Magi when Herod attempts to kill the newborn child, and relate how Jesus is delivered by fleeing with Joseph and Mary to another country.

In the second chapter of Matthew we read that when wise men come to Jerusalem seeking the 'King of the Jews' (Matt. 2:2), Herod is provoked to take action. Being informed that the new king has been born in Bethlehem, Herod tragically gives orders that all male children under two years of age in that town should be put to death (v. 16). To prevent the infant Jesus being numbered among those murdered, God sends an angel to Joseph, instructing him to take Mary and her child and flee to Egypt. They are to remain there until they receive further word (v. 13). Some time later, once Herod has died, Joseph is given permission to return to their home in Nazareth (v. 20).

There are connections with the Old Testament here that are explicit, and there are those that are more subtle, that is to say, allusive. In this context the Gospel-writer (v. 15) gives a formal citation from the book of Hosea. He only quotes the latter half of the verse in question, but in full it reads: 'When Israel was a child I loved him, and out of Egypt I called my son' (Hos. 11:1). Since this is an overt quotation from the Hebrew prophet it does not fall within the category of allusion. Rather, at this particular point Matthew is employing typology, as he does elsewhere, and our primary concern is not with such, important as it may be. Nevertheless, as the quotation forms an important part of the flow of thought, some comment needs to be made on it.

---

[1] Cf. Joseph Ratzinger, *Jesus of Nazareth: The Infancy Narratives* (London: Bloomsbury, 2012), 108: 'In 7 B.C. Herod had had his sons Alexander and Aristobulus executed, as he considered them a threat to his power. In 4 B.C. he killed his son Antipater for the same reason . . . He thought solely in terms of power . . . It was clear from his character that he would stop at nothing.'

In brief, we observe that the words of Hosea are in the past tense ('was', 'called'). This fact, together with the reference to Egypt, makes it apparent that we are not looking at a direct verbal prophecy, but at a description of an event that took place earlier in history from Hosea's temporal perspective (eighth century BC). This is obviously a view back to the exodus, several centuries before Hosea, when God called his people out of Egypt to come to the Promised Land. The words therefore speak of a notable past event, and one that concerned, not an individual, but the whole nation of Israel. While this is so, it is important to recall that at that earlier time of the exodus Israel was expressly described by God as 'my son' and 'my firstborn' (Exod. 4:22, 23). It would appear to be this description that is later echoed by the prophet.

We see, then, that both by God originally and by Hosea some time later, Israel is viewed as God's collective 'son'. This sonship of Israel is not, of course, literal. In calling the Hebrews to be his chosen people, the object of his special care and attention, God was in a sense adopting the nation as his 'son'.[2] Yet from the wider perspective of the ultimate divine purpose as revealed in all Scripture, Israel's special status as God's 'son' serves as a figure for a greater son to come. Here is the essential typological element to be discerned in Hosea's words. In the working out of the divine purpose, the fact is that God's son in the Old Testament, the collective 'son' of the nation of Israel, becomes uniquely embodied in the person of the only-begotten Son of God, namely Jesus himself.[3] This being so, the parallel may be drawn, and is being drawn by Matthew, that just as the son which was Israel of old was at one stage called out of Egypt, so too the divine Son Jesus would be called out from the very same place. There is, however, a very significant difference in the circumstances of these two similar events, as we shall shortly see.[4]

---

[2] A good discussion of Israel's sonship can be found in Douglas K. Stuart, *Exodus: An Exegetical and Theological Exposition of Holy Scripture* (NAC 2; Nashville, TN: Broadman & Holman, 2006), 146, 150–151.

[3] See Richard B. Hays, *Echoes of Scripture in the Gospels* (Waco, TX: Baylor University Press, 2016), 113–114. There is also evidence to suggest that the Jews themselves made a connection between the sonship of Israel, as expressed in Exod. 4:22–23, and the sonship of the Messiah. The midrashic work known as Exodus Rabbah, in a comment on Exod. 13:2 ('Consecrate to me every firstborn male'), records that 'Rabbi Nathan said: The Holy One, blessed be he, told Moses, "Just as I have made Jacob a firstborn, for it says, 'Israel is my son, my firstborn' [Exod. 4:22], so I will make the King Messiah a firstborn, as it says, 'I will also appoint him firstborn' [Ps. 89:27]."'

[4] One of the Fathers of the Orthodox Church, Theophylact, the eleventh-century bishop of Ochrid, anticipating some objection concerning Matthew's use of Hosea at this point, makes the apposite remark: 'The Jews say that this [Hos. 11:1] was said of the people whom Moses led out of Egypt. We reply, is it anything remarkable that something which was spoken in type as a foreshadowing, was realized by Christ in truth? Furthermore, who is the Son of God? The Hebrew people who worshipped the idols and images of Baal Peor, or he who truly is the Son of God?' (See Christopher Stade [tr.], *The Explanation by Blessed Theophylact Archbishop of Ochrid and Bulgaria of the Holy Gospel According to Saint Matthew* [House Springs, MO: Chrysostom Press, 2006], 28).

One further feature regarding Hosea 11:1 that must be pointed out here is the position of the citation within Matthew's narrative. For although the quote concerns God's son coming out of Egypt, the writer of the first Gospel places it at the juncture where Joseph, Mary and Jesus in fact go down into Egypt (Matt. 2:14–15), rather than when they are commanded to depart (vv. 20–21). This is also very relevant to the allusive theme that Matthew is developing, as will become evident.

In this second chapter of Matthew, interwoven with the foregoing typology concerning Israel and Jesus, the son of God brought up from Egypt, there is a more subtle use of allusion, this time with reference to the person of Moses. This is not entirely separate from the former typology, since both themes relate to the contents of the early portions of Exodus. Moses, of course, was the one divinely ordained to lead Israel out of Egypt.[5] So we see both typology and allusion at play in Matthew's narrative, serving a common goal. Each focuses on different aspects of the earlier Exodus account, and each operates on its own literary level, but both enhance our appreciation of what is being recorded of Christ.

By means of allusion, we discover that Matthew's infancy narrative presents Jesus in terms of the man Moses, the divinely ordained leader of the Hebrews, whose life is threatened in the opening chapters of Exodus. The allusions, as is the norm, are both thematic and verbal in character, and certain of them are almost self-evident, while others are more obscure.[6]

The general background of each context is obviously similar. Both consist of a tyrannical king, Pharaoh in Exodus and Herod in Matthew, who has power over the Hebrew people. These two rulers are also bent on destroying male children of the Hebrews, and issue orders to that end (Exod. 1:22; Matt. 2:16).

In the second chapter of the Exodus narrative we find more specifically that the Pharaoh wished to kill Moses (v. 15), while Herod of course seeks the death of Jesus. Each of these two individuals whose lives are sought is divinely appointed, as previously stated, to both deliver and to lead the people of God (Exod. 3:10; Matt. 1:21).

In order to preserve his life Moses fled from Egypt, whereas for his protection from Herod Jesus is taken to Egypt. In the Greek versions of the two texts, we

---

[5] Allison supports the view that Matthew construed the status of Jesus 'as the new Israel and his identity as another Moses as *correlative conceptions*' (italics added). See Dale C. Allison Jr, *The New Moses: A Matthean Typology* (Minneapolis, MN: Fortress, 1993), 142.

[6] These have previously been observed by several other scholars, such as Raymond E. Brown, *The Birth of the Messiah: A Commentary on the Infancy Narratives in the Gospels of Matthew and Luke* (New York, NY: Doubleday, 1993), 113; Aaron M. Gale, *Redefining Ancient Borders: The Jewish Scribal Framework of Matthew's Gospel* (London: T&T Clark, 2005), 152–153.

read that 'Moses departed [*anechōrēsen*] from before Pharaoh' (Exod. 2:15), and that Joseph took his wife and the infant Jesus and 'departed [*anechōrēsen*] into Egypt' (Matt. 2:14). There would have been several other options for a verb of motion to communicate the intended meaning here, yet we find the identical verb used in each case.

Having withdrawn from the place where their lives were endangered, Moses in the one instance and Jesus in the other remained in exile in the same land until the death of the ruler in question.

After a period of time there comes in both narratives a heavenly revelation declaring that the ruler has died (Exod. 4:19, *eteleutēsen*; Matt. 2:19, *teleutēsantos*).[7] At this point the verbal correspondences are so alike that intentional reference is almost certain. With regard to Pharaoh Moses was told, 'Go back to Egypt, for all those who were seeking your life have died' (Exod. 4:19), and in the Gospel Joseph is ordered, 'Get up, take the child and his mother and go to the land of Israel, for those who were seeking the child's life have died' (Matt. 2:20). In the final causal expression the language is extremely close. Exodus has *tethnēkasin gar pantes hoi zētountes sou tēn psychēn*, and Matthew *tethnēkasin gar hoi zētountes tēn psychēn tou paidiou*. The only differences are that the latter lacks the qualifying 'all' and speaks of the 'life' of the child rather than 'your life'. The initial finite verb and subsequent participle are absolutely identical. What is more striking is that they are both plural ('those who were seeking . . . have died'), which is not what would be expected in either case from the previous literary contexts. Exodus had only spoken of Pharaoh, and the Gospel solely of Herod, as the persons seeking the life of the main protagonist. On this occurrence of the plural forms biblical scholar Dale Allison concludes that the plural in Matthew 2:20 is not meant to be taken as indicating Herod's co-executors, there being none specifically mentioned in the text, but rather 'the language of Exod. 4:19 was retained without perfect grammatical adjustment, in order to make the parallel with the sentence from Exodus unmistakable'.[8] Such a conclusion would seem almost unavoidable. Matthew is purposely drawing his readers' attention to the parallel between the death of the king who sought the life of Moses and the king who wished the death of Christ. And in each instance the death in question opens the way for the return of the exile, as directed in the divine communication.

Besides the foregoing statement of the ruler's death, each of the same contexts speaks of taking the family in the act of returning. The older narrative states

---

[7] Again Greek has a variety of verbs and idiomatic phrases to express this idea.
[8] Allison, *The New Moses*, 143.

that 'Moses took his wife and his sons and put them on a donkey, and went back to the land of Egypt' (Exod. 4:20), while in the later Joseph is told to 'take the child and his mother and go to the land of Israel' (Matt. 2:20). Indeed, it may well be the earlier scene that prompted the inclusion of the donkey, not mentioned in the Gospels themselves, in later pictorial representations of the holy family on the move.

The foregoing are the principal points of contact, but mention may also be made of the phrase 'by night' (*nyktos*). This occurs in Matthew's narrative at the point when Joseph, Mary and Jesus flee from Herod (2:14). This night-time flight does not occur in Exodus in relation to Moses, but it does turn up later. In chapter 12 we are twice told that the flight of the Hebrews from Egypt took place 'by night' (vv. 31, 42). This event, of course, is the actual exodus itself, the escape of Israel from the clutches of the king of Egypt. This particular allusive element, therefore, does not connect Jesus with Moses, but with the nation.[9] And that is what we saw above in the matter of Matthew's typological use of Hosea 11:1. The two closely related themes can be seen to intertwine in the set of allusions. At a more explicit level Jesus is the new Israel, God's son, while at a more subliminal level Jesus, as the new deliverer, is primarily seen as corresponding to Moses, as well as to the nation. As stated earlier, the two become merged in the Gospel narrative.

In the matter of seeking out allusions there is always the danger of taking things too far, but in this particular case the allusive data even appears to extend to parallels between the midwives of Exodus 1 and the Magi (wise men) of Matthew 2. Conceptually, both are extra-familial visitors who come to the home of childbirth. In the former account Pharaoh 'summoned' (*ekalesen*) the midwives (Exod. 1:18), while in the latter Herod 'summoned' (*kalesas*) the Magi (Matt. 2:7). The children in question are said to be born before the midwives arrive (Exod. 1:19), as Christ is born before the arrival of the Magi (Matt. 2:2). When they come upon the children neither the midwives nor the Magi do what the king tells them to do (Exod. 1:17; Matt. 2:12). Both contexts further imply or explicitly state that there was some deception involved

---

[9] Allison here anticipates the would-be objector. He helpfully states: 'It is more likely . . . that the cluster of motifs – flight, night, Egypt – should recall the exodus. Tradition held that Moses and the Israelites fled Egypt *at night* (Exod. 12:31–42; the fact was firmly planted in Jewish memory because the Passover was celebrated in the evening; cf. Exod. 12:8). The objection to this reading is that the notice comes in [Matt.] 2:14, not in 2:21, where the family of Jesus leaves Egypt. But this overlooks that the parallelism lies not in the identity of course taken but in the flight itself. It is true that Moses and the Israelites fled *from* Egypt, Jesus and his family *to* Egypt. But the emphasis is on what is shared, that being the act of fleeing from hostility. Moreover, Joseph and his family were only fleeing when they exited Palestine, not when they left Egypt; so the typology is more effective with *nyktos* in 2:14, where there is urgency, instead of 2:21, where haste is unnecessary' (*The New Moses*, 152; italics original).

(Exod. 1:19; cf. Matt. 2:16, 'When Herod saw that he had been *deceived* by the Magi'). The refusal to comply with the king's instructions then immediately results in each instance in his command to kill the male infants of the Hebrews (Exod. 1:22; Matt. 2:16). Perhaps it could also be pointed out that the Greek terms for 'midwives' and 'Magi' bear a phonological resemblance. The first is *maiai* (from the root *mai-*) and the second *magoi* (from the root *mag-*). The connection becomes more evident in the neuter nominal forms, as the craft of the midwife is expressed by the noun *maieuma* and that of the Magi by *mageuma*. These do seem, then, to be further points of detail that connect the two narratives, though I would not insist on the presence of deliberate design in this particular instance.

We may now bring the various threads together and consider what the underlying purpose might be of these Old Testament allusions in Matthew's infancy narrative. First and most apparent, the allusions indicate the fact that a new exodus is soon to transpire. As the early part of the book of Exodus relates the birth of the deliverer of Israel from Egypt, so the opening of Matthew's Gospel records the birth of the one who 'will save his people from their sins' (1:21).[10] The Hebrews in Egypt had waited several centuries, mostly enduring suffering at the hands of their Gentile masters, until the time of redemption eventually arrived with the coming of Moses. So too the events we read in Matthew come after an extended period of Judea's domination under the rule of Gentiles. Here, however, the deliverance set in motion is not going to be merely physical or political, but will be a transcendent spiritual redemption from the overwhelming power of sin and death.

As the life of each appointed saviour is threatened by an evil king, we see that Herod, through the allusions to Exodus, is being portrayed as a 'pharaoh-like' oppressor.[11] There is great irony here, of course. Whereas Pharaoh was the king of a Gentile nation, Herod was the king of the Jews themselves. The one put to death the male infants of foreign slaves, the other the children of his own people. Rather than be the benefactor of the Jewish nation, ruling according to the divine law, in seeking the life even of the one born to accomplish the ultimate act of redemption he had become a greater tyrant than Pharaoh of old had been.

Included in the irony is the direction which the flight takes. For Moses, and then later for Israel, it was *from* Egypt. For the infant Jesus and his family it was

---

[10] It may be significant that Matthew's object phrase 'his people' (*ton laon autou*) and the prepositional phrase 'from sin' echo God speaking of the deliverance of 'my people' (*ton laon mou*) from Egypt in the Exodus narrative (e.g. 3:10, 12). It is noteworthy that in the one instance the possessor is God, and in the other Christ.

[11] Cf. Garrett Galvin, *Egypt as a Place of Refuge* (Tübingen: Mohr Siebeck, 2011), 176.

actually *from* Judea, the Jews' own homeland, and *to* Egypt. It was now Judea that had become the place of oppression and Egypt the place of refuge. This may account for the fact mentioned above concerning the position of the Hosea citation in Matthew's narrative. There it was noted that this quotation regarding the calling of God's 'son' out of Egypt comes at the point where the holy family leave Judea. This is saying, in effect, that the Judea of Christ's day had become like the Egypt of old, spiritually speaking. The allusions, therefore, present an implicit, but unmistakable, condemnation of the spiritual condition of Judea and its king.

We find another positive intention to the allusions. By means of the subtle references to earlier events, readers of the Gospel are given considerable hope. Since Matthew's original Jewish-Christian recipients would be intimately familiar with the exodus account, they would appreciate from the opening chapters of the Gospel the significance of the preservation of the deliverer. In view of such protection from the evil king who sought his death, Moses was then able to proceed and initiate the long-awaited redemption. So, too, the preservation of the Christ-child bodes well in the matter of the greater salvation. Seeing that in the case of Moses, despite the threats to his life and his exile in a foreign land, he succeeded in his calling to bring out Israel, so too in the face of similar dangers Jesus will succeed in the purpose for which he was sent. His people will indeed be saved from their sins. As Moses in times past had accomplished a wondrous deliverance in the physical sphere, so Jesus, the greater Moses-like figure, would now accomplish a more surpassing deliverance in the spiritual.

7

The baptism and temptation

Matthew 3:13 – 4:11; Mark 1:9–13; Luke 3:21–22; 4:1–12; John 1:29–34

The events discussed in the present chapter concern the commencement of Christ's ministry. What is described here forms, in effect, the inauguration of his public preaching among his people. The two events marking this beginning, namely the baptism and temptation, may be treated as inseparable since in all three synoptic Gospels[1] the latter arises out of the former and is inextricably connected with it,[2] as will be made clear.

At approximately thirty years of age (Luke 3:23) Jesus leaves his home in Nazareth to head for the River Jordan in order to receive baptism at the hands of John the Baptist. Immediately upon being baptized, as Jesus emerges from the water, two extraordinary things take place. The first of these is the descent of the Holy Spirit upon him in the form of a dove (Matt. 3:16; Mark 1:10; Luke 3:22; John 1:32), and the second is the heavenly voice declaring Jesus to be God's Son and affirming his Father's delight in him (Matt. 3:17; Mark 1:11; Luke 3:22). Following this, Jesus is led out into the wilderness by the Spirit to be tested by the devil (Matt. 4:1; Mark 1:12; Luke 4:1). There are three specific tests in total, as mentioned by Matthew (4:3–10) and Luke (4:3–12), which in each instance are countered with a passage of Scripture, all three citations interestingly coming from the book of Deuteronomy.

There can be little doubt that in the record of these events allusion is being made to the people of Israel at the time when they came out of Egypt and passed into the wilderness.[3] At this time, as they were about to depart from Egypt, the

---

[1] By 'synoptic' we mean that these three can be viewed together, since they contain much material in common, and also often the order of events. John, the fourth Gospel, has a noticeably distinct character and includes many passages that the others do not.

[2] John speaks only of the baptism and not of the temptation that immediately followed.

[3] Modern biblical scholarship supports such a background to the allusions. See, e.g., G. K. Beale and D. A. Carson (eds.), *Commentary on the New Testament Use of the Old Testament* (Grand Rapids, MI: Baker Academic, 2007), 14–18; 283–287; R. T. France, *The Gospel of Matthew* (NICNT; Grand Rapids, MI: Eerdmans, 2007), 127–128; W. D. Davies and Dale C. Allison Jr, *Matthew 1–7: Volume 1* (ICC; Edinburgh: T&T Clark, 1988), 352–373.

nation was explicitly identified as being God's son: 'Israel is my son, my firstborn' (Exod. 4:22),[4] a matter touched upon in the preceding chapter. Though this sonship was clearly not a physical relation but rather a divine appointment to be the chosen nation, that does not exclude the idea of intimacy.[5] In the Gospels Jesus is presented as the true Son of God, a relationship of actual begettal, spiritually and eternally, according to our confession. As seen previously, Matthew has already identified Jesus as the Son by means of a quote from the prophets back in 2:15, 'Out of Egypt I called my son' (Hos. 11:1). This is highly significant in that the citation is made not simply to claim sonship for Jesus, but to do so in the context of a journey out of Egypt and in a prophetic text which clearly in the first instance relates to the whole nation of Israel, most probably having Exodus 4:22 in mind. And then in our present portion of the Gospels, Jesus is further and more directly confirmed to be God's Son through the voice at his baptism, noted above. This same theme of sonship is, moreover, prominent in two of the three temptations (Matt. 4:3, 6; Luke 4:3, 9). Plainly, then, both Israel at the exodus and Jesus at the inauguration of his ministry are attributed with divine sonship in the manner respectively described.

When the Israelites left Egypt they came to the Red Sea, which they passed through, according to the familiar account (Exod. 14). Reflecting on the meaning of this happening, the apostle Paul later describes it as Israel's baptism: 'They were all baptized into Moses in the cloud and in the sea' (1 Cor. 10:2). In a sense the people did go down into the water and then emerge again, in a way that resembles the rite of baptism. Corresponding to this, in our Gospel passages Jesus presents himself at the River Jordan where he goes down into the water and rises again. The Jordan, as a body of water, here has a distinct relationship with the Red Sea.[6] The sea figures prominently at the beginning of the exodus narrative, the river at its end, and both are parted by miraculous means to allow the Israelites to pass through. Israel is baptized in the former body of water, Jesus in the latter.

Apart from baptism as a rite involving water, for Jesus it was the occasion of his receiving the Holy Spirit. This is a conspicuous element in the Gospel

---

[4] See also Deut. 1:31; 32:5, 6, 18–20; Jer. 31:9. The begettal spoken of in Deut. 32:18 is, of course, metaphorical.

[5] Cf. Terence E. Fretheim, *Exodus: A Biblical Commentary for Teaching and Preaching* (Interpretation; Louisville, KY: John Knox, 1991), 77. Fretheim remarks: 'Israel is here "brought into the closest and dearest relation to God" [citing Driver], with all the intimacy a parent-child relationship implies . . . God as parent enters deeply into the suffering of the children and claims them for life and freedom.'

[6] Ps. 114 (v. 3 and v. 5), we observe, brings together the Red Sea and the Jordan in poetic parallelisms. For other similarities between these two bodies of water and the miraculous events that transpired at each one, see Nicholas P. Lunn, *Jesus in the Jewish Scriptures: How the Old Testament Bears Witness to Christ* (London: Faithbuilders, 2020): 138–147.

accounts. The Spirit first descended upon him, and then led him out into the wilderness (Matt. 4:1; Luke 4:1). It might too quickly be supposed that there is nothing corresponding to this with regard to Israel at the exodus. The narrative of Exodus seems to make no explicit mention of anything similar. Yet upon closer inspection correspondences in the exodus event do in fact emerge. In Exodus 14 itself, while the Israelites are on the shore of the Red Sea, the text states that 'the LORD drove the sea back with a strong east wind all that night and turned it into dry land; and the waters were divided' (v. 21). In Hebrew the word for 'wind' here is *rûaḥ*, which also has the sense of 'breath' and 'spirit', and is the usual word employed to describe the Spirit of God. And, as in the Gospel episode, the activity of this 'wind/spirit' is over water. So there is a parallel here.

However, the chapters in Exodus are not the only biblical source that concern this period in Israel's history. Later Old Testament books also contribute to our understanding of what then occurred. In an oracle of Isaiah, where the context manifestly relates to the exodus, the prophet poses the rhetorical question: 'Where is he who brought them up out of the sea with the shepherd of his flock [Moses]? Where is he who put his Holy Spirit among them?' (63:11). Since the words that precede the reference to the Spirit, along with those in the following verse, describe the events of the exodus, the fact of God putting his Spirit within Israel must also be taken as happening at that same time.[7] Isaiah makes another reference to the Spirit three verses later, still in the same context, in which the prophet says: 'the Spirit came down from the Lord and guided them; thus you led your people' (v. 14).[8] Here is both the idea of the Spirit's descent and that of his role in leading, as also seen in connection with the Spirit as pertaining to Jesus.

Another reference to the Spirit during the exodus is found in a statement made by Nehemiah: 'you gave your good Spirit to instruct them' (Neh. 9:20). While space does not allow a detailed discussion of the exact manner in which the Spirit was operative during this time, it is possible that the term indicates the presence of the angel of the Lord among the people (cf. Isa. 63:9), or the angel in the pillar of cloud and fire who led them. These could very well have been one and the same being. Yet another possibility is that by the Spirit is meant the spiritual endowment of gifts to Bezalel and others, filled with the Spirit of God, who built the tabernacle (cf. Exod. 31:2–3; 35:30–31). Or again it might indicate

---

[7] See the analysis in Gregory K. Beale, *A New Testament Biblical Theology: The Unfolding of the Old Testament in the New* (Grand Rapids, MI: Baker Academic, 2011), 414–415.

[8] In this verse in its Greek (LXX) version, the phrase 'the Spirit [*pneuma*] came down [*katebē*]' contains the same words that describe the descent of the Spirit on Christ at his baptism in all four Gospels (Matt. 3:16; Mark 1:10; Luke 3:22; John 1:32).

the indwelling presence of God that resided within the tabernacle (cf. Exod. 29:45–46; Hag. 2:5).[9] Whatever the precise activity of the Spirit might have been in this setting, it is evident that in the memory of Israel the Spirit was indeed understood to have been granted to the people in some significant manner at the exodus, whether in terms of guidance, gifting or divine indwelling.

In each of our two scenarios, following the baptismal event, the main protagonists are led into the wilderness (Exod. 15:22; cf. Matt. 4:1; Mark 1:12; Luke 4:1). Here they remain for a period of forty years in the case of Israel (Deut. 2:7), and forty days in the case of Jesus (Matt. 4:2; Mark 1:13; Luke 4:2). The quantity of time is here obviously related, especially when it is remembered that the forty years given for Israel to wander in the desert was itself based on a period of forty days, relating to the sending out of the spies who brought back a negative report of the land of Canaan (Num. 14:33–34).

The feature that most closely binds together both occasions, namely the wilderness experience of Israel and that of Christ, has to be that of testing. The concepts of testing and temptation in biblical language are, we observe, expressed by the same words. In Greek the noun *peirasmos* means 'testing, temptation, trial', and the verb *peirazō* has the sense of 'test, tempt, try'. Evidently, a test could readily include an element of temptation also. Therefore, the event in the life of Jesus we generally identify as the 'temptation' could equally well be named the 'testing' of Christ.[10] Deuteronomy offers a clear statement that one of the reasons God led the Israelites into the desert was explicitly to test them. Note the following:

> You shall remember all the way which the LORD your God has led you in the wilderness these forty years, in order to humble you and to test you, to know what was in your heart, whether you would keep his commandments or not. He humbled you and let you become hungry, and then fed you with manna which neither you nor your fathers had known, to make you understand that man does not live by bread alone, but man lives by every word that proceeds from the mouth of the LORD. (Deut. 8:2–3)

---

[9] See the discussions in John N. Oswalt, *The Book of Isaiah: Chapters 40–66* (NICOT; Grand Rapids, MI: Eerdmans, 1998), 607; J. Alec Motyer, *The Prophecy of Isaiah: An Introduction and Commentary* (Downers Grove, IL: InterVarsity Press, 1993), 515. There is the further mention of the Spirit in the wilderness with application to Moses and the leaders of Israel in Num. 11:17. This was how John Calvin, for one, understood Isaiah's remarks here concerning the Spirit (see John Calvin, *Commentaries*, vol. 8, tr. John King [Grand Rapids, MI: Baker, 1998], 349, on Isa. 63:11).

[10] In Matt. 4 and Luke 4 the original edition of the NIV had the traditional title 'The Temptation of Jesus', whereas the updated 2011 edition now has 'Jesus Is Tested in the Wilderness'.

It is scarcely possible to read these verses without thinking of Christ's later experience. Both Israel and Christ were led into the wilderness for a fortyfold time period in order to be tested. And the passage goes on to talk about the people becoming hungry so that they might learn that man does not live by bread alone. These latter words bring us specifically to the first test Jesus faces at the hands of the tempter.

After being in the desert for a substantial length of time without food, Jesus is naturally hungry. The devil uses this opportunity to tempt him, saying, 'If you are the Son of God, tell these stones to become bread' (Matt. 4:3; Luke 4:3). In each of the three temptations Jesus responds with a quotation from Scripture, prefaced by 'It is written', in every instance from the book of Deuteronomy. He first answers his tempter with words from the passage cited above: 'Man shall not live by bread alone, but by every word that proceeds from the mouth of God' (Matt. 4:4; Luke 4:4; cf. Deut. 8:3). Our primary concern here is not how this particular saying countered Satan's trial, but the fact that Christ's quotation is from the very same portion of Deuteronomy that spoke of testing in the wilderness for forty years. This surely puts it beyond all dispute that the Gospel temptation narratives are purposefully evoking the accounts relating to Israel in the wilderness. In the past, following the exodus, the nation was in the wilderness being tested over the problem of the lack of food, as we read in Exodus 16, and the people's response was to grumble (vv. 2–3). Jesus, we see, in a comparable if not more severe situation responded very differently, and resorted to the use of Scripture. Regarding the relevance of Christ's citation, perhaps the intention in using the words 'not live by bread alone, but by every word that proceeds from the mouth of God' was to communicate the important spiritual principle that there is other sustenance able to impart life to human beings than normal physical food. As one biblical scholar puts it: 'This was to teach . . . that there are more important things in life (and especially in the life of God's people) than material provision.'[11]

In the second temptation, according to the ordering in Matthew,[12] the devil brings Jesus to Jerusalem and sets him on the pinnacle of the temple, evidently some high point in the building. He then says to him:

---

[11] France, *Gospel of Matthew*, 131. France continues: 'God's word does not fill the stomach. But it is a question of priority . . . Obedience to God's will takes priority over self-gratification, even over the apparently essential provision of food. God will provide the food when he is ready . . . Jesus' use of this OT text shows that he understood his experience of hunger to be God's will for him at the time, and therefore not to be evaded by a self-indulgent use of his undoubted power as the Son of God. To do that would be to call in question God's priorities.' Note too the use of food and drink in a metaphorical sense in Prov. 9:1–5, where such serve as a figure of what is offered by divine wisdom.

[12] Luke's order transposes the positions of the second and third temptations. I would conclude that Matthew's order is original. Not only is Matthew more probably the earlier of the two Gospels, but his

If you are the Son of God, throw yourself down; for it is written: 'He will give his angels charge over you', and 'In their hands they will bear you up, so that you do not strike your foot against a stone.'
(Matt. 4:6; cf. Luke 4:9–11)

The tempter here himself quotes Scripture, from two verses of Psalm 91 (vv. 11, 12). He appears to be taking words concerning God's protection of the righteous and applying them to Jesus,[13] to whom he suggests that the veracity of what is promised should be confirmed by casting himself down from the high place in order to see the hand of God fulfil the protection pledged. Jesus responds by saying, 'Again it is written: "You shall not test the LORD your God"' (Matt. 4:7; cf. Luke 4:12). Jesus is once more drawing upon words from Deuteronomy, this time from 6:16. This latter verse explicitly refers to the testing that occurred at a location called Massah. This is looking back to the situation described in Exodus 17. There Moses reproved the Israelites for the negative way in which they reacted to the lack of water, asking the rhetorical question 'Why do you test the LORD?' (v. 2). They questioned whether God would intervene to provide for the people he had delivered from Egypt. Moses afterwards called that place 'Massah' (v. 7), meaning 'testing',[14] because there 'the Israelites tested the LORD'.[15] So, whereas the people did not refrain from displeasing God in the wilderness, by testing him, in the Gospel accounts Jesus resolutely abstains from such a course of action, dispelling the tempter's proposal with a firm declaration of the prohibition as stated in Deuteronomy.[16]

In the last of the three temptations, the devil takes Christ to the top of a very high mountain and shows him all the kingdoms of the world and their glory. He says to him, 'All these I will give you, if you fall down and worship me' (Matt. 4:9; cf. Luke 4:6–7). Jesus replies with yet a third quote from Deuteronomy, and says, 'Away with you, Satan! For it is written: "You shall worship the LORD your God, and serve him only"' (Matt. 4:10; cf. Luke 4:8). Jesus is referring back to Deuteronomy 6:13, just a few words away from his

---

(note 12 *cont.*) order also shows a more logical development, ending in the seemingly climactic issue of who is to be worshipped.

[13] Cf. James M. Hamilton Jr, *Psalms, vol. 2: 73–150* (Evangelical Biblical Theological Commentary; Bellingham, WA: Lexham Academic, 2021), 160–161.

[14] The Hebrew noun *massâ* is a cognate of the verb *nissâ*, 'test'.

[15] According to the same verse, the place was also given a second name, Meribah, meaning 'contention', as there the people contended with Moses (cf. Deut. 33:8; Ps. 81:7).

[16] France here remarks (*Gospel of Matthew*, 133): 'The devil's suggestion . . . is to test the literal truth of God's promise of protection by deliberately creating a situation in which he will be obliged to act to save his Son's life.' In such a way, France explains, humankind becomes the master of God, in effect, as if he were there to serve us rather than we him.

previous citation.[17] The context there is provided by the following verse forbidding adherence to other gods for the reason that 'the LORD your God who is in the midst of you is a jealous God; otherwise his anger will burn against you and he will destroy you from the face of the earth' (v. 15). The wording here plainly echoes the tragic affair surrounding the golden calf at Sinai in Exodus 32.[18] There the Israelites had bowed down to the idol, proclaiming: 'These are your gods, O Israel' (v. 8). They had 'made for themselves gods of gold' (v. 31). As a result, God told Moses to leave him alone, 'so that my anger may burn against them and that I may destroy them' (v. 10). Following the incident, the Lord reminds Israel of his jealous nature: 'You shall not worship any other god, for the LORD, whose name is Jealous, is a jealous God' (34:14). In the Gospel scenario, Satan holds the place of the false god and seeks worship from Christ. The latter, of course, refuses and quotes Deuteronomy for the third time to undergird his response – God alone is to be worshipped. At this the efforts of the tempter have been successfully resisted and he receives a brusque dismissal, on this occasion at least.

Without doubt, then, the Gospel records of Christ's temptation deliberately establish a series of parallels with the post-exodus narratives concerning Israel in the wilderness. Not only are the three biblical citations of Jesus all from the book of Deuteronomy relating to that particular time, but also the three historical situations alluded to reoccur in Matthew's account in precisely the same order in which they happened. First, the trial regarding hunger, which is recorded in Exodus 16; second, the putting of the Lord to the test at Massah, found in Exodus 17; then third, the worship of another god, as recounted in Exodus 32.

To what purpose do the temptation narratives allude to these particular happenings in the Old Testament? I think this question can be approached from two different perspectives: from the viewpoint of what actually takes place and from the viewpoint of who it is that experiences these things. It is evident that the testing in the wilderness that Jesus underwent is in some way a counterpart to that faced by ancient Israel in similar circumstances. However, there is of course one enormous difference, which is surely one of the main thrusts of the allusion. Whereas the Israelites were led into the wilderness to be tested and

---

[17] Commentators note the differences between the form of the citation in the Gospels and that appearing in the Greek version of Deuteronomy. The changes are quite justifiable. First, the Gospels replace the Hebrew verb 'fear' by 'worship'. Clearly, the Gospel context presents Satan as seeking to be worshipped, and the idea of that act is indeed conceptually present in the Old Testament use of 'fear' in relation to God. Second, the Gospels add 'only' to the verb 'serve', which is arguably implicit in the meaning of the original Hebrew. The qualifying 'only' or 'alone' is actually added in certain modern English versions of Deut. 6:13, such as NIV, NJB, REB, GNT, NJPS. See also France, *Gospel of Matthew*, 135.

[18] As understood in Andrew Schmutzer, 'Jesus' Temptation: A Reflection on Matthew's Use of Old Testament Theology and Imagery', *Ashland Theological Journal* 40 (2008): 24–25.

failed on all accounts, Christ was brought out into a barren place likewise to be tested and in every instance prevailed. One major purpose of the Gospel passages in question is to demonstrate that Jesus succeeded at every point where Israel had previously stumbled. This surely underscores the idea that Jesus is the new Israel, indeed the perfect Israel.[19] Implicit in this is an important truth. The purpose for which God had called the Israelites of old, the offspring of Abraham, namely that through them all nations on earth should be blessed (cf. Gen. 12:3; 18:18; 22:18; 26:4; 28:14), and yet which on account of their infidelity had not come to fruition, would now finally attain its consummation in a new and obedient Israel, Jesus Christ.

The foregoing is so not just because of what Jesus accomplished, especially in contrast to Israel, but on account of who he is. We have already seen above that in a sense the Hebrews, the people group that God had chosen, constituted his 'son'. As he had called the whole nation to be his own 'treasured possession' (Exod. 19:5), this was a collective national sonship, one based on election. The accounts of Christ's baptism and temptation highlight one fundamental fact about the person involved – his being identified as God's Son. This is first declared to be so when he is baptized (Matt. 3:17; Mark 1:11; Luke 3:22), evidently by the voice of the Father himself. It is then further highlighted in the temptations. Twice the devil says to Jesus, 'If you are the Son of God . . .' (Matt. 4:3, 6; Luke 4:3, 9). It is essential to point out here that the conjunction 'If' (*ei*) does not in this instance denote a hypothetical condition, but one that is real, and should therefore be understood in the sense of 'Since' or 'Seeing that', as explained in the commentaries.[20] The sense of the temptations is not 'If you are the Son of God, which maybe you are or maybe you are not, so prove that you are by doing what I suggest'. Rather the import is 'Since you [actually] are the Son of God, why don't you do what I suggest?' The fact is, then, that both the baptism and the temptations draw attention to Christ's divine sonship. This is the same truth that was previously given publicity in Matthew through his citation of Hosea 11:1, about Israel as God's son in an exodus context, which the Gospel-writer applied to Jesus (Matt. 2:15).

---

[19] Cf. Leroy A. Huizenga, *Behold the Christ: Proclaiming the Gospel of Matthew* (Steubenville, OH: Emmaus Road, 2019), 122: 'St. Matthew [in 4:1–11] is writing Jesus into the story of Deuteronomy 6–8. Jesus, the new Israel, is recapitulating the story of Israel in the desert. But Jesus obeys perfectly, unlike Israel'; also Patrick Schreiner, *Matthew, Disciple and Scribe: The First Gospel and Its Portrait of Jesus* (Grand Rapids, MI: Baker Academic, 2019), 218: 'Jesus not only walks in the footsteps of Israel – he is Israel.' Beale describes Christ here as 'the micro-Israel who has replaced the macronational Israel' (*A New Testament Biblical Theology*, 417).

[20] E.g. Davies and Allison, *Matthew 1–7*, 361. It is the indicative form, rather than subjunctive, of the accompanying verb that determines the nature of the condition as one that is real. The translation 'Since' appears in the text of the ISV and CEB.

The fact of Jesus' success in the various tests he encountered is not to be separated from his identity. The reason he was able to overcome was due to his divine sonship, being not a collective, adopted 'son' like Israel, but the unique ontological Son, *the* Son of God, eternally begotten of the Father. As such, in his incarnate state, in which he nevertheless remained Immanuel, 'God with us' (Matt. 1:23), he rendered a ready obedience to the Father. The allusions demonstrate, therefore, that Jesus is not only the new Israel but also the divine Son in the fullest and most essential sense of the term.

Moreover, since Jesus is the new Israel, led out into the wilderness and tested, resisting with absolute success, then it follows that with the onset of his ministry the symbolism of his baptism and temptation at the same time reveals that a new exodus is about to take place. It is not simply that Jesus is truly Israel, the Son of God, but also that he has come to bring his people out from bondage in a new exodus deliverance, one infinitely more wondrous than that of old, one foretold in centuries past through the prophetic oracles of Isaiah, Jeremiah, Ezekiel and others.[21] Viewed against the background of the Old Testament, all this is implicit in the Gospel passages under discussion.[22]

As a final point, we should draw attention to one other important allusion in the temptation episode. When read against the background of the Old Testament, the tempting of Jesus by the devil must also remind the reader of another instance of temptation that failed to be resisted. We are thinking here of the sin in Eden and the fall of the first man Adam, and of Eve also.[23] Space does not permit a detailed presentation of how, once Adam the head of the human race had fallen, there followed other Adam-like figures through whom there could be a fresh beginning for humankind and its original blessed state hopefully restored. Following Adam himself, the next of these was obviously Noah, since the flood waters evidently brought to an end the old creation and there emerged a new creation, with Noah at its head.[24] To him all the mandates and promises given to Adam were repeated (e.g. Gen. 1:28; cf. 9:1).[25] But like Adam, he too fell.

---

[21] Interestingly, this new exodus in Christ, inaugurated through his baptism, picks up the story at the very location where the Pentateuchal account of the old exodus ends, namely at the River Jordan.

[22] Cf. Joseph Ratzinger, *Jesus of Nazareth: From the Baptism in the Jordan to the Transfiguration* (New York, NY: Doubleday, 2007), 30; also France, *Gospel of Matthew*, 128.

[23] Cf. Beale, *New Testament Biblical Theology*, 222–223.

[24] On the comparison between Adam and Noah, see John H. Sailhamer, *The Pentateuch as Narrative: A Biblical-Theological Commentary* (Grand Rapids, MI: Zondervan, 1992), 129–130; Warren Austin Gage, *The Gospel of Genesis: Studies in Protology and Eschatology* (Eugene, OR: Wipf & Stock, 2001), 11–12; James McKeown, *Genesis* (Two Horizons Old Testament Commentary; Grand Rapids, MI: Eerdmans, 2008), 66. For Noah, Gage uses the designation 'the new Adam' (11).

[25] A particularly useful summary of this aspect of the relationship between these two, and how it later extended into Abraham and his descendants, can be found in Beale, *New Testament Biblical Theology*, 46–48.

From a biblical perspective, we need to understand the creation, status and mission of Israel in this same light. Israel was another Adam figure, another new beginning with the aim of undoing the effects of the fall and re-establishing God's blessing over all his creatures. I believe it to be altogether beyond doubt that the Old Testament narratives set up deliberate parallels between Adam and Israel, and this is precisely because we are to view the divine intention regarding the latter in the light of the creation of the former.[26] Adam had failed; Noah had similarly failed. What now about a whole chosen nation? Would it fail? Plainly, it did. The whole series of new beginnings involving Adam-like figures foundered through sin, until we arrive at the advent in the world of him who was both the new Adam and the new Israel. Against this backdrop we see that the temptations successfully met by Jesus serve to undo the failings, not only of the Israelite nation, but also of Adam, the father of us all.[27] In this way, Jesus can be the head of a new humanity. By resisting the temptations and so being without sin, he extends to us the offer of participating in his righteousness through faith in him. Such, then, is the pivotal nature of the Gospel accounts examined in this chapter.

---

[26] Mention must be made here of the volume by Seth Postell, entitled *Adam as Israel: Genesis 1–3 as the Introduction to the Torah and Tanakh* (Eugene, OR: Pickwick, 2011). Postell's work, to my mind, is unrivalled in its clear laying-out of the biblical correspondence between the first man Adam and the nation of Israel. Nevertheless, my one reservation with the book is that its author sees the relationship between the two back to front. The Old Testament text does not intend us to see Israel in the account about Adam. Rather, we are led to think of Adam in the narratives concerning Israel. Israel is an Adam-like entity in the world, and not Adam an Israel-like figure. Never has a book, in my opinion, been given a more improper main title. It surely ought to be called *Israel as Adam*.

[27] Cf. Beale, *New Testament Biblical Theology*, 479; Beale sees Jesus as being 'both a last Adam and a true Israel figure (i.e., corporate Adam) who obeys at just the points where Adam and Israel disobeyed'.

8

The Sermon on the Mount

Matthew 5:1 – 8:1

Parallels between this portion of Matthew's Gospel and the Old Testament are widely acknowledged. For this reason, those features which are commonly treated in commentaries will be outlined fairly briefly.

The presence of allusion here, existing on several levels, is especially conspicuous. The setting of Christ's sermon, and the content, as well as the narrative sequence leading up to it, are all evocative of a particular episode in the Old Testament narrative. This latter is one of the most prominent events in Israel's history and one that will be brought to mind several times more in Gospel passages to be examined later. We are thinking here of the giving of the law through Moses on Mount Sinai following on the heels of the exodus from Egypt. This occurs in the middle of the book of Exodus and is later recapitulated in the book of Deuteronomy.

That matters relating to Moses should lie behind the celebrated sermon ought not to occasion any surprise. In the same Gospel a comparison has already been made by Matthew between Jesus on one hand and Moses and the exodus on the other.[1] In both the first half of Exodus and the opening chapters of Matthew we observe a distinct correlation in the sequence of events. Set against a background of promised deliverance, each account presents us with a tyrannical king, the slaughter of male infants, the flight of the coming deliverer for safety, his return to his people, a passing through water, a period of testing in the wilderness, and then the ascent of a mountain and the giving of a law.[2] The parallel pattern invites us to see Christ's sermon as in some way a counterpart to the Torah given through Moses.

---

[1] See chapters 6 and 7.

[2] This relationship has long been recognized. See, e.g., Patrick Schreiner, *Matthew, Disciple and Scribe: The First Gospel and Its Portrait of Jesus* (Grand Rapids, MI: Baker Academic, 2019), 138–139, 216–218; W. D. Davies and Dale C. Allison Jr, *Matthew 1–7: Volume 1* (ICC; Edinburgh: T&T Clark, 1988), 424, 427. In the latter we find the comment: 'If in [Matthew] chapters 1–2 the events of Jesus' childhood have their parallels in the childhood events of Moses . . . in chapters 3–4 there is a new exodus: Jesus emerges from the waters to enter the wilderness. Can it then be coincidence that soon after this Jesus goes up on a mountain and there speaks of the Law?' (424).

With regard to the setting, the mountain-top location in which the teaching is imparted is self-evident. For this to be so, the main figure has to ascend the mountain. Here is the first of several verbal linkages between the two. As Moses (Exod. 19:3) 'went up the mountain' (*anebē eis to oros*), in the same way Jesus (Matt. 5:1) 'went up the mountain' (*anebē eis to oros*). Though the particular phrase used might seem quite ordinary in itself, it in fact only appears three times in the entire Greek Old Testament in this precise form, and each relates specifically to Moses ascending Mount Sinai (Exod. 19:3; 24:18; 34:4).

Matthew informs us that once up the mountain Jesus 'sat down' (5:1). According to the Hebrew text of Deuteronomy 9:9, Moses, when referring back to his experience on Sinai, used the words *wā'ēšēb bāhār*. Most English versions translate this as 'I stayed on the mountain' or 'I remained on the mountain', both possible meanings of the verb. The fact is, however, that this is the same verb commonly used for 'to sit', which is actually its primary sense.[3] Interestingly, certain later Jewish writings plainly understood Moses here to mean that he 'sat' on the mountain,[4] as did Jesus.

As Matthew 5:1–2 forms an introductory frame to the sermon, so 7:27–28 and 8:1 form a closing frame, or 'inclusio' as scholars like to call it. Here too it appears that Moses is intentionally being recalled, for we find two distinct phrases relating to him in this concluding section. First, 'When Jesus finished [*synetelesen*][5] these words [*tous logous toutous*]' (7:28) brings to mind 'Moses finished [*synetelesen*] speaking all these words [*tous logous toutous*]' (Deut. 31:1; cf. 31:24; 32:45).[6] Then, regarding the descent from the mountain, the next verse in Matthew begins: 'When he had gone down [*katabantos de autou*] from the mountain [*apo tou orous*]' (8:1),[7] which might reasonably be taken, considered together with the other connections, as a deliberate echo of the words:

---

[3] Cf. Davies and Allison, *Matthew 1–7*, 424.

[4] In the Babylonian Talmud (*Megillah* 21a), for instance, Moses' words 'I *sat* on the mountain' are contrasted with 'I *stood* on the mountain' in Deut. 10:10, both expressive of his specific posture. After his survey of rabbinic and other literature on the matter, Allison remarks: 'The point is simply this: the image of Moses sitting on Sinai . . . was firmly established in the imagination of pre-Christian Jews' (Dale C. Allison Jr, *The New Moses: A Matthean Typology* [Minneapolis, MN: Fortress, 1993], 179).

[5] In the first word there is a variant reading in Greek manuscripts, the critical text reading *etelesen* and the majority text *synetelesen*. The meaning is the same, 'completed, finished', in either case.

[6] Allison, who treats the matter with some thoroughness, here comments that he is 'inclined to accept' that Matthew is deliberately recalling the words at the end of Deuteronomy (*The New Moses*, 194).

[7] Several commentators include 8:1 with what precedes it rather than with what follows, which is suggested by the presence of the inclusio. See, e.g., John Nolland, *The Gospel of Matthew* (NIGTC; Grand Rapids, MI: Eerdmans, 2005), 344–347; Davies and Allison, *Matthew 1–7*, 724. Interestingly, the early Gospel manuscript Codex Washingtonianus (*c.* AD 400), known as W, introduces a division *after* 8:1, and not before.

'When he was going down [*katabainontos de autou*] from the mountain [*apo tou orous*]' (Exod. 34:29),[8] spoken of Moses descending Sinai.[9]

Within the literary framework described, Jesus imparts his new teaching[10] on the mountain top. It cannot be overlooked that the law, here meaning the law of Moses given at Sinai, forms a major, if not the primary, element within his instruction. The whole paragraph of Matthew 5:17–20 concerns the Old Testament law. Here Jesus explains that he has not come to abrogate it but to fulfil it. This leads directly into Christ's treatment of various commandments of the law that follow. In verses 21–48 six separate commandments are expressly cited and their meaning and application discussed. Jesus then turns to the matter of acts of righteousness (6:1), which covers practices such as almsgiving, prayer and fasting. Evidently, what is dealt with here still relates basically to the issue of keeping the Jewish law, for those practitioners that he mentions are patently men such as the scribes and Pharisees (here labelled 'hypocrites'), for whom adherence to the Mosaic law was absolutely fundamental. In all this teaching on the law, Jesus' intention is to highlight the need for correct inner attitude, and not just outward observance.

Towards the end of his teaching Jesus exhorts his audience to obey what he has been teaching (Matt. 7:24–27). He presents two possible responses and their respective consequences, one positive, one negative. This twofold choice, and also the words that Jesus uses to introduce it, provide further echoes of the Mosaic law, particularly of the manner in which it ends. In this final portion of the sermon, Jesus sets before the crowd the only two potential ways one might respond. He speaks of two categories of people in the following terms:

Everyone who hears [*akouei*] these words of mine and does [*poiei*] them . . .
(v. 24)

Everyone who hears [*akouōn*] these words of mine and does not do [*poiōn*] them . . .
(v. 26)

---

[8] Septuagint manuscripts are divided in the matter of the preposition in the phrase 'from the mountain'. Both *apo* and *ek* are attested, though no real difference is made to the meaning. I have followed here the reading of Codex Alexandrinus, one of the major witnesses to the text of the Greek Old Testament. Note too Exod. 32:15, where *apo* occurs in the same phrase without a variant.

[9] Allison (*The New Moses*, 180) accepts this as a parallel.

[10] At Sinai Moses is frequently described as teaching Israel the laws of God (e.g. Deut. 4:1, 5; 5:31; 6:1, etc.). Both Moses and Jesus therefore expound the Torah.

It surely cannot be a coincidence that the law, that is the whole Torah completed in Deuteronomy, contains corresponding statements as it draws to a close. There Moses is recorded as saying:

> Now if you do indeed hearken [*akousēs*][11] to the voice of the LORD your God, being careful to do [*poiein*] all his commandments which I command you today . . .
> (28:1)

> But if you do not hearken [*eisakousēs*] to the voice of the LORD your God, being careful to do [*poiein*] all his commandments and his statutes which I command you today . . .'
> (28:15)[12]

In each case there follows a description of the consequences of each course of action. In the law, Deuteronomy 28:1 leads into a list of blessings that are gained through obedience, while 28:15 leads into a list of curses for disobedience. In Christ's sermon, Matthew 7:24 is followed by the illustration of a man building his house on rock, a house that does not fall, no matter what is thrown against it, but 7:26 compares the person who fails to heed Jesus' words to a man who built his house on sand, which is easily destroyed.[13]

Evidently, then, through the use of allusion Jesus is again being depicted by Matthew as a Moses-like figure.[14] Just as that earlier mighty prophet passed on to Israel the law of God on one mountain, so Jesus performs a complementary act on this later mountain. Since Deuteronomy foretells the coming of a prophet like Moses (18:15, 18), those Jews who perceived the similarities between the Sermon on the Mount and the giving of the Torah, whether by being present at the time or through reading Matthew's account, would no doubt have concluded that Jesus was that prophet.

Jesus, however, cannot simply be another Moses. A key difference in the verses just mentioned is that Moses relates his pronouncement of weal or woe to the utterances of God ('the voice of the LORD your God'), whereas Jesus does

---

[11] Following the reading of Codex Vaticanus, which is closer to the Hebrew. An alternative reading, *eisakousēte*, adds a prefix and makes the verb plural, though still retaining the same basic sense.

[12] The sequence 'hear . . . do . . .' is common in connection with the law generally (e.g. Lev. 26:14; Deut. 4:1; 5:1; 6:3; 7:12; 12:28; 13:18; 15:5). Especially note how Deut. 5:27 relates back to Exod. 24:3, 7 (LXX).

[13] Though Jesus speaks of houses built on rock and sand, since he is expressing a truth in parabolic form, the essential content of his words does in fact relate closely to the blessings and curses of Deut. 28.

[14] Cf. Joseph Ratzinger, *Jesus of Nazareth: From the Baptism in the Jordan to the Transfiguration* (New York, NY: Doubleday, 2007), 65.

so with reference to his own sayings ('these words of mine'). Moses' mediation of the divine words is in keeping with the prophetic role as seen throughout the Old Testament. The words of the prophets were self-consciously attributed to God. Yet Jesus does not conform to this pattern. Although he is no doubt presented as being like Moses in many respects, it is important to discern that he is also distinct in other ways. Plainly, he is not just another prophet, not even one of the status of Moses, through whom the law was given. No mere prophet would make statements such as: 'You have heard that it was said, "You shall not commit adultery." *But I say to you* that everyone who looks at a woman with lust for her has already committed adultery with her in his heart' (Matt. 5:27–28). Jesus utters the phrase 'But I say to you' several times in the sermon in his treatment of how the law is to be understood and applied (see also 5:22, 32, 34, 39, 44). There is nothing comparable in the sayings of the prophets.[15] So it is that when Jesus has concluded his sermon, we read that 'the crowds were astonished at his teaching, because he was teaching them as one having authority' (7:28–29).

What manner of authority was this, if it transcended that of the prophets and even of Moses? Are we to understand this as a specifically messianic authority, since Jesus has already been identified by Matthew as Messiah, the Christ (1:1, 18)? Or is there more to it than that?[16] I believe there to be some indication here of a greater authority still, for in the same sermon Jesus explicitly refers to himself as the 'Lord' (7:21), and he speaks of those who prophesy in his name (v. 22). Seeing that in the Old Testament prophets prophesied expressly 'in the name of' God,[17] should we conclude that Jesus is implicitly claiming himself to be divine? Possibly. One recent biblical scholar, commenting on 7:28–29, holds the view that Matthew 'presents Jesus as God on earth and so stresses his sovereignty'. He concludes that 'his authority to interpret the Old Law and bring the New Law is not derivative but original, rooted in his divine

---

[15] Cf. Ratzinger, *Jesus of Nazareth*, 90: 'Jesus ascribes to his "I" a normative status that no teacher of Israel – indeed, no teacher of the Church – has a right to claim for himself. Someone who speaks like this is no longer a prophet in the traditional sense, an ambassador and trustee of another; he himself is the reference point of the righteous life, its goal and center.'

[16] The important matter in question is appreciated by Davies and Allison, who write: 'Is Jesus here made out to be a new Moses? . . . any alleged comparison with Moses is dwarfed by the ways in which Mosaic categories are transcended . . . Jesus is, among other things, the Son of God, the Messiah, and Lord – titles to which Moses could make no claim. It would thus be a grave injustice to think of him who utters the great sermon as simply a new Moses: Jesus is much more' (*Matthew 1–7*, 423). Interestingly, Jewish scholar Jacob Neusner, who ultimately dismisses Christ's teaching in his sermon, understands these particular words in such a way that '[o]nly God can demand of me what Jesus is asking'. See Jacob Neusner, *A Rabbi Talks with Jesus* (Montreal: McGill-Queen's University Press, 2000), 68.

[17] See, e.g., Deut. 18:20; Jer. 11:21; 26:20; Dan. 9:6; Zech. 13:3; Jas 5:10.

person'.[18] As it was 'the LORD', the God of Israel, who uttered forth his laws for Israel on Sinai, so perhaps here we are to see Jesus, a new Moses-like figure who far surpasses the prophet since he is 'God with us' (Matt. 1:23), pronouncing his new law to the new Israel.

---

[18] Leroy A. Huizenga, *Behold the Christ: Proclaiming the Gospel of Matthew* (Steubenville, OH: Emmaus Road, 2019), 188.

9

Calming the storm

Matthew 8:23–27; Mark 4:35–41; Luke 8:22–25

This chapter deals with that well-known event that took place on the Sea of Galilee in the early part of Christ's ministry. Jesus had been engaged in a good deal of healing and teaching on the western side of the lake, where Capernaum was situated, and so in order to give himself some respite he instructed his disciples to sail him over to the opposite side (Mark 4:35–36; Luke 8:22).

We read in the accounts that upon setting off from the shore Jesus soon falls asleep, no doubt out of extreme tiredness due to his exertions. It is during this crossing that the boat is struck by a sudden storm (Matt. 8:24; Mark 4:37; Luke 8:23). The vessel is threatened with sinking, but when the disciples wake Jesus he rises up and instantly stills the turbulent sea (Matt. 8:25–26; Mark 4:38–39; Luke 8:24), much to the amazement of those with him (Matt. 8:27; Mark 4:41; Luke 8:25). This miracle is recorded for us in all three synoptic Gospels, which present very similar accounts, though with minor variations in detail and wording.

When studied in the light of a particular Old Testament passage, this occurrence takes on a greater significance than that of a mere nature miracle. It is here proposed that behind the recounting of this event lie the matters described in the first part of the book of Jonah, the ancient Hebrew prophet, who lived around eight centuries earlier. The prophet Jonah will also be encountered again towards the end of this book, though in quite a different context.[1]

It does not require a close investigation to realize that what happens in the opening chapter of Jonah bears a distinct resemblance to the event in the Gospels. There is not an absolute identity of course. The former is being alluded to, as a deliberate literary ploy, both by way of sameness to and contrast with certain of its contents, with the purpose of adding to the significance of the latter. Though differences exist, each presents a similar big picture. There is a

---

[1] See chapter 30.

boat on the 'sea' (Jon. 1:4; Matt. 8:24),[2] on board which is the main character along with certain others, including experienced seamen in both instances. In this general scenario a whole stream of other common elements appear.

In both cases the vessel is leaving Hebrew/Jewish territory to go to Gentile lands – to Tarshish in the earlier narrative (Jon. 1:3), and to the region of the Gerasenes in the later (Matt. 8:28; Mark 5:1; Luke 8:26).

Each journey is interrupted by a severe storm: 'a great windstorm' (Jon. 1:4); 'a great storm of wind' (Mark 4:37).

There is considerable danger to the ship and its occupants. The Greek texts here make use of the same particular verb: 'the boat was in danger [*ekindyneuen*] of breaking up' (Jon. 1:4); 'they were in danger [*ekindyneuon*]' (Luke 8:23).

Despite the severity of the storm, the main character lies asleep in the boat: 'he [Jonah] was sleeping' (Jon. 1:5, *ekatheuden*); cf. 'he [Jesus] was sleeping' (Matt. 8:24, *ekatheuden*).

In the face of the danger, the ship's captain 'approached' (*proselthen*) the sleeping Jonah and spoke to him (Jon. 1:6), as the disciples 'approached' (*proselthontes*) the sleeping Jesus and spoke to him (Matt. 8:25).

The words uttered in each instance concern being saved from the threat that those on board the vessel might 'perish'. To Jonah the captain said, 'Call upon your God, that God might save us [*diasose . . . hemas*] and we may not perish [*apolometha*]' (Jon. 1:6). To Jesus the disciples said, 'Lord, save us [*soson hemas*]; we are perishing [*apollymetha*]!' (Matt. 8:25; cf. Mark 4:38; Luke 8:24).

From this point onwards the respective accounts continue to show similarities, but also important contrasts. In both narratives the storm ceases and the sea is calmed (Jon. 1:15; cf. Matt. 8:26; Mark 4:39; Luke 8:24). In this context both make use of the same Greek term meaning 'quieten down' (Jon. 1:12, *kopasei*; cf. Mark 4:39, *ekopasen*). The cessation of the storm results, of course, in each vessel being preserved. How the storm becomes calm, however, varies in the two episodes, as will be explained.

The accounts both end up with those others in the boat being afraid. In the first, the text states: 'and the men feared [*ephobethesan*] the LORD with a great fear [*phobo megalo*]' (Jon. 1:16). In the second we read: 'and they feared [*ephobethesan*] a great fear [*phobon megan*]' (Mark 4:41).[3] The cognate noun (*phobos*) accompanies its verb in each instance, along with an identical adjective, to intensify the degree of fear. But there is a major difference in the object of their fear, which brings us to the main point of the allusions.

---

[2] In their renderings of the Gospel incident, NIV, NJB, REB, CEV and others, are not following the original Greek in putting 'lake' for 'sea' (*thalassa*).

[3] Perhaps also the phrase 'and the men' in Matt. 8:27 is an echo of 'and the men' in Jon. 1:16.

To any unbiased reader the connections between what happened to Jonah and the episode in the Gospels are strong and, upon reflection, even obvious. But what do they signify? Once the correspondences have established a connection between the two occasions, what becomes most striking, and where the chief import of the allusions lies, is in the discontinuities. At a specific point in the flow of events as recorded in the Gospels, there is a notable departure from the story line as it appears in Jonah. What we see is that at the beginning of the allusory schema Jesus is unmistakably occupying the place of Jonah, and so too in what immediately follows. It is Jesus who, like Jonah, gets into the boat, with others, to pass over the sea. It is Jesus who, like Jonah, falls asleep in the boat. It is he whom the others wake up, and so forth. But once he is stirred from sleep, everything changes. Nobody is cast into the sea, as in the story of Jonah. Rather, Jesus himself is the direct cause, simply through his word, of the storm's cessation. He rises in the boat and utters the command, 'Peace! Be still!' And at this 'the wind quietened down, and there was a great calm' (Mark 4:39).

What we are seeing here is not just a miracle affecting nature of the kind performed by the prophets of old. Moses was granted the 'staff of God' by means of which he was able to perform signs and wonders in Egypt, and to exercise control over the waters of the Red Sea (Exod. 4:17, 20; 14:16). Elijah through much prayer was able to stop it raining on the land of Israel and then to bring the rain back again (1 Kgs 18:42–45; Jas 5:17). Yet Jesus required neither staff nor prayer. The natural elements were at his control by a mere word. There is only one who can do such a thing – the one who brought everything into being with a word in the first place (cf. Ps. 33:6, 9). Surely, the miracle is telling us that Jesus is no mere prophet, but much more.

So it is that at the end of the Gospel account of stilling the storm, the fear experienced by those on board the vessel when the storm was miraculously calmed is on account of Jesus himself. In the book of Jonah, we read that 'the men feared *the* LORD with a great fear' (1:16). But in the Gospels the object of the fear is none other than the person of Christ. What has happened in the series of allusions is that a switch, or a huge leap to be more precise, has been made from Jesus corresponding to Jonah in the parallel narrative, to Jesus taking up the place of the Lord God himself. In the earlier event God stilled the storm, and God was feared by the men in the boat. In the later Jesus calmed the storm, and he was the cause of the great fear of those with him. By a skilful employment of allusive similarity and contrast, the Spirit in the Gospel-writers is plainly indicating that Jesus himself is none other than that same God who calmed the elements and preserved the vessel in the book of Jonah. He who in the Gospel narrative is first described in terms of a human prophet is now transformed into one who is divine.[4]

Related to the foregoing, another element that differs between the two events is the position given to the questioning on the part of the others in the boat. In the book of Jonah this comes earlier in the narrative: 'What is your occupation? And where do you come from? What is your country? And from what people are you?' (1:8). The prophet's fellow passengers were evidently determined to know all about Jonah's identity and origins. Here their questioning is situated before the storm is calmed. In the Gospels, however, the questions come at the end, after the storm has ceased. And the questions are much more far-reaching in their import: 'What manner of man is this?' (Matt. 8:27), and 'Who is this?' (Mark 4:41). These are not mere information questions, as in Jonah, but are rather rhetorical questions in which the answer is already implicit. 'What manner of man is this?' – this is no mere man! 'Who is this?' – this is *God* in human flesh! Hence elsewhere Jesus makes the apposite comment, with reference to himself, that 'one greater than Jonah is here' (Matt. 12:41: Luke 11:32).

Alongside the correspondence with the book of Jonah, we may also benefit by reminding ourselves of what the Hebrew poets wrote elsewhere in their Scriptures, where they depict God as the one who, among other wondrous acts, stilled the winds, waves and storm:

O LORD God of hosts, who is mighty like you, O LORD?
Your faithfulness surrounds you.
You rule over the raging of the sea;
when its waves rise up, you still them.
(Ps. 89:8–9)

Some went down to the sea in ships, doing business on great waters;
they saw the works of the LORD, and his wonders in the deep.
For he spoke and raised up a stormy wind, which lifted high the waves
    of the sea.
They rose up to the heavens, they went down to the depths;
their soul melted away in their calamity.

---

[4] Cf. David M. Moffitt, 'God Attested by Men: Echoes of Jonah and the Identification of Jesus with Israel's God in the Storm-Stilling Stories of Matthew's Gospel', in David M. Moffitt and Isaac Augustine Morales (eds.), *A Scribe Trained for the Kingdom of Heaven: Essays on Christology and Ethics in Honor of Richard B. Hays* (Lanham, MD: Lexington Books, 2021), 27. Moffitt argues that these connections with the book of Jonah would lead those reading this Gospel episode to infer 'Jesus's identification with the God of Israel'.

They reeled and staggered like a drunken man, and were at their
    wits' end.
Then they cried out to the LORD in their trouble,
and he brought them out from their distress.
He made the storm be still, and the waves of the sea were quietened.
(Ps. 107:23–29)

In both texts it is 'the LORD' who subdues the storm. The disciples of Jesus, and early Jewish-Christian readers and hearers of the Gospel accounts, would have known these psalms. They confirm what the Gospel allusions to Jonah are indicating – that in being able to calm the storm with a word Jesus is showing himself to be none other than the divine Creator, for in the Old Testament it is to this latter that such an ability is attributed.

In sum, then, the allusions to the Scriptures that lie behind the episode of Christ stilling the storm serve an important theological purpose in pointing to his essential deity. Such a high view of Jesus is seen to be presented even in the three synoptic Gospels, where it is much more subtly expressed than in the more explicit Gospel of John, though present nevertheless. We ought not to ignore, however, the important fact that the episode in question first depicts Christ's plain humanity. Exhausted from his ministerial labours, Jesus fell asleep in the boat. He felt weariness in the same way as any other human being, and succumbed to it. But when the need arose, at the onset of the storm, he rose up and exercised his innate power over creation, as only God can do. Here, then, in a single episode we see the one Person in two natures, the God-Man.

10
The feeding of the multitude

Matthew 14:13–21; Mark 6:30–44; Luke 9:10–17; John 6:1–15

Many readers will be aware that the feeding of the five thousand is the only miracle performed by Jesus, excluding his resurrection,[1] included in all four canonical Gospels. Not only this, but a very similar event also takes place on a later occasion, the feeding of the four thousand, recorded by Matthew (15:32–39) and Mark (8:1–10). We have six passages before us, therefore, that recount the miraculous provision of food. Evidently, what happens on these occasions is of exceptional importance. Our focus will be on the earlier of the two.

In this episode a large multitude attends Jesus in a remote location to hear his teaching, and remains with him for a considerable time. The question then arises about the need for the people to eat (Matt. 14:13–16; Mark 6:30–37; Luke 9:10–12; John 6:1–7). A small quantity of loaves and fish is obtained from among the crowd, which Jesus multiplies to enable the several thousand people to eat until full (Matt. 14:17–20a; Mark 6:38–42; Luke 9:13–17a; John 6:8–12). Baskets are then filled with the fragments left over (Matt. 14:20b; Mark 6:43; Luke 9:17b; John 6:13).

The same basic details are also true of the second similar miracle. The different numbers of people and loaves, and the varying Greek words for baskets involved, show that the first and second feeding accounts are distinct occasions, and not merely a doublet, that is, two variant retellings of the same event. The place where they occur also varies. While this may be so, the two episodes do relate to each other, as one would expect, and much of what will be discussed with regard to the one will also be applicable to the other.[2]

---

[1] According to John 10:17–18 (cf. 2:19), it is Jesus himself who, following his crucifixion, takes back his life again.

[2] The number of basketfuls of fragments gathered on each occasion is possibly significant, and has been taken as such by numerous commentators over the centuries. The second episode involves seven baskets as against twelve on the previous occasion (Matt. 14:20; Mark 6:43; cf. Matt. 15:37; Mark 8:8). Evidently, twelve is a number that relates to Israel, since the nation consisted of twelve tribes descended from the twelve sons of Jacob (cf. the symbolism in Exod. 24:4; 39:14; Josh. 4:8). Seven too is a well-known and

Approaching the record from a purely surface-level perspective, we evidently have Jesus enacting a great miracle concerning food. The cause of this, we are explicitly informed, is the plight of the people, which arouses the compassion of the one they have come to hear (cf. Matt. 14:14; 15:32; Mark 6:35). The miraculous act evidently demonstrates the power of Christ over nature, a power which is used to cater for his people's physical needs. Such an event does, however, already create in the mind of the perceptive reader the issue of his potential to also provide for their greater needs, that is, their spiritual lack. After all, had he not earlier spoken of those who 'hunger and thirst after righteousness' (Matt. 5:6)?

Once we move on to consider the wealth of Old Testament undertones contained within the episode, our appreciation of what transpires is greatly enhanced, especially at the theological level. What Jesus does on this occasion takes the biblically literate reader back in this instance to more than one incident in the Jewish Scriptures. It is proposed here that, on one hand, allusions may be detected yet again to the key events of the Passover and exodus, when the Israelites escaped from Egypt to come into the wilderness, and particularly to the provision of the manna, together with quail, with which they were fed at that time (Exod. 16; Num. 11).[3] On the other hand, we find more overt reference made to one of the miracles performed through the prophet Elisha (2 Kgs 4:42–44), which bears a close resemblance to that done by Christ. These two Old Testament scenarios are not entirely disparate since both involve an act of miraculous feeding.

Looking at the Gospel event, we first consider its general setting. A body of water has just been crossed, bringing Jesus and his disciples to a 'desolate place' (Matt. 14:13; Mark 6:32). The adjective used here is *erēmos*, appearing twice in

---

much-used symbolic number, having connotations of wholeness, completeness, totality or universality. It is perhaps for this reason that seven can relate to the rest of the nations of the world outside Israel, that is to say, the Gentiles. Many readers will be aware that Gen. 10 presents what is commonly referred to as the 'Table of Nations', and that these nations amount to seventy, or 7 × 10. The second feeding episode does indeed appear to have taken place in Gentile territory and, according to Mark, may have been situated in Decapolis (cf. 7:31). What is interesting about this detail is that the latter name means 'Ten Cities'. This being so, we have both numerals, seven and ten, present in connection with the repetition of the miracle. If the twelve basketfuls of the earlier event are symbolic of Jewish recipients of the food provided by Christ, then the seven in Decapolis might reasonably be understood as pointing to a Gentile application of the identical miracle. For further discussion on the possible Gentile nature of the second feeding, see R. T. France, *The Gospel of Matthew* (NICNT; Grand Rapids, MI: Eerdmans, 2007), 600–601.

[3] Here we note that the exodus and wilderness experiences are viewed as a single continuous narrative in the Old Testament. See, e.g., Pss. 78; 105; 106; 114. Bryan Estelle (*Echoes of Exodus: Tracing a Biblical Motif* [Downers Grove, IL: InterVarsity Press, 2018], 102), in discussing what constitutes the 'exodus motif', states that it includes 'both the deliverance from the enemies of Israel in Egypt and the wilderness wanderings as described in the Sinai pilgrimage, which culminate in the arrival at the foot of the mountain of God'.

the Matthean account (14:13, 15) and three times in the Markan (6:31, 32, 35). In this place with Jesus and the Twelve there is also a large multitude of people. With regard to time, the event is set in close proximity to the Passover festival (John 6:4). All these components have correlations in the exodus story. At that time, following the first Passover (Exod. 12:21–28), the people of Israel led by Moses traverse the Red Sea (14:29),[4] and come into the wilderness, a place described as *erēmos* (e.g. 15:22; 16:1, 3).[5] Even these more general features alone could easily have led the Jewish-background reader of the Gospels to think of the exodus narrative.

A good number of other details exist that connect the two situations. The multitude come to Jesus in that place 'on foot'. Matthew 14:13 tells us that 'the crowds followed him on foot [*pezē*] from the towns' (cf. also Mark 6:33).[6] The multitude of the exodus consisted of 'about six hundred thousand men on foot [*pezōn*]' (Exod. 12:37; cf. Num. 11:21). As Jesus is helped in his ministrations by the disciples, so in the wilderness Moses appoints officials to assist him (Exod. 18:25).[7] Also, the great mass of people with Jesus are described as being 'like sheep without a shepherd' (Mark 6:34), precisely the same description used of Israel in the wilderness (Num. 27:17; cf. Ps. 78:52).

In this remote location the multitude in each instance become hungry (e.g. Matt. 14:14; 15:32; cf. Exod. 16:3). Faced with this problem, Jesus asks the question 'Where [*pothen*] are we to buy bread for these people to eat?' (John 6:5). Here there is a distinct echo of the words of Moses who, when confronted with the same situation, said, 'Where [*pothen*] am I to get meat to give to all this people?' (Num. 11:13).

In response to the lack of food, the solution proposed by the disciples is to send the people away so that 'they may get provisions' (Luke 9:12). For 'provisions' the Gospel here uses an extremely rare word, its sole occurrence in the entire New Testament, which is *episitismon*. This is a term with a definite linkage to the Old Testament passages we are considering. When the Israelites came out of Egypt at the Passover, we read that 'they had not prepared provisions for themselves' (Exod. 12:39), where the same noun *episitismon* is found in the Greek version. The psalmist also, reflecting later on the feeding in the

---

[4] In both contexts we observe that the crossing is from west to east.

[5] It is probable that the adjective *erēmos* has different connotations in the two contexts. In the exodus story it no doubt describes an arid desert, while in the Gospels it refers to the desolation of the place, that is, far from any habitation. Cf. Ben Witherington III, *Matthew* (Smyth & Helwys Bible Commentary; Macon, GA: Smyth & Helwys, 2006), 288.

[6] These two references concerning the miraculous feeding in Matthew and Mark are the sole two usages of the adverb 'on foot' in the whole New Testament.

[7] Num. 1:4–16 also speaks of 'twelve' leaders being appointed to help count the people.

wilderness, declares that: 'He [God] rained down on them manna to eat, and gave them the grain of heaven. Men ate the bread of angels; he sent them provisions [*episitismon*] in abundance' (Ps. 78:24–25).

In the Gospel episode, before the feeding takes place, Jesus instructs the multitude to sit down in groups. These groups are said to be of hundreds and of fifties in Mark's version (6:39–40), and of fifties in Luke's (9:14). The allusion to the Israelites in the wilderness has not gone unnoticed.[8] Exodus records that when the people came out into the desert they were likewise organized into divisions, 'of thousands, hundreds, fifties, and tens' (18:21, 25).

At this point in each narrative the miraculous provision of food occurs. In the Old Testament the substance given is identified as 'manna', also described by the regular term for 'bread' (Exod. 16:4, 15 etc.), along with the flesh of birds, namely quails (v. 13). In the Gospels it is, of course, bread that is abundantly provided, together with a few fish (Matt. 14:19; 15:36; Mark 6:41 etc.). A possible factor in determining the particular sort of meat supplied might be the respective localities in which the feedings occurred. In the region of the Sea of Galilee it might be expected that fish would appear on the menu, while in northern Egypt and Sinai the common quail was exceedingly abundant and remains so to this day, where it is subject to ensnaring on a large scale.[9]

The result of the supernatural giving of food was that the people 'ate and were filled'. This extra detail concerning satiety is included in all four Gospels (Matt. 14:20; 15:37; Mark 6:42; 8:8; Luke 9:17; John 6:11, 12, 26). The particular verb found in John is of interest here: 'they were filled [*eneplēsthēsan*]' (6:12). This is the same verb that appears in Exodus 16:12: 'in the morning you shall be filled [*plēsthēsesthe*] with bread'. It further appears in the psalmist's reflections on the miraculous provision of food in the wilderness (Ps. 78:29): 'they ate and were filled [*eneplēsthēsan*] completely'. The psalm itself is evidently looking back to the fact recorded concerning the manna in Exodus 16 that everybody had as much as he or she could eat (vv. 16, 18, 21).

Both contexts speak of the activity of gathering. The Israelites in the wilderness were instructed by Moses to gather up the manna (Exod. 16:16): 'Gather [*synagagete*] as much of it as each of you needs.' In the Gospel miracle Jesus commanded his disciples: 'Gather [*synagagete*] up the fragments that are left

---

[8] See, e.g., James R. Edwards, *The Gospel According to Mark* (PNTC; Grand Rapids, MI: Eerdmans, 2002), 192. Edwards remarks that 'the arrangement certainly recalls God's miraculous provision for Israel in the wilderness'.

[9] We further observe that in providing birds in one instance and fish in the other, reference is being made to two kinds of living creatures that are associated in the Hebrew creation narrative. According to that account, birds and fish were created on the same day, the fifth day of creation (Gen. 1:20–22), and occupy spatial domains also established on the same day, that is, the second (Gen. 1:6–8).

over' (John 6:12; cf. 13). The place given to the actions differs in that the former occurs before the eating and the latter after it but, as stated earlier, allusion is not founded on absolute identity of detail. It is sufficient, especially when considered alongside other common features, that the gathering of food takes place on both occasions, using the same lexical term.[10]

Lastly in this connection, in each of these situations the number of people involved is given, and in each case the text quantifies the men only. When the Israelites came out of Egypt, they amounted to 'about six hundred thousand men . . . besides children' (Exod. 12:37). Interestingly, several modern English versions here state that the number excludes 'women and children' (NIV; cf. REB, NJB, NLT, NET, CEV, NCV, CSB). In this they are surely correct. Later in the wilderness an official count was conducted, and the total came to 603,550 (Num. 1:46; cf. Exod. 38:26), and this is explicitly said not to include women or younger males (Num. 1:3). In the Gospels the miraculous feedings conclude with the number of men who participated (Matt. 14:21; 15:38; Mark 6:44; Luke 9:14; cf. Mark 8:9; John 6:10), while the women and children were not counted.

Moving on from post-exodus Israel in the wilderness, we now consider the second source for Old Testament allusions relating to Christ's feeding of the multitude. This is a miraculous act on the part of the prophet Elisha. In 2 Kings 4:42–44 we read:

> Now a man came from Baal-Shalishah, and brought to the man of God bread of the first-fruits, twenty loaves of barley and fresh ears of grain in his sack. Elisha said, 'Give them to the people that they may eat.' His servant said, 'How can I set this before a hundred men?' But he said, 'Give them to the people that they may eat, for thus says the LORD, "They will eat and have some left over."' Then he set it before them, and they ate and had some left over, according to the word of the LORD.

Since on this occasion a large number of people are fed by an insufficient quantity of food, the miracle enacted by the prophet bears an obvious resemblance to that performed by Jesus. That readers of the latter episode are deliberately being pointed back to the former is suggested by certain of the details.[11] The older text speaks (v. 42), not simply of 'bread', but specifically of

---

[10] This linkage between 'fill' and 'gather' in the Gospel feeding miracle and the manna episode is also proposed in William M. Wright IV, *The Bible and Catholic Ressourcement: Essays on Scripture and Theology* (Steubenville, OH: Emmaus Academic, 2019), 174.

[11] Connections have been noted, for instance, by France, *Gospel of Matthew*, 559: 'An obvious parallel would be with the miracle of Elisha . . . (2 Kgs 4:42–44); there are also verbal echoes of the Elisha story in this pericope, and the nature of Jesus' miracle is the same'; also David W. Pao and Eckhard J. Schnabel,

artous krithinous, that is, 'loaves of barley', just as appears in the feeding of the five thousand (John 6:9), also *artous krithinous* (cf. v. 13). Someone 'brought' these loaves to Elisha (v. 42), as in the Gospel account loaves are brought to Jesus (Matt. 14:18). Elisha's servant posed the question: 'How [*ti*] can I set this before a hundred men?' (v. 43), as compared with the similar question Jesus is asked by his disciples (John 6:9): 'What [*ti*] are these among so many?' Elisha instructed his servant, saying, 'Give [*dote*] to the people that they may eat' (v. 42), as Jesus commands the disciples, 'Give [*dote*] them something to eat yourselves' (Mark 6:37; Luke 9:13).[12] The number of people who are fed is a single group of 100 (v. 43), a number that also appears in connection with the groupings of those who eat in the Gospel miracle (Mark 6:40). There is also the fact that in the earlier account some of the food remained after the meal: 'and they ate [*kai ephagon*] and had some left over' (v. 44), which is likewise a prominent element in Christ's feeding miracles: 'and they all ate [*kai ephagon*] . . . and they picked up twelve basketfuls of fragments that were left over' (Matt. 14:20; cf. 15:37; Mark 8:8; Luke 9:17).

We note too the interesting fact of the sole New Testament usage, in John 6:9, of the diminutive noun *paidarion*, 'young boy', indicating the lad who brought forward the loaves and fishes. This also connects with Elisha in that the prophet's young servant is designated in the same way, not in the actual episode of the multiplication of food, but in the other feeding miracle recorded right before it, and in the immediately preceding verse (2 Kgs 4:41), as well as eighteen more times in the chapter. The occurrence of the noun in the Gospel passage, when taken together with the other verbal resonances and thematic connections, does seem to be a further pointer to Elisha and his miracles.[13]

In addition to the foregoing, I believe we may infer a Passover connection for the Elisha miracle. The feast may not be explicitly mentioned, but the attentive reader would certainly locate it at that time of the year. This is due to the association of the terms 'first-fruits' and 'barley'. The barley harvest was the earliest in the year,[14] taking place in the spring, in the first month of the year

---

'Luke', in G. K. Beale and D. A. Carson (eds.), *Commentary on the New Testament Use of the Old Testament* (Grand Rapids, MI: Baker Academic, 2007), 310: 'the short account of Elisha's feeding of a hundred men in 2 Kings 4:42–44 provides a number of structural parallels'.

12 In the Hebrew text, though absent from the LXX, the Elisha episode also speaks of the food being 'set before them' (v. 44). This phrase appears in the Gospel accounts of Jesus' miracle (Mark 6:41; 8:6; Luke 9:16).

13 Ridderbos, who only observes three of the intertextual features, is of the opinion that 'the combination of these three links – the boy, the barley, and the question – can hardly be regarded as accidental'. See Herman Ridderbos, *The Gospel of John: A Theological Commentary* (Grand Rapids, MI: Eerdmans, 1997), 211.

14 Cf. Hayyim Schauss, *The Jewish Festivals: A Guide to Their History and Observance* (New York, NY: Schocken Books, 1962), 40–41.

according to the religious calendar. This was the month originally called Abib (Exod. 13:4; 23:15), later named Nisan (cf. Esth. 3:7), during which the Passover was celebrated on the fourteenth day. Not only this, but the day when the first-fruits of the barley harvest was celebrated was timed with reference to the Passover itself, occurring on the 'day after the sabbath' following the feast (Lev. 23:10–11). Elisha's miracle, since it speaks of barley loaves made from the first-fruits, must have taken place very shortly after Passover.

It has hopefully been demonstrated, then, that the feeding miracles of Christ, through the allusions they contain, evoke two particular Old Testament scenarios: Moses and the exodus tradition, plus the Elisha narrative. As regards the purpose served by these allusions, I believe we are to discern three distinct, though not entirely unrelated, ideas. Basically, these concern, in the order we shall treat them, first the principal figures involved, namely Moses and Elisha, second the giving of the manna and third the feast of the Passover. Obviously, Moses, the Passover and manna are all elements within a single integrated narrative. Although Elisha stands somewhat separately from these, this prophetic figure does nevertheless show some connection with Moses, and the aforementioned miracle he performed bears a relation to the provision of manna.

A range of commentators agree on the fact that the event of feeding the multitude presents Jesus as a Moses-like figure,[15] a fact noted beforehand in certain passages of Matthew's Gospel.[16] Like that earlier figure, in a desolate place on the far side of the sea, Jesus is at the head of a numerous gathering of people who are hungry, and food is supernaturally obtained to feed them to the full. Readers of the Gospels acquainted with the Old Testament writings would surely not have failed to detect the parallel.

Yet, as in previous allusions to that character, Jesus is not merely being portrayed as a Moses-type figure, nor as a second Moses. Besides the obvious connections between the two persons and situations, there is a notable distinction. Moses himself did not actually perform any miraculous act of feeding. The accounts in Exodus 16 and Numbers 11 make it plain that God, and not Moses, initiated what was to happen and gave the supply of food. Jesus indeed makes this very point when he says, 'Moses did not give you bread from heaven' (John 6:32). In the Gospel feeding of the multitude, however, it is Jesus who both initiates and performs the miracle.[17] The statement concerning the latter that

---

[15] See, e.g., France, *Gospel of Matthew*, 559; Patrick Schreiner, *Matthew, Disciple and Scribe: The First Gospel and Its Portrait of Jesus* (Grand Rapids, MI: Baker Academic, 2019), 151–152.

[16] See chapters 6 and 8.

[17] The reader should understand that when Jesus prays before feeding the multitude, this is described as 'giving thanks' (Matt. 14:19; 15:36). It is not a prayer to God in heaven for a miracle to occur, but rather the regular Jewish blessing pronounced before partaking of food.

'he knew what *he* was about to do' (John 6:6) could in no way be said of Moses. The respective roles therefore essentially differ in this important matter. This fact may even be taken as another pointer to the fact that in being the actual performer of the miracle himself, Jesus is being presented not merely as Moses but as *God*, the miraculous provider of nourishment. Such a correspondence between Jesus and God is a remarkable feature of several of the extended allusions studied in this book.

Besides the foregoing, there is the fact that the bread offered by Jesus has a deeper spiritual meaning, a meaning that concerned himself, as will be considered below. The occasion of the feeding was, to those with eyes to see, much more than a supernatural physical act, and much more could be obtained from it than merely full stomachs. These features therefore again underscore the fact that Jesus is not simply another Moses, but one greater by far than Moses.[18] The latter was indeed a great leader of his people, one appointed to bring deliverance from Egyptian oppression, and to seek provision for his people in the wilderness and intercede on their behalf to God for all their needs. But Jesus is more than all this, and that is what the Gospel episodes before us intend to indicate. The 'feeding in the wilderness' miracle offers a hint that he who surpasses Moses will bring about a new exodus, a deliverance on a much grander scale, as the fourth Gospel will make explicit. There is then both continuity – here is a Moses-like figure – and discontinuity – what he does vastly exceeds what was accomplished through the Old Testament figure of Moses.

The Elijah–Elisha cycle forms a prominent part of the material in the books of Kings. The two prophets ministered in the northern kingdom of Israel at a time of great apostasy. One notable aspect of their respective ministries was miracles, which were not so much in evidence among the other Old Testament prophets. This is one of the features that binds the two men together. Their ministries were, in effect, one – the younger man continuing the work of the older.[19] We see this in Elijah's cloak being left for Elisha (2 Kgs 2:13), in the fact that the spirit of the former passed on to the latter (cf. v. 15, 'The spirit of Elijah is resting on Elisha') and in the close resemblance between the kinds of miracles they perform.[20]

---

[18] Cf. Joseph Ratzinger, *Jesus of Nazareth: From the Baptism in the Jordan to the Transfiguration* (New York, NY: Doubleday, 2007), 264: 'Jesus is the definitive, greater Moses'.

[19] So, e.g., Peter Leithart, *1 & 2 Kings* (Brazos Theological Commentary of the Bible; Grand Rapids, MI: Brazos, 2006), 171. In Leithart's view the oneness between them is so close that he describes Elisha as 'a "reincarnation" (or "reanimation") of Elijah'. For a technical treatment of the compositional unity of the narratives concerning the two prophets, see Michelle L. Bellamy, 'The Elijah-Elisha Cycle of Stories: A Ring Composition', PhD dissertation, University of Boston, 2013.

[20] Both prophets miraculously provide food for widows, both raise a child from the dead, and both help a Gentile in need. See Leithart, *1 & 2 Kings*, 187.

In the Gospels it is significant that Elijah makes an appearance, together with Moses, in the vision on the mount of transfiguration, where the two men were seen with Jesus (Matt. 17:1–8). Together they may be taken as embodying the prophetic witness of the Old Testament.[21] And since Elisha, as was just said, is so closely identified with Elijah, then Elisha too may be taken as a representation of the prophetic ministry of old. This being so, the feeding of the multitude in the Gospels presents Jesus as performing a miracle that transcends the related miracle of the prophet. Elisha fed a hundred with twenty loaves, Jesus fed several thousand with much less. Both events involve the supernatural multiplication of food, but the latter to a more significant degree. Again, there would seem to be the further distinction that Elisha did not perform the act on his own initiative. His words make it clear that God had revealed it to him that he, God, would so provide (2 Kgs 4:43–44, '[T]hus says the LORD, "They will eat and have some left over." Then he set it before them, and they ate and had some left over, according to the word of the LORD'). What results from a comparison of the two miracles, therefore, is evidently the fact that Jesus is by far the more eminent of the two.

We conclude, then, that the feeding of the multitude, as one of its intentions, presents Jesus Christ as one like Moses and Elisha of old, and yet so much greater than them in power, authority and accomplishment. And since these two figures are also representations that embody the Old Testament revelation, it is also to be concluded that here in Jesus is someone whose ministry in one respect bears a continuity with that revelation and yet greatly surpasses it.[22]

Christ's feeding of the multitude, as we have seen, contains allusions that direct readers of the Gospels to the Old Testament passages concerning the manna. Such a connection becomes certain when we continue reading in John 6. There, in a discourse that explicitly refers back to his recent miracle (v. 26), Jesus expounds the relationship between himself and the manna given at the time of Moses (vv. 25–59).[23] In his exposition he draws out a number of

---

[21] See chapter 13.

[22] Jeffrey John (*The Meaning in the Miracles* [Norwich: Canterbury Press, 2001], 5) comments: 'Taking Elisha and Moses together, the story seems to be telling us in an allusive way that in recapitulating what Moses did Jesus fulfils the Law, and in recapitulating Elisha he fulfils the Prophets . . . this miracle [of the feeding] is intended to teach us, in picture-story form, that Jesus is truly the one whom the Law and the Prophets foretold.'

[23] Cf. Romano Guardini, *The Lord* (Washington, DC: Gateway, 1996), 230: 'the nourishing of the bodies is but the prefiguration of the sacred nourishment soon to be proclaimed from Capharnaum', that is, in the following discourse, which took place in that town (cf. John 6:24, 59; also John, *The Meaning in the Miracles*, 68: 'Arguably the best commentary on it [the miracle] is the one that Scripture itself supplies: the discourse of Jesus on the Bread of Life in John 6:25–58.'

comparisons and contrasts between his provision and that of the manna.[24] Both concern what is described as 'bread', or food, and both are said to come 'from heaven' (vv. 31, 32, 50, 51, 58; cf. Exod. 16:4; Neh. 9:15; Ps. 105:40). In each case this does indeed impart life, but of an altogether different kind. The manna sustained the ancient Hebrews for a few short years in the wilderness, but they eventually 'died' (John 6:49). What Jesus provides, however, is the 'bread of life' (v. 35), and whoever eats that bread 'will not die' (v. 50) but 'will live for ever' (v. 51). The reason this can be so is because Jesus does not just 'give' the bread he is speaking of, but he himself *is* the bread (vv. 33, 48). To eat the real bread that comes down from heaven is to partake of his flesh, as he explains: 'the bread that I will give for the life of the world is my flesh' (v. 51), and 'my flesh is true food' (v. 55). In this context, as often elsewhere in John, Jesus is speaking in a figurative manner. To 'eat' his flesh means not to digest him physically in the stomach, as some Jews misunderstood (v. 52), but to receive him spiritually in the heart by faith.[25] To do such would be to receive that which imparts 'everlasting life' (v. 40).

A remarkable irony exists regarding Christ's discourse which further strengthens the link with the manna episode in the wilderness. This relates to the act of grumbling. We read that 'the Jews grumbled [*egongyzon*] about him because he said, "I am the bread that came down from heaven"' (John 6:41), earning them the rebuke from Jesus: 'Don't grumble [*gongyzete*] among yourselves' (v. 43). Even many of those who had been following him up till then, called 'his disciples', 'were grumbling [*gongyzousin*]' about what Jesus had been saying (v. 61). Grumbling (*gongysmos*) is a conspicuous feature of the manna narrative, appearing in both Exodus 16 (the verb and noun occurring eight times in total in vv. 2, 7, 8, 9, 12) and Numbers 11 (v. 1). The irony lies in the fact that in the Old Testament passage it is the lack of food that provokes the grumbling while in the Gospel it is the provision of it! The Israelites grumbled because they wanted physical food to fill their stomachs and keep them alive a while longer. Jesus, according to John 6, came to offer himself as the 'living bread', the spiritual food that would satisfy their souls and cause them to live for ever, and yet at that the Jews grumbled: 'Is this not Jesus, the son of Joseph, whose father and mother we know? How can he now say, "I came down from heaven"?' (v. 42). Therefore they rejected him and his claims on account of their lack of faith. The ironic reversal is sublime, though tragic.

---

[24] For the manna as a designed prefiguring of Christ, see Nicholas P. Lunn, *Jesus in the Jewish Scriptures: How the Old Testament Bears Witness to Christ* (London: Faithbuilders, 2020), 130–133.

[25] Cf. Lunn, *Jesus in the Jewish Scriptures*, 132–133.

The Passover connection of the feeding miracle is dealt with last since it forms a backdrop to the whole, and because it is based on the spiritual understanding of the manna, as just explained. We noted above that the giving of the manna in Exodus 16, the multiplication of bread by Elisha in 2 Kings 4, as well as the feeding of the five thousand in the Gospels, all depict events that happened at a time close to Passover. The temporal correspondence does not of course concern the exact same day, but then it is sufficient for the miracles to be brought into proximity with the Passover feast for an association to be established. As said before, that is how allusion works. It is based on an association of ideas, not precise identity. All the miraculous feedings discussed, therefore, have a distinct link with the Passover.

The way in which Jesus unpacks the spiritual meaning of the feeding in John 6 creates a further pointer to the Passover. This is the matter of eating flesh (vv. 51–56). The observance of the Passover, as is well known, centred on the eating of the flesh of the lamb.[26] And Jesus has been identified as that lamb, 'the Lamb of God', from the beginning (John 1:29, 36).[27] It would appear, therefore, that in his discourse on the miracle Jesus merges the feeding on the manna with the eating of the Passover sacrifice. Thematically, both form part of the one integrated exodus narrative, and both relate to a divinely ordained act of eating. Through the provision of bread in the wilderness the miracle reminds the reader of the manna, while through the explicit reference to 'Passover' (6:4), along with the idea of eating flesh, we are brought to a consideration of this latter festal occasion also.

Here I would bring to the reader's attention a particularly intriguing detail that appears in Matthew's record. According to the Mosaic prescriptions for the celebration of the Passover (Exod. 12:6; Lev. 23:3; Num. 9:3), the lamb was to be slaughtered at a time defined in Hebrew as *bên hā'arbayim*. This phrase consists of a preposition and a noun in the dual number, and literally means 'between the two evenings'.[28] The literal sense is obscured in modern English versions, which generally render the phrase as 'at twilight' (e.g. NASB, NRSV, ESV, NIV, NJPS), though some do footnote the fact that the literal translation would be 'between the two evenings' (e.g. ESV, NET). The time referred to may indeed be 'twilight', but we are interested here in the particular form of the expression. The phrase seems to presuppose that one day ends at sunset, at which point the next begins, in accordance with the common Jewish reckoning.

---

[26] See Exod. 12:8 ('They shall eat the flesh that night').

[27] See also 1 Cor. 5:7; 1 Pet. 1:19; Rev. 5:6, 12.

[28] In the LXX the phrase could be translated as *pros esperan*, 'towards evening' (as Exod. 12:6), or more literally as *ana meson tōn esperinōn*, 'in the middle of the evenings' (as Lev. 23:5).

So 'evening' here could refer to the latter part of the former day and to the onset of the latter, hence 'two evenings'.[29] Whatever the explanation of the grammatical form, the fact is that Matthew seems to pick up on its literal meaning in his presentation of the feeding of the five thousand, as will be explained.

In the Gospel of Matthew the temporal clause 'when it was evening' (*opsias genomenēs*) occurs seven times in total. Of these, two are found in direct speech on the lips of Jesus, one in a saying (16:2)[30] and the other in a parable (20:8).[31] This leaves five instances that appear in Matthew's own narration of the events concerning Jesus. I believe each of these serves to draw special attention to the fact of eventide. In 8:16 the bringing of the demon-possessed and the sick to Jesus is now possible at evening because it implies that with the setting of the sun the sabbath has ended (cf. Mark 1:21) and people are then permitted to carry those needing help. The other four occurrences significantly may be grouped into two pairs. Each of the pair is found in the same extended narrative, just a short interval apart from one other. These come in 14:15 and 23, and in 26:20 and 27:57. I believe not only that each time reference relates to the other of the pair, but that the two pairs by authorial design actually connect with one another, creating what to my mind is a literary allusion of the highest order. What we are looking at in each pair is, in effect, two evenings. Bearing in mind the prescribed time of the Passover offering, we are being called upon to consider what transpired between two evenings on two distinct occasions in Matthew's narrative.

Taking the second pair first, these both come at the end of Passion Week. The first (26:20) concerns the evening on which Jesus shared the last supper with his disciples, and the second (27:57) relates to the approach of the evening on the day he was crucified, which according to the traditional chronology was the evening of the day after the evening of the last supper. This was when Joseph of Arimathea came to remove the body of Jesus for burial. Although a span of daylight hours came between these two, technically speaking these are two evenings of the same day. The meal was held during the evening that began the day at sunset, and Jesus was buried as evening drew near at the end of that same day, before another sunset marked the commencement of the next day, as the

---

[29] In the Babylonian Talmud (*Pesaḥim* 61a) the explanation given is that the first evening is when the heat of the sun begins to decrease, and the second evening is marked by sunset. This would mean that 'between the two evenings' is the period approximately from 3 pm to 5 pm. The Jewish historian Josephus (*Jewish War* 6.423) states that the Passover lamb was sacrificed 'from the ninth hour until the eleventh hour' (that is, between 3 pm and 5 pm).

[30] In 16:2 'when it was evening' does not appear in all manuscripts, so may not be original to Matthew.

[31] Since these two do not form part of the actual narrative, these two appearances of the time phrase do not serve to structure Matthew's account, as the others do.

Jews perceived it. Since this coming day was a sabbath, no work (cf. Mark 15:42; Luke 23:54; John 19:31), such as taking down and burying the victim of crucifixion, was legally permissible. Between these two evenings in question the principal events that took place were the last supper and the crucifixion, which are obviously located at the time of the Passover festival (cf. Matt. 26:19). We further point out the evident fact that the two events occurring within this time frame are inextricably related. At the supper, Jesus gave bread and wine to his disciples, representing his body and blood given for the forgiveness of sins (26:26–28; cf. Luke 22:19). In the morning, what was symbolically portrayed by the meal became actual when Jesus offered up himself, so bringing about the promised forgiveness. The former was anticipatory and preparatory, the latter the full accomplishment, yet both concerned the same essential reality. These two evenings, therefore, embrace what could justly be described as the Passover of the true Lamb, which brings about the ultimate redemption foreshadowed by the first Passover in Egypt.

Regarding the other two references in Matthew 14, it is surely not coincidental that the two evenings here demarcate the feeding of the five thousand. The time phrase 'When it was evening' in verse 15 leads directly into the enactment of the miracle, while in verse 23 the identical expression follows Jesus' dismissal of the multitude after the feeding, upon which he went up a mountain to pray. Chronologically speaking, the most natural way to understand the relationship between the two evenings would be that the first indicates the closure of one day, and the second the beginning of the next. That is to say, they are both essentially part of the same span of evening time, separated by the Jewish division of the day.[32] Whether this is so or not, from a literary point of view the two time phrases definitely serve to bracket the miraculous multiplication of loaves and fishes. Consequently, the feeding miracle is one that falls, according to Matthew's arrangement, between two evenings.

We have, then, in Matthew's account two notable occasions – the feeding of the multitude and Christ's Passover celebration and sacrifice – each enclosed within two evenings. The fact that only these particular happenings are so framed suggests intentional design. This is confirmed by the presence of unmistakable thematic and verbal associations between the two portions of text in question, in Matthew's Gospel itself and when viewed from a broader canonical perspective. Each span of bracketed material obviously depicts a meal at a gathering over which Jesus presides. In each case he takes bread, blesses it,

---

[32] Note the disciples' remark that 'the hour is already late' (v. 15) at the time the miracle was performed. So the miracle took place as the day was declining; then Jesus went up to pray as the night drew on. It does not seem at all likely that a whole period of twenty-four hours passed between these two events.

breaks it and gives it to his disciples (Matt. 14:19; cf. 26:26).[33] Elsewhere, the earlier event is specifically located, like the later, around the time of Passover (John 6:4). And when Jesus explains the significance of the feeding miracle he does so, as we have seen, with reference to eating his own flesh and drinking his blood (6:54–56), which self-evidently relates to the symbolic consumption of his body and blood at the last supper.[34] Even on the former occasion, therefore, though the miracle itself includes no mention of drink, the notion of drinking 'my blood' is present in Jesus' discourse on it. Here the giving of his flesh and blood serves as a metaphor, misunderstood by many of his hearers, for his coming self-sacrifice at his crucifixion.[35]

One further thing may be stated respecting the inclusion of blood, mentioned alongside the flesh, in John 6. On the matter of the eating of flesh, such language fits suitably into a Passover context, since the meat of the lamb was consumed. Yet it has to be said that the drinking of blood appears to be at variance with the original Passover ritual, at which the animal's blood was daubed on the lintel and doorposts of the homes of the Israelites (Exod. 12:7). This first Passover, Jesus' discourse on the feeding miracle, and the last supper do all indeed speak of both flesh, or body, and the disposal of blood. The fact is, however, that in the two New Testament events in question the blood is spoken of as applied in an entirely different manner from that in the Old. I believe that there is a good reason for this. Why this is so will be explained in more detail in our chapter on the last supper.[36] Suffice it to say for now that in both Gospel passages the 'blood' is said to be drunk, that is, consumed inwardly, unlike at the original Passover where it had a purely external application. Here I believe is great theological significance with regard to the nature of Jesus' Passover offering. In speaking of the drinking of his blood, along with eating his flesh, in John 6, and in the command to drink 'my blood', as well as to eat 'my body', at the last supper, we are being told, through figurative speech and action, that the

---

[33] The closeness between the sequence of Jesus' actions in each instance is noteworthy: 'Taking [labōn] . . . he blessed [eulogēsen] . . . having broken [klasas] . . . he gave [edōken] to the disciples' (14:19); cf. 'Taking [labōn] . . . having blessed [eulogēsas] . . . he broke [eklasen] . . . giving [dous] to the disciples' (26:26). It is difficult not to conclude that the resemblance is purposeful.

[34] Cf. D. A. Carson, The Gospel According to John (PNTC; Leicester: Apollos, 1991), 295. Carson opines that the language of John 6 equating the bread with Christ's flesh 'inevitably calls to mind the institution of the eucharist'. This is not to say that the 'bread of life' discourse is to be interpreted sacramentally. Rather, both the feeding of the multitude and the last supper point to the event of Jesus' giving of himself in his death on the cross. The former does so by means of a miracle, replete with Old Testament allusions to manna and the Passover, and the latter by means of a symbolic meal. Since both are precursors to Christ's sacrifice they relate to each other also, while each finding its ultimate fulfilment only at the cross.

[35] Cf. Ridderbos, Gospel of John, 238; the author states that 'the vivifying power of the bread (that he [Jesus] both is and gives) consists in that he gives himself for the world, in his self-surrender in death'.

[36] See chapter 19.

Old Testament ritual of animal sacrifice has now ceased, and that the true and perfect human life-giving offering, foreordained from the foundation of the world, is now given. With respect to this latter sacrifice, it is both his body and his blood that are to be received for eternal life to be imparted. More on this in due course.

From what we have examined in this chapter, we conclude that, when viewed against the backdrop of the ancient Scriptures of Israel, the Gospel miracles in which food is supernaturally multiplied and given for the sustenance of the multitudes present Jesus in a multifaceted way. By means of allusions to related miracles involving Moses and Elisha, he is being portrayed as one greater than older prophetic revelation, indeed as one who is himself the divine provider. Christ, moreover, himself explains that what is represented by the bread from heaven provided of old, namely the manna, is fulfilled in his own person, the giving of his own flesh, and blood also. The meaning of the miraculous provision of food is further enhanced through allusions to the Passover, both retrospectively to that in Exodus and prospectively to the coming Passover in Jerusalem. From this we understand that the lamb slain at the liberation of the Israelites from bondage in Egypt is now replaced by the true Lamb of God whose offering, of both his flesh and blood, is able to set us free from the sin of the world and grant life everlasting.

11

Walking on the water

Matthew 14:22–27; Mark 6:45–52;
John 6:16–21

The event of Jesus walking on water is narrated in three of the four canonical Gospels. In each case it is placed immediately after the feeding of the five thousand. It stands to reason, therefore, that there is an inextricable connection between the two episodes, and that what we now investigate in some sense depends on the earlier event for a full and proper interpretation.

After the miraculous feeding, while he stays to dismiss the crowd, Jesus sends his disciples by boat back across the Sea of Galilee (Matt. 14:22; Mark 6:45; John 6:16–17). He then ascends a mountain alone to pray into the night (Matt. 14:23; Mark 6:46). During this time a storm descends on the lake, causing considerable difficulty for the disciples, who are attempting to row to the other side (Matt. 14:24; Mark 6:48a; John 6:18). In the early hours of the morning Jesus comes to them walking on the sea, much to their consternation since they think he must be a ghost (Matt. 14:25–26; Mark 6:48b–49; John 6:19). He speaks to identify himself and to reassure them (Matt. 14:27; Mark 6:50; John 6:20). He then climbs into the boat, at which time the wind ceases (Matt. 14:32; Mark 6:51a). The disciples respond in utter amazement to all they have witnessed (Mark 6:51b), declaring Jesus to be the Son of God (Matt. 14:33). The vessel soon arrives at its destination (John 6:21). Matthew alone includes the additional matter of Peter getting out of the boat to walk on the water to Jesus (14:28–31).

According to the plain meaning of what happens here, we appear once more to be reading about a nature miracle. To be able to perform wonders of this kind is, of course, in itself a significant testimony to the person of Christ. However, once the allusions present in the accounts are discerned, they considerably augment what is communicated on the surface level. Not a few commentators have detected allusions here to certain Old Testament passages. Chief among these is a poetic passage from Job (Job 9), and the experiences of Moses (Exod. 33 – 34) and Elijah (1 Kgs 19) on a particular mountain. All three of these passages interrelate closely, as we shall see. Further to this, a secondary set of allusions are to be perceived having reference to the crossing of the Red Sea during the Israelite exodus from Egypt (Exod. 14 – 15). These latter are not commonly noticed in the commentaries.

First, then, we are reminded of a text from the book of Job. There Job himself addresses his three companions with the following words about God (9:4–11):

> ⁴He [God] is wise in heart and mighty in strength.
> Who has defied him and succeeded?
> ⁵He moves the mountains, though they do not know it,
> overturning them in his anger.
> ⁶He shakes the earth out of its place,
> and its pillars tremble.
> ⁷He speaks to the sun, and it does not shine;
> he seals up the stars.
> ⁸He alone stretches out the heavens,
> and he treads on the waves of the sea.
> ⁹He is the Maker of the Bear, Orion, and the Pleiades,
> and the chambers of the south.
> ¹⁰He does great things that cannot be fathomed,
> and wonderful things without number.
> ¹¹If he passes by me, I cannot see him;
> and if he moves past, I do not perceive him.

Looking more closely at verse 8, the original Hebrew text declares that 'he treads on the waves of the sea'. Its Greek equivalent here translates the line as 'he walks [*peripatōn*] upon the sea [*epi thalassēs*] as upon firm ground'. In the Gospel episode the same verbal phrase is applied to Jesus. There we are told that he came to the disciples *peripatōn epi tēn thalassan*, 'walking upon the sea' (Matt. 14:25; Mark 6:48). As we continue in the verses from Job we soon discover another connection. In the second line of verse 11, the LXX has *ean parelthē me*, 'If he passes by me'. Mark's version of the miracle includes the unique feature that as Jesus came walking on the water towards the disciples, 'he wished to pass by them' (6:48). Here the verb is *parelthein*, as in Job. Obviously, in Job both verse 8 about the one walking on the sea and verse 11 about one who passes by are referring to actions attributed to God himself. The images employed in the passage – the earth trembling, its pillars shaking, the darkening of the heavenly bodies, and the like – are all conventionally associated with manifestations of the divine presence, that is to say, theophanies.[1] On such occasions God is unmistakably present in some special way, yet his being is not seen (cf. v. 11, 'I cannot see him . . . I do not perceive him').[2]

The term 'pass by' in relation to God has a particularly distinct Old Testament heritage. First and foremost, it harks back to what may be considered one of the primary theophanies found in Israel's Scriptures, that at Sinai. There God descended on the mountain amid thick cloud and strokes of lightning (Exod. 19:16). The whole mountain trembled and smoke rose up like that of a furnace (v. 18). It was clear, however, that no form of God was seen.[3] Later, after the apostasy involving the golden calf, Moses was alone on the mountain with God, and there Moses asked to see his glory (33:18). By way of reply God told him, 'I will make all my goodness pass by [*pareleusomai*][4] before you, and I will proclaim my name, the LORD' (v. 19). He then added, 'But you cannot see my face, for no human being may see me and live' (v. 20). In fulfilment of this, Moses was instructed to 'stand [*stēsē*] upon a rock' (v. 21), and then the Lord came to him and 'proclaimed his name and passed by [*parēlthen*] before Moses, proclaiming, "The LORD, the LORD . . ."' (34:5–6). We note in this context the twofold use of the verb 'pass by', as well as the emphasis on the personal divine name, 'the LORD', that is, the ineffable tetragrammaton YHWH, represented by *kyrios*, 'Lord', in the LXX. Clearly, then, Moses was privileged to witness a theophany of the closest order possible under the Old Testament economy.[5]

This mountain-top encounter with the divine undergoes a kind of rehearsal in the life of the prophet Elijah several centuries later. In 1 Kings 19, Elijah fled to Mount Horeb, an alternative name for Mount Sinai,[6] to avoid death at the hands of the impious queen Jezebel (vv. 1–3, 8). Here God spoke to him, saying, 'Go out and stand [*stēsē*] on the mountain before the LORD, for the LORD is about to pass by [*pareleusetai kyrios*].' Again we note the prominence of the

---

[1] Hartley describes Job 9:5–13 as a 'hymn' that contains 'language descriptive of a theophany' (John E. Hartley, *The Book of Job* [NICOT; Grand Rapids, MI: Eerdmans, 1988], 169; cf. 172). Clines likewise identifies the text as a 'traditional description of theophany' (David J. A. Clines, *Job 1–20* [WBC 17; Dallas, TX: Word, 1989], 232).

[2] Cf. Hartley (*Book of Job*, 173): 'God himself is not visible in the natural phenomena'.

[3] See Deut. 4:12, 'Then the LORD spoke to you from the midst of the fire. You heard the sound of words, but you saw no form; there was only a voice' (cf. v. 15).

[4] The LXX gives the simple sense of 'I will pass by', whereas the Hebrew has the causative, 'I will make pass by', with the divine goodness as the direct object. For the benefit of readers unfamiliar with Greek, the form *pareleusomai* is the future tense of the verb *parelthein*, which occurs in relation to Christ in Mark 6:48.

[5] For a discussion of what the text means when it says that Moses saw only God's 'back' (Exod. 33:23), see Thomas J. White, *Exodus* (Brazos Theological Commentary on the Bible; Grand Rapids, MI: Brazos, 2016), 280–282.

[6] The description 'mountain of God' is applied to both Sinai (Exod. 24:13; cf. 15) and Horeb (1 Kgs 19:8), these being two names for the same mountain. Cf. also Exod. 33:6; Deut. 1:6; 4:10; Ps. 106:19.

divine name and the fact that the Lord 'passed by'. And similarly there were natural phenomena typically associated with theophanies – a tearing wind, an earthquake, and fire (vv. 11–12) – but the Lord himself was not seen.

The Gospel episode we are considering evidently relates back to the poetic description of theophany in Job 9 as well as to the theophanies granted to Moses and Elijah. What the disciples were experiencing was likewise such a manifestation of the divine presence. They had an encounter with the one 'walking on the sea', as spoken of by Job, the same one who passed by Moses and Elijah. Remarkably, we also find in the Gospel accounts the personal name of God to be in evidence, though it could easily be overlooked in English translation. In all three versions, as Jesus approaches the boat, he calls out to the disciples, 'It is I' (Matt. 14:27; Mark 6:50; John 6:20). The Greek words here are *egō eimi*, literally 'I am'. On the surface, the words function as a simple act of self-identification: 'It's me', that is, 'I'm your master, whom you know', and not a phantom as they supposed. Yet at a deeper level, taken against the background of the Jewish Scriptures, the words convey a much more profound meaning. Jesus here is doing nothing less than alluding to the personal name of God.

The divine name was revealed to Moses back in Exodus when God commissioned him to return to Egypt to liberate his people from slavery. There (Exod. 3:13–14) we read this all-important exchange between Moses and God:

> Moses said to God, 'Behold, I am going to the people of Israel, and I will say to them, "The God of your fathers has sent me to you", and they may say to me, "What is his name?" What shall I say to them?' And God said to Moses, 'I AM WHO I AM'. Then he said, 'Thus you shall say to the people of Israel, "I AM has sent me to you."'[7]

This name of God, 'I AM', is here disclosed to Moses, and later proclaimed to him in the form of YHWH, as we have seen in the theophany Moses witnessed on the mountain.[8] Now, on the Sea of Galilee, Jesus takes this same name on his lips and applies it to himself, so claiming identity with the One so named.[9]

---

[7] 'I AM' appears as the translation of the divine name in NRSV, ESV, NASB, NIV, NKJV, AV, ASV, REB, NJB, NLT, NET, CEV and others.

[8] We note too the prominence of *egō eimi* as uttered by the person of God in certain portions of the book of Isaiah (41:4; 43:10, 25; 46:4; 48:12; 51:12; 52:6).

[9] Cf. Richard B. Hays, *Reading Backwards: Figural Christology and the Fourfold Gospel Witness* (London: SPCK, 2015), 26. Commenting on Mark 6 in particular, Hays states: 'In this narrative context, there is little doubt that we should also hear Jesus' comforting address to the disciples ("It is I [ἐγώ εἰμι]; do not be afraid" [6:50]) as an echo of the self-revelatory speech of the God of Abraham, of Isaac, and of Jacob speaking from the burning bush in Exodus 3:14: "I AM WHO I AM" (LXX: ἐγώ εἰμι ὁ ὤν). Thus, when Jesus speaks this same phrase, "I am," in his sea-crossing epiphany, it serves to underscore the claim of *divine identity* that

It is, then, more than the walking on the sea and the act of passing by amid the phenomena of nature that creates the theophanic overtones of this event. As the name of God was central to the theophanies experienced by Moses and Elijah, so too here in Galilee, and its reference to Jesus himself makes his own person the focus of this encounter. In seeing him in this manner, the disciples were beholding none less than God in human form. The self-manifestation of God that was denied to Moses and Elijah, the God described by Job as unseeable (Job 9:11), and the one that Moses was told he could not see (Exod. 33:20), was granted to them. The one they followed was being displayed to them in a radically new light and they were utterly astounded (Mark 6:51).[10]

At this new revelation of their master, his disciples in the boat 'worshipped [*prosekynēsan*] him' (Matt. 14:33). While this word can simply mean 'do obeisance', there can be little doubt that in this present context, in view of what they had just witnessed and heard, it actually means the worship of one who is divine.[11]

What we have considered so far makes the occurrence of what took place on the Sea of Galilee theologically charged to a profound degree. It is seen to be one of many indicators, though often subtly expressed, that all four Gospels present Jesus as divine. In various places and in diverse ways, Matthew, Mark and Luke, together with John, each testifies to that wonderful truth. But now as we come to explore another layer of meaning, also hinted at by means of allusions, the content of the episode becomes deeper still. Here we examine the Gospel incident in the light of the Passover and exodus, and more specifically in the light of the passage through the Red Sea that occurred at that time.

As stated above, in all three of its versions the account of Jesus walking on the water immediately follows the feeding of the five thousand (Matt. 14:13–21; Mark 6:30–44; John 6:1–15). This association would seem to contribute to its meaning. That prior miracle, we saw earlier,[12] was one that took place near the time of Passover (John 6:4), and one that made explicit reference to the manna (cf. 6:31, 49, 58). It also occurred after a previous crossing of the sea (Matt. 14:13; Mark 6:32). The fourth Gospel tells us that earlier 'Jesus crossed to the far shore

---

is implicitly present in the story as a whole' (italics added). Cf. also Daniel Fanous, *Taught By God: Making Sense of the Difficult Sayings of Jesus* (Rollinsford, NH: Orthodox Research Institute, 2010), 201. Fanous connects Christ's use of 'I am' with the attempt of the Jews on another occasion to stone him for blasphemy (John 8:59). This seems to put it beyond doubt that his use of the title was an implicit claim to deity.

[10] Cf. Joseph Ratzinger, *Jesus of Nazareth: From the Baptism in the Jordan to the Transfiguration* (New York, NY: Doubleday, 2007), 352: 'The Jesus who walks upon the waters is not simply the familiar Jesus; in this new Jesus they suddenly recognize the presence of God himself.'

[11] Hays (*Reading Backwards*, 44) remarks: 'The worship of the disciples acknowledges and declares Jesus' identity with the one God of Israel, present in the midst of his people.'

[12] See chapter 10.

of the Sea of Galilee' (John 6:1). That was the journey from west to east. Then there took place the miraculous feeding of the multitude. It was after dismissing that multitude that the episode of walking on the water occurred, namely on the return journey back over the sea.

When the Israelites came out of Egypt they crossed the sea and then enjoyed the miraculous provision of food, the 'bread from heaven', in the wilderness. It was following on from this that they experienced the theophany of the Lord at Mount Sinai, and Moses received his own special theophany. The same basic sequence is found in the Gospels: the crossing of the sea, the feeding in the wilderness, and the theophany, the 'passing by' that relates to what was seen by Moses. Though the Gospels present two sea crossings, necessary for the flow of the narrative,[13] the allusory associations are generally clear. Furthermore, within this broad sequence of events we may detect other more specific allusions to elements in the same portion of the Old Testament.

The obvious connection, it is almost needless to point out, is that the miraculous happening we are examining in the Gospels is one that took place when the people of God, here the disciples, were traversing a sea. Circumstantially, therefore, we are looking at an occurrence related to that which occurred during the exodus, and one which, like that one also, was around the time of Passover. This general relationship is considerably strengthened by the presence of a series of common details and lexical similarities.

The two events of crossing the sea and walking on the water are both located temporally in the night (Exod. 14:21; Matt. 14:23; Mark 6:47). But we can be more precise. One detail of the latter episode that is found in both Matthew and Mark is the time at which it occurred. Each of the two versions tell us that the incident happened in 'the fourth watch [*phylakē*] of the night' (Matt. 14:25; cf. Mark 6:48). Ancient sources inform us that night-time was divided into four watches of the same length, namely three hours.[14] This means that the 'fourth watch' was the last period of the night. It was the watch during which the new day dawned, and it was therefore also known as the 'morning watch'.[15] Back in Exodus a similar time phrase is given. There we read that it was 'in the morning watch [*phylakē*]' that the Lord discomforted the Egyptian host and brought back the waters of the sea upon them (Exod. 14:24). The two events,

---

[13] Since Jesus had to return to the Galilean, i.e. Jewish, side of the sea to the west.

[14] See, e.g., Jerome, *Commentary on Matthew*, on 14:25: 'Guard duties and military watches are divided into intervals of three hours'; cf. R. T. France (*The Gospel of Matthew* [NICNT; Grand Rapids, MI: Eerdmans, 2007]), 569, n. 13, where the 'fourth watch of the night' is explained as '[a] Roman term covering the period 3 A.M. to 6 A.M.'. The main text of the GNT actually gives: 'Between three and six o'clock in the morning'. Also see REB, NCV.

[15] As found, for instance, in Josephus, *Jewish War* 4.63.

then, as well as relating to the crossing of a sea, both took place during the same portion of the night.

The narrative tells us that the disciples 'saw' Jesus coming to them on the water, *kai ephobēthēsan*, 'and they were afraid' (John 6:19), and 'they cried out' (Matt. 14:26; Mark 6:49). At this Jesus called out to them, 'Take courage, it is I; do not be afraid' (Matt. 14:27; Mark 6:50). Here the words appearing in Matthew and Mark are identical, consisting of three distinct elements: *tharseite*, *egō eimi* and *mē phobeisthe*. The middle item, 'I am', has already been discussed. Of these three, John records for us only the latter two, 'It is I; do not be afraid' (John 6:20), but again using the same wording. I believe at this point we are again being directed to the Old Testament account of the Red Sea crossing. There we read that the Israelites 'saw' the Egyptian host coming towards them, 'and they were afraid' (*kai ephobēthēsan*), and 'they cried out' (Exod. 14:10). After they vented their feelings at Moses (vv. 11–12), he said to them, 'Do not be afraid. Stand still and see the salvation of the LORD' (v. 13). The first clause is particularly relevant, as well as interesting. Our English translation here, 'Do not be afraid', is a literal rendering of the Hebrew *'al tîrā'û*. This has the same meaning of course as the words spoken by Jesus to the disciples. The Greek Old Testament, however, at this point has *tharseite*, 'Take courage', identical to what Jesus said. In other words, the words Jesus uttered to the disciples on the sea reflect both the Hebrew and Greek readings of the words spoken by Moses to encourage the Israelites at the Red Sea. I am convinced that this is a deliberate literary ploy, and that it is intended to further reinforce the exodus association and to bring to mind the obstacle then caused by the sea.

As we read the narration of the events at the Red Sea, we encounter several times in the LXX the phrase *en mesō tēs thalassēs*, 'in the midst of the sea' (Exod. 14:29; 15:8, 19). This evidently relates to a key element in the story, namely the fact that God's people made their passage in the middle of the waters. The phrase is attested only once elsewhere in the entire Old Testament (Neh. 9:11), and it is noteworthy that this appears in a later recounting of the very same incident. This sole usage of the expression in connection with one specific occurrence makes its single New Testament appearance stand out all the more. In the Gospel episode of Jesus walking on the sea, the disciples are said to be situated in a boat *en mesō tēs thalassēs*, 'in the midst of the sea' (Mark 6:47). Though when taken alone it might seem inconsequential, when considered along with the other connections, this phrase surely has to be one further item in an intentional strategy to evoke the earlier event.

In the older account, God's people walk through the parted water; in the Gospel the disciple walks on it, like Jesus. As Peter is walking on the sea, he is distracted by the strength of the wind and his faith wavers. The account says: 'and beginning to sink [*katapontizesthai*] he cried out, "Lord, save me!"' (Matt. 14:30). At their passage through the sea the Israelites celebrated the fact that the Lord 'drowned [*katepontisen*]' the Egyptians in the Red Sea (Exod. 15:4). This verb, meaning 'sink, drown' in water, or 'swallow up', is rare in both Testaments, especially in the former sense. There is only one other New Testament usage (Matt. 18:6).[16]

In the Gospel we read that Jesus 'stretched out his hand' (*ekteinas tēn cheira*) in order to prevent Peter from drowning (Matt. 14:31). This action is prominent in the Red Sea episode. There we find the same phrase used several times in connection with Moses (Exod. 14:16, 21, 26, 27). First he 'stretched out his hand' (*exeteinen . . . tēn cheira*) to part the waters (v. 21), and once Israel had crossed he 'stretched out his hand' again (v. 27) to bring the waters back upon the Egyptians in order to destroy them. In the Song of the Sea that follows, however, it is explicitly the Lord who is said to have stretched out his hand (15:12). In the Old Testament event the stretching out of the hand is both to save God's people and then to drown the enemy. In the Gospel it is only to save a follower of Jesus from drowning.[17]

We additionally note that the element of 'wind' (*anemos*) plays a part in each setting (Exod. 14:21; Matt. 14:24, 30, 32; Mark 6:48, 51; John 6:18), and the 'waves' (*kymata*) likewise (Exod. 15:8; Matt. 14:24), each further contributing to the similarity between the two occasions.

John's Gospel provides the way in which the episode on the sea ends: 'and immediately the boat was at the land where they were going' (6:21).[18] Needless to say, the Israelites, in fleeing from Egypt and crossing the Red Sea, were making their way to a particular place, the land that God had promised them, and in the wider exodus narrative phrases like 'the land where you are going' appear several times (e.g. Exod. 34:12; Num. 32:7; Deut. 28:21). We might also

---

[16] I would not want to make too much out of it, but it is interesting to note that Peter's name, in its original Aramaic, was *kēphâ*, usually anglicized as 'Cephas' (cf. John 1:42). One of the most authoritative dictionaries, that of Jastrow, informs us that this can mean both 'rock' and 'stone' (Marcus Jastrow, *Dictionary of the Targumim, the Talmud Babli and Yerushalmi, and the Midrashic Literature* [New York, NY: Judaica Press, 2007 (repr. of 1903 edn)], 634). The second meaning appears, for example, in Prov. 17:8, where the Hebrew *'eben*, 'stone', is translated as *kēphâ* in the Aramaic Targum. Now at the Red Sea we are told regarding the Egyptians that 'the deep waters covered them; they went down into the depths like a *stone* [*'eben*]' (Exod. 15:5). It is hard to resist pointing out that the Syriac Peshitta, an early Aramaic version, renders this latter part as 'like *kēphâ*', which could, potentially at least, be read as 'like Cephas', the disciple who sank in the sea! The one episode, therefore, has the Egyptians sinking like a stone, and the other a 'stone' sinking. The former perish, whereas the latter is rescued.

[17] The idea of salvation is therefore also present in both scenarios (Exod. 14:13, 30; 15:2; Matt. 14:30–31).

[18] A good many commentators suggest that the immediate reaching of land was also a miracle, or 'a miracle within a miracle'. See, e.g., C. K. Barrett, *The Gospel According to St. John: An Introduction with Commentary and Notes on the Greek Text* (Philadelphia, PA: Westminster, 1978), 281.

remark on the fact that in the Gospel the arrival was 'immediately' after the incident on the sea, while in the Old Testament there was a considerable delay, namely forty years, due to the people's unbelief. Perhaps the contrast is deliberate.[19]

All the foregoing details serve to establish a secondary layer of allusive content, all relating specifically to Israel passing through the sea at the exodus. Considering the broader significance of that event, we see that it encapsulated death on one hand, and new life on the other. It saw the death of the Egyptians, that is, the enemy and oppressor, and freedom and a new beginning for Israel, the people of God. Thus it serves as a fitting figure of Christian baptism, as the apostle Paul takes it (1 Cor. 10:1–2). I believe that what is happening to Peter relates closely to this same theme. Nobody actually dies in the Gospel episode, but the idea of death is nevertheless not far away, being present in a widely used symbolic understanding of the element that forms the obvious setting for the whole incident, namely the sea. The waters of the sea, and deep water in general, are frequently employed in Scripture as a symbol of death, and also perhaps of the closely associated forces of evil and chaos (cf. Job 26:5; Pss 18:4; 74:13–14; Jon. 2:2–6, etc.). To walk on the sea, therefore, signifies having dominion over the power of death.[20] In figurative form, it is this that Peter desired, and that Jesus was able to grant him. At the surface level he wanted to experience what it was like to walk on water, to not be overwhelmed by that natural element. Viewed at a deeper level, against the Old Testament background of the sea, and especially the Red Sea, representing death, we see a human being wanting to overcome death itself.

It is further important to appreciate that it is not just the sea that has a symbolic significance, but also Peter himself. He, as the lead disciple,[21] stands as a representation of all the disciples, and indeed of all believers.[22] The experience he undergoes, therefore, relates to every follower of Christ. And what happens to Peter, to all intents and purposes, is his own 'baptism', or his symbolic death and resurrection if you prefer. He goes down into the water and figuratively dies, in what in actual fact is a potentially life-threatening

---

[19] That is to say, the journey with Moses under the old covenant took a lengthy period of time, with most of the people dying on the way, while with Jesus under the new covenant the arrival is instant, with all the disciples intact.

[20] Cf. N. H. Tur-Sinai, *The Book of Job: A New Commentary* (Jerusalem: Kiryath Sepher, 1967), 157. Here the treading on the sea of Job 9:8 (see above) is interpreted as the vanquishing of a hostile power.

[21] Cf. France, *The Gospel of Matthew*, 623.

[22] Cf. Jeffrey John, *The Meaning in the Miracles* (Norwich: Canterbury Press, 2001), 79: 'Peter here is the representative disciple'; cf. O. Wesley Allen Jr, *Matthew* (Fortress Biblical Preaching Commentaries; Augsburg, MN: Fortress, 2013), 158: 'This is the first scene in Matthew in which Peter begins to gain a special voice and thus take on a representative role for all disciples.'

experience, and without intervention certainly so. Then Jesus, like God in the miracle at the Red Sea, stretches forth his hand, exercises his strength, and the disciple is brought up again. Life, new life that is, is imparted.[23] What is portrayed symbolically therefore through this event is required of all who would follow Jesus and enter into new life. As the Egyptians died in the Red Sea, so the old nature that binds us to sin needs to die. It is this that our baptism signifies, and the meaning of that sacrament is illustrated for us dramatically in the events concerning Peter on the Sea of Galilee as interpreted against the background of the Old Testament allusions.[24]

---

[23] Compare the Old Testament experience of Jonah, who underwent a symbolic death in the ocean, without actually dying physically, and then was brought up from the depths again. It ought perhaps not to go unremarked that the apostle Peter was in fact the 'son of *Jonah*' (Matt. 16:17), a matter to be discussed further in chapter 30.

[24] I quote here the very apposite comments of Joseph Ratzinger: 'The crossing of the Red Sea was above all a symbol of salvation for Israel, but of course it also points to the danger that proved to be the destiny of the Egyptians. If Christians consider the crossing of the Red Sea as a prefiguring of Baptism, there in the immediate foreground is the symbolism of death: It becomes an image of the mystery of the Cross. In order to be reborn, man must first enter with Christ into the "Red Sea," plunge with him down into death, in order thus to attain new life with the risen Lord' (Ratzinger, *Jesus of Nazareth: From the Baptism*, 239; Ratzinger appears to be alluding here to *The Catechism of the Catholic Church*, secs. 1220–1221).

12

The Syro-Phoenician woman

Matthew 15:21–28; Mark 7:24–30

The passage we turn to next concerns the healing, or more strictly speaking, exorcism, of a young girl. This event is unusual in that it takes place outside the borders of Judea and Galilee in the region of Tyre and Sidon to the north (Matt. 15:21), an area known in the days of the Roman Empire as 'Syro-Phoenicia'.[1] In this Gentile locality a mother approaches Jesus on behalf of her daughter, who is afflicted by an evil spirit (Mark 7:25).[2] Mark (v. 26) calls the woman a 'Greek' (*Hellēnis*), clearly indicating that she herself is a Gentile, and not a Jew living abroad.

Most readers will be familiar with the way the encounter goes. At first Jesus ignores the woman, and his disciples urge him to send her away (Matt. 15:23). When the woman persists, Jesus utters the proverbial saying, 'It is not right to take the children's bread and throw it to the dogs' (Matt. 15:26; Mark 7:27), apparently meaning that he had come to God's children, the people of Israel, and not to those classed as 'dogs', namely the Gentiles. In the face of this the woman is not thwarted but counters with the words, 'Yes, Lord, but even the dogs eat the crumbs that fall from their masters' table' (Matt. 15:27; cf. Mark 7:28). Jesus then remarks on her great faith, and tells her to return home, which she does, to find her daughter completely restored (Matt. 15:28; cf. Mark 7:29–30).

This episode, I believe, makes a more subtle use of allusion. We find here allusions that point not so much to a localized event recorded in the Old Testament, but more generally to a somewhat broader theme. Lying behind the account in the Gospels there are, I would argue, events and persons at the time of Israel's conquest of the Promised Land.

The land God chose to give to the Israelites was then occupied by Canaanites. These were not just any Gentile people. Through their progenitor they were, we

---

[1] Cf. Arthur J. Bellinzoni, *The Building Blocks of the Earliest Gospel: A Roadmap to Early Christian Biography* (Eugene, OR: Wipf & Stock, 2018), 96.
[2] The spirit is also described as a 'demon' (Mark 7:26, 29).

recall, placed under a curse (Gen. 9:25, 'Cursed be Canaan') long before the time their land was promised to Israel. And then, when the time of the conquest drew near, God determined that they should be annihilated, or at least driven from their land, to make way for the Israelites (e.g. Exod. 23:23; Num. 35:51–52; Deut. 4:38).[3] Canaan was then to be the 'everlasting possession' of God's chosen people (Gen. 17:8; 48:4).

The conquest of Canaan was undertaken at the time of Joshua, who was the divinely appointed leader of the nation of Israel at that time. As explained before,[4] when the LXX and the New Testament speak of this Old Testament character they employ the identical proper noun (*Iēsous*) by which Jesus is later known. So, for early Jewish-Christian believers acquainted with the writings of the old covenant, when the name Jesus was mentioned the thought of his earlier namesake could not have been far behind, especially when other factors were present to help activate that line of thinking.[5]

It is also highly significant that Matthew identifies the woman who approaches Christ specifically as a 'Canaanite' (15:22), rather than as the more contemporary 'Syro-Phoenician'.[6] This happens to be the only use of the term 'Canaanite' in the entire New Testament, a remarkable fact in itself.[7] It would therefore seem to be a deliberate move to bring to mind the ancient Gentile population of the Promised Land. And this term would doubtless still have evoked extremely negative feelings on the part of the Jews in New Testament times.[8] In this Canaanite they would have seen a Gentile woman, one from a nation that was cursed, that was consigned by God to destruction or expulsion,

---

[3] Such a divine decree was not arbitrary. Old Testament descriptions of the Canaanites make it clear that at the time of the conquest they had become a nation of abhorrent moral and religious practices. This was not a case of genocide, but an act of divine judgment.

[4] See chapter 3 regarding Jeshua the priest.

[5] Seeing Jesus in this particular Gospel episode as a new Joshua figure is an idea found among a number of Christian commentators, ancient and modern. We find it, for example, in the writings of the fourth-century Eastern Church Father Ephrem the Syrian (Carmel McCarthy [ed. and tr.], *Saint Ephrem's Commentary on Tatian's Diatessaron* [Journal of Semitic Studies Supplement 2; Oxford: Oxford University Press, 2000], 197) and in a much more recent study by Richard Bauckham (*Gospel Women: Studies of the Named Women in the Gospels* [London: T&T Clark, 2002], 44).

[6] The Phoenicians were basically northern Canaanites. They shared the same language, culture and worship of Baal as those living in Canaan to the south. It is noteworthy that in the LXX the Hebrew term for 'Canaan' is sometimes translated as *Phoinikē* (e.g. Exod. 16:35; Josh. 5:1), that is, 'Phoenicia'. In one place 'the land of Canaan' is rendered as 'the land of the Phoenicians' (Josh. 5:12).

[7] The word appearing in some of the more traditional English translations (e.g. AV, NKJV) as 'Canaanite' in Matt. 10:4 is in fact a different word, not *Chananaios* but *Kananaios*. This latter would seem to relate to the Hebrew adjective *qannâ*, meaning 'zealous'. Hence the rendering 'Simon the Zealot' (e.g. NIV, NASB, NJB).

[8] Blomberg remarks that: 'No one in the first century used that term [Canaanite] anymore; Matthew is deliberately conjuring up distasteful memories' (Craig L. Blomberg, 'Matthew', in G. K. Beale and D. A. Carson [eds.], *Commentary on the New Testament Use of the Old Testament* [Grand Rapids, MI: Baker Academic, 2007], 54).

and whose remnant had proved a snare to earlier generations of Israelites. Not only so, but the particular Canaanite who needed help was one who was, literally, 'evilly [*kakōs*] possessed by a demon' (Matt. 15:22). It would be difficult to imagine someone towards whom the Jews would feel more ill-disposed.[9]

When Joshua entered the land of Canaan he was at the head of the twelve tribes that made up the Hebrew nation. As Jesus comes into this Gentile region where the 'Canaanite' lives, he is, of course, bringing with him his twelve disciples (Matt. 15:23), emblematic of the community that constituted the new Israel.[10]

As the conquest was about to begin, God decreed to his people with regard to the Canaanites, 'You shall utterly destroy them. You shall make no covenant with them and have no mercy on them [*mē eleēsēte autous*]' (Deut. 7:2). In the Gospel episode the Canaanite woman comes to Jesus and, in a manner that contrasts starkly with the command given to Israel of old, she appeals to this new Joshua with the words 'Have mercy on me [*eleēson me*], Lord' (Matt. 15:22).

At first Jesus completely ignores her plea, while the disciples respond by telling him to 'send her away', or 'dismiss her' (Matt. 15:23). They obviously do not see her as being worthy of Christ's attentions. Then, as the woman continues to cry out, Jesus declares to her, 'I was sent only to the lost sheep of the house of Israel' (v. 24). Despite this she still persists (v. 25). At this stage in the exchange Jesus utters that well-known, and almost offensive, saying: 'It is not right to take the children's bread and throw it to the dogs' (v. 26). Up to this point, then, Jesus and the disciples have together all responded as their fellow Jews would typically have done to a woman labelled a Canaanite.

The woman, however, remains undeterred, and retorts with the words 'Yes, Lord, but even the dogs eat the crumbs that fall from their masters' table' (Matt. 15:27). When he hears this reply, Jesus' attitude instantly turns to one of commendation, and he says: 'O woman, great is your faith! Be it done for you as you wish.' Her daughter receives healing at that moment (v. 28). What begins as an extremely negative reaction to the Canaanite woman in the end becomes wholly positive, both regarding herself and her afflicted daughter.

In view of the woman's Canaanite origin and the circumstance of Jesus (Joshua) entering a Gentile land with the Twelve, I believe we can detect three separate allusions to the book of Joshua, each one presenting Gentiles, or more precisely ethnic Canaanites, who were actually favoured at that time. Because there exists not one but several sources for the allusions, the points of contact

---

[9] Even in the case of the Roman centurion (Matt. 8:5–13), a representative of the forces that oppressed the Jews, Jesus and the disciples do not respond so negatively as in this instance.

[10] Cf. N. T. Wright, *Jesus and the Victory of God* (London: SPCK, 1996), 300.

with the Old Testament for each are less extensive than if just one single passage had been in mind. Yet the fact is that each of these concerns a subject that is evidently closely related at the conceptual level, and indeed these are the only three instances of this particular kind found at this time in Israel's history.

First, I would consider that someone familiar with Israel's Scriptures, upon reading or hearing the episode about the Canaanite woman in the Gospels, could not have failed to think of another Canaanite woman, who appears in the book of Joshua. This of course is Rahab (Josh. 2:1–21; 6:22–25). Here was a woman from the condemned race that lay in the path of Joshua and the twelve tribes as they were about to enter the Promised Land.[11] As such, the divine decree was that she and her kinsfolk be destroyed or driven out. Yet her words to the Hebrew spies amounted to a profession of faith in their God,[12] and so she and the members of her household were preserved. The epistle to the Hebrews reminds us that it was 'by faith' that Rahab did not perish (Heb. 11:31). Faith was her most conspicuous virtue, as it evidently was of the woman in the Gospel episode. Rahab, then, provides a biblical precedent of a Canaanite woman finding favour among the people of God. If the Old Testament Joshua and Israel welcomed Rahab (cf. Josh. 6:25), how could Jesus refuse the Canaanite woman who came to him?[13]

We further point out that Rahab is explicitly referenced just once in all the Gospels, and that is in Matthew, the Gospel which also speaks of the 'Canaanite woman'. Rahab is listed among the names in the genealogy of Christ in the first chapter (v. 5). There it is stated that she was the wife of Salmon, who fathered Boaz, ancestor of David who became king (cf. Ruth 4:21–22; Luke 3:31–32). Rahab is thus presented as David's great-great-grandmother. This fact entails that Jesus himself was likewise descended from Rahab, the woman of Canaan. Such a lineage invests the Gospel allusion to Rahab with a measure of irony. For when the woman approaches Jesus she addresses him by the title 'Son of David' (Matt. 15:22). At the literal level it is quite remarkable that a Gentile, and one of female gender at that, should attribute such a messianic title to Jesus when even many Jews failed to do so. But functioning as an

---

[11] As Rahab and her fellow Canaanites had 'heard' of the works of God that he had previously performed on behalf of Israel (Josh. 2:10), so too the woman had 'heard' about Jesus (Mark 7:25).

[12] Cf. Rahab's words: 'the LORD your God, he is God in heaven above and on earth below' (Josh. 2:11).

[13] One wonders if the phrases occurring in the second half of Mark 7:24 are also intended to be taken as elements of the allusion: 'He entered a house and did not want anyone to know it. Yet he could not be hidden'. In Joshua 2 the Hebrew spies sent by Joshua also 'entered a house' (v. 1). They did not wish their presence to become known, but it was (vv. 2–3), and in this case the woman herself hid them (v. 4). If allusion is present here, it is in the manner of a reversal with respect to this latter detail. Regarding Rahab, the woman successfully hid those sent by Joshua, while the Canaanite woman was able to find the later Joshua who attempted to remain hidden. Admittedly, this is somewhat tentative.

allusion to the Canaanite woman Rahab, it serves as a reminder that without her there would in fact be no son of David, for she herself was a link in the chain that led to David. Rahab was, in the Hebraic sense, David's mother. And this being so, she was a mother to Jesus as well – no Rahab, no Messiah! Since an earlier Canaanite woman had so contributed to the Davidic lineage, there are some just deserts in a later woman of the same ethnic group receiving a blessing back from David's greater son.

The second allusion to events in Joshua is more subtle, indeed barely hinted at, but to my mind it is present nonetheless, and would readily have been discerned by the biblically literate reader once the Joshua background for the literary allusions was recognized. Joshua 9:3 introduces us to the people from the Canaanite town of Gibeon. These play a central role in the narrative up to 10:6. Like the Canaanite woman in the Gospel, the Gibeonites 'heard' and 'came' to the Joshua figure (9:3–4, *ēkousan . . . elthontes*; cf. Mark 7:25, *akousasa . . . elthousa*). They explained that they had come because of the 'name of the LORD', adding that 'we have heard the report of him and all that he has done' (Josh. 9:9). These Canaanites were coming to Joshua in the first instance simply to preserve themselves. They knew what had happened to other cities in the land, and to avoid a similar destruction they pretended to be from a distant country and to seek a covenant of peace with Joshua and Israel. After some initial hesitation on the part of the Israelites, for fear that they might be local inhabitants of Canaan (v. 7), the covenant was agreed. When the Israelites discovered that the Gibeonites were in actual fact Canaanites, they were greatly displeased and grumbled against Joshua and their leaders, who nevertheless honoured the covenant of peace made with them and ratified by an oath (vv. 15–20). The life of these Gentiles was to be one of service to Israel (cf. v. 21), but Joshua, we are told, 'delivered them' nonetheless (v. 26).

Shortly afterwards, as recorded in the next chapter, when the Gibeonites were attacked by their fellow Canaanites for joining with Israel, they appealed to Joshua, saying, 'Come up to us quickly; save us and help us!' (Josh. 10:6). Here we see the same appeal, 'Help us' (*boēthēson hēmin*), addressed to Joshua as the woman made to Jesus (Matt. 15:25), 'Help me' (*boēthei moi*). Joshua responded swiftly and delivered the Gibeonites from the hands of those who threatened them.

There is one feature in the Joshua account that ought to be mentioned, as it does establish at least some connection with the Gospel episode. When the Gibeonites came to the Israelites, they actually brought the remains of bread in the form of 'crumbs'. The Hebrew word *niqqudîm*, occurring in Joshua 9:5 and 12, has this particular meaning, according to one of the standard lexicons.[14] In claiming to be from a distant land, the Gibeonites had carried with them this crumbled bread, among other things, to give the impression that they had been travelling for some time. They presented it to the Israelites (v. 12), and then we read that the men of Israel 'partook of their provisions' (v. 14); in other words, they ate their crumbs. If the Gospel narrative is intending the reader to think of this passage, then the allusion, as seen on several other occasions, is one of reversal. The woman, we remember, argued that even the dogs, the Gentiles, eat the crumbs dropped by their masters. In the account in Joshua it is the Hebrews who ate the crumbs of Canaanites! The allusive connotation might therefore be that if, in the days of the old Joshua, the Canaanites let God's people partake of the crumbs left over from their meagre supplies, then now, in the days of the new Joshua, this Canaanite ought at least to be allowed to share the crumbs of the much more abundant provisions granted to God's people. Did not the Israelites once share the Canaanites' crumbs, even when it was all they had? Then why should Israel not now share their crumbs with Canaanites? Though a mere hint, the literary linkage is perhaps sufficient to draw the perceptive reader's mind back to those Canaanites of Gibeon who approached the earlier Joshua.

So, while explicit verbal correspondences are admittedly sparse, the broad picture we are given concerning the Gibeonites does bear a relation to what we read of the woman in the Gospels. In each instance we read of Canaanites coming on the basis of what they have heard to one named Joshua, seeking help in the face of an extreme situation. Although at first meeting with a negative response, each party is persistent and is eventually granted what they seek. And even though the Gibeonites had succeeded through deception rather than on account of an explicit faith as in the case of the woman, they were still received in peace and helped against their enemies when attacked. Here, then, by way of implication, is another firm precedent for those who were ethnic Canaanites being received into the covenant blessings enjoyed by Israel.

Our third consideration is the person of Caleb.[15] Joshua and Caleb are very closely associated in view of their faithfulness during the rebellion in the wilderness (Num. 14:6–9, 30, 38). Caleb also figures prominently in the book of Joshua, especially in the chapters (14–15) concerning the dividing up of the Promised Land. We observe in certain passages that Caleb is associated with the Israelite tribe of Judah (e.g. Num. 13:6; 34:19), although he was not native

---

[14] See Francis Brown, S. R. Driver and Charles A. Briggs, *A Hebrew and English Lexicon of the Old Testament* (Oxford: Clarendon, rev. edn, 1953), 666b, where the definition is given as 'what is crumbled or easily crumbles, crumbs'. The term is translated by the ESV as 'crumbly' and by NASB as 'crumbled'.

[15] This is 'Caleb son of Jephunneh' (Josh. 14:6), not to be confused with 'Caleb son of Hezron' (1 Chr. 2:18).

to that tribe. Indeed, ethnically he was not a Hebrew at all. In several instances Caleb is designated a 'Kenizzite' (e.g. Num. 32:12; Josh. 14:6). What is remarkable about this fact is that the Kenizzites were actually one of the several tribal groups occupying the land of Canaan (Gen. 15:19), concerning which God had promised Abraham: 'To your offspring I give this land' (v. 18).[16] Although it would seem that Caleb, and perhaps his ancestors also, had been joined to the Israelites for some time,[17] the fact remains that he was a Gentile in origin, and not just any Gentile but one belonging to those occupants of Canaan who were consigned to destruction and the dispossession of their land.[18]

However, it is not merely Caleb's ethnic origin that has relevance in this context; it is also his actual name. Those with an elementary knowledge of Hebrew will know that the name Caleb (*Kālēb*) means 'dog'.[19] This is the term used in the Gospels by the Canaanite woman as a metaphorical description of herself and others like her – 'even the dogs eat the crumbs that fall from their masters' table' (Matt. 15:27).[20] In the Old Testament, then, we are presented with Caleb, a Gentile 'dog', and more particularly a Canaanite 'dog', just like the woman according to her own figurative self-estimation.

There are two further matters regarding Caleb of great importance for our purposes. First, he and his family were fully incorporated within the Hebrew tribe of Judah. That is to say, despite his racial origins, he was numbered among the Jews.[21] His family genealogy is actually inserted into the genealogies of the Judahites in 1 Chronicles (4:15). Here was a man of Canaan who, to all intents and purposes, had become a Jew. Then, second, being ranked among those of Israel, he was given an inheritance as such. The book of Joshua gives considerable emphasis to the fact that when the Promised Land was divided up and

---

[16] Harstad states that: 'Thrice he is called "Caleb son of Jephunneh the Kenizzite" (Num 32:12; Josh 14:6, 14). Some interpreters have suggested that "Kenizzite" designated a clan of Judah, though no Scripture passage names such a clan. It is more likely that both Caleb and his father were descendants of the Kenizzites, who were some of *the original Canaanite inhabitants of the land* (Gen 15:19; that is the only other Scripture passage with "Kenizzite" besides the references to Caleb . . .)' (Adolph L. Harstad, *Joshua* [Concordia Commentary; St Louis, MO: Concordia, 2004], 518; italics added).

[17] This is evident in that the rebellion of Num. 14 had taken place forty years before the Israelites actually entered the land, and Caleb was central to both narratives.

[18] Cf. the comments of Coote: 'Caleb is said to have descended from the Kenizzites, one of the "pre-Israelite" peoples of Canaan (Gen 15:19; cf. Gen 36:11). Apparently the Calebites came to prominence among the Israelites (cf. the example of Uriah "the Hittite", 2 Sam 11:3–12:20; 23:39) and were worked into the genealogy of Judah' (Robert B. Coote, 'The Book of Joshua', in Leander E. Keck, ed., *The New Interpreter's Bible*, vol. 2 [Nashville, TN: Abingdon, 1998], 673).

[19] See Brown, Driver and Briggs, *Hebrew and English Lexicon*, 477a.

[20] That the Greek word (*kynarion*) does not here mean 'puppy', as some have argued, is affirmed in Daniel Fanous, *Taught By God: Making Sense of the Difficult Sayings of Jesus* (Rollinsford, NH: Orthodox Research Institute, 2010), 100. The term simply denotes a domestic dog.

[21] Judah (*yĕhûdâ*) was that tribe of Israel from which the designation 'Jew' (Heb. *yĕhûdî*; Gk *Ioudaios*) was derived.

distributed to the Israelite tribes, Caleb received his fair share.[22] Of all the numerous towns allotted to the families of Judah, Caleb received Hebron (earlier known as Kiriath Arba), one of the major cities in that region, and the locality in which the Hebrew patriarchs were buried.[23] Together with such a significant possession, Joshua, we read, gave Caleb his own personal blessing (Josh. 14:13). All this was not bad for one who was a 'dog'! Evidently he was being treated as one of the 'sons of Israel', as one of God's own people.

In Caleb, then, we find one who ethnically was classed as a Canaanite and yet who partook fully in what was promised to Israel. Although a 'dog', literally by name and metaphorically by race, he did not merely have to content himself with the 'crumbs' that fell from the children of Israel's table. On the contrary, he was granted a choice possession among them, as one of them.

To this Caleb, therefore, the episode about the Canaanite woman makes a highly meaningful allusion. If he, considering his ethnicity and name, could share in the divine blessings promised to Israel, then here was another good reason why the Canaanite woman should be granted what was in the first instance promised to the Jews.

Rahab, the Gibeonites and Caleb were all of Canaanite origin, and all, as portrayed within the pages of the book named after Joshua, received blessings with Israel – three precedents that show the Canaanite woman's case should be heard. And if a Canaanite, the worst of the Gentiles to the Jewish mind, can share in God's promises, then it opens up the way for all Gentile peoples to likewise receive the same.

In response to the woman's words about the dogs eating crumbs, and in accordance with the subtle allusions within the text, Jesus gives her what she asks, and her daughter is freed from the spirit that afflicted her. The mother had begged him to 'cast out [ekbalē] the demon' (Mark 7:26). Here perhaps we have a final allusion to the Old Testament Canaanites. For the divine intention for Israel of old was that the inhabitants of Canaan should be either destroyed or 'cast out' (e.g. Exod. 23:28; Num. 21:32; Deut. 11:23; Josh. 24:12).[24] They were

---

[22] When one reads the passage about the apportioning of land to Judah (Josh. 14 – 15), it is Caleb's name that is by far the most conspicuous, both in its frequency and in the fact that his inheritance is listed first (14:6–15). This cannot simply be due to his being one of the faithful spies, alongside Joshua. When this latter receives his portion, considerably shorter space and attention are given to it (19:49–50), and he was also the leader of all Israel. The reason, therefore, for the place in the record given to Caleb's possession most probably lies in the uncommon fact of his Canaanite origins. Here was a Canaanite himself inheriting a portion of Canaan (and, from what we know of the matter, probably a part of the land, in the south, which his ancestors, the Kenizzites, had previously inhabited).

[23] Genesis describes the location as 'the cave of the field at Machpelah facing Mamre (that is, Hebron) in the land of Canaan' (23:19).

[24] In all these instances the LXX uses the same verb, ekballō, as appears in Mark 7:26.

occupying the possession that God had promised to his chosen people, and they therefore needed to be dispossessed. In the woman's child in the Gospel we find a daughter of Canaan, not cast out herself, as her ancient ancestors had been, but being herself delivered through the casting out of the evil spirit that had taken hold of her. A Canaanite is set free from the clutches of Satan, who in a sense is the one dispossessed. The human being occupied by the malign spirit is now rid of its previous possessor. So, with respect to this new Joshua, it is not the Canaanites themselves who are cast out, but the evil forces that control them, and they themselves, the most reprobate of the Gentiles, through faith are made free to inherit the divine blessings along with the new Israel.

13

The transfiguration

Matthew 17:1–9; Mark 9:2–10; Luke 9:28–36

This event is evidently of a momentous nature, and yet it remains one of the most underrated occurrences in the Gospel story, especially, sorry to say, within the evangelical Christian community. It finds a place in all three synoptic Gospels forming an approximate midway point, from a literary if not a chrono-logical point of view, between the commencement of Christ's ministry at his baptism and the climax of that ministry at the cross. On each of these earlier and later occasions a voice is heard proclaiming the divine sonship of Jesus, first from his Father in heaven when he is baptized (Matt. 3:17; Mark 1:11; Luke 3:22) and then through the Gentile centurion at the crucifixion (Matt. 27:40; Mark 15:39). Similar to these utterances, at the transfiguration a voice also designates Christ to be God's Son (see below). The three events are therefore related conceptually, with respect to this declaration of sonship, as well as positionally. But it is not only the words that are heard that gives the transfiguration its importance. As its usual title suggests, the episode predominantly concerns something that was seen, leading one scholar to claim that of all that is recorded in the Gospels there is nothing, not even the resurrection appearances, that is as 'visually spectacular' as the transfiguration of Christ.[1]

The Gospel narratives inform us that one day Jesus took three of the disciples, Peter, James and John, to go up a certain unnamed mountain with him. Trad-itionally, the place in question has been identified as Mount Tabor (575 metres) in Lower Galilee, though it was more probably Mount Hermon (2,815 metres) some 70 miles to the north. The reasons for this are the description of the moun-tain as 'high' (Matt. 17:1; Mark 9:2), and the fact that the Gospels state in the preceding context that Jesus and those with him were then in the vicinity of Caesarea Philippi (Matt. 16:13; Mark 8:27), a town situated at the foot of Hermon. On top of this elevated peak, where Christ has gone to pray (Luke 9:28), he is transfigured in the presence of his three followers, meaning that he

---

[1] Stephen N. Williams, 'The Transfiguration of Jesus Christ', *Themelios* 28.1 (2002): 14.

begins to radiate some kind of supernatural light (Matt. 17:2; Mark 9:3; Luke 9:29). Equally supernatural is the sudden appearance of the Old Testament figures of Moses and Elijah, who begin to converse with him (Matt. 17:3; Mark 9:4; Luke 9:30–31). In this situation Peter offers to build shelters for the three of them (Matt. 17:4; Mark 9:5; Luke 9:33). But then a cloud covers them all, and the divine voice issues forth from the cloud declaring Jesus to be 'my Son' (Matt. 17:5; Mark 9:7; Luke 9:34–35). At this the disciples fall face down (Matt. 17:6), and when Jesus tells them to arise, they see nobody but him alone (Matt. 17:7–8; Mark 9:8; Luke 9:36).

Before considering the allusive elements in the accounts of this event, a few words ought to be said regarding the others who are present to see Christ transfigured. Two come right out of the Old Testament, and had therefore been dead for centuries, and three are from among the band of apostles. Historically, commentators have discerned, and rightly so to my mind, a symbolic or representative element in the identity and number of these individuals. A very common understanding of Moses and Elijah is to see them as representing the whole Old Testament, or old covenant, dispensation. Some would be more specific and take the two as emblematic of the law and the prophets respectively.[2] I am not sure that we should go so far as to make such a precise distinction since Moses, as well as Elijah, was a great prophet, perhaps even greater than the latter.[3] We would here do well to remember the important fact that in the Jewish mind Elijah and Moses were closely associated. This was partly due to the very last oracle of the prophetic books, Malachi 4:4–6, in which these two feature together, and partly due to a tradition circulating among the Jews that Moses did not actually die and undergo burial, as Deuteronomy 34:5–6 states, but rather he experienced a translation up to heaven in a similar way to Elijah (2 Kgs 2:11).[4]

There is additionally the fact that the Old Testament itself created a certain future expectation regarding both these men, and these two only apart from the

---

[2] Cf. Joseph Ratzinger, *Jesus of Nazareth: From the Baptism in the Jordan to the Transfiguration* (New York, NY: Doubleday, 2007), 311.

[3] Cf. Num. 12:6–8; Deut. 18:15, 18; 34:10. Though Moses certainly dominates the Pentateuchal literature (excepting Genesis), the same cannot be said for Elijah with respect to the prophetic corpus, since the narratives depicting his ministry only appear in the historical books, that is, the Jewish 'former prophets', while there is almost no mention of him at all in the books of the 'latter prophets'.

[4] This tradition is preserved, for example, in Josephus, *Antiquities of the Jews* 4.326: 'while he [Moses] bade farewell to Eleazar and Joshua and was yet conversing with them, a cloud suddenly descended upon him and he disappeared'. See also Ryan E. Stokes, 'Not over Moses' Dead Body: Jude 9, 22–24 and the *Assumption of Moses* in Their Early Jewish Context', *JSNT* 40.2 (2017): 192–213. An ascension into heaven is also claimed for Moses in the Babylonian Talmud (*Sotah* 13b). Such traditions aside, it is evident that the Old Testament presents the final departures of Moses and Elijah as events of an extraordinary nature, and both occurring in the same locality, in the region east of the River Jordan, opposite Jericho (Deut. 34:1; cf. 2 Kgs 2:5, 15, 18).

coming messianic figure. Among the Jews there existed an anticipation of the arrival of a prophet like Moses (based on Deut. 18) and also the coming of Elijah before the day of the Lord (based on Mal. 4). Another common factor between these two, and one that is evidently relevant to our purposes, is that they uniquely had mountain-top encounters with God, that is to say, theophanies, and each took place on the very same mountain, namely Mount Sinai,[5] with similar attendant circumstances.[6]

As Moses and Elijah may be considered to represent the old covenant, so the apostles evidently represent the new. Both covenants bear witness to Jesus Christ, and it is in him that they find their true and fullest meaning. This, I believe, explains the numbers. The Hebrew law had laid down the rule that for the truth to be established in a legal inquiry there should be 'two or three witnesses' (Deut. 17:6; 19:15), a prescription also taken up by Jesus and the apostles (Matt. 18:16; 2 Cor. 13:1; 1 Tim. 5:19). We are expressly told that the law and prophets bear witness to Christ and the gospel (Rom. 3:21). The apostle Peter similarly described his role and that of his two apostolic companions on the mount of transfiguration as being 'eyewitnesses of his majesty' (2 Pet. 1:16). So what this key event signifies, I would suggest, is borne witness to by the Scriptures of the earlier covenant in the form of *two* men present, being less distinct in its testimony, in seeing things from afar, than that of the new-covenant witnesses, those who saw the truth up close, and who are therefore *three* in number, yet both the two and the three being valid in their witness.

In the accounts of the transfiguration, Old Testament allusions are apparent even at the surface level, especially in the words spoken from the cloud. It is widely recognized that in the declaration 'This is my beloved Son, with whom I am well pleased; listen to him' (Matt. 17:5), there are references to at least three Old Testament texts. These, in order, are Psalm 2:7 ('you are my son') concerning the messianic king; Isaiah 42:1 ('in whom my soul is pleased') concerning the servant of the Lord, and Deuteronomy 18:15 ('you shall listen to him') regarding the future prophet like Moses.[7] A more extensive series exists, however, of less overt allusions which all point to a particular portion of Jewish Scripture. In this case, the backdrop to the allusory schema is Moses on Mount Sinai as recorded in the latter part of Exodus, principally the account in chapter 24, but also the similar scenario in the latter portion of chapter 33 and

---

[5] See chapter 11, n. 6.

[6] The period of 'forty days and forty nights' occurs in connection with Moses and Elijah (Exod. 24:18; 34:28; 1 Kgs 19:8). Both were leaders who were rejected by many of their own people, even to the point of having their lives threatened.

[7] See David L. Turner, *Matthew* (BECNT; Grand Rapids, MI; Baker, 2008), 417–418.

its continuation in 34.[8] Many of the allusions that now follow appear in earlier commentaries and studies.[9]

Before coming to the main passage, we first observe how the Gospel event is bracketed. The episode opens by referring to a period of 'six days' (*hēmeras hex*) before the transfiguration occurs (Matt. 17:1; Mark 9:2),[10] and then once Jesus and the three disciples descend from the mountain the very next text concerns the failure of the other disciples to cast out an evil spirit from a young man (Matt. 17:14–21; Mark 9:14–29; Luke 9:37–43). The first of these, though not exactly parallel, nevertheless brings to mind the 'six days' (*hex hēmeras*) that passed before the Lord spoke to Moses on Mount Sinai (Exod. 24:16). Later, when Moses came down from the mountain, it was to discover that the golden calf debacle was in full flow (Exod. 32). While at first sight this seems to bear no relation to the demon-possessed boy in the Gospels, there is in fact a similarity. At the broad conceptual level, both relate to a foreign entity, namely a false god or demon, that had taken hold of the persons concerned and driven them to wild behaviour (Exod. 32:25; cf. Mark 9:20). The Greek term for 'demon' (*daimonion*), we find, may also denote lesser divine beings.[11]

Both incidents importantly further include the lack of faith manifested on the part of those who remained at the foot of the mountain. In response to this Jesus issues the rebuke: 'O faithless and perverse generation' (Matt. 17:17; Luke 9:41; cf. Mark 9:19), which echoes the words uttered by Moses concerning the Israelites in the wilderness: 'a crooked and perverse generation' (Deut. 32:5) and 'a perverse generation' (v. 20). These latter phrases are closely linked to the worship of the golden calf through the use of the Hebrew verb *šiḥat*, 'have become corrupt' (v. 5), which also appears in God's description of the earlier idolatrous conduct at Sinai (Exod. 32:7).[12] Rebukes expressed in this particular

---

[8] Cf. Patrick Schreiner, *Matthew, Disciple and Scribe: The First Gospel and Its Portrait of Jesus* (Grand Rapids, MI: Baker Academic, 2019), 154.

[9] See, e.g., Schreiner, *Matthew, Disciple and Scribe*, 154–156; A. D. A. Moses, *Matthew's Transfiguration Story and Jewish-Christian Controversy* (Journal for the Study of the New Testament Supplement Series 122; Sheffield: Sheffield Academic Press, 1996), 4–49. Attention should be drawn to the fact that modern scholarly treatments tend to deal with the allusions under the discussion of the transfiguration account recorded in one particular Gospel. Yet some do so with respect to Matthew, such as the two afore-cited works, others in the context of Mark (e.g. G. K. Beale and D. A. Carson [eds.], *Commentary on the New Testament Use of the Old Testament* [Grand Rapids, MI: Baker Academic, 2007], 186–187), and others still in relation to Luke (Beale and Carson, *Commentary on the New Testament Use of the Old Testament*, 311–313). All this serves to demonstrate the drawbacks of such a restricted approach to biblical theology, and overlooks the obvious fact that the same allusory framework can cross the boundaries of individual human authorship.

[10] Luke's time period, 'about eight days later' (9:28), necessarily entails an inclusive reckoning of the days.

[11] See Henry George Liddell and Robert Scott, *A Greek Lexicon* (Oxford: Clarendon, rev. edn, 1940), 322a.

[12] What makes this linguistic connection reasonably certain is the fact that in both instances the verb is used intransitively, that is, without a direct object, which is unusual for this verb in the particular form it bears in these two occurrences.

manner are found nowhere else in the whole of Scripture apart from in these instances, and more specifically each includes the collocation 'perverse generation' (*genea diestrammenē*), suggesting that Jesus is deliberately echoing the words in the Old Testament, which would at least take the minds of informed readers back to Israel's post-exodus unfaithfulness. Intriguingly, both incidents beneath the respective mountains also make reference to something or someone being cast into fire and water (Exod. 32:20, 24; cf. Matt. 17:15; Mark 9:22), perhaps further cementing the association. We conclude, then, that the framework in which the transfiguration is set in the Gospels itself constitutes an allusive element within the larger literary schema.

Looking at the transfiguration event itself, we see that in both Exodus 24 and in the Gospel narratives the main character, Moses on one hand and Jesus on the other, first ascended a mountain, *anebē . . . eis to oros* (Exod. 24:15; Luke 9:28), accompanied by certain others.[13] At Sinai there was a larger group of seventy anonymous elders of Israel who also went up, but before this there appear three named persons mentioned alongside Moses, these being Aaron, Nadab and Abihu (Exod. 24:9). These three exhibit a remarkable correspondence to Peter, James and John, who went up with Jesus in the Gospel accounts. Each trio consists of a leading figure, Aaron the high priest and Peter, whose name consistently heads up the list of apostles,[14] followed by a pair who were in fact brothers (e.g. Exod. 6:23; cf. Mark 1:19). The greater mass of people remain at the foot of the mountain in both settings.

On Mount Sinai those who have ascended experience a theophany, that is, a manifestation of God. The text says: 'they saw the God of Israel' (Exod. 24:10; cf. v. 11). From what transpired later in this mountain-top encounter, we learn that when it states that they saw God, it does not mean they actually saw his very person, for at that time Moses was told by God, 'No one may see me and live' (33:20). Perhaps it was some kind of phenomenal or angelic representation of God. Whatever the case, Moses and the others were evidently party to an extraordinary sight. What Moses himself beheld on the mountain is specifically described as the Lord's 'glory' (33:18),[15] a term that is applied more generally to the divine manifestation on Sinai, as in the words 'the appearance of the glory of the LORD was like a consuming fire on the mountain top' (24:17). On that other mountain in the Gospels, Jesus is transformed and his own

---

[13] In the LXX the text of Exod. 24:15 actually reads: 'Moses *and Joshua* [*Iēsous* = Jesus] went up the mountain'. This combination of the two names in itself has the potential of leading later Christian readers of the transfiguration accounts to think of this passage.

[14] See Matt. 10:2; Mark 3:16; Luke 6:14; Acts 1:13 (cf. Matt. 16:18).

[15] In the verse that follows (33:19), the LXX makes God say: 'I will pass before you in *my glory*'.

appearance is depicted in theophanic terms. His face shone like the sun and his clothing became brilliant white (Matt. 17:2; Mark 9:3), or 'as bright as a flash of lightning', as Luke puts it (9:29 NIV). We then read that Peter, James and John 'saw his glory' (Luke 9:32). We are reminded too of the fact that on Sinai the face of Moses 'was glorified' (LXX) in that it reflected the divine glory that he beheld (Exod. 34:29–30). An intriguing fact concerning this latter is that several ancient Jewish sources state that on this occasion Moses' face shone like the sun, as did that of Jesus.[16]

Immediately following this transfiguration, two men, identified as Moses and Elijah, appeared alongside Christ (Matt. 17:3; Mark 9:4; Luke 9:30–31), the significance of which has already been discussed. The element worthy of note as far as the presence of allusion is concerned is the fact that these two men are described as 'speaking with him', that is, with Jesus (Matt. 17:3; Mark 9:4; Luke 9:30). At this point all three Gospels employ the same Greek verb, *syllalein*, 'to speak with'. This is not a common verb in biblical Greek, occurring only six times in the New Testament, three of which relate to the transfiguration, and only four times in the much longer Old Testament.[17] One of these latter, notably, concerns Moses on Sinai, where he ascended 'to speak with him' (*syllalein*), that is, with God (Exod. 34:35). Accordingly, Moses is found speaking with God on the one mountain, and later Moses and Elijah with Jesus on the other.[18]

In this connection, we note that Luke informs us that the topic of the conversation between Jesus and the other two was 'his departure that he was about to accomplish in Jerusalem' (Luke 9:31). What interests us here is that the word commonly translated in English versions as 'departure' is the Greek term *exodos*. From this of course we obtain the name of the book of Exodus, being the portion of the Old Testament from which our series of allusions is derived. It would seem that the Gospel account is definitely drawing the attention of the reader back to that period of Israel's history.

---

[16] This tradition occurs in the first-century writings of Philo of Alexandria (*The Life of Moses* 2.70), and in the later Babylonian Talmud (*Baba Bathra* 75a) and Midrash (Deuteronomy Rabbah 207c).

[17] Besides the four mountain-top episodes, the other six references are Prov. 6:22; Isa. 7:6; Jer. 18:20; Luke 4:36; 22:4; Acts 25:12. In the New Testament the verb is evidently a distinctly Lukan term, only used by Matthew and Mark in connection with the transfiguration.

[18] At this juncture, having noted the exceptional manner of Christ's glory and the appearance of two Old Testament figures, one may wonder whether what was seen by the disciples here was an actual sensory occurrence, in which Moses and Elijah were physically present, and therefore resurrected, or whether it was a visionary experience of some kind. I am inclined towards the latter, as suggested by the words of Jesus immediately after the event: 'Tell the vision [*orama*] to no one until the Son of Man has risen from the dead' (Matt. 17:9). The same term is found with regard to supernatural visions in Acts 7:31 and 10:17. If simply a vision, the literal resurrection of Moses and Elijah would not be required, just as in the Acts 10 example no literal animals appeared before Peter.

Upon seeing the two others with Jesus, it is Peter who proposes the construction of shelters for them. He says to his master, 'If you wish, I will make three shelters here – one for you, one for Moses, and one for Elijah' (Matt. 17:4; cf. Mark 9:5; Luke 9:33). The relevance of this for our allusory schema becomes apparent when one learns that the noun *skēnē*, here translated 'shelter', is the same word that appears in the Greek Old Testament for 'tabernacle'. When Moses was conversing with God on the top of Sinai, after the theophany of Exodus 24, the latter commanded him: 'You shall make [*poiēseis*] the tabernacle [*skēnēn*]' (Exod. 26:1; cf. 25:8). This is echoed in the words of Peter: 'I will make [*poiēsō*] three tabernacles [*skēnas*]'. In the case of Moses, the tabernacle in question was to serve as a dwelling-place for God among the Israelites. What Peter was thinking of we cannot be completely certain, for the text adds: 'he did not know what he was saying' (Luke 9:33).[19] As an allusion, however, the words are extremely meaningful, as will presently be shown.

In the account of Moses and his companions going up Mount Sinai in Exodus we read there of a cloud on the top of the mountain (24:15). Each of the Gospel accounts also depicts the descent of a cloud that envelops all those on the mountain (Matt. 17:5; Mark 9:7; Luke 9:34). In all three versions the verb describing the coming of the cloud is 'overshadow' (Matt. 17:5 [*epeskiazen*]; Mark 9:7 [*episkiazousa*]; Luke 9:34 [*epeskiazen*]), a term which undoubtedly has connotations of theophanic activity.[20] We are told, moreover, that Moses 'entered [*eisēlthen*] the midst of the cloud [*nephelēs*]' (Exod. 24:18), just as on the mount of transfiguration those present are said to 'enter [*eiselthein*] the cloud [*nephelēn*]' (Luke 9:34).

From within the aforementioned cloud the divine voice spoke to Moses on Sinai ('out of [*ek*] the midst of the cloud [*tēs nephelēs*]', Exod. 24:16; cf. 19:9; 34:5). The voice in the transfiguration episode also issues from the cloud ('out of [*ek*] the cloud [*tēs nephelēs*]', Matt. 17:5; Mark 9:7; Luke 9:35).

Lastly, mention may be made of the element of fear that is felt by those who witnessed the glorification of Moses' face (Exod. 34:30, *ephobēthēsan*, 'they were

---

[19] Some commentators see in Peter's words a reference to the feast of Tabernacles which, they claim, was being celebrated at that time, as a part of which Jewish families would build tent-like structures for themselves. Yet, if this were so, I personally cannot see why the sudden appearance of Moses and Elijah would provoke Peter's suggestion. If it were the time of the festival, then tabernacles would be required for the disciples as well as for Jesus, regardless of whether Moses and Elijah were present or not. More probably, we are to view the constructions proposed by Peter simply as shelters from the elements to make the time of their visit and conversation with Jesus more comfortable. This would be similar to the shelter (also *skēnē*) made by Jonah (Jon. 4:5–8). Cf. R. T. France, *The Gospel of Matthew* (NICNT; Grand Rapids, MI: Eerdmans, 2007), 649.

[20] In Exodus, once the Israelites had completed the construction of the tabernacle, the text states that 'the cloud overshadowed [*epeskiazen*] it, and the glory of the LORD filled the tabernacle' (40:35).

afraid') and by those who witnessed Christ's transfiguration (Matt. 17:6; Luke 9:34, both *ephobēthēsan*).

We discover, then, a series of correlations, deliberately conceived I would submit, between what took place on the mountain as recorded in the Gospels and what had occurred centuries earlier at the top of Sinai. We shall soon reflect on what their intended purpose might be. Evidently, as the nature of the event in question is so remarkable, we are to look for a suitably extraordinary meaning in the allusions that the accounts bear, and I believe they do not disappoint us.

First, however, we are required to consider the transfiguration with respect to its more explicit significance. This is because the allusory sense is inextricably linked to the surface meaning of the text. Indeed, it arises out of it and develops it, or perhaps it would be more accurate to say it *transcends* it. In order to correctly appreciate the plain meaning, the context is naturally crucial. An important fact we observe respecting the three synoptic versions of the transfiguration is that each Gospel has preserved the same order of material before and after the main event. In sum, we find that preceding the incident on the mountain all three Gospels contain, in uniform sequence: Christ's question about his identity (Matt. 16:13–14; Mark 8:27–28; Luke 9:18–19), Peter's confession (Matt. 16:15–16; Mark 8:29; Luke 9:20), the first passion prediction (Matt. 16:21; Mark 8:31; Luke 9:22), the saying about taking up one's cross (Matt. 16:24–26; Mark 8:34–37; Luke 9:23–25), immediately leading into a saying about the Son of Man coming in his glory or his kingdom (Matt. 16:27–28; Mark 8:38; Luke 9:26). Then, following the descent from the mountain and the cure of the demon-possessed boy, all three Gospel-writers place the second passion prediction (Matt. 17:22–23; Mark 9:31–32; Luke 9:44–45). Outside the passion narrative, this is by far the longest series of distinct passages that are recorded in identical order by the synoptic authors. This must mean that they are all meant to hang together, and that the same interpretative thread runs through them collectively.

The sequence begins with the question about who people say Jesus is. In each Gospel his disciples reply with the three alternative ideas popularly proposed: John the Baptist, Elijah or one of the prophets. This relates to the transfiguration narrative through the mention of Elijah, and also in Matthew's version to John the Baptist, whose relationship with Elijah is discussed on the way down the mountain (17:10–13). Demonstrably, in Christ's estimate the answer given is inadequate, for he then asks his disciples a contrastive question: 'But who do you say that I am?' At this point Simon Peter steps in with his famous confession, recorded in varying lengths in each of the three accounts: 'You are the Christ, the Son of the living God' (Matthew), 'You are the Christ' (Mark), 'You are the Christ of God' (Luke). This connects, in its fullest expression, both to the transfiguration and to Psalm 2 which, as mentioned above, is also alluded to on the mountain. The heavenly voice from the cloud identifies Jesus as the Son, or more specifically as 'my Son' (Matt. 17:5; Mark 9:7; Luke 9:35), as does Psalm 2:7, 'You are my Son', where 'the LORD' himself is speaking.[21] And in the psalm this same one here addressed as God's Son is, a few verses before, termed 'his anointed' (v. 2),[22] that is to say, his 'Christ', *Christos* in Greek, or 'Messiah' in its more Hebraic form.[23]

What Peter confesses, therefore, namely that Jesus is both the Messiah and the Son of God, is further affirmed in the mountain-top vision. However, it is very probable that Peter and the other disciples then understood the messianic role in a similar manner to the contemporary expectation in common vogue among the Jews of the time. Psalm 2 itself pictured this kingly figure as coming to possess the nations of the earth as his inheritance (v. 8), and ruling over them with an iron sceptre (v. 9),[24] with the kings of the world submitting to him in fearfulness (vv. 11–12). Such a depiction of the all-conquering Messiah, which was not entirely lacking in a biblical basis, was predominant during this late period of the second temple when Christ's ministry took place. Yet this was only one part of what the complete messianic task would involve. Jesus needed to apprise his disciples of the all-important other aspect.

Without doubt Peter's confession was an unparalleled high point in the pre-passion career of the disciples, but immediately afterwards Jesus' teaching apparently takes a radically different turn. Having been honoured with the titles 'Christ' and 'Son of the living God', he next proceeds to inform his disciples for the very first time of his coming rejection and the suffering and ultimate death that await him in Jerusalem. Though not obviously fitting in with the messianic portrayal of Psalm 2, this was nevertheless a further element in what the Messiah would be required to accomplish, for he was not only an all-powerful king but also one called upon to suffer for his people, a suffering servant. This equally essential component of Jesus' messiahship is also affirmed in the transfiguration, both when Christ speaks with Moses and Elijah of his own 'exodus' and in the allusion to Isaiah 42:1 in the utterance from the cloud. Contextually, the term *exodos* on the lips of Jesus makes unambiguous reference to his coming death. This we understand from the fact that, as in the foretelling of his passion

---

[21] Ps. 2:7 is further cited in the New Testament with reference to Jesus in Acts 13:33; Heb. 1:5; 5:5.

[22] Quoted in Acts 4:25–26.

[23] It is interesting to note that the *Common Lectionary* assigns the reading of Ps. 2, together with Matt. 17:1–9, to Transfiguration Sunday (Year A). See Roger E. van Harn and Brent A. Strawn (eds.), *Psalms for Preaching and Worship: A Lectionary Commentary* (Grand Rapids, MI: Eerdmans, 2009), 55.

[24] Cf. Rev. 2:27; 12:5; 19:15.

(Matt. 16:21), this is something he is to undergo in Jerusalem (Luke 9:31), and because the same noun 'exodus' occurs elsewhere in the New Testament with the sense of 'death' (2 Pet. 1:15).[25] The Isaianic text is taken from what is universally recognized as the first of the 'servant songs' (Isa. 42:1–4), a series of oracles in the latter part of Isaiah that culminate in 52:13 – 53:12, focusing on the servant's extreme suffering and death.

The same Peter who acknowledged Jesus as the Christ responds negatively to Jesus' prediction. 'This will never happen to you,' he exclaims (Matt. 16:22). For this he earns his master's stern rebuke, and the words 'your mind is not set on divine matters, but on human' (Matt. 16:23). Such shows the degree to which the disciple's thinking was removed from a correct comprehension of true messiahship, and how serious this ignorance was. The death that was foretold was plainly as intrinsic to the role as the dominion over the nations.

This leads directly into the saying of Jesus that takes the issue of suffering even further. For having affirmed that he, the Messiah, would indeed be put to death, he then teaches that those who would follow him should also be prepared to take up their own cross. Christ teaches the ironic principle that 'whoever wishes to save his life will lose it, but whoever loses his life for my sake will find it' (Matt. 16:25). Life, true life that is, only comes through undergoing death.[26]

In the sequence of Gospel material being traced, we have now come very close to the transfiguration itself. But there yet remain other final sayings of Christ before that event unfolds. These occur, in slightly different form, in all three synoptic Gospels at this same point (Matt. 16:27–28; Mark 8:38; Luke 9:26), and they speak of the Son of Man coming in his glory and his kingdom coming with power. Such words are accompanied by that enigmatic saying of Jesus to the effect that not all those standing there with him at that moment in time would taste death before they saw this coming of Christ in glory and in his kingdom, or 'kingship', as the term (*basileia*) may also be translated.[27] There can be little doubt that Jesus here is making some reference at least to what is about to transpire on the mountain just six days later, according to the texts. The form of his words, 'some standing here will not taste death before they see . . .', has puzzled commentators and various explanations have been offered. If Jesus were talking about something that would happen just a week or so later, then why speak of some present still being alive to witness it? Surely, none of

---

[25] Note too how some English Bible versions render the noun in Luke 9:31, e.g. 'death' (CEV, HCSB); 'decease' (NKJV, ASV); 'dying' (GNT).

[26] On this principle, see G. K. Beale, *Redemptive Reversals and the Ironic Overturning of Human Wisdom* (Short Studies in Biblical Theology; Wheaton, IL: Crossway, 2019), 121.

[27] Cf. France, *The Gospel of Matthew*, 640–641. It does not therefore necessarily denote the territory ruled.

them would die during such a short interval. The way I understand the saying and the following time phrase is that the former refers to the actual future glory and kingdom power of Christ, while the six days relates to the coming trans-figuration in which that glory and authority would be portrayed by means of a vision. The visionary representation, therefore, was just a few days away, but the realization of it lay in the more distant future.

To explain a little further, I do not consider that the glory and kingdom concerned is primarily that of Christ's second advent, as some interpret the passage. It does, of course, include that, but I do not believe that such matters relate solely to the ultimate end times. This latter is the crowning culmination of Jesus' glory, power and kingdom which actually began during his first advent. From a biblical perspective the ideas of glory and power pertain in fact first to Christ's resurrection, when he emerged triumphant over sin and death. He was 'declared to be the Son of God with power by the resurrection from the dead' (Rom. 1:4) and 'raised in glory . . . raised in power' (1 Cor. 15:43). His resurrected body is described as 'the body of his glory' (Phil. 3:21). But then his ascension to the right hand of the Father a few weeks later further enhanced that glory, for we read that 'he was taken up in glory' (1 Tim. 3:16). The vision of Daniel 7, often assumed to depict the second coming, in actual fact concerns the arrival in heaven of the Son of Man (Jesus), who 'came to the Ancient of Days [God] . . . and he was given dominion, glory, and a kingdom . . . his dominion is an everlasting dominion, which will not pass away, and his kingdom will not be destroyed' (7:13–14).[28]

Yet another important stage in the establishing of Christ's kingdom came several decades later when, in AD 70, Jerusalem was overthrown in the Jewish revolt against Rome, when the temple was destroyed and the old-covenant manner of worship once and for all ceased. I admit that I can offer no explicit citation of a specific chapter and verse to support such a view, but I am persuaded that it is nevertheless a truly biblical notion, and one, I believe, that would be sustained by a careful reading of the prophecy later uttered by Jesus on the Mount of Olives (Matt. 24; Mark 13; Luke 21). There are also a number of scholars who hold to this interpretation.[29] Accordingly, Christ's words about

---

[28] See how Jesus himself employs this prophetic passage in Matt. 26:64. He clearly relates it to the culmination of his first advent. Cf. France, *The Gospel of Matthew*, 640–641.

[29] E.g. Thomas R. Hatina, 'The Focus of Mark 13:24–27: The Parousia, or the Destruction of the Temple?' *BBR* 6.1 (1996): 43–66; N. T. Wright, *Jesus and the Victory of God* (London: SPCK, 1996), 339–368. Wright (346) sees the disciples' question that inaugurates the Olivet prophecy as virtually tantamount to meaning: 'When will you come in your kingdom?', and the events foretold there by Jesus as a vindication of his kingship and of his people (351, 360–362). This does not, of course, entail that there will be no second advent at the time of the end in which the kingdom will be consummated.

some not tasting death indicate that just a certain number of his apostles would live to see all these wondrous events come to pass that would affirm his glory, power and kingship. For sure, several of the original twelve apostles, and possibly most, had been martyred by AD 70.

At this point in each Gospel account, the transfiguration itself takes place. In its most basic sense, therefore, it consists of an anticipatory vision of Jesus in his glory.[30] Such a vision seems to have been given in view of the foregoing prediction of his suffering, an element of messiahship the disciples had not taken into consideration. Evidently, the revelation that he was going to suffer and die in Jerusalem was incredibly difficult for them to factor into their understanding of who he was and what he had come to do, since this understanding comprised a faulty, or at least a partial, view of what the messianic role entailed. In such a situation the vision of Jesus transfigured into glory would be a powerful assurance that beyond the rejection and death he had foretold would come the glory and power of his kingly rule. The heavenly declaration likewise confirmed that kingship through its allusion to Psalm 2. But to this it immediately adjoined the allusion to the servant of Isaiah's prophecies, a servant who would ultimately undergo great suffering. Jesus' discussion of his 'exodus' with the two prophets of old was in a similar vein – prior to a coming in glory there needed to be a departure in death. In short, then, the disciples were presented with a strong affirmation, in the form of a preview, as it were, of Christ's ultimate glory, with the added dimension of the suffering that necessarily preceded it. This, I would consider, is the significance of the transfiguration at its most elemental level.

An important corollary of the foregoing is the superiority of Jesus as a revelatory figure over the older revelation, as represented by Moses and Elijah. If he is indeed the Christ, the one to be invested in kingdom glory, then his teaching comes with an authority greater than that of any other previous divine spokesman. This is the relevance of the third Old Testament allusion in the heavenly utterance from the cloud: 'listen to him'. These words are plainly taken from Deuteronomy 18:15 concerning the eschatological prophet like Moses,[31] a prediction now shown to also be fulfilled in Jesus.[32] In the eventual

---

[30] Cf. Daniel Fanous, *Taught By God: Making Sense of the Difficult Sayings of Jesus* (Rollinsford, NH: Orthodox Research Institute, 2010), 17: 'The transfiguration was a taste, a kind, a parable, a prefiguration of the glorious kingdom that would come in the future.'

[31] That the expectation of such a figure was prevalent among the Jews at that time is evinced by John 1:21, 25; 6:14; 7:40. The fact that Jesus was clearly not satisfied with being identified merely as 'one of the prophets' (Mark 8:28) demonstrates that this anticipated prophetic figure was not simply another of the same kind, hence the grammatically definite designation '*the* prophet'.

[32] Acts 3:22–23 also applies the prediction in Deut. 18 to Jesus.

disappearance from the vision of Moses and Elijah and the fact that Jesus remained 'alone' (Matt. 17:8; Mark 9:8; Luke 9:36), we further see how the latter has superseded the former in the matter of being the revelatory mouthpiece of God.[33] Not that Jesus would in any way contradict the earlier revelation, for as he himself had explained earlier he had come 'not to abolish the law and the prophets . . . but to fulfil' (Matt. 5:17). The detail that Jesus, Moses and Elijah were 'speaking together' strongly suggests the mutual agreement between them.

The events that directly follow the transfiguration also appear to relate back to it. Coming down the mountain, the three disciples question Jesus about Elijah (Matt. 17:10–13; Mark 9:11–13). Since they had just beheld this prophet in the vision, it was natural that such questions should arise in their minds, though it was perhaps unexpected that Jesus should answer their queries with reference to John the Baptist. Then a short while later Jesus repeats the prediction of his coming passion (Matt. 17:22–23; Mark 9:31–32; Luke 9:44–45). Between the descent from the mountain and this latter prediction all three Gospels place the healing of a demon-possessed boy (Matt. 17:14–21; Mark 9:14–29; Luke 9:37–43). Since all the occurrences and teachings in this portion of each Gospel seem to be related in some way to the transfiguration, it is likely that this latter miracle story likewise concerns a similar theme. In what way this is so cannot now be treated at length. There is much to suggest, however, that the miracle depicts a manner of symbolic death and resurrection. This we understand both from the literal surface reading of the episode, in which the boy is said to be 'dead' (Mark 9:26), and from its close literary connections to the raising of Jairus's daughter,[34] which obviously recounts a literal death and resurrection.

---

[33] Cf. Heb. 1:1–2, 'God, who at various times and in various ways spoke long ago to the fathers in the prophets, in these last days has spoken to us in his Son'. Those English versions that express these two stages of revelation in the form of a contrast are mistaken. There is no 'but' present in Greek (cf. NASB, NKJV).

[34] In these two miracle accounts significant resemblances may be identified: it is the father of the child that seeks the healing (Mark 5:6; 9:21); the daughter and the son are described as the 'only' (*monogenēs*) child (Luke 8:42; 9:38); the question of faith on the part of the father finds a place in both (Mark 5:6; 9:23–24); Jesus arrives at the location where the afflicted child is with the same three disciples, Peter, James and John (Matt. 17:1; Mark 5:37); exactly the same verb (*apethanen*), 'died', is used to describe each child's condition (Mark 5:35, 39; 9:26; Luke 8:52, 53); Jesus takes each child by the hand (Matt. 9:25; Mark 5:41; 9:27); two distinct verbs of 'raise up' (*egeirō* and *anistēmi*) occur in both accounts (Matt. 9:25; Mark 5:42; 9:27; Luke 8:54), appearing elsewhere in resurrection contexts; and each miracle is a cause of astonishment (Mark 5:42; Luke 8:56; 9:43). Evidently, by such literary means some correlation is being deliberately created between the two events. Perhaps – here just thinking out loud – the miraculous exorcism of the young boy, in context, is to be viewed as a representation of the state of the Jewish people and their need of deliverance (from an evil 'spirit' that possesses them) through a spiritual death and resurrection. This fits well with the previously noted allusion to the golden calf incident. The nation had become unfaithful to its God and was in need of a radical awakening from its deadness. If this interpretation is correct, then in this sequence of passages under discussion we have, in order, the necessity of Messiah's own death and resurrection, the death (in the form of taking up the cross) and gaining of life on the part of the disciple, and the need for the healing of Israel through a similar death and resurrection.

This overview of the purpose and meaning of the transfiguration at the primary level of interpretation in its larger context has been essential in order that the underlying set of allusions, which is our chief concern, may be correctly understood and appreciated. What, then, do the indirect references back to Moses and his encounter on the mountain add to the foregoing? First, it has to be said that while both episodes portray theophanies in which the appearance of some form of 'glory' is central, it would be a mistake to see them as being on an equal footing in this respect. Without question, when we move from what is depicted in the old-covenant Scriptures to the event recorded in the Gospels we are obliged to conclude that movement to be an upwards one. The transfiguration, therefore, is not just more of the same. Neither can we say that the transfiguration simply is, as one scholar puts it, 'an enhanced repetition of the glorification of Moses'.[35] I believe that what is signified by the allusions, though plainly affirming a connection between the two occasions, places the glorification of Jesus in a wholly different category, something other than a mere 'enhanced repetition'.

First and foremost, what happened on Sinai was a theophany of the God of Israel, which Moses witnessed, along with others – 'they saw the God of Israel' (Exod. 24:10). With this glorious divine manifestation Moses interacted at a distance, albeit in closer proximity than the others who were also on the mountain. As far as this event was concerned, the glory originated in and pertained to the divine appearance. Moses' face did indeed subsequently radiate a degree of glory, but it is evident that this was a reflection of the divine glory he beheld and in no sense could be identified as his own,[36] nor was it a lasting glory. When we consider the transfiguration, one obvious fact is that Jesus himself forms the primary focus of the vision. Through the allusions the scene on Mount Sinai has been evoked, but with radical divergences. While Christ's ascent of the mountain in the company of certain others initially leads the reader to think of him in the role of Moses ascending Sinai, once the summit is reached and the encounter there takes place we find a marked inversion of roles. Jesus is not going up, like Moses, to meet the divine glory, but rather he in his own person becomes the subject of glory. And in this latter scene, Moses, as on Sinai, stands to one side as a witness, in the same place as the prophet Elijah.

In other words, we come across the same feature found elsewhere in such extended allusions[37] where the narrative commences with us thinking of Jesus as an Old Testament character, here a Moses-like figure, which indeed he is in

---

[35] D. F. Strauss, cited in Dale C. Allison Jr, *The New Moses: A Matthean Typology* (Minneapolis, MN: Fortress, 1993), 293.

[36] Exod. 34:29 states of Moses that 'his face shone because he had spoken with the LORD'.

[37] See, e.g., chapters 10, 19 and 26.

several respects, but he is then suddenly transposed, so to speak, into a figure of an altogether different nature. Plainly, Jesus, unlike Moses, occupies the centrepiece of the narrative and assumes the role that corresponds to the Sinai theophany itself. Contrary to Moses, whose glory was one that was merely reflected, the glory of Jesus issues forth from within himself. As one commentator remarks: 'Jesus shone with his own heavenly glory. Moses' radiance was derivative, Jesus' essential.'[38] We are surely confronted here once again with an exalted Christology which portrays Jesus as inherently divine. For here the glory of the Godhead is made visible through the human nature of the Son, the second Person of the Trinity, who came into the world as the man Jesus of Nazareth. What was seen on the mount of transfiguration for the benefit of his three apostles was the veil of his flesh momentarily being drawn aside to allow a glimpse, in a vision at least, of his divine glory. Understood in this way, the fact that he was 'transfigured' relates only to his human appearance. Within that humanity there abode an unchanging being, whose essence was Deity, and whose glory remains the same from everlasting to everlasting.[39]

We cannot here deal with all the theological implications of what is involved here. The vision was given to grant the disciples a display of Christ's glory beyond his approaching rejection and death. Yet, viewed from a different perspective, he already possessed an all-surpassing glory. As far as his Godhead was concerned, the glorification that followed his suffering added nothing to the fullness and perfection of his innate glory. With regard to his humanity, however, there was a very real increase. As touching his manhood, an abundance of glory would be ascribed to Jesus in the coming events – for his self-sacrifice, his conquest of death, and in the exaltation of his human body into heaven and its session at the right hand of the Father. In a real sense, then, the human nature of Jesus did attain a glory that it did not previously possess. I doubt very much if the three disciples present would have then had any notion of such a distinction,[40] yet for them the main thrust of the vision was, despite the looming suffering, the sure fact of Christ's ultimate glorification.

---

[38] France, *The Gospel of Matthew*, 647.

[39] Cf. John 17:5, where Jesus speaks to his Father of 'the glory that I had with you before the world was'.

[40] It is possible, however, that one of the three, the apostle John, later had some appreciation of what the transfiguration meant at a deeper level. Interestingly, his Gospel does not recount this event. Nevertheless, in his prologue he does say, 'The Word became flesh and made his dwelling among us, and we beheld his glory, the glory as of the only begotten from the Father' (John 1:14). This clearly refers to his divine glory, and John does not tie it down to a particular event, but it is rather the attribute of the Son's essential unchanging glory. This has been taken by some commentators to be the Johannine replacement for the transfiguration episode. Rather than just recount a single occasion in which that glory became visible, the fourth Gospel assigns the glory to Christ's very person, a 'perpetual theophany' as it has been labelled. See Williams, 'The Transfiguration of Jesus Christ', 25.

Evidently, then, Jesus and Moses can in no sense be viewed in equal terms. The former is not simply a new Moses, as we discovered in the feeding of the multitude,[41] nor does he merely enjoy an enhanced revelation of God exceeding that of his predecessor. No, he is one that far transcends the man Moses, being very God in human form, who appears in theophanic terms.[42]

Some brief comments are also necessary concerning the allusive significance of the term for 'shelter' or 'tabernacle' (*skēnē*). The suggestion of Peter that the disciples make three such items for Jesus, Moses and Elijah is plainly an improper one. To accommodate all three men in such structures, which possess an obvious association with the Old Testament sanctuary, would be to grant the three of them a certain equality of status. For reasons just demonstrated, this could in no way be admissible. The disparity between two prophets on one hand and the Son of God on the other would be too great to even think of such a thing. Given the connotation of the tabernacle of old, the only one of the three properly deserving such a structure would of course be Jesus. And yet he does not require a man-made tabernacle of any kind. For Jesus already possessed a tabernacle that was well-suited to its purpose. I mean here his flesh, that is, his human body. This was the sanctuary in which the divine Person took up residence. Indeed, the apostle John, one of the disciples present here, speaks of 'the temple of his [Christ's] body' (John 2:21), as that is exactly what it was.[43]

Not only does Jesus far excel the person of Moses, but the 'exodus' that he came to accomplish also eclipses that conducted by Moses. In the latter case, the departure in question was limited to benefits for the Hebrews solely with respect to the physical realm – release from slavery to Pharaoh and the promise of their own land. The exodus that Jesus was to effect in Jerusalem, however, frees his people from the corruption of sin, from the oppression of the devil, and even from death itself, and brings them into an eternal possession.

Finally, attention should be drawn to the fact that in the transfiguration we are told that the 'face' (*prosōpon*) of Jesus emitted light (Matt. 17:2). On Mount Sinai, we recall, Moses asked God: 'Show me your glory' (Exod. 33:18), which

---

[41] Chapter 10.

[42] Here it is worth recalling the words of the writer to the Hebrews: 'Jesus . . . was faithful to the one who appointed him, just as Moses also was faithful in all God's house. Yet Jesus is worthy of more glory than Moses, just as the builder of a house has more honour than the house itself . . . Now Moses was faithful in all God's house as a servant, testifying to the things that would later be spoken. But Christ was faithful over God's house as a Son' (Heb. 3:1–3, 5–6). In this context we think too of the reversal of status in the figures of Moses and the one named Joshua on Mount Sinai. There Joshua, whose name in Greek corresponds to 'Jesus', is merely the 'servant' of Moses (Exod. 24:13). In the transfiguration the one bearing the name 'Joshua' is Lord, and Moses his attendant. The significance of this inversion could hardly be lost to Jewish-background readers.

[43] The apostle Paul, as noted in an earlier study (chapter 5), also spells out the wondrous fact that 'in him [Christ] dwells all the fullness of Deity in bodily form' (Col. 2:9).

would include seeing God's 'face'. This degree of manifestation, however, was denied. 'You cannot see my face,' said God (v. 20). A view of God's 'back' only was permitted (v. 23).[44] But now in the transfiguration, Moses' request is portrayed as being fulfilled in the vision. For there in the human face of Christ he was allowed the sight of the face of God radiant with divine splendour, for in that very human visage the one and the same God who descended on Sinai was manifested. Both Moses and Elijah shared in a similar privilege, for in the Old Testament they both experienced a mountain-top theophany which, although it brought them in a sense into the awesomeness of the divine presence, nevertheless left the person of God obscured to them. On the mountain with Jesus, as the vision depicted for the two prophets and as an actual real-life occurrence for the three apostles, that obscure presence was finally given wonderful definition.[45]

---

[44] For a discussion of what it means to see God's 'back', see Thomas J. White, *Exodus* (Brazos Theological Commentary on the Bible; Grand Rapids, MI: Brazos, 2016), 280–281. While the Old Testament employs the phrase 'face to face' (Exod. 33:11; Num. 12:8) in connection with Moses' communication with God, in the light of the passage under discussion this cannot be taken with complete literality, for the same expression is used with reference to God speaking to the entire people of Israel at Sinai (Deut. 5:4). See further White, *Exodus*, 278.

[45] A second set of allusions has been proposed by some with regard to the transfiguration. It has been argued that the account of Abraham and Isaac on Mount Moriah in Gen. 22 is also being evoked by literary means. Such a view is advocated, for example, in Leroy A. Huizenga, *The New Isaac: Tradition and Intertextuality in the Gospel of Matthew* (Leiden: Brill, 2009), 79–80, 209–235. I personally was not entirely convinced by the parallels that were drawn and so have not included this view in the present volume. The two scenarios are located on mountain tops, but so are many others in both Testaments. The theophanic element, which is strongly present, if not central, on both Sinai and the mount of transfiguration, is absent from Moriah (where there is a heavenly voice, but no appearance). The strongest link is the phrase 'beloved son', which occurs in each context: 'Take your beloved son [*ton hyion sou ton agapēton*]' (Gen. 22:2) and 'This is my beloved Son [*ho hyios mou ho agapētos*]' (Matt. 17:5; Mark 9:7). Such a close similarity is not without significance, for it is indeed the case that the person of Isaac prefigures the Messiah in many respects. And we shall in fact discover later, when we come to the events of Passion Week, that Gen. 22 is distinctly alluded to in an extensive manner.

14

The parable of the rich fool

Luke 12:16–21

This chapter will be briefer than usual since the allusion involved is one that is quite apparent, or at least would have been so to early Jewish-Christian readers familiar with Hebrew. It also concerns a very short passage from a single Gospel. In this instance we are dealing not with an event involving Jesus but with one of his parables. As explained in the introduction, since parables invariably take the form of a story of some kind, albeit fictional, they may therefore allude to Old Testament narratives which are factual. Certainly, this is the case here.

The particular parable that Jesus tells here in Luke is sparked off by a request from someone in the crowd. A man says to him, 'Teacher, tell my brother to divide the inheritance with me' (12:13).[1] In reply Jesus says, 'Man, who appointed me a judge or arbitrator between you?' (v. 14). He then declares to the crowds, 'Beware, and be on your guard against every kind of greed; for a person's life does not consist in the abundance of his possessions' (v. 15). Jesus next proceeds to tell them the parable we are considering (vv. 16–21).

In this parable, Jesus tells the crowd about a rich man whose fields were so bountiful that he had no place to keep his crops. He came up with the idea of building bigger barns to store his grain and 'his good things' (v. 18). The man then told himself, 'Soul, you have many good things laid up for many years. Take it easy, eat, drink, and be merry' (v. 19). But then God spoke to the man, saying, 'Fool! This night your soul is required of you. Then those things you have prepared, whose will they be?' (v. 20). After the parable Christ ends with the comment: 'So it is with anyone who stores up treasures for himself but is not rich toward God' (v. 21).

There can be little doubt that allusion is being made here to what is related in 1 Samuel 25:1–38 concerning the character of Nabal. In this chapter of the Old Testament we read how David, as a fugitive from King Saul who sought his life, moved with his men into the region of Maon. Not far from there was a

---

[1] This would seem to mean 'to give me a share of our inheritance' (as NJB).

well-to-do man called Nabal, married to one Abigail. When out in the countryside David's men would mix with Nabal's shepherds, and although it was within their power to seize whatever they wanted, none of Nabal's sheep went missing (v. 7). On the contrary David's men even protected his shepherds (v. 16). Then one day David sent messengers to Nabal to wish him good health and, on the basis of how his men had treated Nabal's shepherds, to request some provisions: 'Please give whatever you have at hand to your servants and to your son David' (v. 8).

Now Nabal is described as 'very wealthy' (v. 2). He was not lacking in livestock, for he possessed a thousand goats and three thousand sheep. This was an enormous amount by any standards. David's men numbered six hundred (v. 13), and so not too many animals would have been required to give them a good meal,[2] and even thirty or forty would not have been greatly missed out of such a large quantity. Not only this, but Nabal also owned property at Carmel, a highly fertile area of northern Israel. So besides his flocks he must have been well supplied in other produce. Yet when he heard David's request he was unwilling to provide anything at all. 'Should I take my bread and water,' he asked, 'and the meat I have slaughtered for my shearers, and give it to men who come from I do not know where?' (v. 11).

When Nabal's response got back to David his anger was roused and he gathered armed men to go and wreak havoc on Nabal (v. 13). The situation was saved, however, by Nabal's good wife, Abigail. Loading up donkeys with provisions, she went and met David on the way with his men, and managed to appease his wrath by the gift of food and drink.

There are several lessons to be learned from this episode, but for our purposes we are focusing on Nabal himself. He was a rich man, such as Jesus was talking about in the parable. In fact, for those hearers of Jesus who understood Hebrew, probably the vast majority, their minds would have immediately gone to 1 Samuel 25. This is simply because of the main character's name. There Abigail said to David, 'Please let not my lord pay any attention to this worthless man, Nabal; for as his name is, so is he. Nabal is his name, and folly is with him' (v. 25). English readers will not readily see the play on words here. The wife is punning on her husband's name, for Nabal, *nābāl* in Hebrew, means 'fool'. Abigail declares that 'as his name is, so is he'. In other words he is a 'fool' by name and a 'fool' by nature. She further says 'folly is with him', the Hebrew word for 'folly' being *něbālâ*.

---

[2] From what I have been able to discover, the meat from a full-grown sheep could feed forty people or more.

Now in Christ's parable, God addressed the rich man as 'Fool' (v. 20). The crowds listening to the parable would have heard here the word *nābāl*, and prompted by the rich man in the parable, himself a fool, the Old Testament rich man Nabal, also explicitly called a fool, must surely have sprung to mind.

But it is not just their wealth and foolishness that connect these two characters. We have not yet touched upon the climactic element of the parable and its correspondence in the Nabal narrative. The foolishness of the man in the parable lies in the fact that he makes plans to store up all his wealth, and once that is done he believes a life of ease and merriment lies before him. As it turns out, however, that very same night he hears God's words: 'Fool! This night your soul is required of you.' That night would see the termination of his life, and God would have him consider the question: 'those things you have prepared, whose will they be?' This rich man, then, met an untimely end in the parable. It was not his destiny to gain enjoyment from all those many good things. To store them up for himself was wholly in vain.

A similar early death befell Nabal. When Abigail, having returned from her encounter with David, told her husband what she had done, that is, the gifts she had made to David of Nabal's animals and produce, we read that 'his heart died within him and he became like a stone' (1 Sam. 25:37). Then after a few days 'the LORD struck Nabal and he died' (v. 38). Here, then, was another man of substance unable to enjoy the benefits of his wealth.

While there are details that differ, as is the case generally when allusion is being made in one text to another, the same basic moral lesson is being taught. If one is blessed through the abundance of possessions, one's intentions on how to use them should not be limited to oneself. It is not simply our own life, or the lives of our family members, that should benefit. The rich ought to hold what they own with a loose hand. After all, what is important in life far exceeds material prosperity. Ultimately, it is spiritual riches that count, which entails seeing one's wealth as a God-provided means of helping others.[3] Neither Nabal nor the rich man had it in his heart to share from the abundance of his wealth. Hence the tragedy that happened to them – neither of them ended up enjoying it for himself.

It is hard to avoid the conclusion that Jesus is deliberately referring his listeners to the Old Testament character. As he is describing this fictitious rich man, he is making his audience take a sideways or, more accurately, backwards glance at Nabal. The reason for this is surely to enforce the point he is making.

---

[3] It is significant that later in the same Gospel Jesus actually tells a rich man directly to 'give to the poor' (18:22).

Through the allusions to the Old Testament account in 1 Samuel 25, the parabolic story is given grounding in a real-life situation. The earlier passage therefore is evoked to provide an illustration, in the form of an actual historical event, of what the fictional parable portrays in the form of a figure. Jesus is in effect saying, 'What I'm talking about is not purely theoretical, but look for yourself – it has actually happened!' His warning about the dangers of great wealth are not hypothetical but, through the use of the specific allusions, are made real.

15

The woman taken in adultery

John 7:53 – 8:11

The next passage we consider is one that has been the cause of some controversy. Since the passage, often dubbed the *pericope adulterae*, is absent from a number of ancient Greek manuscripts, it is widely held not to be an original part of John's Gospel. To further support this claim arguments have been put forward to the effect that the style of language differs from the rest of the Gospel. As far as our purposes are concerned, the genuineness of the text is not the major issue. Our primary aim is to detect Old Testament allusions, and it has to be said that such are found in this passage also. For that reason, and since there have been many, and there still are many, who accept its authenticity, it will be included here. For my part, I am inclined to regard the verses as Johannine. I believe this first on the basis of the language. Although some have argued for Lukan authorship, I find scant linguistic grounds for such an opinion. On the contrary, the passage contains some quite specific features which are found elsewhere only in the fourth Gospel.[1] Second, the passage, properly interpreted, does seem to have something pertinent to say in its particular context within the narrative of John, as will be explained in due course. But while this is my personal judgment on its authenticity, my intention is chiefly to highlight the allusions present within the passage, regardless of the identity of its author.

---

[1] Three elements of linguistic data in particular point strongly, in my view, to Johannine authorship. These are the presentational strategy: 'The scribes and the Pharisees brought [to him] a woman caught in adultery' (8:3). It consists of the clause-initial verb *agousin*, 'bring', in the third person plural and specifically in the historic present tense-form. The identical verb in the initial position and in the historic present tense occurs twice more in John, both in similar presentational contexts (9:13; 18:28), and is found nowhere else outside the fourth Gospel. The clause 'This they said testing him' (8:6) exhibits a very particular form and function. It consists of an initial demonstrative pronoun, *touto*, followed by a verb of speech to which is attached a present participle. Precisely such a structure is found three times in other Johannine texts (6:6; 12:33; 21:19) and nowhere besides in the entire New Testament. In all these instances the post-positive particle *de* likewise occurs. The strategy is not only exclusively Johannine in form but is also thoroughly Johannine in function. A distinct feature of John's Gospel is the authorial practice of inserting short explanatory clauses offering an interpretation of the immediately preceding words in the narrative. Finally, we note the exact sameness of 'sin no more' in 8:11 and the earlier 5:14, both *mēketi hamartane*.

In this episode the scribes and Pharisees bring a woman caught in the act of adultery to Jesus and set her before him (John 8:3).[2] These men present her case to his attention, pointing out that the law demands her execution by means of stoning. They then ask him, 'Now what do *you* say?' (vv. 4–5). In Greek the addition of the independent pronoun 'you' (*sy*) suggests a challenge. Would Jesus dare oppose the law? The whole thing is explicitly stated to be a test, since if Jesus expressed a view contrary to what is prescribed in Israel's ancient law then his opponents would have something with which to accuse him (v. 6), and so expose him as a false messiah. Such an eventuality is obviously what they are hoping for. The outcome, however, is not what they expect. After writing on the ground for a few moments, Jesus straightens himself up and declares, 'He who is without sin among you, let him be the first to throw a stone at her' (v. 7). He then stoops down again to continue writing (v. 8). As is well known, the woman's accusers are convicted in their consciences and begin to depart, starting with the oldest (v. 9). The passage ends with Jesus addressing the woman on the matter of her accusers, telling her to go and sin no more (vv. 10–11).

In this case, I believe the Old Testament text alluded to is quite apparent, even though the majority of modern commentators seem to overlook it. The passage in question is the Torah injunction regarding, appropriately enough, a woman who is suspected of having committed adultery (Num. 5:11–31). This is an ordinance, incidentally, that will be alluded to again in a later episode recorded in all four Gospels.[3] The law in question begins by stating: 'If any man's wife goes astray and is unfaithful to him, and another man sleeps with her . . .' (vv. 12–13). The situation presupposed in the law specifically concerned a husband who wished to ascertain the guilt or innocence of his wife in the face of such a suspicion. In this circumstance the woman was to be brought to the priest at the sanctuary for the various rituals to be performed. Prominent among the proceedings was the preparation of a vessel of water mixed with dust from the tabernacle floor (v. 17) and the placing of the woman under an oath by the priest. This latter in effect invoked a curse upon the woman in the event that she was actually guilty of what her husband suspected (vv. 19–21). Once the woman had responded to the imprecation with a twofold 'Amen' (v. 22), the priest was to write the curse on a scroll and rub off the writing into the vessel (v. 23). The woman was then made to drink this 'bitter water that brings a curse' (v. 24) and the result was awaited. If she were innocent she would suffer

---

[2] John 7:53 – 8:1 are here taken as transitional verses that serve to connect the final pericope of ch. 7 (vv. 45–52) with the passage concerning the woman taken in adultery.

[3] See chapter 22.

no harmful effects. If she had been unfaithful, however, she would be punished in a manner that suggests permanent sterility,[4] and 'become a curse in the midst of her people' (v. 27).

We first note the obvious thematic relationship between the Torah text and the Gospel passage. Both deal with the moral offence of adultery. More than this, both focus on the actions of the woman, and not the man (a matter for further discussion later on). Alongside this fundamental connection, we may discern a whole range of more specific conceptual and linguistic correspondences, as will be demonstrated.

Each of the two passages locates the happenings within Israel's sacred precincts. In the law this is the 'tabernacle' (Num. 5:17), while in the Gospel it is the 'temple' (John 8:2), both uniquely being the divinely appointed sanctuaries of their respective times.

To this particular holy place men bring the woman concerned: 'The husband shall bring his wife [*axei . . . tēn gynaika autou*] to [*pros*] the priest' (Num. 5:15), as compared with: 'The scribes and Pharisees brought a woman [*agousin . . . gynaika*] to [*pros*][5] him [Jesus]' (John 8:3).[6]

In both texts the phrase 'caught in the act' is used in connection with the woman: 'she was not caught in the act [*syneilēmmenē*]' (Num. 5:13); and 'a woman who had been caught in the act [*kateilēmmenēn*] of adultery' (John 8:3; also v. 4).[7] As this descriptive participle bears this particular sense only in these two passages in the whole of canonical Scripture, it creates a strong linkage between them.

The woman is brought to one specific individual male, the priest or Jesus, to deal with the matter. In the former circumstance to approach the priest is to come 'before the LORD (*kyriou*)', a phrase appearing several times (Num. 5:16, 18, 25, 30). In the latter the woman ends up standing before Jesus alone (John 8:11), whom she addresses as 'Lord' (*kyrie*).

When the woman is presented, the phrase 'make her stand' appears in each instance. In fact, this is almost a characteristic feature of the Numbers text: 'he shall make her stand [*stēsei autēn*]' (Num. 5:16, 18, 30); as compared with 'they made her stand [*stēsantes autēn*]' (John 8:3). The location, moreover, in which the woman was made to stand is more precisely said to be 'in the midst [*en mesō*]' in both instances (Num. 5:21, 27; cf. John 8:3, 9).

---

[4] Cf. Timothy R. Ashley, *The Book of Numbers* (NICOT; Grand Rapids, MI: Eerdmans, 1993), 132–133.

[5] Here following the majority reading.

[6] The reader should be aware that *axei* and *agousin* are different tenses of the same Greek verb (*agō*).

[7] Both texts contain the feminine perfect participle of the same root verb, differing only in their prefixes, a fact which does not alter their basic meaning.

An act of writing figures prominently in what takes place, performed by the principal male character to whom the woman has been brought. In the law, the text states that 'the priest shall write [*grapsei*]' (Num. 5:23), while in the Gospel we read that 'he [Jesus] . . . wrote [*egraphen*]' (John 8:8; also v. 6).[8]

The ground features in a significant, that is, not merely incidental, way in each passage. The first speaks of 'the dust from the floor of the tabernacle', where in its Greek version 'the dust' is replaced simply by 'the ground [*tēs gēs*]' (Num. 5:17). In the second 'the ground [*tēn gēn*]' is where Jesus wrote (John 8:6, 8). Needless to say, unless there was dust of some sort on the ground where the incident took place he would not have been able to write anything legible.[9] The fact is that according to the Greek of each passage the 'ground' plays an important part, and in each case it is the ground of the sanctuary.

An intriguing textual variant in the Gospel also connects the two texts. In fact, the correlation it makes seems so apposite that I think it hard to deny that the reading is original. In its Greek translation of the Numbers text the water that the woman is made to drink is termed *to hydōr tou elegmou*, 'the water of conviction'. This phrase occurs there five times (5:18, 19, 24 [twice], 27).[10] In John 8:9 a participial clause appears in many manuscripts which states *kai hypo tēs syneidēseōs elenchomenoi*, 'and being convicted by their conscience'.[11] This clause contains the participle (*elenchomenoi*), 'convicted', which is cognate to the noun 'conviction' (*elegmou*) in the Numbers text. We will return to this presently.

Then, lastly, each of the two texts concludes with a reference to the sin of the woman who has been brought: 'the woman shall bear her sin [*tēn hamartian autēs*]' (Num. 5:31); cf. 'Go and sin [*hamartane*] no more' (John 8:11). Indeed, these are the very last words of each passage.

In view of the extremely strong conceptual relationship as well as the parallels in language and other details, it is not implausible to suppose that the presence of allusions in the Gospel pericope is intentional. It is interesting to discover that, while unnoticed by modern scholars, a number of older commentators did in fact detect the connection, though none unpacks it in any depth.[12]

---

[8] The subsequent phrase denoting the place where the writing is done is also in each instance constructed with the same preposition (*eis*).

[9] The NLT, we observe, includes 'dust' in the text of vv. 6 and 8.

[10] More fully, it is described as 'the water of conviction that brings a curse'.

[11] The clause is found in a sizeable portion of the Byzantine textual tradition and in the later Received Text of the Greek Testament.

[12] See, e.g., John Lightfoot, *A Commentary on the New Testament from the Talmud and Hebraica*, vol. 3 (Peabody, MA: Hendrickson, 2003 [repr. of 1859 edn]), 327–330; John Albert Bengel, *Gnomon of the New Testament*, vol. 2 (Eugene, OR: Wipf & Stock, 2004 [repr. of 1877 edn]), 349, 351; John W. Burgon, *Plain Commentary on the Four Holy Gospels, Volume 4, Part 1: St. John I–XI* (London: John Henry Parker, 1855), 294–297.

Accepting the presence of deliberate allusion, we need to enquire as to its purpose. Here I first ought to stress that although I believe the ordinance of Numbers to be clearly in mind in the *pericope adulterae*, I am not at all claiming that the two scenarios are identical. Differences, of course, also exist. Though both passages involve women accused of adultery, that in Numbers treats it only as a suspicion, while in the Gospel the woman was discovered in the performance of the act. In this latter case the law of Moses required a completely different course of justice, namely death by stoning (Deut. 22:22–24). The scribes and Pharisees implicitly appeal to this penalty of the law in John 8:5. In the Numbers situation, as there were no witnesses, no judicial penalties were imposed. By means of the drinking of 'the water that brings a curse' the consequences were left in the hands of God. It was an act to establish her guilt or otherwise, with serious consequences if her husband's suspicions were confirmed. This drinking therefore forms no part of what transpires with respect to the woman in John 8, since her guilt could be confirmed by witnesses, and so, strictly speaking, from the perspective of the Torah what the Pharisees wish to do to her is right. That the guilt of the adulteress was never in doubt is an important component of the episode. However, as will become apparent, the issue of the woman's guilt is not the primary concern of the passage.

From the foregoing, it is evident that, while the law of Numbers 5 is almost certainly being alluded to, the reason for this is definitely not in order for it to be enacted upon the woman brought to Jesus. It must be stressed, then, that no application of this law's stipulations to the woman's actions is in view. This being so, the reader's attention is nevertheless being drawn to that particular ordinance, and to appreciate why requires a deeper understanding of the Numbers passage.

Regarding the law of suspected infidelity in Numbers 5, the observation has been made that the regulation only touches upon the marital unfaithfulness of the woman, and not of the man.[13] One explanation for this lies in the fact that the woman may also function as a representative figure. In her classic work on the anthropology of the book of Numbers, Mary Douglas concludes that the woman in this law is in fact not just an individual wife but a female figure who at the same time serves as a picture of the whole nation of Israel.[14] A number of modern theologians and biblical scholars concur.[15] One such scholar

---

[13] E.g. Roland K. Harrison, *Numbers: An Exegetical Commentary* (Grand Rapids, MI: Baker, 1992), 107.

[14] Mary Douglas, *In the Wilderness: The Doctrine of Defilement in the Book of Numbers* (Oxford: Oxford University Press, 2001), 160–163, 168–169.

[15] E.g. David L. Stubbs, *Numbers* (Brazos Theological Commentary on the Bible; Grand Rapids, MI: Brazos, 2009), 61; also Iain M. Duguid, *Numbers: God's Presence in the Wilderness* (Wheaton, IL: Crossway, 2006), 73–75; Jacob Milgrom, *Numbers* (JPS Torah Commentary; Philadelphia, PA; Jewish Publication Society, 1992), 37.

remarks that 'several aspects of the text suggest that this law should also be read figurally, pointing to the important and powerful image of Israel as the bride of YHWH'.[16] The evidence that supports such a conclusion may be summarized as follows:

1 The marriage relationship is a well-known metaphor in Old Testament language for the relationship between YHWH and Israel his covenant people. Infidelity to the God of Israel, in the form of idolatry, is frequently expressed in terms of 'playing the harlot' (e.g. Deut. 31:16; Jer. 3:6), which is spiritual adultery. To go after other gods is comparable to a married woman going after other men.[17]

2 The Hebrew verb which appears in Numbers 5:12 and 27 speaking of the potential offence of the woman is *mā'al*, 'act unfaithfully'. In both instances this is followed by a prepositional phrase with *b*- relating to the husband.[18] Elsewhere in the Old Testament, *mā'al b*- occurs overwhelmingly with reference to God as the one being unfaithfully treated. It is Israel as a nation who is the main perpetrator of such a crime.[19]

3 Corresponding to this infidelity on the part of the 'woman', the husband responds with *qinâ*, 'jealousy'. This Hebrew noun and its cognate verb occur ten times in the law of Numbers 5:11–31 (vv. 14 [four times], 15, 18, 25, 29, 30 [twice]). The same term is used of the Lord, and indeed is characteristic, on occasions when Israel commits apostasy against him.[20]

4 Hebrew verbs derived from the root *ṭāmē'*, 'be unclean, defiled', occur several times in the Numbers law (vv. 13, 14 [twice], 19, 20, 27, 28, 29) and also in connection with Israel's relationship with its God. Note Psalm 106:39: 'They were defiled [*wayyiṭmĕ'û*] by their works, and played the harlot in their deeds.' Here, through poetic parallelism, defilement and 'harlotry' (i.e. sexual misconduct) are brought into close association.

5 A comparison can be made between what the law states concerning the woman among her people with various other texts in the Jewish Scriptures concerning Israel among the nations. The former tells how the

---

16 Stubbs, *Numbers*, 61.

17 For a detailed discussion of this theme, see Deborah W. Rooke, 'Wayward Women and Broken Promises: Marriage, Adultery and Mercy in Old and New Testaments', in Larry J. Kreitzer and Deborah W. Rooke (eds.), *Ciphers in the Sand: Interpretations of the Woman Taken in Adultery (John 7:53–8:11)* (Sheffield: Sheffield Academic Press, 2000), 17–52, esp. 32–43.

18 This preposition literally means 'in', but in English it would need to be rendered as 'towards'.

19 E.g. Lev. 26:40; Num. 31:16; Deut. 32:51; 1 Chr. 5:25; 2 Chr. 12:2; Ezra 10:2; Ezek. 20:27.

20 E.g. Deut. 6:15; 32:16; 1 Kgs 14:22; Ezek. 8:3; 16:38.

woman, found guilty of infidelity to her husband, will become 'a curse ['ālâ] and an oath' among her people (Num. 5:21, 27). In the latter, the people of Israel, proving themselves unfaithful to their God, will become a 'curse ['ālâ]', a 'horror' and a 'reproach' among all the nations (Jer. 24:9; 26:6; 29:18; 42:18; 44:8, 12; cf. Deut. 28:37; Isa. 65:15; Zech. 8:13). In the LXX the Greek equivalent for 'curse' in these prophetic texts is either *ara* or its longer form *katara*, a fact we will return to shortly.

6 Finally, the similarity surely cannot go unnoticed between the drinking of water by the woman in Numbers 5:11–31 and the drinking of water by the Israelites following the golden calf apostasy in Exodus 32. Following that act of gross idolatry, Moses forced the people to drink water mixed with the ashes of the idol they had worshipped (v. 20), being not too dissimilar from the water mixed with dust drunk by the woman, as noted by certain commentators.[21]

These facts make it reasonable to suppose that the woman of the Numbers 5 law is to be taken as a figure of Israel itself and the jealous husband as a figure of Israel's God.[22] When viewed at this figural level, the law assumes quite a different character, and becomes an intimation of the Lord's relationship with his people, and the possible trials that they may be put through.[23] That, however, is another story. Suffice it to say, this corporate identity of the woman in the Numbers text is important for our interpretation of the episode of John 8 *in situ*.

In the light of the foregoing I believe that we are to understand the woman of the *pericope adulterae* in a symbolic manner. I would stress that at the literal level I take it that she was first and foremost a real individual woman, and the act of which she was accused was an actual event that took place at that time. However, the meaning of Scripture, as seen many times previously, is located at different levels. By means of allusion to the law of Numbers 5, a text in which the female figure emerges as a representation of Israel, the immoral woman of

---

[21] Commenting on this event, Nahum Sarna makes reference to the Talmud, saying: 'In Avodah Zarah 44a this move [of Moses] is seen as a trial by ordeal modeled on that administered to the *sotah*, or suspected adulteress, whose treatment is described in Numbers 5:12–31. She was forced to drink bitter water mingled with dust taken from the floor of the sanctuary . . . The purpose of the ordeal was to identify the transgressors' (Nahum M. Sarna, *Exodus* [JPS Torah Commentary; Philadelphia, PA; Jewish Publication Society, 1991], 207). See also Douglas, *In the Wilderness*, 164.

[22] Duguid (*Numbers*, 92), interestingly, develops the matter further by pointing out the contrast between the figure of the woman and that of the Nazirite in the immediately following passage in Numbers (6:1–21). The Nazirite is interpreted as 'a perfect picture of what Israel was intended to be', in contrast to the Israel needing to be tried for infidelity in 5:11–31.

[23] See Stubbs, *Numbers*, 63.

the Gospel pericope may also be interpreted as a representative figure. But a figure more exactly of what, or whom?

At this point we consider the placement of 7:53 – 8:11 within John's narrative. The immediately preceding passage concerns a discussion among the chief priests, the Pharisees, and those officers who had been sent to arrest Jesus but failed to do so (John 7:45–52). During the course of this exchange the question is posed whether any of the rulers or the Pharisees believe in Christ (v. 48). The Pharisees are then reported to have declared, 'No, but this mob[24] which does not know the law is accursed' (v. 49). The final word here is the adjective *epikataratoi*,[25] formed from the basic noun *ara*, 'curse', modified by various affixes, giving the sense 'under a curse'. Now, as seen above, the idea of being cursed is central to the ordinance of Numbers 5. There it occurs no fewer than ten times altogether (Num. 5:18, 19, 21 [twice], 22, 23, 24 [twice], 27 [twice]), either as the noun *ara* or as the cognate verb *epikataraomai* in the LXX. This latter verb is obviously directly related to the adjective appearing in John 7:49. What makes this significant is the fact that in the entirety of John's Gospel 7:49 is the only verse that speaks of a curse in any shape or form. This means, then, that the pericope alluding to the woman in the law who is placed under a curse is situated directly after another pericope which contains the only occurrence of the term 'curse' in the whole Gospel. This does not seem, to me at least, to be mere coincidence. Rather, it hints at deliberate design, having the effect of making the two passages interrelated.

We argue, then, that the location of the *pericope adulterae* is meaningful. It appears where it does because it needs to be interpreted in the light of what precedes it. In that previous text the Pharisees claim that the great mass of the Jewish laity are under a curse because of their ignorance of the Torah. Then in the next episode the Pharisees, together with their associates the scribes,[26] bring a woman who has committed an immoral act, contrary to the commandments, in a passage that exhibits allusions to that legal ordinance in which a woman is potentially placed under a curse should she be guilty of the very same act. In the former, the Jewish 'mob' is placed under a curse for its neglect of the law; in the other, by means of the allusions, the text evokes an adulterous woman put under a curse for transgressing the law. The Jewish legalists, the

---

[24] Greek *ochlos*, 'crowd, multitude, throng, mass, populace, mob'. The word itself is neutral, but it is often used with strongly negative connotations.

[25] Or *eparatoi* in a small number of manuscripts.

[26] The 'scribes' obviously bear a close relationship to the Pharisees as the two parties often appear together (e.g. Matt. 5:20; 12:38; 23:2; Mark 2:16; 7:1; Luke 5:21; 11:53). Both showed a particular concern for the law. In some modern translations 'scribes' actually appears as 'teachers of the law' or 'experts in the law' (e.g. NIV, NLT, NET, CEV).

Pharisees, are the prime operatives in each instance. They both pronounce against the people and bring the woman forward.

To my mind the two passages are connected in that the woman of the second serves as an embodiment of the 'mob' of the first. We have already seen that the woman of Numbers 5 is almost definitely to be viewed as a representative of the Jewish nation, as is often the case in prophetic and poetic literature of the Old Testament. We find that the same figurative function of the woman in the earlier text transfers into the later text making the allusions. At the surface level of the text the woman of John 8 is an individual guilty of adultery; at the deeper level she is the collective 'woman' of the Jewish people, against whom the Pharisees have pronounced a curse for their neglect of the law, that is, for their spiritual unfaithfulness. Both are viewed, one explicitly, the other implicitly, as being under a curse.

When the *pericope adulterae* is read with this new level of meaning, it takes on an altogether different character. The woman the scribes and Pharisees bring to Jesus, the woman they want to condemn and whose sin is a matter on which they desire to hear Jesus' own verdict, is now a figure of the mass of common folk of their own nation upon whom they themselves have just passed a damning sentence. Taken in this manner, for Jesus to condemn the woman would be for him to concur with the Pharisees' own attitude towards the mass of Jews. Figuratively, to pronounce against the sin of the one would be to acknowledge the spiritual state of the other. But this Christ does not do. He does not overlook the fact that the woman has broken God's law, but he offers no condemnation, and gives her the opportunity to go and sin no more (John 8:11). In so doing, Jesus is, in a figure, extending absolution from guilt to all those whom the women figures, namely the Jewish masses, seen by the Pharisees as nothing but accursed sinners.

This leads on to a remarkable twist in the story. We have previously stressed that, although allusion would seem to be definitely made to it, the law of Numbers 5 is not being evoked in order to apply it to the woman. Rather, in the Gospel pericope this particular law is being applied to her accusers! At the heart of the Torah passage is the preparation and application of certain elements that will determine the guilt or innocence of the woman. The woman is made to imbibe a specially prepared drink which consists basically of water in an earthen vessel to which two other substances have been added. The first of these is some dust from the ground of the tabernacle (v. 17). The second is more involved. Having uttered the curse formula verbally (vv. 21–22), 'the priest shall write these curses on a scroll', after which 'he shall wipe them off into the water' (v. 23). The drink therefore takes the form of water containing dust and the words of the curse. In this mixture I take it that the primary elements are the dust and the ink of the curse. The water chiefly serves to make the substances consumable.[27] In sum, then, the prescriptions of the law bring together as the two principal components of the ritual the dust of the ground and the written curse, which the woman is obligated to consume.

John 8 includes details that correspond to the same two elements appearing in the law. We read there both of the ground and of the act of writing (vv. 6, 8). As the Numbers text brought the dust of the ground and the writing together in the single earthen vessel, the two are joined together in John 8 in that Jesus writes on the ground. As noted above, in both situations it is the main officiant, the priest and Jesus, who does the writing. These connections between the *pericope adulterae* and the ritual of the law, to my mind, explain the oft-asked question about what Jesus wrote on the ground. Solutions proposed by various commentators and scholars have been numerous.[28] For my part, it does seem evident that Jesus would have been writing those words of the curse as prescribed for the woman in Numbers 5. Considering the strength of the allusions between the two passages, this surely has to be the case. The writing in the latter hearkens back to the writing of the curse in the former. Yet it seems apparent from the narrative that the words Jesus was writing were in no way directed at the woman, but at the men who had brought her. Verses 5–8 of the pericope, in which the act of writing is mentioned twice, plainly concern the interaction between Christ and the woman's accusers, not the woman herself. It is in response to their questioning him that he begins to write, and it is after he continues writing that they gradually depart. The twist lies in this fact, that having put the curse down in writing the priest administers it to the woman, whereas Jesus obviously intends his writing to have an effect on the scribes and Pharisees. The action is entirely aimed at them.

We see, then, that in the law the writing and the dust relate to the woman, while in the Gospel the writing *in* the dust relates to the woman's male accusers. I believe this to be the main point of the allusion. The old-covenant ordinance was designed to make trial of the woman. In the Gospel, however, while the Pharisees supposed they were testing Jesus, he in fact was the one subjecting them to examination. At the centre of each passage is the bringing together of

---

[27] This does not mean that the water is without any symbolic significance. While the Hebrew text refers to it as 'holy water', it is interesting to observe that the Greek text describes it as *hydōr katharon zōn*, 'pure living water' (Num. 5:17 LXX). In John's Gospel 'living water' is of course a familiar image (4:10, 11; 7:38), where it has particular associations with the Holy Spirit, which in turn is portrayed as a Spirit who convicts of sin (16:8).

[28] For a survey of different interpretations, see Jennifer Knust and Tommy Wasserman, 'Earth Accuses Earth: Tracing What Jesus Wrote upon the Ground', *HTR* 103.4 (2010), 407–446.

writing and the ground. It is the symbolism of this act that provides the meaning to what transpires. For the woman in Numbers 5 this is plain. It clearly represents the curse that she herself will experience if she is guilty. The symbolism in John 8 is somewhat altered, as is often the case in literary allusion, yet it retains the two most essential elements. The men Jesus is addressing are not made to drink anything, as was done in the legal ritual. But the writing and the ground are still highly meaningful from a figural perspective.

We have already suggested that the writing bears the same significance as in the law. Indeed, it is that very law of Numbers 5 that allows us to interpret the act of writing. It was the pronouncement of a curse against an adulteress, who represented, at a higher level, a people charged with spiritual infidelity against their God. Jesus was writing the words of that same curse on the ground. In making the ground the specific place where the words are written, we find further symbolism which takes our minds to well-known texts of Scripture.

In the creation of the first human being, God took the basic material 'from the dust of the ground' (Gen. 2:7). At death we humans 'return to the ground, since from it you were taken; for you are dust and to dust you shall return' (3:19; cf. Job 17:16; Pss 22:29; 30:9; Eccl. 3:20; 12:7; etc.).[29] Man and woman are intimately, even intrinsically, bound to the ground beneath their feet. In viewing the ground we behold the essential substance from which our bodies are formed. Even the Hebrew terms underline this connection, *'ădāmâ* being the word for 'ground', and *'ādām* for 'human being'. Accordingly, the ground makes a fitting figure for humankind in general.[30]

When Jesus wrote on the ground, therefore, he was writing on something that represented human nature, and the words he was writing on it were those of a curse. What else could his actions mean other than that the entire race of humankind was affected by the same all-embracing curse? I believe that this was the point he intended to communicate, and that those men who witnessed it understood his meaning, or at least they eventually did. As Pharisees and scribes they would have been perfectly familiar with the ordinance of Numbers 5,[31] as well as with the significance of the ground in terms of the Genesis creation. They themselves had claimed that it was the ignorant

---

[29] In Ps. 30 the psalmist protests: 'What profit is there in my blood, in my going down to the pit? Will the dust praise you? Will it proclaim your faithfulness?' (v. 9). Note that in the poetic diction here 'dust' is personified, indicating the state of dead humanity.

[30] It is interesting to recall that in the parable of the sower it is the ground that receives the seed of the word of God. Since the actual recipients are men and women, Jesus would seem to have this same figurative connotation in mind.

[31] Later in the Mishnah, a compendium of the oral law, a whole treatise, called *Sotah* ('a woman who has gone astray'; cf. Num. 5:12), was devoted to this particular ordinance of the Torah.

'mob' which was cursed, but Jesus was correcting this and reminding them that in fact the whole of humanity was under a curse, themselves included.

At the figural level, those men who had a short while before pronounced a curse upon the Jewish common folk enact a significant role in the *pericope adulterae* that follows. In bringing the woman to Jesus they are playing the role of the husband in the original law, for it is he that brings forth his wife for judgment (Num. 5:15). Taken in its figural sense, if the woman to whom he is espoused is Israel, then the husband represents God. The Lord himself, the spiritual 'husband' of the nation, is the one who experiences the jealousy and brings the woman. Yet in John 8 it is the Pharisees who take on this responsibility. Viewed in the light of the allusions to the Numbers ordinance, it is they who figurally assume the place of God in the matter. And this indeed is quite in keeping with the preceding Gospel passage, in which they declare the people 'accursed' (7:49). For that act too is legitimately something that only God can carry out. In their words there is perhaps an echo of the original curse in Eden. The term they use, namely *epikataratos*, repeats the term used in God's post-fall declaration of the curse (Gen. 3:14).[32]

In two respects, then, in the act of cursing the people and in bringing the woman forward, the Pharisees are implicitly taking upon themselves the role of God himself. But Jesus soon puts them in their proper place. By writing the curse on the ground itself, he symbolically reminds them of the absolute nature of the curse. All of humanity falls within its influence, the adulterous woman and the Pharisees alike. It is not with God that these self-righteous and self-important men should be identified, but with the sinful woman. Like her they too are all sinners. The older ones among them, as perhaps having more insight than their juniors, cannot deny the truth of what Christ's actions imply and are the first to quit the scene (John 8:9). It is precisely at this point in the narration of the incident that the phrase 'being convicted by their conscience' occurs, echoing the phrase 'the water of conviction' from the law in Numbers. The ritual, in its figural sense, has been applied to the accusers, and it has been effective. They stand convicted.

This chapter has hopefully demonstrated that the *pericope adulterae* makes good sense in its context. That is not to claim its originality, which is a separate issue, since it could still possibly have been added later, by John or his associates, as a supplementary unit to that concluding John 7. Nevertheless, its interpretation, along the lines proposed here, shows just how powerful its message is

---

[32] This Edenic curse is significantly of the 'ground' (*'ădāmâ*), another reminder of the relationship between human beings and the earth.

when placed in its traditional location. Through the allusions to the law of Numbers 5, which itself offers a figural interpretation, the episode concerning the adulterous woman also presents us with a considerable depth of symbolism. By means of symbolic actions, relating back to this law, Jesus is proving that the Pharisees, and by way of implication all who share in the same attitude, are ill-advised to condemn other sinners for their conduct when they themselves are equally guilty. To me, the disputed pericope, however we might understand its origins, is a masterpiece in its meaningful blending together of both allusion and symbolism.

16
The conversion of Zacchaeus
Luke 19:1–10

In this short chapter we will examine the well-known passage in Luke's Gospel about a tax collector named Zacchaeus.[1] This man, we recall, is the rather short fellow who needs to climb a tree in order to see Jesus passing by, and who later entertains Jesus in his home (19:3–4). His genuine repentance and coming to faith is indicated by his own words: 'Look, Lord, I give half of my possessions to the poor, and if I have cheated anyone out of anything, I will give back four times the amount' (19:8). At this Jesus responds, 'Today salvation has come to this house, because he too is a son of Abraham' (v. 9).

It is here proposed that forming a backdrop to the account of Zacchaeus there are the Old Testament passages concerning the figure of Rahab that are found in the early part of the book of Joshua, particularly in chapters 2 and 6.

On the surface, the Old Testament character and the New seem quite distinct. One is a Gentile, a Canaanite, the other a Jew. One is a woman, the other a man. Yet both of them, as we shall see, would be viewed extremely negatively by the Jewish people in general.

One obvious connection between Rahab and Zacchaeus is that both were inhabitants of precisely the same city, Jericho (Josh. 2:1; Luke 19:1), the former when it was a Canaanite settlement, the latter a long time later when it was a Jewish habitation.

Significantly, there is also a major protagonist in each wider context who bears the same name and a comparable role. The Rahab story is set against the background of the advance westwards towards Jericho of Joshua at the head of the twelve tribes of Israel (e.g. Josh. 4:8). At one point in that narrative the nation is represented symbolically by means of twelve individual men.[2] The Zacchaeus episode depicts the arrival in Jericho of Jesus, likewise journeying west, with his twelve disciples (cf. Luke 18:31, 'the Twelve'). As previously noted, the names

---

[1] Some older English versions (e.g. AV) call tax collectors 'publicans'.
[2] See Josh. 3:12 ('twelve men from the tribes of Israel').

Joshua and Jesus go back to an identical original name. Both leading figures, therefore, are called *Iēsous* in Greek.

With respect to the time of year, we find that the events in each account take place shortly before the feast of Passover (Josh. 5:10; Luke 22:1).

Already in these details we have a considerable resemblance: the same exact location, the same time of year, the leader with the same name, the group of twelve that he leads, and the two characters in focus being of such a kind that was despised by the Jews. These facts alone establish a strong association between the two narratives. But there are a number of other features that bind them together even more closely.

The characters in question, in both cases, show hospitality to some who have arrived in their home town. At this point the verbal parallels between the LXX text of Joshua and the Greek of the New Testament are very much alike. Regarding the Israelite spies we read that 'they entered into the house of a prostitute whose name was Rahab, and lodged there' (Josh. 2:1). Here the verbal phrases are 'entered the house' (*eisēlthosan eis oikian*) and 'lodged there' (*katelusan ekei*).[3] The same sequence, 'enter' and 'lodge' (not a common verb) appears in Luke's narrative: 'He has entered in to lodge . . .' (*eisēlthen katalusai*), containing precisely the same two verbs (19:7).

Rahab is noted for the fact that she took in the Israelite spies. Looking slightly further afield for a moment, we find that when this act is taken up in the epistle of James as an example of good deeds, the apostle says that 'she received [*hupodexamenē*] the messengers' (2:25).[4] Luke uses similar language of Zacchaeus, who 'received' (*hupedexato*) Jesus gladly (19:6). Though not directly taken from the text of Joshua, the occurrence of the verb 'receive' as an act of welcome predicated to Rahab elsewhere strengthens the idea that the account of Zacchaeus was written with her in mind.

Both accounts give prominence to the 'house' of the host (Josh. 2:1, 3, 15, 18 [*eis tēn oikian sou*], 19 [*en tē oikia sou*]; Luke 19:5 [*en tō oikō sou*], 9). Together with this, the narratives speak explicitly of those people or things that belong to Rahab and Zacchaeus. This fact is slightly obscured in translation. In connection with Rahab, the phrase 'all that was hers' is found twice (6:22, 23). In Hebrew this may denote either persons or property. The LXX translators here decided to render this phrase by *hosa estin autē*, that is, 'what things were hers'. The same phrase, however, could equally well have been translated using the noun *huparchonta*, meaning 'possessions'. This is actually how the same Hebrew

---

[3] The first of these is repeated two verses later: 'the men who entered your house' (v. 3).

[4] The writer to the Hebrews expresses the same idea: 'Rahab . . . having received [*dexamenē*] the spies in peace' (11:31).

phrase is rendered in the following chapter (7:24, *panta ta huparchonta autou*) and a good number of other places (e.g. Gen. 25:5; 39:5; 45:11). In the Lukan passage (19:8) Zacchaeus makes mention of 'my possessions' (*mou tōn huparchontōn*).

Each narrative results in the character's deliverance, together with his or her household: '. . . that you will deliver us from death' (Josh. 2:13); 'Joshua let Rahab the prostitute live, with her family . . .' (6:25); 'Today salvation has come to this house' (Luke 19:9), obviously meaning the household, that is, the family. This is a significant outcome, for in each case there is an element of unexpectancy at such a thing, according to the prevailing Hebrew view.

From the foregoing we see that the Gospel passage clearly intends that its readers associate the conversion of Zacchaeus, a Jew, with that of Rahab, a Gentile.[5] Perhaps the main reason for this association lies in the fact that in contemporary Jewish society tax collectors were seen as collaborators with their Roman masters, and therefore, although Jews, they were regarded with much the same disdain as the Gentiles. We detect this from certain sayings of Jesus, which reflect, no doubt, not his own attitude but how the Jews generally viewed such people. In the Sermon on the Mount he said:

> For if you love those who love you, what reward do you have? Do not even the tax collectors do the same? If you greet only your brothers, what are you doing more than others? Do not even the Gentiles do the same? (Matt. 5:46–47)

Observe the parallelism here between 'tax collectors' and 'Gentiles'. Later, regarding a fellow Christian who has sinned against another and refuses to be reconciled, Jesus said: 'Let him be to you as a Gentile and a tax collector' (Matt. 18:17). Again the two classes of people are grouped together. It is important therefore to appreciate from the outset how Zacchaeus would have been seen by other Jews, especially as he was in fact a *'chief* tax collector' (Luke 19:2).[6] The pairing of 'tax collectors and sinners' is also commonly found (e.g. Matt. 9:10–11; 11:19; Luke 7:34; 15:1). The term 'sinners' frequently appears in the Gospels for those not adhering to the Mosaic law. Among such, for sure, would

---

[5] Although overlooked by modern commentators, the connection was, however, appreciated in the patristic age. One of the Greek Church Fathers, Amphilochius of Iconium (*c.* AD 340–400), in his address *On Zacchaeus* (*Patrologia Graeca* 39), notes the relationship and particularly makes much of their both, in a sense, having 'received Jesus'. See H. F. Stander, 'The Greek Church Fathers and Rahab', *Acta Patristica et Byzantina* 17 (2006): 44.

[6] In keeping with this the Mishnah declares that 'If a tax collector enters a house, the house is unclean' (*Tahoroth* 7.6).

have been women of ill repute, that is, prostitutes. Note the comment of the Pharisee about the woman who wiped Christ's feet with her hair: 'If this man were a prophet, he would have known who and what kind of woman this is who is touching him – for she is a sinner' (Luke 7:39).

Now the Greek Old Testament narrative labels Rahab a *pornē*, a 'prostitute' (Josh. 2:1), a fact which is reiterated in the New (Heb. 11:31; Jas 2:25).[7] Rahab was a woman, then, who without doubt would be classed as a 'sinner', doubly so since she was also a Canaanite. Neither a tax collector, nor a prostitute, especially not a Canaanite one, would, to the first-century Jewish mind, be characters expected to find a place in the kingdom of God. As we saw when discussing the Syro-Phoenician woman, in Old Testament times the Canaanites had been consigned to death or banishment,[8] and at the time of Jesus tax collectors were considered as being beyond the pale.[9]

By echoing the account concerning Rahab, the Gospel of Luke is, with subtle skill, reminding its readers that long ago even an actual Gentile 'sinner' was welcomed into the congregation of Israel.[10] If God could show mercy to a Canaanite prostitute, then how much more to an ethnic Jew, despite the many immoral acts, especially of extortion, of which he was evidently guilty (Luke 19:8). Though his previous deeds may have made him, in effect, a Gentile in the eyes of his fellow Jews, the case of Rahab provides grounds for believing that such a person could nevertheless be saved. So, despite popular opinion regarding Zacchaeus, expressed in the present context through the grumbling of the onlookers (v. 7, 'a man who is a sinner'), Jesus reinstates him as a genuine 'son of Abraham' (v. 9).[11]

---

[7] The particular profession in which Rahab engaged herself has, by some, been altered to that of innkeeper on the basis of a possible second meaning of the Hebrew term (*zônâ*). The Greek term (*pornē*), however, allows no such move. See the discussion in Robert G. Boling and G. Ernest Wright, *Joshua: A New Translation with Introduction and Commentary* (AB 6; New York, NY: Doubleday, 1982), 144.

[8] See chapter 12.

[9] See Darrell L. Bock, *Luke 1:1–9:50* (BECNT 3A; Grand Rapids, MI: Baker, 1994), 312.

[10] Cf. Josh. 6:25, 'she lives among the Israelites to this day'.

[11] It is interesting to observe that Rahab is brought into proximity to the Hebrew patriarch Abraham in two passages of the New Testament. In Matt. 1 her name appears in the genealogy that extends from Abraham to Christ (v. 5), while in Jas 2 she is cited alongside Abraham as an example of one justified by her deeds (v. 25). Perhaps one could therefore say that Rahab was a spiritual daughter of Abraham.

17

Jesus comes to Jerusalem

Matthew 21:1–10; Mark 11:1–11; Luke 19:28–44; John 12:12–19

We next consider the arrival of Jesus in Jerusalem a few days before the climax of his ministry in the crucifixion and resurrection. This event is related by all four Gospel-writers, who give much attention to the manner of his approach to the city. The occasion of the 'triumphal entry', as it is often called, is well known to Bible readers, when Jesus made his entrance into Jerusalem on the back of a donkey to the acclaim of the crowds. At the literal level this was accomplished in fulfilment of the prophecy in Zechariah: 'Rejoice greatly, O daughter of Zion! Shout aloud, O daughter of Jerusalem! Behold, your king comes to you; he is just and able to save, humble and riding on a donkey, on a colt, the foal of a donkey' (9:9). This prophetic fulfilment aspect is highlighted in two of the Gospels (Matt. 21:5; John 12:15).

Alongside the prophetic significance of this important event, there is also the presence of allusions to the ancient Scriptures of Israel, functioning at a deeper level. A recognition of these will once again give a more profound under-standing of the episode in question. On this particular occasion, the portion of the Old Testament to which allusion is being made is that which relates the approach of Joshua and the Israelites to the city of Jericho as appears in the early chapters of the book of Joshua (Josh. 1 – 6). There we read how Joshua and the people of Israel crossed the River Jordan and drew near to Jericho, which was subsequently destroyed. As in all cases discussed in this volume, the Gospel accounts in question can be seen to allude to the earlier text through a variety of means.

To begin, we encounter once again the all-important fact that the chief protagonists in each narrative bear the selfsame name. Mention has been made several times before that the name *Iēsous*, the Greek designation for 'Jesus' in the New Testament, also translates the Hebraic 'Joshua'.[1] The connection

---

[1] See chapters 3, 12 and 16.

between the figures of Jesus and Joshua is made more apparent by several of the accompanying circumstances.

We observe an essential likeness in the topographical framework of each narrative. With regard to both events, the main protagonist approaches a major walled city of the same land from an easterly direction. There are in fact several similarities in the details here. Joshua came from the eastern side of the Jordan Valley, across the river, and on to the city of Jericho. This latter city, significantly, appears in all three synoptic Gospels as being the place Jesus visited immediately prior to his arrival at Jerusalem (Matt. 20:19–34; Mark 10:46–52; Luke 19:1–10). So, along with the name 'Jesus', the previous 'Jericho' context contributes somewhat to establishing a link with the Joshua 1 – 6 narrative. Moreover, now that Jesus approaches his city, he too has traversed a valley, that lying to the east of Jerusalem, and must needs have crossed the Brook Kidron at some point in his journey (cf. John 18:1), as Joshua crossed the Jordan.[2]

Further still, this final stretch of Christ's journey began, we are told, in the environs of Bethany (Mark 11:1), about one and a half miles to the east of Jerusalem. What is noteworthy about this is that it would bring to the minds of those readers familiar with the geography of the Holy Land a different Bethany. We are informed of another place having the identical name located 'across the Jordan' (John 1:28), that is to say, on its eastern bank, in the approximate locality from which Joshua and Israel passed westwards. In fact, the descriptive phrase found in the Gospel locating this other Bethany, *peran tou Iordanou*, is one that appears several times in the Joshua narrative, in its Greek version, with reference to the area where that earlier journey commenced (e.g. Josh. 1:15; 2:10). In sum, therefore, we have in the Old Testament account Joshua crossing a river from the east, where there would later be a location called Bethany, and coming to the city of Jericho, while in the Gospel narrative we have another Joshua who, having come from the east via Jericho, takes his departure from the vicinity of a second Bethany to cross another watercourse on his approach to the city of Jerusalem. Surely, these connections would not be lost on the attentive early Jewish readers of the Gospels.

The principal character, of course, is not travelling alone. One comes at the head of the twelve tribes of Israel, the other accompanied by twelve disciples

---

[2] This watercourse is strictly a wadi, and therefore seasonal. Since the primary rainy season in Israel is in January and February, and lasts until the middle of March, there can be no doubt that Kidron flowed with water at this time, which was probably in the latter half of March, shortly before Passover. Early Jewish writings (e.g. Mishnah, *Middot* 3.2) speak of the blood of the Passover lambs sacrificed in the temple flowing down to mingle with the water in Kidron. See Brant Pitre, 'Jesus, the New Temple, and the New Priesthood', *Letter & Spirit* 4 (2008): 65. We observe that at Israel's crossing of the Jordan the river was in full flood (Josh. 3:15) at this same season.

and a multitude (arguably the beginnings of the new Israel). We pointed out in the foregoing chapter that the former narrative does distinguish 'twelve men', men specifically appointed by Joshua (Josh. 3:12; 4:2, 4), as representing the whole.

Temporally speaking, each account describes events occurring around the time of the Passover (Josh. 5:10–11; cf. Mark 14:1; John 12:1). The earlier account, which relates events transpiring over a period of several days, actually contains a precise date. We are informed that 'the people came up from the Jordan on the tenth of the first month and camped at Gilgal on the eastern edge of Jericho' (Josh. 4:19). This would be the tenth day of the month Nisan. While mention of this does not strictly fall within the ambit of allusion, as far as the present chapter is concerned, what is extraordinary about this time reference is that it is one of the dates traditionally given for the entry of Christ into Jerusalem.[3] Whether this is accurate or not, there evidently remains, at any event, a close association in the calendrical placement of the two narratives.

A notable correspondence of language can be seen in the sending out of two men before the main event: 'Joshua son of Nun sent [apesteilen . . . Iēsous] two [dyo] men . . . saying [legōn] . . . they went [poreuthentes]' (Josh. 2:1); as compared with: 'Jesus sent [Iēsous apesteilen] two [dyo] disciples, saying [legōn] . . . they went [poreuthentes]' (Matt. 21:1–2, 6). The verbal connections here are extremely close, the five lexical items Iēsous, apesteilen, dyo, legōn, and poreuthentes, playing a part in both narratives and, it should be stressed, in precisely the same grammatical forms. This would be hard to explain as mere coincidence. In this context we also draw attention to the term 'opposite' (katenanti)[4] in all three synoptic accounts used in connection with the place to which the two disciples are sent (Matt. 21:2; Mark 11:2; Luke 19:2). This alludes to the comparable phrase 'opposite Jericho' appearing in the Old Testament record (Josh. 3:16, apenanti; cf. Deut. 34:1). Both pairs of men are therefore sent by their leader, Joshua–Jesus, to a place opposite them.

In ancient times Jericho was known as 'the city of palms [phoinikōn]' (Deut. 34:3; cf. Judg. 1:16 etc.). When going up to Jerusalem the crowds accompanying

---

[3] There is some evidence to suggest that, prior to the Council of Nicea, 10 Nisan was the commonly held date for the observance of Palm Sunday. See H. St John Thackeray, *The Septuagint and Jewish Worship: A Study in Origins* (London: Oxford University Press, 1921), 111. This same date is still widely advocated; cf. Darrell L. Bock and Mitch Glaser, *Messiah in the Passover* (Grand Rapids, MI: Kregel, 2017), 85; and Kenneth F. Doig, *New Testament Chronology* (Lewiston, NY: Edwin Mellen, 1990), who states that 'Nisan 10 was the day for the selection of the Paschal lamb to be sacrificed for the Passover supper (Exodus 12:3). On that day Jesus entered Jerusalem riding on a colt' (available online at <www.nowoezone.com/NTC20.htm> [accessed 23 Jan. 2023]).

[4] The Byzantine Text, the Greek text contained in the majority of later manuscripts, has the synonym *apenanti* in Matt. 21:2.

Jesus were holding 'branches of palms [*phoinikōn*]' (John 12:13; cf. Matt. 21:8; Mark 11:8). It is, of course, from this particularly visually prominent detail that the designation 'Palm Sunday' for the day of this event was later derived. And so, while Jerusalem in itself has no special association with palms, through this great mass of people bearing the branches of such trees and spreading them on the road, it is temporarily transformed for this occasion to become, as it were, a metaphorical city of palms.

An important element in the Joshua passage is that the host of Israel were instructed to 'shout' (Josh. 6:5 [*anakragontōn*], 16 [*kekraxate*], 20 also) as they paraded around the city. The crowds attending Jesus did the same thing as they processed towards the city (Matt. 21:9 [*ekrazon*]; Mark 11:9 [*ekrazon*]; John 12:13 [*ekraugazon*]). Not only this, but the same phrase 'with a great shout', descriptive of the manner in which the people gave voice, occurs in both accounts (Josh. 6:5; Luke 19:37). Accordingly, the Joshua figure is accompanied in each narrative by a shouting multitude.

A major component of the earlier narrative is the fact that the city is encircled and subsequently collapses (Josh. 6:3–5, 7, 11, 13, 14–15, 20). Note especially the verb appearing in the clause, 'all the rest of the people encircled [*periekyklōse*] the city' (v. 13). In Luke's version of the triumphal entry, the author appends an additional section beginning, 'As he [Jesus] drew near, he saw the city and wept over it' (19:41). In the words of Jesus that follow he addresses the city, foretelling the event in which Jerusalem's enemies would 'encircle [*perikyklōsousin*] you and close you in on every side' (v. 43). This is the sole New Testament occurrence of this particular verb. Both cities, then, were to be encircled by their enemies as a prelude to their destruction.

Within this same aforementioned Lukan section, in speaking to Jerusalem Jesus further declares that her enemies 'will level you to the ground . . . and will not leave in you one stone upon another' (19:44). Though there is no direct lexical relationship, what is here foretold for the Judean capital is distinctly reminiscent of the fate that befell Old Testament Jericho.[5]

One final element worthy of note is that towards the end of the Jericho narrative, there comes the uttering of a curse by Joshua in connection with the city (Josh. 6:26, *epikataratos*, 'cursed'). In Mark's version the entry into Jerusalem is immediately followed by Jesus' cursing of the fig tree (11:12–14, 20–21, *katērasō*,[6]

---

[5] We also note in Luke the use of the verb *parembalousin*, 'throw up a fortification' (19:43), with respect to Jerusalem's encircling enemies. This possibly echoes the repeated *parembolē*, 'encampment', of the Hebrews outside Jericho in the Joshua account (e.g. 6:11, 14, 18).

[6] From the verb *kataraomai*.

'you cursed'), a recognized symbol of the Jewish state which the city of Jerusalem embodied.[7]

What, then, do these literary associations contribute to our understanding of the episode in the Gospels? There are perhaps two distinct matters that arise from their presence. First, there are the two places in question. A clear correspondence is being drawn between the cities of Jericho and Jerusalem. What is remarkable about this is that one is a Canaanite city, the first to be destroyed in the Promised Land, while the other is the holy city of God, the focal centre of divine worship for the Jewish nation. To the Judaic mind in the first century it would have been hard to conceive of two more different cities. Such allusions to Jericho in the Gospel passages can only mean that Jerusalem is being presented in an extremely negative light. By means of this literary device the narrative is stating, in effect, that the civil and religious capital of Judea had fallen to such a depth of moral and spiritual degradation that a drastic comparison of this nature was warranted. Such a comparison must have struck home deeply with those Jewish readers who detected the allusions. Not only had the capital of the Jews failed to live up to its calling and function as the dwelling-place of God in his temple, but also the city was equally as depraved as that of the Canaanites before them, who had been subject to divine destruction on account of their abominable practices. Jerusalem had become, to all intents and purposes, a pagan city, a virtual Jericho.

As a consequence of Jerusalem's state being comparable to that of Jericho, there comes a comparable destruction. While this punishment is depicted in similar terms, with not one stone left standing on another, there is at this point a notable difference. What transpired at Jericho happened there and then, upon the arrival of Joshua and the Israelite tribes with him. With regard to Jerusalem, however, the judgment spoken of overtly in the lamentation of Jesus (Luke 19:43–44), and signified more covertly through the series of allusions, is not instant. Rather, this latter-day Joshua is foretelling a destruction to come. Evidently, the reference is to the Roman overthrow of Jerusalem in AD 70, four decades later. The Jewish population of the city, therefore, are given an opportunity that the inhabitants of Jericho did not, by and large, receive.[8] The ancient Canaanite city was consigned to immediate destruction, while the later

---

[7] Cf. C. E. B. Cranfield, *The Gospel According to St. Mark: An Introduction and Commentary* (Cambridge: Cambridge University Press, 1959), 356–357. Cranfield states, making reference to the commentary of Victor of Antioch, that 'the withering of the fig tree was an acted parable in which Jesus "used the fig tree to set forth the judgement that was about to befall Jerusalem"'.

[8] With the exception of Rahab, who hid the Hebrew spies and was subsequently delivered along with her family, as discussed in the preceding chapter.

had a period of grace in which to repent. During this interval several thousand people at least, as we learn from the early chapters of Acts (e.g. 4:4), availed themselves of this opportunity.[9]

Lastly, we may discern another aspect to the allusions, one that is highly consequential, this time relating to the person of Jesus himself. One conspicuous item in the Jericho narrative that has not yet received any mention is the ark of the covenant. As the Israelites marched around the city this sacred object was transported in their midst, preceded by one portion of the people (Josh. 6:6–8) and followed by the remainder (6:9). Both groups are mentioned together in Joshua 6:13 (here cited according to the MT):

The seven priests carrying the seven trumpets of rams' horns before the ark of the LORD went on continually and blew the trumpets; and the armed men went before them and the rear guard came after the ark of the LORD.

From this we see that there were those among the people who 'went before' and those who 'came after' the ark. Now with regard to the person of Jesus himself, the Gospel records speak of 'the crowds going before him and those that followed' (Matt. 21:9; Mark 11:9).

It would appear, then, that through the allusions appearing in the Gospel accounts it is Jesus who is made to occupy the place of the ark in the Old Testament narrative. This connection is perhaps more understandable in the light of the fact that the Greek text of the LXX actually renders the Hebrew 'before the ark of the LORD' as simply *enantion kyriou*, 'before the Lord' (Josh. 6:7, 13; cf. 7:6). The sacred object is described by a phrase denoting a divine person, which person in the Gospels is Jesus himself. Thus the literary allusion we have detected in the Gospel accounts is polyvalent with respect to the figure of Jesus. That is to say, the one Jesus of the New Testament narrative corresponds to not just one but two elements in the earlier account, a feature we have observed several times elsewhere. Jesus is here presented both as Joshua, the human leader of Israel, and as the ark, the token of God's presence among his people.[10] Jesus does not only carry out the role that Joshua played in the Old Testament narrative; in addition, as the Word incarnate, he is the divine presence in the midst of his people, alluded to in the crowds processing before and after him

---

[9] Not only were the members of the early Jewish-Christian community in Jerusalem saved spiritually, but they were also afforded the opportunity of physical deliverance from the devastation of the city through the prior warning of Jesus to flee to the mountains (Matt. 24:16).

[10] Cf. John I. Durham, *Exodus* (WBC 3; Waco, TX: Word, 1987), 360.

in their approach to Jerusalem, shouting with loud voices, as the hosts of Israel did with respect to the ark before Jericho.[11] Here is one further instance of allusion that would appear to underscore the fact of Christ's deity.

[11] By implication, therefore, it would have to be understood that it is Jesus who would later bring about the downfall of Jerusalem. This, I believe, is how we are to interpret Rev. 6:16 (cf. Luke 23:30).

18

The parable of the wicked tenants

Matthew 21:33–46; Mark 12:1–12; Luke 20:9–19

In this chapter we consider the parabolic teaching of Jesus concerning certain evil tenants, recorded in a text sometimes also referred to as the parable of the vineyard. It seems to have been told on the day after his triumphal entry into Jerusalem. The context in all three of the Gospels which include the parable is very clearly that of conflict with the religious leaders, who have just questioned his authority (Matt. 21:23–27; Mark 11:27–33; Luke 20:1–8).[1] Each rendition of the parable also ends up with the same leaders looking for a way to seize Jesus (Matt. 21:46; Mark 12:12; Luke 20:19).

The parable concerns a landowner who planted a vineyard and provided it with all that was necessary. He then rented out the plot to tenant farmers (Matt. 21:33; Mark 12:1; Luke 20:9). At harvest time he sent messengers to the tenants to claim his share of the produce (Matt. 21:34; Mark 12:2; Luke 20:10a). These men were beaten and even killed. So the owner sent more messengers, who met the same fate (Matt. 21:35–36; Mark 12:3–5; Luke 20:10b–12). Lastly, he decided to send his son to them, thinking that they would respect him (Matt. 21:37; Mark 12:6; Luke 20:13). But when they saw him coming they determined to kill him and take his inheritance. The tenants took hold of the son and murdered him (Matt. 21:38–39; Mark 12:7–8; Luke 20:14–15a). After telling the parable Jesus poses the question, 'When the owner of the vineyard comes, what will he do to those tenants?' (Matt. 21:40; cf. Mark 12:9; Luke 20:15b). His audience replies that 'he will bring those wretches to a wretched end' and then 'he will rent out the vineyard to other tenants, who will give him his share of the produce at the proper seasons' (Matt. 21:41).

The plain meaning of the parable is not hard to deduce. Once Jesus has finished speaking here, we next read that: 'The scribes and the chief priests looked for a way to arrest him immediately, because they knew he had spoken

---

[1] The intervening parable of Matt. 21:28–32 is on a similar theme to that concerning the wicked tenants, the older son indicating those Jews who refused to respond to Christ with faith.

this parable against them' (Luke 20:19). The leaders understood that the vineyard was the nation of Israel and that they themselves were the tenant farmers to whom its owner, God, had entrusted it. The image of the vineyard, or vine, representing Israel, would have been well known from Old Testament passages such as Isaiah 5:1–7 and Psalm 80:8–19. It would not have been difficult for the rulers to have recognized the messengers as the prophets whom their ancestors had rejected,[2] and that Jesus was presenting himself as the owner's son.

It is here proposed that beneath the surface of the parable, Jesus is making allusions to a particular Old Testament character, this being the patriarch Joseph, specifically in the context of his dealings with his brothers as recorded in Genesis 37.[3]

Once pointed out, the connections with the Joseph narrative seem, to me at least, to be quite unambiguous. In the parable, the owner has a son, showing the owner to also be a father. His son is described as 'a beloved [*agapēton*] son' (Mark 12:6; Luke 20:13). In Genesis 37 we encounter the father figure of Jacob, of whom it says that, while having many sons, 'he loved [*ēgapa*] Joseph more than all his other sons' (v. 3). Because of this special love, and because of the divine revelations Joseph received that foretold his pre-eminence over them, these other sons hated their brother (v. 4) and were jealous of him (v. 11).

The occasion came when, as the brothers were together out in the countryside grazing the flocks, Jacob, the father, sent Joseph to his brothers. 'Come,' he said, 'I am going to send you [*aposteilō*] to them [*pros autous*]' (Gen. 37:13), and so 'he sent [*apesteilen auton*] him' (v. 14). In a similar fashion, in the parable the landowner declares his intention to send his son to the tenants (Luke 20:13), and then 'he sent [*apesteilen auton*] him to them [*pros autous*]' (Mark 12:6; cf. Matt. 21:37).

As Joseph came to the place where his brothers were, the text says: 'When they saw him from a distance . . . they plotted against him to put him to death' (Gen. 37:18). They said to one another, 'Come, let us kill him' (v. 20), where in the Greek version these latter words are *deute apokteinōmen auton*. In the parable the tenants likewise see the son coming, and say to one another, 'Come, let us kill him' (Matt. 21:38; Mark 12:7; cf. Luke 20:14). Here we find exactly the same words, *deute apokteinōmen auton*, as spoken by Joseph's brothers.[4]

---

[2] Cf. Matt. 23:34.

[3] Samuel Emadi has recently affirmed the same connection; see *From Prisoner to Prince: The Joseph Story in Biblical Theology* (NSBT 59; London: Apollos, 2022), 138–145. Emadi presents a list of scholarly publications that maintain such a view (142, n. 54).

[4] The resemblance is not just in the exact correspondence of what they say but also in the preceding sequence of 'saw . . . said to one another', adding even more confirmation to the intentional nature of the verbal echo.

The connection is enforced by the fact that the parable next continues with the words *kai labontes auton*, 'and taking hold of him' (Matt. 21:39; cf. Mark 12:8), identical to the phrase, *kai labontes auton*, that appears in the Greek version of the Joseph account (Gen. 37:24).

At this point in each story there is a significant divergence in detail. In Genesis the brothers planned to kill Joseph, but in fact did not carry it through. 'For he is our brother,' they say, 'our own flesh and blood' (37:27). Apparently, their kinship to Joseph pulled them back from the brink of murder, and they sold him as a slave instead. However, since the report they gave to their father made it seem as though Joseph were actually dead (vv. 33–34), and as they did not know what would become of him following his subjection to slavery, Joseph became, as far as his family were concerned, as good as dead (cf. 42:13, 32). Later in the account, the brothers stated categorically that Benjamin's brother, Joseph, was 'dead' (44:20), for so they conceived him in effect to be. By way of contrast, in the Gospel parable the son who is sent is said to actually be killed (Matt. 21:39; Mark 12:8; Luke 20:15). What the wicked tenants plan to do, they carry out. This is a noteworthy distinction.

In short, then, both the Joseph episode and Christ's story contain a series of major elements in common. Both concern a father sending a son, one especially loved, to a group of ill-disposed persons who, when they see him coming, declare their intention to kill him. They then seize the son and dispose of him, in the one case by selling him into slavery, making him to all intents and purposes 'dead', while in the other they really do take his life.

To reiterate the primary level of meaning, as stated above, the son in the parable represents Jesus himself, and it is a parable concerning his rejection. This can be known for certain from the fact that the parable is immediately followed by a citation from Psalm 118:22–23 regarding 'the stone that the builders rejected' (Matt. 21:42; Mark 12:10; Luke 20:17), a prophetic reference to Jesus (cf. Acts 4:11; 1 Pet. 2:7). This means that the vineyard owner in the parable, the one who sends his son, is God the Father, and the tenants are the religious leaders of the Jews who are presently confronting Jesus and plotting against him.

Into this situation, through subtle literary allusion, comes the Old Testament character of Joseph, particularly in relation to his brothers, the sons of Israel.[5] The account of Genesis 37 presents Joseph as an especially beloved son of his father, of whom the others were jealous, aggravated by the fact that he received special revelations telling of his future supremacy over his brothers. Jesus came

---

[5] 'Israel', of course, being Jacob's other name (Gen. 32:28).

to the Jews as the 'Son of God',[6] being the one foretold in the prophetic oracles, and he spoke as one with greater authority than even the Jewish religious leaders. This provoked them to envy (cf. Matt. 27:18; Mark 15:10).

As the tenants of the vineyard determined to do away with the owner's son, so the Jewish leaders sought to dispose of Jesus. The two respective groups had the same evil intentions. Yet at this point we encounter an important difference. Whereas Joseph's brothers, when it comes to it, cannot bring themselves to murder one of their own, the Jewish rulers can. These latter have no qualms about ridding themselves of Jesus once and for all. While the former handed their brother over to Gentiles for enslavement (Gen. 37:28), the latter delivered up one of their own to Gentiles for execution (Matt. 27:2).[7] The discontinuity between the two therefore has a particularly important point to make. It is, in effect, declaring that the present Jewish authorities are acting far more harshly than Joseph's brothers, who, although jealous and filled with hate, at the end of the day relented from such a heinous act.

Another element within the parable, related to the foregoing, is that of the coming retribution on the part of the owner, the murdered son's father. The Genesis account culminated in the eventual reconciliation of Joseph and his brothers (Gen. 45:1–15). For them there was restoration. The parable, however, speaks of judgment. The more severe reception of the 'son' entails a more severe outcome for those who violently rejected him. For those 'wretched' tenants, responsible for his death, there will be a 'wretched end', and the vineyard will be given over to other tenants (Matt. 21:41). In the 'stone' analogy that immediately follows, those who reject this stone 'will be broken to pieces . . . and be crushed' (v. 44). The reference here is no doubt to the events of AD 70 when the whole religious and political system of the Jews would cease with the destruction of Jerusalem and the temple at the hands of the Romans. In murdering Christ, the Son, the Jewish leaders would seal the terrible fate of the nation.[8]

---

[6] Craig Blomberg suggests that Jesus' identification of the 'son' with himself in this parable 'is probably his first public claim to be the "Son of God"' (Craig L. Blomberg, *Matthew: An Exegetical and Theological Exposition of Holy Scripture* [NAC 22; Nashville, TN: Broadman, 1992], 323). This may be true, at least as far as the synoptic Gospels are concerned. Shortly afterwards, in Matt. 22:41–46, Jesus more openly affirms his divine sonship in his treatment of Ps. 110:1, and this specific issue seems to be one of the chief reasons for his condemnation by the Sanhedrin (26:63).

[7] This corresponding detail, the handing over to the Gentiles, ostensibly falls outside the scope of the parable Jesus is telling. It is, however, one of several other links between Joseph and Christ that suggest the former to be a 'type', or prefigurement, of the latter. See, e.g., Sidney Greidanus, *Preaching Christ from Genesis: Foundations for Expository Sermons* (Grand Rapids, MI: Eerdmans, 2007), 344.

[8] This is not to deny, of course, that there would be a substantial number of Jewish followers of Christ within that state. The apostle Paul speaks of such a 'remnant' (Rom. 9:27; 11:5). Nor is it to exclude the possibility of a yet-future, eschatological deliverance of Israel (cf. Rom. 11:26).

Implicitly, for the reader familiar with the Joseph story, there is also the idea of coming vindication for Jesus himself. As Joseph's dreams of exaltation were finally realized in his being promoted to 'lord' (*kyrios*) of Egypt (Gen. 45:9), so too beyond his rejection Jesus would be even more exalted, being made 'Lord' (*kyrios*) of all (cf. Acts 2:36).

We can see, then, that the allusions to what befell the patriarch Joseph add a new interpretative dimension to the parable. The chief priests and elders of the Jews are being compared with the envious and hate-filled brothers of Joseph, and sadly found to be even worse. And so for their act of rejecting the Son, beloved of his Father, they are held to a greater account.

We will discover further Gospel allusions to the person of Joseph in later chapters.

19
The last supper

Matthew 26:17–30; Mark 14:12–26; Luke 22:7–20; John 13:1 – 14:31

The crucial event of the last supper is recounted in all three synoptic Gospels. There is no direct account of it in John, but there is at least some hint of it (cf. 13:2, 26). At this point in his narrative John instead relates a lengthy farewell discourse on the part of Jesus. Yet it would seem that this discourse commences at the same venue as the supper – in the upper room (cf. Mark 14:15). In John 14:31 Jesus says, 'Come, let us leave,' apparently indicating their departure from the location where the supper had been held. Following this the discourse continues elsewhere, probably en route to and within Gethsemane. John 13 and 14 may therefore be taken as set against the background of the last supper.

We remember how Jesus, on this evening before his death, reclines at table to share a meal with the twelve disciples. During this meal Jesus institutes the ceremony of communion, the eating of bread and the drinking of wine as symbols of his body and blood, an act which was to later be done in remembrance of him (Matt. 26:26–28; Mark 14:22–24; Luke 22:17–20). Behind this significant occasion there lie two corresponding events in the Old Testament to which allusion is made: the Passover of Exodus 12 and the ceremony that took place at Mount Sinai as narrated in Exodus 24. As the relevance of the Passover to the last supper has been discussed, at least to some degree, in a previous chapter,[1] our focus here will be on the latter event.

First and foremost is the fact that Exodus 24 and the Gospel episode in question both depict the instigation of a *covenant*. Moreover, these are not just any covenants, but the two are what we mean when we speak of the old and the new covenants, or 'Testaments', of the Bible. The former is that made at Sinai with the nation of Israel, the latter that made by Jesus with his followers on the very same day, according to Jewish reckoning,[2] that he was to be crucified. In view

---

[1] See chapter 10.

[2] Since the Jews then counted a day as the period from one sunset to another, it would mean that the last supper in the evening would be on the same calendar day as the crucifixion the following morning.

of this special place that these two passages have in common, the existence of literary connections between them should come as no surprise.

In each of the two covenants we first note the presence of one who mediates. On the occasion of the earlier covenant the mediator there was Moses, one who was placed between the people and God, and at the second there was obviously Jesus, who elsewhere in the New Testament is described as 'the mediator of a new covenant' (Heb. 9:15; 12:24).[3]

Also present, of course, was the community with which the covenant was to be made. In Exodus 24 this was the nation of Israel, made up of twelve tribes, represented in symbol by twelve pillars (v. 4). At the last supper, this was the new community of Christ, the church, there represented by the twelve disciples.[4]

At the making of the Sinai covenant an important place was given to the reciting of laws. It was expected that the Israelites should adhere to these divine regulations. Prior to Exodus 24 God had revealed to them the Ten Commandments (20:1–17), and also a series of casuistic statutes and more specific laws (21:1 – 23:19). Before the covenant ceremony Moses repeated all these laws to the people, who replied by saying that they would do everything the Lord had said (24:3). The laws were again recited during the ceremony itself (v. 7). All these laws are elsewhere summed up by the command to love (Lev. 19:18; Deut. 6:5; cf. Matt. 22:37–40). At the last supper Jesus declared a law to his disciples, which was also one related to love: 'A new commandment I give to you, that you love one another; as I have loved you, you also love one another' (John 13:34).

The ratification of the covenant entails sacrifice. At Sinai this was animal sacrifice, as is spelt out in Exodus 24:5. In the upper room, the covenant ceremony was also overtly a Passover meal, as Jesus instructed his disciples to 'prepare the Passover' there (Matt. 26:19). Under normal circumstances the sacrifice of a lamb would have been expected on such an occasion (cf. Exod. 12:1–11). However, here at the last supper it would appear that Passover and covenant institution are merged into one.[5] No ordinary Passover was being celebrated that evening. This was *the* Passover, the ultimate paschal event, which would result in more than just Israel being released from slavery to its oppressor. This meal inaugurated the deliverance of humankind from its greater bondage to sin. To attain such a goal an altogether different kind of lamb would

---

[3] Cf. Heb. 8:6, 'the mediator of a better covenant'.

[4] Later to be known as 'pillars' of the church (Gal. 2:9).

[5] It is not an uncommon feature in literary allusion, as seen elsewhere, that more than one earlier text is alluded to.

be required: 'the Lamb of God who takes away the sin of the world' (John 1:29), that is, Jesus himself. A short while after the supper, indeed later on the selfsame day, as noted, he would die that all-important sacrificial death.

In both the original Passover and the Sinai covenant ritual, the application of blood played a central part in the proceedings. On the former occasion, it was collected in a bowl and put on the doorframes of the houses where the Israelites lived (Exod. 12:7, 22). On the latter, the blood of the animal sacrifices was collected in bowls and sprinkled by Moses on the people (24:6, 8). At the last supper, in being both a Passover and the making of the new covenant, blood is also highly significant, though there is a notable difference. In this ceremony the blood of the offering is represented by wine. The bowl of literal blood of the Old Testament ceremonies becomes a chalice of symbolic blood in the new. But more importantly than that, the blood that is disposed of externally in the former, to house or people,[6] is internally disposed of in the latter. In the one the blood is applied on the outside only; in the other it is received on the inside.[7] The meaning of this is readily discerned from the fact that with respect to the blood of sacrifices 'the life . . . is in the blood' (Lev. 17:11). The blood at one and the same time spoke of the death of the sacrifice, but also of its life, since blood is life-giving.

Yet for Israel under the old covenant, the sacrifices that were merely of an animal nature were completely unable to impart life to sinful mortal humans. Hence the blood, being emblematic of life, was never consumed. When sacrifices were offered in the sanctuary the blood was poured out on the ground (cf. Lev. 1:15; 4:7; 8:15). And when the covenant was made, the blood was merely sprinkled externally on the people, showing symbolically that, though this was a covenant that bore witness to the life,[8] this was not to be the covenant that actually imparted it. But under the new covenant, Jesus offers his own blood to the people, and this time the command is 'Drink' (Matt. 26:27).[9] Life is in the blood, and those who follow Jesus drink his blood in symbol, showing forth that his life, which is an everlasting life, is now in them also.

Together with the application of the blood, another major component of the covenant-making ritual is the utterance of a particular formula of declaration. In the case of Moses at Sinai, as he sprinkled the blood on the people he pronounced the words, 'This is the blood of the covenant that the LORD has made

---

[6] The house protected by the blood of the Passover doubtless stands for those living in it. Obviously, it was not the actual house that required protection.

[7] We touched on this matter earlier in the context of the feeding of the multitude (chapter 10).

[8] Cf. Rom. 3:21.

[9] This also brings to mind the words of Jesus recorded in the Gospel of John: 'Whoever eats my flesh and *drinks my blood* has eternal life' (6:54).

with you' (Exod. 24:8). At the last supper, when Jesus offered wine to the disciples he explained, 'This is my blood of the covenant, which is poured out for many for the forgiveness of sins' (Matt. 26:28), or in another version, 'This cup is the new covenant in my blood, which is poured out for you' (Luke 22:20; cf. 1 Cor. 11:25). The resemblance between the two utterances has long been remarked by biblical scholars.[10]

Since a covenant is the formal binding of a relationship between two parties, it is appropriate that it be accompanied by a meal. In Middle Eastern culture the meal, both then and still now in many places, signifies an act of fellowship, or the sealing of a relationship. When Isaac made a covenant with Abimelech, we read that 'they ate and drank' (Gen. 26:30). Again, when Jacob entered into a covenant with Laban, we are told that 'they ate there' (31:46). Similarly, at Sinai Israel enjoyed a meal. This was done representatively for practical reasons. Since the nation probably numbered well in excess of a million people, it was seventy chosen elders who ascended the mountain on which the Lord came down, and there 'they ate and drank' (Exod. 24:11). In the Gospels the new covenant is instituted, of course, within the context of a meal. Eating and drinking are prominent elements in what transpired on that occasion when Jesus reclined at table with his followers.[11] The sharing of the food and drink was not accidental to what was taking place, but as at Sinai was an intrinsic part of the inauguration of a covenant.

One final correspondence exists between Exodus 24 and the New Testament passages, one that has not been previously noticed as far as I am aware, and yet one that is of great theological consequence. At Sinai, again representatively through the seventy elders, Israel was allowed to view God. We recall that those same elders who ate and drank also 'saw God' (24:11; cf. v. 10, 'they saw the God of Israel'). As discussed in our treatment of the transfiguration,[12] this was a theophany, a special visible manifestation of God for the benefit of the leaders of Israel. Remarkably, the matter of seeing God also finds a place at the last supper, with an important theological twist. On that occasion the apostle Philip requested of Jesus: 'Lord, show us the Father' (John 14:8). To this Jesus responded: 'Have I been with you so long, and yet you have not come to know me, Philip? *He who has seen me has seen the Father.* How can you say, "Show us

---

[10] E.g. Thomas J. White, *Exodus* (Brazos Theological Commentary on the Bible; Grand Rapids, MI: Brazos, 2016), 212; Leon Morris, *The Gospel According to Matthew* (PNTC; Grand Rapids, MI: Eerdmans, 1992), 660–661.

[11] Since Judas Iscariot was in attendance at this covenant meal (cf. John 13:30), this makes his act of betrayal all the more blameworthy. The meal denoted the precise opposite of what he was about to do.

[12] Chapter 13.

the Father"?' (v. 9). To this Jesus adds: 'Do you not believe that I am in the Father and that the Father is in me?' (v. 10).

At the earlier covenant ceremony, the Hebrew elders were granted a theophany – 'they saw God' after a fashion, remotely as it were, by means of a temporary visual depiction. At the making of the new covenant, the disciples asked to see God the Father and they saw Jesus. To see Jesus, he himself declares, was to see God the Father. This was no mere theophany but an incarnation (cf. John 1:14), God become man in the person of Jesus of Nazareth. The covenant mediator was at one and the same time the God he was representing. In fact, he was uniquely qualified to act as the perfect mediator of the new covenant since he shared in both divine and human natures. In his own humanity, therefore, there existed very God ('the Father is in me'). It is for this reason that Jesus could tell his disciples that to see him was to see the Father. Only at this all-important institution of the new covenant is this momentous fact explained to them: 'From now on, you know him [the Father] and have seen him' (John 14:7). God is now both known and seen in Jesus.[13]

It is hoped that the allusions explained in this chapter demonstrate once again how much the detection of such features can enhance our understanding of a biblical passage. They are not there merely as literary ornaments, but rather serve to draw attention to important truths, frequently Christological, implicit within the text.

---

[13] It might be possible to extend the allusions even further. In Exod. 24, once the covenant had been established, Moses and Joshua ascended to the top of the mountain (v. 13). The elders were not to accompany them. Before going, Moses had told them: 'Wait here for us until we come back to you' (v. 14). Both Moses and Joshua are well-known figures who foreshadow Christ, one as lawgiver and mediator, the other as saviour, for the name 'Joshua' means 'the LORD saves', being the Hebrew version of the Greek name 'Jesus', as frequently noted. In the last supper discourse, Christ speaks of the fact that he is going to a place where the disciples cannot follow (John 13:33, 36). But he additionally says, 'I will come back and take you to be with me' (14:3; cf. v. 28, 'I am going away and I am coming back to you'). Both passages entail a period of waiting before the return. While Moses was absent in the height of the mountain with God, much of Israel became apostate, though some remained faithful. What will happen, we may therefore wonder, during the absence of Jesus, who is now at the right hand of God in heaven? We find it moreover to be the case that the absence of both Moses and Jesus relates to the building of a sanctuary. From Exod. 25 onwards, Moses was receiving the instructions for making the tabernacle, the construction of which would commence after his return to the people below. In John 14, Jesus informs his disciples that he goes to prepare a place, called 'my Father's house', that is, a sanctuary (vv. 2–3). The interrelations between these two would deserve a lengthy treatment of their own.

20

Gethsemane 1

Matthew 26:36–46; Mark 14:32–42; Luke 22:39–46; John 18:3–12

As the time of Christ's passion draws near, the Gospel accounts show an increase in references to Old Testament prophecies and figures which relate to the coming sacrifice, and this also holds true with regard to the kind of allusions we are considering.

The first three Gospels all give an account of Jesus going to the garden of Gethsemane after the last supper in order to spend time in prayer alone in view of his approaching ordeal. The fourth Gospel, that of John, does not include this event, though at that particular juncture in the narrative it does present a prayer of Jesus (John 17), which is principally an intercessory prayer for his disciples and those who would believe in him.[1] It seems clear, then, that on the night before his death our Lord spent a good deal of time, as we might expect, in prayer.

My contention in this chapter is that certain features of what transpired in Gethsemane bring to mind aspects of the ritual described in Leviticus 16, the regulations concerning what came to be known as Yom Kippur,[2] that is, the annual Day of Atonement.

The levitical instructions regarding this particular Hebrew holy day explicitly locate the ceremony within the tabernacle. In later times, once the larger and more solid stone temple had been built, the same ritual would have taken place there. Whether it be the tabernacle or the temple, each of these is the divinely ordained sanctuary of God, and both share the same basic structure and contain similar items. What these two sacred places have in common is an essential threefold pattern. Each consisted of an outer court, a holy place and a most holy place (or 'holy of holies', as some prefer to call it). These three are

---

[1] That this is not precisely the same occasion as the prayer recorded in the synoptic Gospels is shown by the fact that in John it is *after* this prayer that he then proceeds to the garden (18:1).

[2] This is the later (post-biblical) and more familiar Hebrew designation of what was originally *yôm hakkippurîm* (Lev. 23:27), the latter form being an abstract plural.

161

graded, from the outer to the inner, and from the larger to the smaller. Corresponding to these distinct areas there were three different tiers, or ranks, of minister. First, there were the Levites. These performed duties in the outer court and were forbidden from going further into the sanctuary. The priests, who were taken from one specially selected family of the tribe of Levi, were able to move inwards from the outer court and to enter into the holy place, but they were not to pass beyond that. Then there was the sole figure of the high priest, the head of the priestly family. He alone was permitted to have access to all three areas of the sanctuary. And what directly relates to the Day of Atonement is the fact that the high priest was uniquely allowed to enter the third and most holy chamber of the sanctuary on that specific day. At no other time was this permissible.

Therefore, with regard to the three kinds of minister and the three areas of the sanctuary, there was a diminishing of the numbers involved. The Levites were by far the larger group, consisting entirely of able-bodied males of the tribe of Levi between certain ages. The priests were comparatively few. In Old Testament times they were typically the sons of the high priest. Then the high priest was a single man. So as we proceed through the sacred spaces, there is basically a movement from the many (the Levites), to the few (the priests), to the one (the high priest), as well as a corresponding advance towards that place which is the holiest of all.

In the Gospel record of the prayer in Gethsemane, we find a similar progression. As Jesus and his companions come to the garden, first the larger group of disciples are left in a certain place (Matt. 26:36; Mark 14:32). Then Jesus continues further with just three others, Peter, James and John (Matt. 26:37; Mark 14:33).[3] Lastly, Jesus alone goes on 'a little further' (Matt. 26:39; Mark 14:35), which is described as 'about a stone's throw' away (Luke 22:41), to the place where he would meet his Father. Here too, then, we move from the many, to the few, to the one, and the latter single individual comes into the presence of God, as only the high priest was privileged to do on the Day of Atonement.

Also like that particular ritual, Jesus did not simply remain in the place where he communed with God until he was finished, and then return to his disciples. During the course of his time of prayer he went back to the others twice, and then a third time once his prayer was completed. This too significantly mirrors the ritual of the Day of Atonement. The high priest did not enter the most holy place and remain there for the duration. Leviticus 16 describes

---

[3] Note that these three stand out as a particular distinct group among the larger band of twelve disciples. It was these three whom Jesus took with him when he raised up the daughter of Jairus (Mark 5:37), and the same three he chose to accompany him up the mount of transfiguration (Mark 9:2).

three specific tasks that the high priest performed within the most holy place, and the nature of these, by way of implication, allows us to conclude that each required its own separate visitation into that inner chamber of the sanctuary. On his first entrance the high priest burned incense (v. 13), on the second he sprinkled the blood of a bull, the sin-offering for himself (v. 14), and the third time he sprinkled the blood of a goat, the sin-offering for the people (v. 15). Explicit mention is made of the fact that the latter two necessitated two separate visits. Yet it does not take a great deal of thought to realize that the first did also. The offering of incense itself necessitated the use of both hands (see v. 12), so it would not have been possible for him to have also brought in the blood of the bull at the same time. Jewish commentators are clear on the fact that, just like the third element of the ritual, the first two also required a separate entrance and exit, making three in total.[4] Consequently, here is another connection: on that particular day the high priest went into the most holy place and came out again on three separate occasions, while in Gethsemane Jesus went to pray and returned three times (Matt. 26:44; Mark 14:41).

Before we proceed to compare what the high priest did within the inner sanctum with what Jesus did in Gethsemane, there is the significant fact that the whole of this latter activity took place in what is described as a 'garden' (cf. John 18:1, 26). For those readers immersed in the symbolism of their ancestral Scriptures, the connotations of this would have readily been appreciated. Today, biblical scholars have come to understand that the garden of Eden was perceived to be a kind of sanctuary in which the first man and woman met God. There is a close conceptual association, therefore, between the garden of Eden, on one hand, and the tabernacle and temple, on the other.[5] This explains the garden imagery present in the latter two. The golden lampstand, a prominent feature of both sanctuaries, was plainly tree-like in design, including

---

[4] See, e.g., Baruch A. Levine, *Leviticus* (JPS Torah Commentary; Philadelphia, PA: Jewish Publication Society, 1989), 103: 'He [the high priest] left the Holy of Holies momentarily, took the bowl of bull's blood, and reentered the Holy of Holies'; Bernard J. Bamberger, 'Leviticus', in W. Gunther Plaut (ed.), *The Torah: A Modern Commentary* (New York, NY: Union of American Hebrew Congregations, 1981), 865: 'After offering the incense, the officiant went outside, got the bowl of bull's blood, brought it into the Shrine, and sprinkled some of the blood . . . Then he went out again, the goat "for the Lord" was slaughtered, and he brought its blood into the Shrine and sprinkled it.' These observations by recent Jewish scholars agree with the Mishnah, where tractate *Yoma* 5.3 similarly indicates an exit and another entrance between the offering of incense and the sprinkling of bull's blood. The whole of this section of the Mishnah (5.1–4) unambiguously speaks of three entrances and three exits during the course of the ritual.

[5] The classic treatment of this subject in recent times is G. K. Beale, *The Temple and the Church's Mission: A Biblical Theology of the Dwelling Place of God* (NSBT 17; Leicester: Apollos, 2004); see esp. 66–80. Beale concludes that 'parallels between the Garden of Genesis 2 and Israel's tabernacle and temple indicates (*sic*) that Eden was the first archetypal temple, upon which all of Israel's temples were based . . . when all are viewed together they have a significant collective effect, pointing to Eden as the first temple in garden-like form' (79–80).

branches, buds and blossoms (Exod. 25:31–36), while the inside of the temple was decorated with flowers, gourds and trees (1 Kgs 6:18, 29). It also explains why images of cherubim were embroidered on the veil of the tabernacle (Exod. 26:31), and on the wooden doors of the temple (1 Kgs 6:32), which faced east like the entrance to Eden, where God had stationed cherubim (Gen. 3:24; cf. Exod. 27:13–15).[6]

We learn, then, that the tabernacle and temple, the sacred spaces in which the ritual of the Day of Atonement was carried out, were reminders of Eden, the garden where human beings had originally shared fellowship with God. In the Gospel passages under discussion, Jesus is in a garden, with trees on all sides, as the high priest was encompassed by decorative trees when he entered the sanctuary. And in this garden Jesus comes into the presence of God, an experience enjoyed in Eden, and he performs actions, as we shall see next, that evoke the rituals of the day when the high priest made atonement for Israel in the innermost part of the sanctuary.

In the instructions of Leviticus 16 there were just two ritual elements that the high priest carried into the most holy place. As stated above, these were incense and blood (vv. 13–15). These were two substances which in themselves could in fact attain nothing. One was simply a compound that emitted a sweet-smelling odour when set alight, and the other an organic red liquid that flowed in the veins and arteries of living creatures. What was important about them was not their intrinsic worth but their symbolic value. And Scripture makes it quite apparent what it was that they represented.

In the ceremonies of the sanctuary and in wider biblical imagery, incense speaks of prayer.[7] Why this should be so is evident from the fact that when burned it sends smoke rising upwards, as prayers rise heavenwards, and also gives out a fragrant smell, indicating the pleasing nature of prayer to God. Both Testaments make the connection between incense and prayer: 'May my prayer be set before you like incense' (Ps. 141:2); 'The twenty-four elders fell down before the Lamb, and each one had a harp and they were holding golden bowls full of incense, which are the prayers of the saints' (Rev. 5:8; cf. 8:3–4).[8] Accordingly, when the high priest burned the incense, it pictured his own prayers and those of the people he represented ascending to God.

---

[6] Mention may also be made of the 'serving and keeping' of those in the garden or sanctuary (Num. 3:7–8; 8:25–26; cf. Gen. 2:15) and the reference to gold and precious stones (Exod. 25:3, 7; cf. Gen. 2:12). For these details and others, now widely recognized, see Beale, *The Temple and the Church's Mission*, 66–71.

[7] Cf. C. F. Keil, 'The Pentateuch', in C. F. Keil and F. Delitzsch, *Commentary on the Old Testament* (Peabody, MA: Hendrickson, 1996 [repr. of 1866 edn]), vol. 1, 586: 'burning incense was a symbol of *prayer*' (italics original).

[8] Luke 1:10 specifically relates the burning of incense inside the temple with the time of prayer.

The connection between incense and the events of Gethsemane is immediately obvious, for once Jesus withdrew from his disciples he gave himself expressly to the matter of prayer. This praying of Jesus is a major part of the narrative (Matt. 26:39, 42, 44; Mark 14:35, 39; Luke 22:41, 44). It was for this express reason that he had come to this place. So, what was symbolized in the burning of incense, Jesus did in actual fact.

Besides the incense, the high priest brought in blood. This, too, within the context of the ceremonies of Leviticus, had its own particular meaning, one that is highly important. Elsewhere in the same book, speaking of the blood of animal sacrifices, we are told: 'I have given it to you on the altar to make atonement for your lives, for it is the blood that makes atonement for a life' (Lev. 17:11). The blood, then, represents a sacrificial death, the death of a victim that assumes the identity of the offender, and a death for the purposes of atonement, which means the removal of sin and the acceptance of the sinner by God. This was true of several of the various kinds of animal sacrifices prescribed in Leviticus (e.g. 1:4, 4:20; 5:6). However, Yom Kippur was the supreme occasion on which atonement was attained for Israel (cf. 23:28). It was, above all else, *the* time of atonement, hence its name. This is why the disposal of the blood featured so prominently in its ceremony, and it was the only time when blood was brought into the inner sanctuary.

In Gethsemane, Christ's prayer centred very much on the subject of sacrificial death, in this case his own, which was just a few hours away. It was to this event that all the animal offerings of the law of Moses, and especially those of the great Day of Atonement, were pointing. The sacrifice of animals was a temporary measure until the true sacrifice came. That sacrifice had to be human, like those who had offended, not animal in nature. For the blood of bulls and goats could not take away sin (Heb. 10:4), but the blood of Jesus could, and does. Now as he prayed in Gethsemane, this ultimate sacrifice was to take place the very next morning, and it was concerning the prospect of this coming death that Jesus prayed. In this death he was to be identified with humanity, he was to be sacrificed for human beings as one of them, and his prayer was very much that of a human being. Although divine in nature, he was also human, and that humanness clearly expresses itself in this prayer that, if it be the Father's will, this cup of suffering might be taken from him.

At this point there is one particularly fascinating connection. When the high priest entered the most holy place, one of the actions performed was the sprinkling of blood before the lid (the 'mercy-seat' or 'atonement cover') of the ark of the covenant (Lev. 16:14). This meant that during the ceremony, blood was sprinkled on the ground.[9] In Gethsemane we read of Jesus that, 'being in anguish,[10] he prayed more earnestly, and his sweat became like drops of blood falling upon the ground' (Luke 22:44). This detail, in the context of the allusion, functions as a literary symbol to indicate that the death which will achieve the true atonement is that of Christ's own human body. The blood in the levitical ritual was that of animals; here, the blood-like sweat of Jesus falling on the ground shows that the suffering and death are to be his. It is only by this dreadful means that atonement will be fully accomplished.

Lastly, each occasion involves some manner of heavenly appearance. In Leviticus 16, as the prescriptions concerning the Day of Atonement begin, God declares to Moses: 'Tell your brother Aaron not to come just at any time into the sanctuary inside the curtain before the atonement cover that is upon the ark, or he will die; for I will appear [LXX: *ophthēsomai*] in the cloud over the atonement cover' (v. 2). Exactly how or in what form this took place is unstated. Sometimes God's appearance in Old Testament times was through some kind of angelic manifestation (cf. Exod. 14:19). Whatever it was that was seen, the fact is that this appearance relates to what the high priest (here Aaron) would see specifically on the occasion in question, the Day of Atonement. In the case of Jesus at prayer in Gethsemane, there was a corresponding visual phenomenon. There we read that 'an angel from heaven appeared [*ōphthē*] to him and strengthened him' (Luke 22:43).

At this point certain details occurring in the Mishnah seem very relevant. As stated in the introduction, there is a strong probability that much of the material in the Mishnah, although written down later, reflects earlier practices. In the two instances about to be mentioned, there is such a close connection with what appears in the Gospels that I find it hard not to conclude that these latter narratives were written with the Judaic traditions regarding Yom Kippur in mind. First, there is the matter of sleep. In the Gospel accounts the sleepiness of the disciples is a conspicuous feature, and it is similarly prominent in the opening section of *Yoma*, the Mishnah tractate that deals with the Day of Atonement. There reference is made to the problem of staying awake on the part of the high priest during the preceding night. As the chief celebrant of the coming ceremonies, he was not permitted to succumb to sleep the night before to prevent the possibility of contracting ritual uncleanness in his sleep.[11] It was,

---

[9] Cf. Keil, 'The Pentateuch', vol. 1, 586–587: 'he was to sprinkle some of the blood . . . upon the ground in front of it [the lid of the ark]'.

[10] The Greek noun translated 'anguish' (*agōnia*) also means 'agony'.

[11] Uncleanness might be contracted during sleep by several means, such as contact with an unclean creature like a mouse or a lizard. However, according to the tradition recorded in the Mishnah, the high priest was obliged to stay awake so that he would not inadvertently become defiled through a nocturnal

we read, the duty of the younger priests to prevent the high priest from falling asleep (*Yoma* 1.4, 7). The allusion in the Gospel accounts at this point is one of reversal, as is sometimes the case. This creates a sense of irony owing to the fact that it is Jesus (Matt. 26:40, 43, 45; Mark 14:37, 40; Luke 22:45–46), corresponding to the high priest, who endeavours to keep his sleepy disciples awake, rather than vice versa. They ought to be supporting him at this crucial time as the making of atonement approaches, but it is he who exhorts them to stay awake to give themselves to prayer and vigil.

Later in the same tractate of the Mishnah there comes a section concerning the utterance of the divine name by the high priest. This was the only time of the entire year when the sacred tetragrammaton, YHWH, was spoken. The priest uttered the name, not when he was inside the most holy place, but when he was outside, so that he could be heard by the people standing there. And we are told that 'when they heard the Name pronounced from the mouth of the high priest, they would bend their knees, bow down, and fall on their faces' (*Yoma* 6.2). John's Gospel has a remarkable correspondence to this. When the men arrived who had been sent to Gethsemane by the Jewish leaders, we read that Jesus went out and asked them, 'Who are you looking for?' (John 18:4). They replied, 'Jesus of Nazareth'. In response to this, Jesus uttered the words 'I am [he]' (v. 5). There is, however, no pronoun 'he' present in the original Greek,[12] which simply says 'I am' (*egō eimi*). On hearing Jesus say those words, 'I am', John tells us that 'they drew back and fell to the ground' (v. 6). Clearly, they were totally awestruck. But why?

The answer lies in the fact, treated in a previous chapter, that 'I am' is the meaning given to the divine name when it is explained to Moses back in Exodus.[13] The God of Israel, named YHWH, is the great 'I AM'. This is the name that the high priest spoke in public hearing solely on the Day of Atonement, and the meaning of that name is what Jesus uttered in Gethsemane. The Mishnah informs us that the response of those who heard the name was to fall on their faces, while the Gospel tells us those who heard Jesus say 'I am' fell to the ground. We further observe that on the Day of Atonement the high priest uttered the divine name three times altogether (*Yoma* 6.2, 'Please O YHWH . . . Please, O YHWH . . . before YHWH'), while 'I am' likewise appears three times in John 18 (vv. 5, 6, 8). Here, then, it seems to me, is not just another link between

---

emission. Such would render him unfit to carry out the next day's proceedings (cf. Lev. 15:16–17; 22:4; Deut. 23:10–11). See David Instone-Brewer, *Traditions of the Rabbis from the Era of the New Testament, vol. 2A: Feasts and Sabbaths: Passover and Atonement* (Grand Rapids, MI: Eerdmans, 2011), 259.

[12] Hence the pronoun appears in italics ('*he*') in some of the older English versions (e.g. AV, NKJV, NASB; cf. NRSV, ESV footnotes).

[13] See Exod. 3:13–14, quoted and discussed earlier in chapter 11.

the events of Gethsemane and the atonement festival, but one that is theologic-ally charged. Not only is Jesus, in expressing these words, fulfilling the role of the high priest in the latter ritual, but at one and the same time he is also appropriating that name to himself. The 'I' of the 'I AM' is Jesus.

Why, we may ask by way of conclusion, should the record of this event in the Gospels evoke this particular Old Testament holy day, and why at this point in the narrative? The answer is not difficult to conceive. In the Gospels the events concerning the death of Christ are explicitly placed at the time of the Passover festival. Jesus is already identified as the 'Lamb of God' from the beginning of his ministry (John 1:29), the lamb being the central element in the celebration of Passover. Jesus died as *the* Lamb of God, as is shown, for example, by the citation of the injunction that none of the lamb's bones should be broken with direct application to Christ's body on the cross (John 19:36; cf. Exod. 12:46; Num. 9:12). Hence the apostle Paul can say that 'Christ, our Passover, has been sacrificed' (1 Cor. 5:7). At the surface level, therefore, the death of Jesus is closely and explicitly associated with that of the Passover lamb, and is indeed the ultimate fulfilment of what that earlier animal death prefigured – the blood that protects from divine judgment and the death that sets free from spiritual bondage. Yet, at the same time, Christ's death fulfils what is enacted in the ritual of the Day of Atonement. He is the one true atoning sacrifice. It is his offering that once and for all gives access to the divine presence, symbolized by the most holy place (cf. Heb. 9:11–12).

As the time of Jesus' death approaches in the Gospel narratives, where every-thing revolves around the Passover festival, how is it indicated that this death is also highly relevant to what transpired at the Day of Atonement? This latter holy day, we recall, occurred in the seventh month of the year, while Passover was in the first (Lev. 16:29; Exod. 12:6). So the way in which the two are brought together is that while the narrative makes direct reference to the one, at the same time it makes allusive reference to the other. This is what is going on in the Gospel pas-sages in question. On Passover night we detect a series of textual hints that make us think also of Yom Kippur, since Jesus came to enact what was foreshadowed not just by the former but by the latter too.[14] This is further confirmed, we shall note here, by the presence of other allusions to the Day of Atonement in other Gospel passages, to be considered later, relating to other events in Passion Week.

Further to this, two specific allusions to the atonement ritual mentioned above are quite exceptional and serve to underline the key significance of what

---

[14] Cf. Dorothy A. Lee, 'Paschal Imagery in the Gospel of John: A Narrative and Symbolic Reading', *Pacifica: Australasian Theological Studies* 24 (2011): 16–17.

is about to happen in the Gospels. One differs from the ritual of the holy day. While the high priest took with him on that day a bowl of animal's blood to secure a provisional atonement, Christ had nothing of this kind. In his case, we saw that the blood-like drops of his sweat falling to the ground represent the fact that it is with his own blood that the atonement will be made, not with that of an animal, and for that reason the atonement will be one that is perfect and permanent. Under the new-covenant fulfilment of the old-covenant ritual, this greater high priest[15] himself offers his own blood as the sacrifice. The allusion clearly indicates the significance of Christ's own death within the context of the Day of Atonement ceremony.[16] The other remarkable allusion points us to the mind-boggling fact that the one who undergoes this sacrificial death identifies himself as none other than YHWH in person, the 'I AM' God in human flesh.

---

[15] For Jesus as our high priest, see Heb. 5:10; 6:20; 7:26; 8:1 etc.

[16] It is noteworthy that in the levitical description of the regulations for the Day of Atonement the stress is on the high priest taking the necessary precautions so that he might *not* die (Lev. 16:2, 13), which is what the high priest of the new covenant comes expressly to do!

21
Gethsemane 2
Matthew 26:36–46; Mark 14:32–42; Luke 22:39–46; John 18:3–12

Having viewed the events of Gethsemane against the background of the Day of Atonement ceremony, we now review the same happenings in the light of an important incident in Genesis. We have previously seen that it is sometimes the case that the allusions discernible in a Gospel episode may hearken back to more than one Old Testament source. When this occurs, it appears that the two or more passages from the earlier Scriptures are related thematically. At first sight this may not seem to be so with what we are about to discuss. An event from the patriarchal narratives and the levitical ritual do not initially strike the reader as having much in common. Further examination, however, reveals that early readers of the Gospels, especially those from a Jewish background, would have been able to detect a significant relationship at a deeper level, and indeed Jews before the time of Christ already seemed to be making this connection.

Our thoughts are here directed to Isaac, son of Abraham, and specifically to the occasion recorded in Genesis 22 in which his father receives command from God to offer him up as a sacrifice. Among the Jews this event is generally designated 'The Binding of Isaac' (*ăqêdat yiṣḥaq*) or simply the 'Aqedah',[1] from the occurrence of the Hebrew verb 'bind' in verse 9. An indicator of its particular importance is the considerable treatment it received in early Jewish literature (see below), and still continues to receive. The incident is likewise explicitly referenced in the New Testament in Hebrews (11:17) and James (2:21).[2] There is also a very probable implicit reference, that is to say, an allusion, to it in Romans (8:32).

---

[1] Sometimes anglicized as 'Akedah'. The event is also commonly termed 'The Offering of Isaac' or 'The Sacrifice of Isaac'.

[2] To these we may add the references appearing in the earliest post-apostolic writings of the First Epistle of Clement (10.7; 31.3) and the Epistle of Barnabas (7.3). The former most probably dates from the end of the first century and the latter from the early second.

As one reads through the patriarchal narratives, it may fairly be concluded that aside from his long-awaited, divinely ordained birth, the occasion of the Aqedah forms the most notable event concerning Isaac. The reader will recall that allusions to Isaac were previously observed in the Gospel passages recounting the birth of Jesus (Matt. 1:18–25; Luke 1:26–38).[3] If this literary stratagem is employed in the event that saw the commencement of Jesus' human life, then it is altogether credible that it should be put to further service in the crucial and climactic event of his death.

Even at the most general level there is considerable correspondence between the two episodes, the Aqedah and Gethsemane. With respect to the person whose death is concerned, each is a son of Abraham, indeed that particular son through whom the divine purpose is carried forward,[4] born by supernatural means. Regarding the location, both events relate to a specifically designated place on a mountain, Mount Moriah in one case (Gen. 22:2), the Mount of Olives in the other (Matt. 26:30). The activity and the occasion also correlate closely. Both depict the principal character as being accompanied by others, and, upon arrival, certain of these others remain behind, leaving the son alone with his father. The dealings of these latter two centre on the death of the one, the son, as a sacrifice. To these general features can be added a number of distinct correlations in both concept and language that inextricably link the two happenings.[5]

The son in question is described in the words of the Lord to Abraham as 'your only son, whom you love' (Gen. 22:2). In the common Greek version of the Old Testament (LXX), here (and in vv. 12 and 16) the adjective *agapētos*, 'beloved', appears in the phrase 'beloved son'. Of course, 'beloved son' in the Gospels brings to mind the person of Jesus, who is designated such by his Father (e.g. Matt. 3:17; 17:5; Mark 1:11; 9:7). However, what is obscured in the Septuagint translation is the presence in the original Hebrew of the descriptive term *yāḥîd*, meaning 'only, unique'. In other verses of the LXX this word can be found translated as *monogenēs*, meaning 'sole, single, unique' (e.g. Judg. 11:34; Ps. 22:20). Significantly for our purposes, it is also the New Testament term traditionally rendered as 'only-begotten' with respect to the Son of God (e.g. John 1:14; 3:16; 1 John 4:9). Moreover, apart from the Son, there is only one other person to

---

[3] See chapter 4.

[4] With regard to Isaac, see Gen. 21:12; Rom. 9:7; Heb. 11:18. Such would not have applied to Ishmael.

[5] As with previous discussions relating to Isaac, much of the contents of the present chapter leans heavily on the work of Leroy A. Huizenga, especially *The New Isaac: Tradition and Intertextuality in the Gospel of Matthew* (Leiden: Brill, 2009). Huizenga's focus is entirely limited to the Gospel of Matthew. Other scholars, to be mentioned in subsequent footnotes, express their essential agreement with his findings, and detect similar allusions in the parallel passages of Mark, Luke and John.

whom the New Testament writings apply this particular adjective, and that is Isaac himself, where the offering of Isaac is explicitly in view: 'He [Abraham] who had received the promises was ready to offer up his only [*monogenē*] son' (Heb. 11:17).[6] In short, in the divine instruction for Abraham to sacrifice Isaac in Genesis 22:2 we find the idea of the one to be so offered as being a 'beloved son' and an 'only[-begotten] son', descriptions which both have an obvious connection with Christ.[7] Though the Gospel accounts of Gethsemane do not directly employ either of these phrases, once the biblically informed reader begins to detect the several allusions to the Genesis incident the significance of these terms should readily spring to mind, especially as Jesus has been so described prior to that occasion. It soon becomes evident that the 'beloved/only' son which was Isaac in the Aqedah is now replaced by Jesus in the passion.

Looking at more specific details, we see that when the respective parties arrive at the place to which they have been heading, the lead figure gives similar instructions to certain of those who had accompanied him. In the earlier event Abraham said to his servants, 'Sit here [*kathisate autou*] . . . we will go over there [*heōs hōde*]; and we will worship and return to you' (Gen. 22:5). In Gethsemane Jesus said to his disciples, 'Sit here [*kathisate autou*] while [*heōs hou*] I go over there and pray' (Matt. 26:36). There can hardly be any doubt that an allusion is intended here.[8] This is because the spatial use of the adverb *autou*, 'there', is extremely rare in the Old Testament and the New alike. There are only three other occurrences in the whole of the latter, all in Luke–Acts.[9] Our two verses in question are the sole places in Scripture where the two specific words, an imperative and the adverb ('Sit' and 'here'), are juxtaposed in this manner. But more than this, there is also the conceptual similarity of what follows the command. In one case it is to go and worship and in the other to go and pray, and to return afterwards.

We find the notion of testing to be prominent in each setting. The episode in Genesis is headed up by the statement (22:1) that God 'tested' (*epeirazen*) Abraham, and accordingly that theme forms a backdrop to the whole story. The same is there too in the Gospels. Ironically, perhaps, in the garden Jesus warns his disciples (Matt. 26:41; Mark 14:38; Luke 22:40, 46) to pray that they do not come 'into testing' (*eis peirasmon*). However, the emotional state (Matt. 26:37;

---

[6] Here NASB and NKJV translate the final phrase as 'only begotten son'.

[7] Just to note in passing that the Latin Vulgate shows more consistency than the Greek in using the same term *unigenitus* in Gen. 22:2, 12, 16 and Heb. 11:17 of Isaac and in the several New Testament references to Jesus.

[8] Huizenga (*The New Isaac*, 251) describes the allusion as 'near indubitable'.

[9] Luke 9:27; Acts 18:19; 21:4.

Mark 14:33) and strenuous prayer (Luke 22:44) of Jesus strongly suggest that he is first and foremost the one then being tested.

Implements are involved in each episode that are represented in Greek by identical terms. In the Aqedah a 'knife' (Gen. 22:6, 10) and 'wood' (vv. 3, 6, 7, 9) are necessarily brought to the place in order for the sacrifice to be enacted. The first of these appears in the LXX as the noun *machaira*, indicating a 'knife' or 'dagger', particularly a large one. The second word is the plural noun *xyla*, meaning 'pieces of wood', which may be used of firewood or more substantial logs. These items are brought to the top of Moriah, the knife by Abraham and the wood by Isaac, in readiness for the act of offering. The very same two words likewise occur in the Gethsemane narrative, where they are translated 'swords and clubs' (Matt. 26:47, 55; Mark 14:43, 48; Luke 22:52), being *machairōn kai xylōn* in every instance. These objects form the weapons carried by the men who have come to arrest Jesus.[10] Although the two words feature in both scenarios, and in each case the items serve as instruments able to cause death, there is an obvious distinction in usage. In the former we find it to be Abraham who requires these things, while in the latter the band of soldiers. Yet it is the evident intention of each of the two parties, Abraham on one hand, acting on God's instructions, and the soldiers on the other, acting on the orders of the Jewish rulers,[11] to bring about the death of the victim in question. It seems probable, therefore, that the difference in the bearers of the implements of death is a deliberate contrivance in order to underscore where the responsibility lies, at the human level at least,[12] for the coming event.

In the Genesis passage Isaac addresses his father through the Hebrew vocative form *'ābî*, 'My father' (22:7). Both of the two standard Jewish Targums (Onkelos and Jonathan)[13] of the Pentateuch render this word by the Aramaic *'abbâ*, 'O father'. In the New Testament this latter term appears in the Greek as *abba*, transliterated into English as 'Abba', in a small number of places, three

---

[10] According to the Johannine version they were also carrying 'torches' (John 18:3), that is to say, the 'fire' which is the third element brought to Moriah (Gen. 22:6, 7).

[11] These rulers, we are explicitly informed, wanted Jesus dead (cf. Matt. 26:4, 59; 27:1, 20; Mark 14:1, 55; John 11:53 etc.).

[12] Further to this there is the matter of ultimate causation, which in the case of both Isaac and Jesus is the divine will. There is good reason to believe that the father-figure of Abraham portrays *the* Father. Ultimately, it is part of the divine purpose that God will send his Son, as an act of supreme goodness for the salvation of humankind, to the cross (cf. Isa. 53:10). Yet, in the working out of this divine plan, there is the exercise of an evil will on the part of fallen human beings. This is what the allusion in question is intended to convey. Note Peter's remark in his Pentecostal sermon: 'this man, delivered over by the predetermined plan and foreknowledge of God, by the hands of godless men you put to death by nailing him to a cross' (Acts 2:23). At this point in the speech both the ultimate divine causality and the accountable human agency are to be observed.

[13] The same holds true in the important Targum Neofiti.

173

to be precise. In the Gospels there is just one sole instance of 'Abba', and that happens to be on the lips of Jesus calling on his Father in the garden, as recorded in Mark's account (14:36).[14] In Matthew's parallel we find the twofold occurrence of *pater mou*, 'My Father' (Matt. 26:39, 42).[15] This corresponds more exactly to the Hebrew form in Genesis 22:7, and is, moreover, the only New Testament usage of this specific vocative phrase. Therefore, in Christ's invocation of the Father in Gethsemane, Matthew echoes the precise form of the Hebrew original of Isaac's words, and Mark its Aramaic form.[16] Regarding the terms in question, the uniqueness of the one and the rarity of the other make it highly probable that there is deliberate design in this textual feature. Though perhaps not of considerable significance in itself, when placed alongside the several other allusions it may be taken as yet one more link with the offering of Isaac.

In the Aqedah we see that Abraham, as he was about to bring down the knife to slay Isaac, was told by the angel of the Lord, 'Do not lay your hand upon [*epibalēs tēn cheira epi*] the lad' (Gen. 22:12). This is a particular idiomatic expression in which the verb involved has the literal meaning of 'cast' or 'throw'. This heavenly utterance, of course, marks the pivotal moment in the story. At this point it becomes apparent that God did not in fact wish Abraham to slaughter his own son. And so the hand of Abraham is stayed. As we read of what transpired in Gethsemane, the identical idiom occurs. There the soldiers approached and 'laid their hands upon [*epebalon tas cheiras epi*] Jesus' (Matt. 26:50; cf. Mark 14:46), the corresponding son. This time their hand is not divinely restrained. Whereas it was not the divine will that Isaac should be harmed, Jesus was indeed to be seized and led away to his execution. This had to be so for the promised blessing to become a reality. So it was that God let wicked men lay hands on his Son.

Angels also receive mention in both contexts. In this, however, there is something of a contrast, one that is meaningful given the respective occasions. In the case of Abraham offering up his son, the angel enters the scene as an intervention, with the express purpose of preventing the death of Isaac (Gen. 22:11–12). When it comes to God's Son, the angels are available and capable of thwarting his death, for Jesus said, 'Do you think that I cannot call upon my

---

[14] The two remaining New Testament instances are Rom. 8:15 and Gal. 4:6. For an overview of Mark's connections with Gen. 22, see Stephen P. Ahearne-Kroll, 'Genesis in Mark's Gospel', in Maarten J. J. Menken and Steve Moyise (eds.), *Genesis in the New Testament* (LNTS; London: Bloomsbury, 2012), 27–30.

[15] These two references in Matthew's account of Gethsemane are the sole instances in the entire New Testament where we find Jesus directly addressing God (i.e. through a vocative) as 'My Father'.

[16] This matter is also discussed in Matthew S. Rindge, 'Reconfiguring the Akedah and Recasting God: Lament and Divine Abandonment in Mark', *JBL* 131.4 (2012): 768–769.

Father, and he will at once send me more than twelve legions of angels?' (Matt. 26:53). However, he did not summon them to forestall it. In the former, one angel is all that is required to stop the act, a possibility that was undoubtedly not within Abraham or Isaac's authority to demand and yet was freely given from above. In the latter, Christ has the authority to call down tens of thousands of angelic beings,[17] and yet freely forgoes doing so in order that the sacrifice of himself can proceed. Where there is no entitlement to such, an angel intervenes and the son of Abraham lives on, but where the one involved has the prerogative, the myriads of angels do not intervene, and *the* son of Abraham goes to his death.[18] The reader will recall that in Luke's version we find that an angel was nevertheless sent, by no means to deliver Jesus, but to strengthen him in the face of his impending suffering (Luke 22:43).

In the Genesis account, the act of binding Isaac, although just mentioned in a single verse, is made prominent through the title given to the incident. To prepare his son for sacrifice we read that Abraham 'built an altar there and arranged the wood, and he bound his son Isaac and laid him on the altar, on top of the wood' (22:9). Binding was not a typical part of regular sacrificial ritual, since by the time the victim, an animal, was placed on the altar it had already been slain. Here the victim was a living human being and Abraham felt the binding was necessary to prevent the possibility of escape. It was against Isaac in this bound condition that Abraham proceeded with the intention of delivering the fatal blow. The act of binding similarly takes place in Gethsemane, carried out by those same men who came bearing swords and clubs. We are told that 'the band of soldiers and its commander and the Jewish officials arrested Jesus and bound him' (John 18:12).[19] There is some consistency in the employment of allusion here. As Abraham, the one to make use of the knife and the wood, also bound the victim to be offered, so the same band of soldiers, equipped with swords and wooden clubs, bound the one they desired to lead away to his death. In this restrained state Jesus was presented first to the high priest (John 18:24) and then to Pilate (Matt. 27:2; Mark 15:1). Therefore, though not a conspicuous element in the overall sequence of events, the fact of Christ being bound nevertheless receives mention several times as the crucifixion draws near.

---

[17] It is interesting to observe that Targum Jonathan (on Gen. 22:10) speaks of a plurality of angels, in saying, 'the eyes of Isaac looked to the angels on high'. The same appears in Targum Neofiti.

[18] Rindge ('Reconfiguring the Akedah', 770) proposes that the tragedy of the Gethsemane experience, in which Jesus is depicted as 'sorrowful and distressed' (Matt. 26:37 etc.), is compounded by 'the clear disparity between God's intervention to save Isaac and the lack of a divine rescue to save Jesus'.

[19] The two verbs for 'bind' may differ in the LXX and New Testament, yet they are obviously synonymous.

The connection between the two occasions is further cemented linguistically by similar movements to take hold of a *machaira*, 'knife, sword'. On Moriah, Abraham 'stretched forth his hand [*exeteinen . . . tēn cheiran*] to take the knife [*labein tēn machairan*]' (Gen. 22:10). In the garden of Gethsemane, we read, 'behold, one of those who were with Jesus stretched forth his hand [*ekteinastēn cheiran*] and drew his sword [*machairan*], and struck the slave of the high priest, cutting off his ear. Then Jesus said to him, "Put your sword back into its place; for all who take the sword [*labontes machairan*] shall perish by the sword"' (Matt. 26:51–52). The unnamed disciple in this verse is identified in the fourth Gospel as Simon Peter (John 18:10). On reflection it would seem that a correlation exists at more than merely the level of language, yet it is not one of mere sameness. Abraham and Peter are indeed both characters who align with what is good and right in their respective scenarios. Abraham took the knife to kill his son, which was in obedience to the divine command and hence a righteous act. Peter drew his sword to defend God's Son against the wicked who would seize him, a well-intentioned act motivated by loyalty to his Master. Nevertheless, in this latter case he was in fact working against God's will, which was that Jesus should be taken and suffer. This very thing is implied in the rebuke he received from Jesus (Matt. 26:53) and the following words: 'How then will the Scriptures be fulfilled which say that it must happen in this way?' (v. 54; cf. also 16:22–23). When he raised the knife against his son Isaac, Abraham was prevented from acting. Ironically, when Peter lifted his sword against the enemy in defence of the Lord, he too was soon restrained. The one act of intervention ensured that Isaac remained unharmed; the other allowed Jesus to be taken away to his execution.[20]

One matter that receives no mention in the relevant scholarly literature, as far as my knowledge goes, is the possible presence of allusion with respect to the role of Judas Iscariot in what transpires in Gethsemane. Here there are admittedly no linguistic parallels with Genesis 22, but it is tempting to see some correlation at a deeper conceptual level, especially in the light of other connections noted above. With regard to the Aqedah, as we have seen, Abraham himself was the one set to carry out the slaying of Isaac, and it was he who bound the young man and was ready to lay his hand on him, though he was withheld from doing so. Abraham, then, fulfils the role of the officiator of the sacrifice, or the executioner. Now one element in the account is the fact that Abraham did not know the place where his son was to be offered up. At the beginning of the

---

[20] Huizenga comments (*The New Isaac*, 258): 'Hearing echoes of the Akedah here in Matt 26:51 involves high irony: Abraham's action would fulfill the will of God, while this disciple's would thwart it.'

narrative, God instructed him to go to 'one of the mountains of which I will tell you' (Gen. 22:2). Here in Genesis it was God himself who directed Abraham, the one to be responsible for Isaac's death, to the appointed place. In the Gospels we have explained how the instruments of death, corresponding to Abraham's knife and wood, are now put in the hands of evildoers. The mob of armed men are the ones to take Jesus away to his execution. In this scenario, it is these same men who lay their hands on him and who bind him as the agents of his demise. But how did they get to be in that place? They needed to be shown. And the one who showed them was Judas, one of Christ's own disciples: 'Now Judas, who betrayed him, knew the place', we are told, 'and taking a band of soldiers . . . he came there' (John 18:2–3; cf. Matt. 26:47; Mark 14:43; Luke 22:47).[21]

In the allusive schema not only has the agency of death, formerly in the hands of righteous Abraham, been transferred to the wicked; so too, it would seem, has the guidance to the very place where Christ was delivered up into their hands been similarly transposed. Whereas the holy and all-righteous God led Abraham to the place, the treacherous and self-serving Judas led the soldiers. This could be another textual means of stressing where the human responsibility for Jesus' coming death lies. As the implements of violence appear in the hands of the ungodly, hands which are permitted to be laid on the Son, so the task of bringing them to that place falls similarly to the ungodly, this being the traitor Judas.[22] This was truly the hour of darkness.[23]

Lastly, regarding the connections, an intriguing point of contact has been observed between Mark's version of Gethsemane and a non-biblical writing dealing with the life of Abraham. Mark presents Jesus as praying the words: 'Abba, Father, all things are possible for you [*panta dynata soi*]; remove this cup from me; yet not what I will, but what you will' (Mark 14:36). There is nothing in Genesis 22 that corresponds to the idea that 'all things are possible' for God. Scholarly research has discovered,[24] however, that the saying closely relates to something that features in the treatment of the Aqedah by the well-known Jewish philosopher and commentator Philo of Alexandria,[25] active in the early part of the first century AD. Philo was a highly influential figure, his writings even making a deep impression on the theologians of the early church. In discoursing on the offering of Isaac, Philo puts into the mouth of Abraham words bearing a remarkable resemblance to those Jesus prays. When Isaac

---

[21] Also Acts 1:16, which speaks of 'Judas, who became a guide for those who arrested Jesus'.

[22] Acts 1:18 describes his actions as 'wickedness'.

[23] Cf. the words of Jesus: 'this is your hour, and the power of darkness!' (Luke 22:53).

[24] See Rindge, 'Reconfiguring the Akedah', 769.

[25] Also known as Philo Judaeus.

questioned his father, saying, 'Where is the lamb for the burnt-offering?' (Gen. 22:7), Abraham is made to reply: 'Know all things are possible for God' (*On Abraham*, 175). The relevant words in Philo's Greek are *panta . . . theō dynata*, which consist of exactly the same subject (*panta*) and predicate (*dynata*) as the Markan utterance, similarly qualified by a dative prepositional phrase referring to God (*soi*, 'for you'; *theō*, 'for God'). In both contexts it seems that the statement is made in an implicit effort to divert the course of action that is about to take place – the offering up of Isaac in the one instance, and the passion of Christ in the other. In stating that everything is possible for God, each utterance has the effect of asking, 'Is there no other possible way?'[26]

We see, then, that both Philo on the Aqedah and Mark on Gethsemane include an almost identical saying. And in view of the other notable allusions of the happenings in Gethsemane to the Genesis event, one wonders whether this is also to be numbered among them – not as alluding to the biblical text itself but to one of the then-current Jewish expositions of it. In this regard, the question here naturally needs to be considered as to whether or not this interpretative insertion on the part of Philo could have been known to one of the Gospel-writers a short while later in the same century. It is not altogether impossible that Mark should have been familiar with the writings of the Alexandrian scholar. As early church history informs us and as local ecclesiastical tradition affirms, the person of Mark had a close association with the city of Alexandria where Philo had lived and composed his works.[27] Perhaps Mark came by the writings of Philo through the Jewish community there, or if he did not get to read the actual works themselves, he might at least have come to learn certain of the ideas they contained. While this is possible, I do not consider that this is the origin of the statement in Mark's account. Though I cannot prove it, I feel it is more probable that Philo's addition to the text of the Aqedah was not merely his own invention but rather reflected the wider interpretation of the passage among the Jews.

I find it interesting that Josephus, the Jewish historian writing around AD 90, expands the biblical text significantly at this same point. In response to Isaac's enquiry he has Abraham declare, 'God will provide for himself an oblation,

---

[26] Cf. the remark of Rindge ('Reconfiguring the Akedah', 769): 'The respective comments by Abraham and Jesus (that all things are possible with God) can likewise be read as an attempt to persuade God to intervene so as to remove death from the "beloved son"'.

[27] Such sources tell us that Mark departed from Rome, where he had assisted the apostle Peter, and came to Alexandria in Egypt, where he was eventually martyred and buried. To this day the Coptic Archbishop of Alexandria oversees the ecclesiastical dominion known as the 'See of St Mark'. For details, see Thomas C. Oden, *The African Memory of Mark: Reassessing Early Church Tradition* (Downers Grove, IL: InterVarsity Press, 2011).

since he is able[28] to make a bountiful provision for men out of what does not exist, and to take away from others what does exist, when they put their confidence in it.'[29] The overall meaning of the latter part amounts to a proposition that in substance does not differ considerably from 'all things are possible for God'.[30] Where there is nothing, God can bring something into being, and where something has being he can make it not so, all expressed within the context of God providing an offering for himself.[31] On Moriah the question amounts to: does it have to be Isaac who is slain? In the garden the question is: does Jesus have to drink the cup of suffering? Surely, God who is omnipotent can work out an alternative way?

So, while the matter is far from conclusive, I am inclined to the view that Mark is following some particular aspect of traditional Jewish understanding of the Aqedah, reflected in Philo and also perhaps Josephus, in inserting these words into his account of Gethsemane. One other factor that makes this specific point of contact between Mark and Philo seem more than coincidence is the meaningfulness of the utterance against the backdrop of the Aqedah. In answer to the question posed concerning Isaac – would he himself have to be slain? – the answer is 'No'. Although his death had been prescribed by God, another way was in fact possible. God showed Abraham a ram, which was then sacrificed in the place of his son (Gen. 22:13). With regard to God's Son, however, though it remained true that 'all things are possible for God', in this case there was to be no change in his predetermined plan. Jesus would go to his death.

In the light of the foregoing evidence, it would seem that what took place in the garden on the Mount of Olives with respect to Jesus is intended to evoke what transpired on Mount Moriah with respect to Isaac. Through the subtle deployment of literary allusions the reader is being informed that in the events about to be set in motion, that is, the impending crucifixion and resurrection,

---

[28] While the Greek term *hikanos* varies from that appearing in Philo and Mark, *dynatos*, the meaning is not so distinct. While the latter has the basic sense of 'able' and the former 'sufficient', the lexicon does also list 'capable' as one of the possible meanings of *hikanos* (Henry George Liddell and Robert Scott, *A Greek Lexicon* [Oxford: Clarendon, rev. edn, 1940], 825).

[29] Josephus, *Antiquities of the Jews* 1.227.

[30] I do wonder if the source for this particular addition to the text of the Aqedah is the not-too-dissimilar saying in the announcement of Isaac's birth (Gen. 18:14), discussed in chapter 4, which also has a counterpart in the Gospel account of Christ's birth (Luke 1:37).

[31] Three centuries later, Augustine of Hippo introduces a similar theme in a sermon on Gen. 22 entitled 'Abraham, Tested by God'. Augustine stated: 'After all, what is beyond hoping for from God, to whom nothing is difficult? . . . What can be difficult for him to make who makes with a word? . . . It was supremely easy for him to make everything out of nothing' (*Sermons* 2.7). For a heading to this section of the homily, Augustine's modern editor has appropriately chosen '*Everything is possible with God*', the very words found in Philo and Mark (Edmund Hill and Michele Pellegrino, *The Works of Saint Augustine, Part III, vol. 1: Sermons 1–19* [Brooklyn, NY: New City Press, 1990], 179). Was Augustine aware of an exegetical tradition similar to that known earlier to Philo and Josephus, and Mark too?

the reader is to recognize that the true son of Abraham had come and the promise of blessing in him was about to be accomplished. The allusions to Isaac seen at Christ's birth now receive further confirmation that he is indeed that special 'seed' of Abraham. And we will find the same truth to be further underscored once we come to the crucifixion itself in a subsequent chapter.

As has been shown, the allusions have not consisted of a mere correspondence of like to like. In this case, certain elements of the original Old Testament text that concerned Abraham have been transferred to those who came to take Jesus to the death awaiting him. It has been proposed, also, that a similar transference of role, though this time respecting the original role of God, is to be discerned with regard to Judas, as the wicked one who directed the band of the ungodly to the place where their victim could be found. By such means, as well as to identify Jesus as the ultimate son of Abraham, the allusions function to highlight where the responsibility, humanly speaking, for his execution lies.

Much more could be said regarding the Binding of Isaac and Jesus, but to pursue all avenues of interest would have made the chapter far too long for such a volume. Suffice it to make brief reference to one other important matter: the evident willingness of the victim. Much early Jewish commentary on the Aqedah applauds the virtuousness of Isaac in willingly submitting to Abraham. One might think that this is entirely absent from the original biblical text, but the idea is in fact present implicitly. Though we are not told how old Isaac was at the time, he is described (Gen. 22:5, 12) by the Hebrew noun *na'ar*, meaning 'youth, lad, young man'. The same term is used of the two servants who accompanied Isaac and his father, *šĕnê nĕ'ārāw*, literally 'two of his young men' (v. 3). The word may refer to a teenager, or even someone in his twenties. Not infrequently, it denotes young men old enough for military service (e.g. Gen. 14:24; Judg. 7:10; 2 Sam. 2:21). Whatever Isaac's precise age, when we consider that Abraham himself was well over 100 years old at this time, it becomes apparent that Isaac could very easily have gained the upper hand in any physical contest with his father. He would have had no problem escaping the old man's clutches, if he had so desired. Evidently, then, Isaac voluntarily allowed himself to be bound and laid on the altar. This willing consent on Isaac's part forms a significant element within the story according to a good many ancient Jewish interpretations of it.[32] The counterpart to this in the Gospels is, of course, the

---

[32] These include 4 Macc. (13:12; 16:20); the Qumran document 4Q225; Pseudo-Philo, *Liber Antiquitatum Biblicarum* (32.2–3); Josephus, *Antiquities of the Jews* (1.232); Targum Jonathan (on Gen. 22:10); and the influential midrash Genesis Rabbah (56.8). For more details, see Huizenga, *The New Isaac*, 89–90, 104–126. Willingness is similarly attributed to Isaac in the early Christian document 1 Clement (31.3, 'Isaac gladly allowed himself to be brought forward as a sacrifice').

total submissiveness of Jesus to the will of his Father. Though the prospect of suffering causes him considerable distress, he nevertheless prays, 'May your will be done' (Matt. 26:42; cf. Mark 14:36; Luke 22:42).[33]

The reader may have been wondering about the ram caught in the thicket (Gen. 22:13). This has only been mentioned here in passing and yet is surely an important feature of the Aqedah. As the account concerning Abraham and Isaac progresses, the first-time reader is relieved to discover that Isaac's life is not in fact required by God. When it comes to the sacrifice, the focus is taken away from Isaac and placed on a ram, conveniently situated at hand and unable to get away. It is of great significance that no allusion is made to this ram and its predicament in Gethsemane. I believe this to be a deliberate omission. This is because the Gospel narrative is saving up such an allusion for the more appropriate time of the crucifixion itself. During that event, as will be explained,[34] there is a subtle, but potent, allusion to the ram divinely provided on Mount Moriah.

In this and the preceding chapter, then, we have detected the presence of two distinct schemas of allusion in the events of this night. At the plain level, all that is happening occurs around the time of the feast of Passover, so the reader already has that festival and its significance in view. At the level of allusion, the mind of the reader has now been drawn to both the Day of Atonement and the offering of Isaac. We may ask: why these two? Taken individually, the reason why each of these should be evoked at this point in the Gospel accounts is not, to my mind, at all difficult to discern. The events of Gethsemane mark the beginning of the day of Christ's death, recalling that once the sun had set that evening, the new day, that day on which the crucifixion took place, had already commenced. During the first few hours of that day, in the allusions of Gethsemane the reader is further given the ritual of Israel's atonement to complement that of the Passover. As previously remarked, Jesus will die as the Lamb of God, but also as the atoning sacrifice of the goat offered to the Lord. And now too he is being depicted as the ultimate son of Abraham who would bring in the divine blessing, and this through the actual offering up of himself, which Isaac was not obliged to undergo.

From what scholars have discovered about these various themes as expressed in ancient Jewish literature, there would seem to be a single underlying, unifying

---

[33] On the theme of Christ's willingness vis-à-vis Isaac in Matthew's Gospel, see Leroy A. Huizenga, 'Obedience unto Death: The Matthean Gethsemane and Arrest Sequence and the Aqedah', *CBQ* 71.3 (2009): 507–526; and for John's Gospel, see Mitchell Alexander Esswein, 'Is He Going to Kill Himself? The Willing Self-Sacrifice of Jesus and the Akedah in the Fourth Gospel', *Sacra Scripta* 11.2 (2013): 231–261.

[34] See chapter 24.

concept. Evidence suggests that the Jews perceived the offering of Isaac as the foundational offering on which all later sacrificial offerings were based. Although Isaac did not actually die, his willingness to offer up himself, according to Jewish perceptions, was to such a degree that to all intents and purposes he was considered dead.[35] In a sense, the later offerings of Israel were re-enactments of Isaac's offering, or were at least powerful memorials of it.[36] Such a relation in thought was considerably reinforced by the belief that the locality of the Aqedah, namely Mount Moriah, was in fact the later location of the Jerusalem temple, as suggested in the Old Testament itself (2 Chr. 3:1), as well as in extrabiblical writings.[37] But of all Jewish sacrifices the offering of Isaac was especially closely associated with that of the Passover.[38] The Gethsemane accounts in the Gospels which allude to the Aqedah are, of course, set within the context of the Passover celebration.

To the Jewish mind, the nature of Isaac's offering was such that it was able to attain atonement.[39] This therefore establishes a connection with the Day of Atonement, the regular annual atoning ritual of the Jews. More than this, since the temple was built, as was believed, at that same locality, the very rock on the summit of Moriah on which Isaac's offering was enacted became the bedrock on which the most holy place of the temple was constructed. That is to say, the Binding of Isaac occurred on the identical spot where centuries later the blood of the goat brought into the sacred inner chamber on the Day of Atonement was sprinkled.

We note finally on this matter that the rabbis of old liked to speculate on the exact date of the Aqedah. One line of thought held that it fell precisely on what was to become the day of Passover. In one of the standard midrashic texts, it is written: "'As on the day when you came out of Egypt, I will show them wonders'"

---

[35] Some ancient sources speak as if Isaac had actually died. See the texts and discussion in Kathleen Troost-Cramer, *Jesus as Means and Locus of Worship in the Fourth Gospel: Sacrifice and Worship Space in John* (Eugene, OR: Pickwick, 2017), 28–29; also C. T. R. Hayward, 'The Sacrifice of Isaac and Jewish Polemic against Christianity', *CBQ* 52.2 (1990): 292. The Neofiti Targum, for example, here states that 'Abraham sacrificed his son Isaac', as if it were an accomplished act. More significantly, perhaps, *Pirkei de Rabbi Eliezer* (31.10) describes Isaac's soul as departing from his body and then returning.

[36] Cf. Huizenga (*The New Isaac*, 241), who speaks of Isaac as 'the patriarchal prototype and paradigm of all Jewish sacrifice'.

[37] E.g. *Jubilees* 18.13; Josephus, *Antiquities of the Jews* 1.226.

[38] There is much in the scholarly literature that supports this view. See, e.g., the remarks of Huizenga (*The New Isaac*, 241): 'In Jewish tradition, as we have seen, the Akedah was linked to Passover and all temple sacrifices'; Troost-Cramer (*Jesus as Means and Locus of Worship*, 28): 'The Passover lamb, therefore, recalls and represents the Akedah, with Isaac as the "lamb"'; Esswein ('Is He Going to Kill Himself?', 237): 'one should also note a link between the *Akedah* tradition and the Passover . . . as time progressed, there arose a tradition that Passover and Isaac's near-sacrifice were connected'.

[39] Troost-Cramer (*Jesus as Means and Locus of Worship*, 32; cf. 33–34), for example, speaks of 'the meaning and effect of the Akedah as an atoning sacrifice'.

[Micah 7:15], for on it [the Passover] Isaac was born, and on it he was bound [*ne'ĕqad*]'.[40] Yet another school of rabbinic thought claimed an alternative timing for the Aqedah, saying that 'the expiatory sacrifice was brought once a year, on the Day of Atonement, the day on which the offering of Isaac took place'.[41] It was not in the least bit uncommon for more than one interpretation to be in circulation among the rabbinic schools. The point we are making is that ancient Jewish traditions existed that closely associated the Aqedah thematically as well as temporally with both the feast of Passover and the Day of Atonement. As we have seen in this and the previous chapter, the Passover event of Gethsemane, marking the onset of Christ's physical passion, evokes through its allusions both the Day of Atonement and the Aqedah. Thus, all three Old Testament elements are brought together in a skilfully woven literary web in the New Testament narration of what Jesus underwent in the garden.

In the present chapter, then, we have seen how Jesus enters his day of suffering as the new Isaac, the true son of Abraham in the fullest sense, the one who would offer himself wholly up to death, according to the divine foreordained plan, and bring the blessing of forgiveness and eternal life to all who put their faith in him.[42]

[40] Exodus Rabbah 15.

[41] Louis Ginzberg, *Legends of the Jews*, vol. 1 (Philadelphia, PA: Jewish Publication Society of America, 1909), 283.

[42] Leroy Huizenga, commenting specifically on Matthew's version ('Obedience unto Death: The Matthean Gethsemane and Arrest Sequence and the Aqedah', *CBQ* 71.3 [2009]: 526), concludes by saying: 'The Aqedah thus plays a major role in the Matthean Gethsemane and arrest sequence. It emphasizes Jesus' general obedience by appropriating a specific type [namely, Isaac]; reveals that his death resulted from obedience to the divine plan, not a mere human conspiracy; gives his sacrifice as a rationale for his nonviolence; and functions as positive apologetic. The subtle mechanism of allusion increasing its very force, the passage powerfully demonstrates more than that Jesus is not brigand nor magician nor coward. Jesus is in fact cut from the same cloth as Isaac, who faced his sacrificial death with incomparable obedience and courage.'

22

Peter's denials

Matthew 26:69–75; Mark 14:66–72; Luke 22:54–62; John 18:15–18, 25–27

After his arrest in Gethsemane, Jesus was carried off to the house of Annas, the high priest (John 18:13).[1] We read that though most of the disciples had fled when Jesus was seized, Peter and one other disciple followed behind the band of soldiers and servants that had taken him (v. 15a). This other disciple is not identified, but seeing that he is only referred to in the Gospel of John the traditional view that this is John himself does not seem unreasonable. For argument's sake we will call him by that name.

Jesus was brought into the courtyard of the high priest's house (v. 15b), and John, 'who was known to the high priest', spoke to the serving woman at the door and gained access for Peter (v. 16). It was there, gathered around a fire in the courtyard (v. 18), that Peter's interrogation began. Earlier that night Jesus had warned Peter that his faith was going to be tested (Luke 22:31–32), and that time of trial had now come.

With regard to the Gospel record of Peter's denials, it is here proposed that allusion is being made to a particular passage in the Jewish Torah. This is that ordinance found in Numbers 5:11–31, the test for an unfaithful wife.

First we examine the setting. Since we have examined the law of Numbers 5 in a previous chapter,[2] we here repeat only its salient features. The law concerns a possible situation where a 'man's wife goes astray and is unfaithful to him' (v. 12) but there is no witness to her infidelity and she has not been caught in the act of adultery (v. 13). Where such unfaithfulness was suspected, the wife was to be brought 'to the priest' (v. 15). All that follows then was to take place within the tabernacle. This is evident from the fact that a grain-offering was presented (vv. 15, 25), something which required the fire on the bronze altar (v. 26; cf. Lev. 2:1–2). Also, the woman was made to stand 'before the Lord'

---

[1] Annas was the father-in-law of Caiaphas, yet both are called 'high priest' in the Gospel of John (18:13, 19, 24; cf. Acts 4:6).

[2] See chapter 15.

(Num. 5:16), again suggestive of the sanctuary.[3] There is mention of 'holy water' (v. 17a), which most probably refers to the water of cleansing contained in the tabernacle's bronze laver,[4] and the transaction involved the use of dust from the tabernacle floor (v. 17b). Since the woman would not be permitted to enter the tent-like structure itself, into which only priests could go, we may conclude with some certainty that these proceedings were enacted within the court of the tabernacle.

In the case of Peter in the Gospels, we find that he has come into a 'court' (*aulē*), the same term used to describe the tabernacle court in the Greek version of the Hebrew Bible (e.g. Exod. 27:9; Num. 4:32). There is a priestly figure present, in the person of Annas; it is in fact his courtyard. Within that area there is a fire (John 18:18). The word used here is a rather specific one (*anthrakia*), one that gives the idea of something where coal or charcoal could be burned. Such a term has an association with the altar in the tabernacle's courtyard, on which were 'burning coals' (Lev. 16:12, *anthrakōn*; cf. Isa. 6:6). In both accounts, then, there is a priest and a court, in which there stood a fire of burning coals.

Possibly the serving woman who let Peter in is another element within the same allusion. In the Gospel she is termed a 'doorkeeper' (*thyrōros*) and evidently had control over the doorway leading into the court of the high priest. This same word may be used of those who kept the doors of the temple (cf. Ezek. 44:11). We remember too that there were 'women who served at the entrance [LXX: *thyras*, 'doors'] of the tabernacle of meeting' (Exod. 38:8; cf. also 1 Sam. 2:22).

From a thematic point of view, we perceive a striking similarity. In each instance we have a principal character whose loyalty to another is in question – the husband's wife and the Lord's disciple. In each respective priestly courtyard setting, both of these undergo an ordeal to determine their faithfulness. A deep-level relationship, therefore, can be seen to exist between the two different situations. But there is not simply a one-to-one correspondence between the parties involved, as is often the case with such a literary device. As we have stressed before, part of the skill of allusion involves change, and sometimes reversal or contrast. In the law of Numbers 5 a woman is being subjected to trial by a man, whereas in the Gospels we have a man examined by a woman,[5] in

---

[3] Elsewhere in the law of Moses the phrase 'before the LORD' has particular reference to activities at the sanctuary (e.g. Exod. 23:17; 27:21; 28:30; Lev. 1:5; 6:25; 14:11; Num. 3:4; 16:40). Hertz remarks that 'before the LORD' indicates 'near the altar of burnt-offering' (J. H. Hertz, *The Pentateuch and Haftorahs: Hebrew Text, English Translation, and Commentary* [London: Soncino, 1981], 590).

[4] For 'holy water' Targum Onkelos reads 'water from the laver' and Targum Jonathan 'holy water from the laver'. The same source for this water is found, among other sources, in the Mishnah (*Sotah* 2.2), in the commentaries of Rashi and Ibn Ezra (on v. 17), and more recently in that of Hertz (*Pentateuch and Haftorahs*, 590: 'holy water . . . from the bronze laver which stood near the altar').

[5] Note Luke 22:57, where Peter addresses her simply as 'woman'.

a society that was very much male-dominated. In the law an ordained priest, invested with sacred authority, instigates the trial; in the Gospels it is a serving-girl. For sure this woman has a priestly association, being a member of the high priest's household, yet she is just a lowly servant nonetheless, and a female one at that. Although in the employ of the high priest, she is completely lacking in the authority of the sacerdotal office. These distinctions between the original law and the later event recorded in the Gospels have a similar effect, which is to greatly diminish the severity of the challenge. In contrast to the woman in Numbers 5, for Peter the situation is made into one that is far less foreboding – not a male officiant but a woman, not an actual priest but merely a servile member of a priest's household, and all in the context of an informal conversation rather than a formally prescribed ritual.[6] We further note that the woman in Numbers was in that place according to a legal requirement, while Peter was there voluntarily.

Another important distinction is that the purpose of the legal ordinance was to ascertain whether the woman had been unfaithful prior to the moment of trial, while for the apostle his presence in the courtyard was itself the actual occasion of his trial, to see whether he would be faithful in that very situation.

So, when faced with a less threatening circumstance, the fact is that Peter crumbles. Although just a short while earlier he had declared that he would never forsake Jesus, even if threatened with death (Matt. 26:35; cf. Luke 22:33), he fails the test and demonstrates infidelity to his Master. Questioned three times by the servant-girl, in each instance he denies his relationship with Jesus.

One prominent feature in each setting is that of swearing an oath and the pronouncement of a curse. In Numbers 5 we read that 'the priest is to put the woman under an oath' (v. 19). If she were guilty of unfaithfulness to her husband, a 'curse' would come upon her (vv. 20–22). In the Gospel account it is Peter who, of his own accord, swears an oath and pronounces a curse – 'then he began to curse and swear' (Matt. 26:74; Mark 14:71) – which can only be taken as actions applicable to himself.[7] Peter, we see, disowns Jesus despite his

---

6 There seems to be no indication in the Gospels that at this stage the followers of Jesus were also liable to be arrested and harmed. The men who came to Gethsemane were seeking none but 'Jesus of Nazareth', and he alone was taken. Of the twelve disciples Jesus said, 'Let these go' (John 18:7–8), and we read of no attempt to seize any of them. This being so, though understandably fearful due to his Master's arrest, Peter had no great reason to fear conviction and punishment himself for the mere fact of being a disciple. John, after all, along with several women followers, was present at the crucifixion, where it would have been publicly known that he was a disciple, since Jesus addressed him from the cross (John 19:27).

7 R. C. H. Lenski, *Commentary on the New Testament, vol. 1: Matthew* (Minneapolis, MN: Augsburg, 1961 [repr. of 1943 edn]), 1073: 'He called down all manner of evil on himself and with oaths called God to witness that he did not know him [Jesus].'

previous protestations to the contrary, and despite his present swearing of an oath, making his denial all the more acute.

Peter's oath-bound remonstration took the form of 'I do not know the man' (Matt. 26:72, 74; cf. Mark 14:71). The verb used is in fact grammatically perfect,[8] a verbal form which could also technically bear the sense of 'have known' (as in 2 Tim. 3:15). What is interesting about this term is that besides its plain meaning of 'knowing' someone, it also possesses an idiomatic sense in which it indicates not simple mental knowledge but a more intimate manner of relationship. And when the direct object is 'man', in 'to know a man', the expression can be that used with reference to a woman sleeping with a man (e.g. Gen. 19:8; Judg. 21:12). Here, of course, this potential secondary layer of meaning in Peter's words bears a direct connection with the situation in Numbers 5. For there the whole matter revolved around the question of whether or not the woman concerned had known a man in this other sense. In both cases, for the one undergoing examination to deny knowing the particular man would be a declaration of innocence in the mind of the examiner, and yet in Peter's case his denial of such knowledge makes his confession one of guilt, since he does indeed know Jesus.

Finally, among the allusions, there remains what strikes me as a most artful association between the two passages. The trial that the woman was to undergo is generally referred to as that of the 'water of bitterness' (cf. Num. 5:18, 19, 23, 24 in NRSV, ESV, NASB, NKJV, NJB). The reason for this is that she was made to literally drink water that would result in bitter suffering if she were indeed guilty. To my mind, it is more than mere coincidence that the incident involving Peter ends with the words 'wept *bitterly*' (Matt. 26:75; Luke 22:62). Here we have a bitter consequence of Peter's failure to remain faithful, and here that is also expressed by means of water, shed in the form of tears.[9]

Before we draw matters to a conclusion, it is essential that we recall what was stated in our earlier consideration of the law of Numbers 5. There it was noted that the wife in the Torah passage functions as a symbol of the nation of Israel, marriage being a commonly used metaphor of the relationship between the Lord and his people. When seen in this way, the contents of the law in question become somewhat more relevant to what we read about Peter, who is being represented allusively as the wife figure in Numbers. His infidelity is not marital, but

---

[8] *oida*, first-person singular perfect indicative active.

[9] Before this concluding scene we are told that Peter 'went outside'. Interestingly, according to ancient Jewish tradition on Num. 5, if the woman was found to be guilty of infidelity, as Peter in fact was, then the offender was to be immediately taken out of the court so as not to defile the sacred area (Mishnah, *Sotah* 3.4, 'Remove her, so that she does not make the court of the temple impure'). In the analogy, once his guilt was known to him, Peter instantly departed from the court.

it can properly be perceived as unfaithfulness in a spiritual relationship. This becomes all the more pertinent when we realize that the marriage metaphor of the Old Testament regarding Yahweh and Israel undergoes a transformation in the New. The bridegroom is now Christ, and his bride the corporate body of those who believe in him, the church (cf. John 3:29; 2 Cor. 11:2; Rev. 21:9), of which Peter is a leading member. Peter is unfaithful to his 'Lord' (cf. Luke 22:61), another term which could fit well into a marital metaphor.[10]

In sum, then, it would appear that the denials of Peter draw allusively upon the Mosaic law of marital fidelity. This does not mean, lest there be any misunderstanding, that in this episode we are seeing the rule of Numbers 5 actually being applied to Peter. That, of course, would not be allusion but would be part of the surface meaning of the text. Clearly, the apostle is not literally being subjected to the ordeal prescribed. Rather, what we see here is a series of verbal and conceptual pointers to that law. In so doing another dimension of meaning is subtly added to the Gospel narrative. And this helps us appreciate more the significance of Peter's actions and experience on this sad occasion.

The presence of the allusions reinforces the fact that the event was one of a trial, a test to discern the apostle's afore-confessed absolute loyalty to his Lord. The differences with the law – his confrontation being not with a priest but with a servant, not with a high-status male but with a woman of much lower rank – serve to indicate that Peter gives way too readily, even under a moderate degree of pressure. In the light of the allusions, we further see that his denial of Jesus is comparable to that of infidelity within marriage, the most intimate of human relationships. It constitutes a betrayal of the relationship, of love, and of trust, in a union with no mere human husband but with the Lord himself, the heavenly Bridegroom. And then, in bringing down a curse on himself in the face of his manifest unfaithfulness, he shows himself to be altogether deserving of undergoing the contents of that curse.

From the perspective of the broader context, considering that whatever it was that Peter uttered in his curse did not in actual fact come upon him, the story betokens the wonder and magnitude of divine grace. Evidently, Peter was forgiven, as shown by the fact that after the resurrection he was reinstated and affirmed by the Lord he had denied, an event to be dealt with in a subsequent chapter.[11]

---

[10] In Hebrew the term 'Lord' (not 'LORD', which represents the divine name) may also connote the idea of 'husband'. This is so whether the original term is *'ādôn* or *ba'al*. For the former, see Francis Brown, S. R. Driver and Charles A. Briggs, *A Hebrew and English Lexicon of the Old Testament* (Oxford: Clarendon, rev. edn, 1953), 11a (meaning 2.c *husband*), and for the latter, 127a (meaning 2. *husband*). Both of these nouns would be rendered in Greek as *kyrios*, as used with reference to Jesus in the Gospels.

[11] See chapter 30.

23

The trial and crucifixion 1

Matthew 26:57 – 27:56; Mark 14:53 – 15:41; Luke 22:63 – 23:49; John 18:19 – 19:37

The Gospel accounts of this crucial day in the purpose of God are replete with both Old Testament citations and allusions, as we might expect. Already in the upper room Jesus has quoted directly from Psalm 41:9 concerning the one who would betray him (John 13:18), and alluded most clearly to the ceremony of the old covenant (Exod. 24) in the institution of the new.[1] In that same room he discoursed to his disciples and told them about the predictions in the Psalms (35:19; 69:4) of the unmitigated hatred that he would experience (John 15:25). Already as they walked to the garden he has cited the prophecy of Zechariah 13:7, which foretold how his companions would desert him at the time of his suffering (Matt. 26:31; Mark 14:27). Already in Gethsemane both the ritual of the Day of Atonement and the offering of Isaac have been evoked. Now, as his captors bring him to the authorities for a mockery of a trial and a cruel execution, the Scriptures of old persist in being called to mind, both directly and indirectly.

As the narrative progresses we encounter more overt Old Testament references relating to the heavenly Son of Man (Dan. 7:13; cf. Matt. 26:64; Mark 14:63), the suffering servant (Isa. 53:12; cf. Mark 15:28; Luke 22:37), the innocent afflicted one of the Psalms (Ps. 22:1; cf. Matt. 27:46; Mark 15:34; Ps. 22:18; cf. John 19:24; Ps. 31:5; cf. Luke 23:46; Ps. 69:21; cf. Matt. 27:34),[2] the Passover lamb (Exod. 12:46; Num. 9:12; cf. John 19:36) and the one who was pierced (Zech. 12:10; cf. John 19:37). Alongside such direct references the allusions likewise continue. Not surprisingly, the more extensive manner of allusion that forms our main consideration once again leads us back to the Day of Atonement and the offering up of Isaac, both alluded to in the Gethsemane narrative previously treated. We shall devote a chapter to each of these two.

---

[1] See chapter 19.

[2] For a detailed analysis of references to the Psalms, see U. P. McCaffrey, 'Psalm Quotations in the Passion Narratives of the Gospels', *Neotestamentica* 14 (1980): 73–89.

With regard to the Day of Atonement there are at least three distinct elements in the trial and crucifixion accounts that hearken back to the ritual of that important religious festival described in Leviticus 16. We will first give our attention to the figure of Barabbas in relation to Jesus. Second, we will investigate the clothing that was removed from Jesus before he was crucified, especially his seamless tunic. Then, third, we will consider the tearing of the veil in the temple.

Barabbas appears in the trial accounts in all four Gospels. These records tell us that Pilate, the Roman governor, was reluctant to condemn Jesus and have him crucified, as he suspected the Jewish leaders had delivered him up out of envy (Matt. 27:18; Mark 15:10). Pilate thought up a way of freeing Jesus, which ultimately backfired. Apparently there was a custom at Passover time to release a prisoner, chosen by the people (Matt. 27:15; Mark 15:6; John 18:39).[3] The crowd are given the choice between Jesus and one Barabbas, a 'notorious prisoner' (Matt. 27:16). The Gospels provide details of the crimes the latter had committed, including rebellion and murder (Mark 15:7; Luke 23:19, 25). Unfortunately for Pilate, the chief priests and elders persuade the people to request the release of Barabbas and not Jesus (Matt. 27:20; Mark 15:11). At this the former is set free, while the latter is handed over to be crucified (Matt. 27:26; Mark 15:15).

A number of biblical scholars, as well as preachers, have remarked on the connection here, at the conceptual level, with the ceremony of Yom Kippur.[4] At the heart of the latter were two goats (Lev. 16:5). The pair of goats were presented in the courtyard of the sanctuary and the officiating high priest was to cast lots over them to determine the fate of each (vv. 7–8). One of them was to be sacrificed to the Lord (v. 9), while the other was to be sent out into the wilderness (v. 10). We can immediately see a basic similarity here with the situation in the Gospels, where it is explicitly specified that we are dealing with another 'two'.[5] Here before the presiding official are two prisoners; a choice is made between the two, with the result that one is put to death and the other dismissed, all in a public setting that includes the Jewish people. Since the reader of the Gospels has very recently been alerted to allusions involving the ceremony of atonement, his or her mind will be ready to pick up further allusive elements relating to the same portion of the Torah.[6]

---

[3] Note that in John 18:39 Pilate is recorded as saying, 'You have a custom that I release someone to you at the Passover.' It was not, then, a Roman custom, but a Jewish one that the governor continued to observe.

[4] For recent scholarly work on Jesus and Barabbas in comparison with the two goats of the Day of Atonement, see Hans M. Moscicke, 'Jesus as Goat of the Day of Atonement in Recent Synoptic Gospels Research', *Currents in Biblical Research* 17.1 (2018): 59–85.

[5] Note Pilate's question to the crowd: 'Which of the *two* do you want me to release to you?' (Matt. 27:21).

[6] Even without reference to earlier allusions to the Day of Atonement, one scholar has claimed that the parallels between the atoning ceremony and the Barabbas narrative are 'obvious'. See Jennifer K. Berenson

In order to appreciate why the Day of Atonement is being alluded to here, it is crucial that we understand the respective roles of the two goats. Failure to do so might easily lead to a misinterpretation of what is going on in the Gospels, and in many cases has in fact done just that. The first thing we need to be aware of is that both the text of Leviticus and the traditional Jewish interpretation of that text speak of the two goats in a unified way. Though there is a different outcome for each of them in the ceremony, there is also a sense in which the two are identified. In Leviticus 16 the goats used for the ritual are specified as 'two male goats' (v. 5), not one of each gender, or two females. The same verse informs us that these two goats were to be 'for a sin-offering'. It does not say 'for sin-offerings', but 'two male goats for *a sin-offering*' in the singular. In other words, the two together both comprised the same essential offering. In keeping with this is the fact that both goats are explicitly said to be involved in the atoning process, both the one that was sent out (v. 10) and the one that was slain (vv. 15–16), a point that is often overlooked.

Later Jewish interpreters of the law recognized that the two goats fulfilled, in a way, a single function, and therefore were to be identified as a unity. For this reason the Mishnah determined that the two should actually look the same: 'The two goats of the Day of Atonement – it is a requirement that they be alike in appearance and in stature and in value and in their being taken at the same time [lit. 'as one', *kě'eḥād*]' (*Yoma* 6.1).[7] This essential sameness between the two animals came to be seen as one of the distinctive features of the ceremony.[8]

I believe this resemblance between the goats finds a counterpart in the Gospel accounts of Jesus and Barabbas. Not only are they two males presented in order that a particular fate be chosen for each of them, but the two are much more closely associated in another way. Anyone acquainted with Aramaic will understand that the name Barabbas (*bar* 'Abbâ), conveys the meaning 'son of the father'.[9] The other of the two men is, of course, by nature *the* Son of the Father. The name Barabbas is simply a patronymic, or a kind of surname, identifying the man's father, here a person called Abba, in order to distinguish a

---

Maclean, 'Barabbas, the Scapegoat Ritual, and the Development of the Passion Narrative', *HTR* 100.3 (2007): 313.

[7] It is interesting to observe that early Christian interpreters showed familiarity with this Jewish tradition concerning the likeness of the goats. Note the following descriptions in Christian writings of the second and early third centuries: 'two fine goats that are alike' (Epistle of Barnabas 7.6); 'two identical goats' (Justin Martyr, *Dialogue with Trypho* 40.4); 'two goats . . . of the same age and appearance' (Tertullian, *Against Marcion* 3.7).

[8] Another relevant expansion found in the Mishnah (*Yoma* 4.1) concerns the high priest laying a hand on the head of each of the two goats and declaring, 'The sin-offering of the Lord', emphasizing the statement in Leviticus (16:5) that both goats together constituted this one offering.

[9] Cf. R. T. France, *The Gospel of Matthew* (NICNT; Grand Rapids, MI: Eerdmans, 2007), 1053, n. 32.

man with a common first name from others bearing the same name. What, then, was the actual first name of Barabbas? A textual variant exists in the Greek manuscripts of Matthew 27:16 and 17 which provides that name. While some ancient copies read *Barabbas* alone, others contain *Iēsous Barabbas*, that is, 'Jesus Barabbas'. The authenticity of this latter is highly probable, and is being recognized more and more as the original reading. It is hardly likely that a later Christian scribe could of his own accord enter the name of Jesus as being also that of a notorious criminal and for it to then find popularity. The inclusion of 'Jesus' is accepted in a range of modern English versions, including NRSV, NET, REB, CEV and GNT.[10] Significantly, although it was omitted in the original edition of the NIV, it was entered in the new edition (2011). As far as one recent scholarly study is concerned, '[t]he vast majority of modern scholars have accepted this reading'.[11]

We have then two males for the crowd to decide between, one Jesus Barabbas and the other Jesus, the Son of the Father. Both could legitimately share one and the same name: Yeshua bar Abba.[12] In this way the Gospel narrative is identifying the two, just like the goats of the Day of Atonement where the two are one.

Aside from the close conceptual association between the two male goats and the two men called Jesus, we may also detect a number of verbal connections. There are not so many of these, perhaps because the whole scenario is so evocative of the levitical enactment, and perhaps because there have already been notable allusions to the same Old Testament festival a short while before in the Gospel narrative.

In the matter of the release of one prisoner to the crowd, the words of Matthew contain a construction reminiscent of the election of the goats on Yom Kippur. Back in Leviticus the text states that 'Aaron shall cast lots over the two goats, one lot for the LORD [*hena tō kyriō*] and one lot for the one sent away

---

[10] The explanatory note in the online NET Bible states: 'Although the external evidence for the inclusion of "Jesus" before "Barabbas" . . . is rather sparse, being restricted virtually to mss of what was formally labeled the "Caesarean" text (Θ *f*1 700* sys arm geo2; Ormss), the omission of the Lord's name in apposition to "Barabbas" is such a strongly motivated reading that it can hardly be original. There is no good explanation for a scribe unintentionally adding Ἰησοῦν (*Iēsoun*) before Βαραββᾶν (*Barabban*), especially since Barabbas is mentioned first in each verse (thus dittography is ruled out). Further, the addition of τὸν λεγόμενον Χριστόν (*ton legomenon Christon*, "who is called Christ") to Ἰησοῦν in v. 17 makes better sense if Barabbas is also called "Jesus" (otherwise, a mere "Jesus" would have been a sufficient appellation to distinguish the two).'

[11] Hans M. Moscicke, 'Jesus, Barabbas, and the Crowd as Figures in Matthew's Day of Atonement Typology (Matt 27:15–26)', *JBL* 139.1 (2020): 132; cf. Maclean, 'Barabbas, the Scapegoat Ritual, and the Development of the Passion Narrative', 325.

[12] Of course, even if one has doubts about 'Jesus' being the first name of Barabbas, the meaning of this latter name in Aramaic still ties him to the person of Jesus.

[*hena tō apopompaiō*]' (16:8). In the Gospel we read that 'at the feast the governor was accustomed to release one prisoner to the crowd [*hena tō ochlō*] whom they wanted' (Matt. 27:15). Each exhibits the same particular Greek construction (*hena* plus dative), the only occurrence of such in the entire New Testament. Some scholars take this, as seems reasonable, to be a deliberate 'verbal echo'.[13]

Then there is the linguistic fact that the idea of 'sending away' in Leviticus would be expressed by the selfsame verb that also means 'release' in Hebrew. There is a single verb, *šillaḥ*, signifying 'send away, release, dismiss'. We see this, for instance, in certain English translations of Leviticus 16, where 'send away' (NASB, NIV, REB) in verse 21 renders the same Hebrew word as 'release' (NASB, NIV, REB) in verse 22. In the Gospels the Greek verb that is used with respect to the release of one of the two prisoners is *apolyō*, 'release, set loose' (e.g. Matt. 27:15, 21; Mark 15:11, 15; Luke 23:18; John 18:39). In the Greek text of the LXX the live goat is described (Lev. 16:8, 10) by the adjective *apopompaios*, which is a derivative of the verb *apopempō*, meaning 'send away'. However, in another ancient Greek translation of the Old Testament, that known as Aquila's version, this goat is termed *tragon apolelymenon*, 'a goat released'.[14] In this case the animal is described by the participle of *apolyō*, the same verb as that occurring with reference to Barabbas in the Gospel passages. Consequently, the action relating to the living goat in the law is not essentially different from that relating to Barabbas in the Gospels.

This brings us now to the all-important matter of the significance of the goats on the Day of Atonement. The ritual, like most under the Mosaic law, abounded in symbolism, and therefore what was enacted with respect to the slaughtered goat as well as this second goat must have represented meaningful truths to the people of Israel, who observed the proceedings. It has already been demonstrated that although two goats were involved there was an essential unity between them, both together making up a single sin-offering and both being involved in the act of atonement. This suggests that in the ritual of the goats we are looking at two aspects of the same basic truth, and that truth obviously centres on the idea of making atonement.

In short, one goat was to offer up its life in sacrificial death and its blood employed in various rituals in the sanctuary (Lev. 16:9, 15–16). This intimated the principle that 'without the shedding of blood there is no forgiveness' (Heb. 9:22). Put simply, atonement for sin required death, namely the death of an innocent victim. Once this sacrifice and disposal of blood was completed, the

---

13 E.g. Moscicke, 'Jesus, Barabbas, and the Crowd', 140.
14 See Hans M. Moscicke, *The New Day of Atonement: A Matthean Typology* (Tübingen: Mohr Siebeck, 2020), 115, n. 78.

high priest was to take the other goat, lay hands on its head, and confess over it all the sins, iniquities and transgressions of Israel. In so doing, we read, 'he shall lay them [the sins etc.] on the head of the goat and send it away into the wilderness by the hand of a man standing ready' (v. 21). The laying on of hands therefore symbolized the transference of sin to the second animal.[15] In watching this goat depart from their encampment, the people were seeing their sins being removed, even disappearing. This goat, we must bear in mind, was not a wild goat accustomed to the harshness of the desert, but a domesticated animal. The man who led it away abandoned it some distance from the camp and returned alone. Unable to fend for itself there, the creature would almost certainly perish. But even if not, the point is that it was gone for good, and the nation's sins with it.[16]

The main idea, then, behind the second goat was a strongly negative one with respect to the animal itself – it was laden with the sins placed on it and was brought to a place far away in an exceedingly inhospitable environment where it would be irretrievably lost.[17] Yet for the people what was being symbolized by the goat was altogether positive. They were, in ceremonial form, seeing the sin of the nation being taken and removed far from them, permanently annulled. Accordingly, viewing the goats as a twofold representation of the act of atoning for sin, we could say that the first goat signified the sacrificial *means* of atonement, and the second the expiatory *effect* of that means. In plain words, the death of the innocent victim (depicted in the first goat) brought about the removal of sin (depicted in the second).

Some further enquiry is necessary into the sending away of the goat. When lots were cast over the animals, the two options are described as being either 'to the LORD' or, literally, 'to Azazel' (Lev. 16:8; cf. vv. 10, 26). In Hebrew these two phrases are *lyhwh* and *la'ăzā'zēl* respectively, where the initial *l-* is a preposition meaning 'to', 'for', or 'belonging to'. This is represented in the Greek of the LXX by the grammatical dative case, which essentially covers the same range of meanings, the relevance of which will be seen presently. There is an evident balance between these two phrases, and since the former includes a name, the

---

[15] Cf. Baruch A. Levine, *Leviticus* (JPS Torah Commentary; Philadelphia, PA: Jewish Publication Society, 1989), 106: 'By laying his hands on the scapegoat, the High Priest transferred to it the sins of the people'.

[16] Gordon J. Wenham (*The Book of Leviticus* [NICOT; Grand Rapids, MI: Eerdmans, 1979], 233) sees the symbolism of the ceremony as 'transparent', stating that 'this ceremony removes the sins from the people and leaves them in an unclean place, the desert'. Levine (*Leviticus*, 106) summarizes the principal significance of this aspect of the ritual as 'riddance'. Cf. Jacob Milgrom, *Leviticus 1–16: A New Translation with Introduction and Commentary* (AB 3; New York, NY: Doubleday, 1991), 1021: 'The banishment of evil to an inaccessible place is a form of elimination amply attested in the ancient Near East'.

[17] As is well known, in later times the practice was for the man leading the goat away to fully ensure that it did not return by tipping it over a precipice to its death (Mishnah, *Yoma* 6.6).

divine name 'Yahweh', it could be argued that the latter similarly consists of a name, which would be 'Azazel'. This is precisely how a good many English versions render it (e.g. NRSV, ESV, NAB, NET, NJB, REB, CEV, GNT, as well as the Jewish NJPS translation). According to this view, Azazel would be understood as some spirit, of a malign nature, that was conceived of as inhabiting the desert regions. This conception no doubt originated in the popular folklore of the ancient Near East. The use of the term, it should be stressed, need not be making a comment on a people's belief in such a demon. We are talking here more about a convention of language based on certain primitive theological convictions, not about the accuracy of those convictions themselves.[18]

Elsewhere in the Old Testament the writers speak of 'Leviathan', it seems to me, in a similar fashion. This was the primeval sea monster of ancient myth that represented the forces of chaos. It finds a place in the idiom of Hebrew poetry (e.g. Job 3:8; Ps. 74:14; Isa. 27:1), but that is not to say that the prophets actually believed in such a mythical creature. To my mind, to be brought into the dominion of 'Azazel', whether an actual or fictional being, simply means to go to perdition, that is, to be irrevocably lost.[19] Why this particular term, which only appears here in Leviticus 16 in all of Scripture, was employed might be due to the contextual factor of the physical circumstances that the Israelites were in at that time, right in the middle of such a wilderness location.

The main alternative to taking 'Azazel' as a proper name is to give it the meaning of 'scapegoat'. Such a sense was first introduced into English by William Tyndale, the sixteenth-century translator of the Bible, finding its way into the King James Version a short while later. This view takes the first syllable, 'ǎz, to be the Hebrew noun for 'goat', 'ēz, and the remainder to be the verb 'āzal, meaning 'depart', so yielding the overall sense of 'departing goat'. Though this has gained some following among certain exegetes and translators, including those of the original LXX, it is quite doubtful that it is correct. Biblical Hebrew is not a language that forms compound words in this manner. To take it in this way, moreover, destroys the balance between the two prepositional phrases. If the lot cast for one goat results in it being 'to the LORD', what sense does it make

---

[18] Cf. Theodor H. Gaster, 'Demon', in George A. Buttrick (ed.), *Interpreter's Dictionary of the Bible*, vol. 1 (Nashville, TN: Abingdon, 1962), 818: 'demons often survive as figures of speech . . . long after they have ceased to be figures of belief. Accordingly, the mention of a demon's name in a scriptural text is not automatic testimony to living belief in him'. Similarly, speakers of English might use utterances such as (the reader is begged to excuse the strong language) 'Go to hell!' or 'To the devil with you!', without it reflecting their personal views on the afterlife or the existence of the evil one.

[19] The goat, of course, was in no sense an offering to a demon. Cf. Milgrom, *Leviticus 1–16*, 1021: 'the goat sent [to] him [to Azazel] is not an offering . . . the goat is simply the vehicle to dispatch Israel's impurities and sins to the wilderness/netherworld'.

for the other to be 'to a scapegoat'? It would require giving the latter use of the preposition an altogether different meaning from the former.

A third alternative, which has not enjoyed much popularity, is that the word conveys the idea of 'rugged' or 'craggy' terrain, such as would be common in a desert. This too is extremely doubtful.[20]

When all is said and done, it is probably best to adopt the first interpretation. Historically, this has been the most prevalent understanding among the Jews themselves.[21] And with regard to modern biblical scholarship, the NET Bible tells us that: 'The most common view among scholars today is that it [Azazel] is the proper name of a particular demon (perhaps even the Devil himself) associated with the wilderness desert regions.'[22]

With the foregoing in mind, we now come to consider the import of the allusions to the goats within the context of the trial of Christ. With respect to Jesus himself, he is clearly pictured as the first goat, that which is to be offered up as a sacrifice. It is his blood, a metaphor for his death, that will provide the means of atonement. Such a truth is unpacked in some detail by the writer to the Hebrews, where the sacrificial death of Jesus is expounded largely with reference to the ritual of the Day of Atonement.[23]

If in Jesus Christ himself we are to discern an allusion to the first goat, then the second must correspond to the other Jesus present in the context, namely Barabbas. Regarding the person of Barabbas, however, there has been a very common misunderstanding in the minds of expositors who detect and attempt to interpret the allusions. Time and again I have either heard or read expositions of Barabbas that are sadly erroneous, and the reason for this is that their authors confuse the surface-level features and the allusive elements of the text. Typically, in such a presentation Barabbas is interpreted as a sinner going free, which does

---

[20] Levine (*Leviticus*, 102) describes the second and third alternatives as 'contrived'.

[21] See, e.g., Robert Alter, *The Five Books of Moses: A Translation with Commentary* (New York, NY: W. W. Norton & Co., 2004), 612–613: 'the most plausible understanding – it is a very old one – is that it is the name of a goatish demon or deity associated with the remote wilderness ... Azazel is not represented as a competing deity (or demon) rivalling YHWH, but the ritual depends upon a polarity between YHWH/the pale of human civilization and Azazel/the remote wilderness, the realm of disorder and raw formlessness'; Milgrom, *Leviticus 1–16*, 1021: 'The most plausible explanation is that Azazel is the name of a demon'; Bernard J. Bamberger, 'Leviticus', in W. Gunther Plaut (ed.), *The Torah: A Modern Commentary* (New York, NY: Union of American Hebrew Congregations, 1981), 859: 'Azazel ... was probably a demonic being, residing in the desert, whose abode was regarded as a focus of impurity.'

[22] NET, note on Lev. 16:8. Among modern Bible versions, CEV makes this interpretation explicit in the text: 'to the demon Azazel'.

[23] Cf. Rowan Williams, *God with Us: The Meaning of the Cross and Resurrection, Then and Now* (London: SPCK, 2017), 26: 'The epistle to the Hebrews ... is an immensely sophisticated meditation on the Day of Atonement, and how Jesus has now performed a Day of Atonement ritual not just for one year but for ever.' An excellent discussion of Christ's fulfilment of the atonement in Hebrews can be found in Andrei A. Orlov, *The Atoning Dyad: The Two Goats of Yom Kippur in the Apocalypse of Abraham* (Leiden: Brill, 2016), 65–72.

indeed open up the possibility for some wonderful gospel preaching, though regrettably founded on a false interpretation of the Scriptures. As regards the plain meaning, this does indeed seem close to what is going on. I say 'close', because even at that level of meaning Barabbas is not strictly speaking a 'sinner' experiencing freedom from his sin. Rather, he is a condemned criminal being released from the temporal punishment of his crimes. The Roman governor may have allowed Barabbas to walk free, but that does not at all entail that his sins were forgiven. Barabbas had a far greater Judge who would hold his murder and other lawless activities to account.

At the surface level, therefore, there seems little valid reason to regard Barabbas as a sinner set free from his sins. But what about at the deeper level, at the allusory level that invokes the Day of Atonement? Cannot Barabbas be taken as representing the living goat that was released? Well, yes he can. But, as we have seen, that is not at all a positive thing as far as the animal was concerned. This second male goat was not one that was set free to enjoy life, but one that was abandoned in a desolate place and lost for ever. And the reason for that, we learned, was because the creature was conceived in the ceremony to be a bearer of sin. The regulations of Leviticus 16 have indicated that the goat that is sent away symbolizes not what is happening to the *sinner*, but what is happening to the *sin*, which the creature in question is bearing. At this allusive level, then, it is certainly not possible that Barabbas may be taken as depicting a sinner going free.

So, if not as a freed sinner, how is Barabbas to be understood within the allusory schema relating to the two goats? Here is where the phrase 'to Azazel' becomes crucial for a correct interpretation. As mentioned above, this phrase serves to specify where, or more precisely, to whom, it was that the second goat was sent, and by means of that goat the sin of the people was being conveyed to that destination. We saw that with regard to the atoning ceremony, going 'to Azazel' had the basic connotation of being lost for ever. Now one often unremarked detail of the trial narrative is the fact that Barabbas is not simply 'released'. More precisely, the text consistently speaks of him being released 'to', or '*for*', if you prefer. Note the following:

'Which of the two do you want me to release *to you*?' asked the governor.
'Barabbas', they answered.
(Matt. 27:21)

Then he released *to them* Barabbas.
(Matt. 27:26)

> But the chief priests stirred up the crowd that he should rather release *to them* Barabbas.
> (Mark 15:11)

> They all shouted together, 'Away with this man! Release *to us* Barabbas!'
> (Luke 23:18)

In each instance the Greek contains a phrase that is grammatically dative, as appears in the Greek version of Leviticus 16 in the phrases 'to the LORD' and 'to Azazel'. Also, each occurrence is adjoined immediately to the verb 'release'. Many English translations place the name of Barabbas in between, as in 'he released Barabbas to them', whereas the order is actually 'he released to them Barabbas'. This brings the idea of destination into closer association with the verb.

What we find then is that as the sin-bearing goat was led forth specifically to Azazel, Barabbas, who corresponds to this goat in the allusions, is brought forth to another explicitly identified entity. In the foregoing dative phrases, 'to you', 'to them', 'to us', the pronouns all have an identical reference, namely to the Jewish multitude, including their leaders who were inciting them. 'Release *to us* Barabbas' is what they cry out, and eventually the governor yields to their wishes, and 'he released *to them* Barabbas'. At the level of allusion this action has a significance of great importance. According to the original regulations of Yom Kippur, the goat was supposed to convey the people's sin far away from them. As they watched it disappear into the distance, they were seeing their sins being removed from them, in symbol at least. But now note the direction in which Barabbas, the allusory sin-bearing goat, is heading. To the people! In other words, sin is not being taken away from them, but is coming right at them. The goat was released *to Azazel*; Barabbas was released *to the people*. In the one their guilt is entirely removed; in the other it goes forth directly among them. What idea can this express other than that in this allusive Day of Atonement ceremony the people are, in quite the opposite way to the original aims of the festival, actually made to bear their guilt themselves? In the proceedings of the Day of Atonement, the second goat depicted the results that issued from the sacrificial death of the first goat. In that death, sin was expiated, or taken away. At the trial of Jesus, he, the first goat, goes to his death, but the sin of the Jewish multitude is not removed. Rather it comes to them. The release of Barabbas, the second goat, specifically to the people portrays the terrible truth that the people have to bear the consequence of their sin.

And what exactly was that sin? I believe the sin in question was precisely the handing over of Jesus, that is, the rejection of their own Messiah, the Son of God, to be executed. Remember that the two goats were identical and represented different aspects of the same truth. So, too, Jesus and Barabbas are in a sense one. Just as the second goat bore away the sins dealt with by the death of the first, so Barabbas brings upon the people the sin which was their instigating of the death of Jesus. As it pertained to the people, this death, far from being a holy offering to God on their part, was an act of betrayal born out of envy, hatred and unbelief. In return for this malicious deed the second 'goat' bore the guilt of their sin directly to them.

Such an interpretation does seem to fit well with the words that the crowds themselves utter right at this stage in the proceedings. Pilate actually declares to the Jewish multitude that the responsibility for Christ's death does not rest upon himself (Matt. 27:24), and says to them, *hymeis opsesthe*, literally 'You shall see [to it]'. This has the sense of 'The responsibility is yours' (as NIV, NLT; cf. GNT, CEV, NCV). All the people, we are told, then answer with the words, 'Let his blood be on us and on our children!' (v. 25). When they say 'his blood' they are obviously using a metaphorical expression. By this phrase they are explicitly stating that they accept the responsibility for Jesus' death.[24] So it is that the people acknowledge that the death of the Son of God should be held to their account and their children's also. And such an awful claim of responsibility tragically worked itself out in the years to follow. As a nation, that generation of Jews remained firmly unbelieving in Christ and the gospel message, as did the generation of their sons and daughters, until finally a terrible judgment came upon them in the form of the Roman destruction of the Jewish nation in AD 70.[25] Thus the Gospel allusions here to the ritual involving the two goats on Yom Kippur are particularly poignant.

The Barabbas episode, then, provides a prominent allusion to the atonement ceremony in the context of Christ's trial and execution. There are other details in the accounts that would appear to point in the same direction. All four Gospels record how the clothing of Jesus was removed before his crucifixion

---

[24] France (*Gospel of Matthew*, 1056) remarks that the formula '*x*'s blood on *y*' is 'a statement of responsibility for death'.

[25] There is a basic agreement between the exposition presented here and that of Peter Leithart (*Jesus as Israel: The Gospel of Matthew through New Eyes*, vol. 2 [Monroe, LA: Athanasius Press, 2018], 292–293). Leithart, however, goes on to make the intriguing proposal that the Jewish multitude, having requested and received Barabbas, and having declared their responsibility for Jesus being crucified, themselves become, as it were, the second goat. It is for this reason that they are shortly to be scattered among the nations, which corresponds to the goat being sent out into the wilderness (296). We could say that if the second-goat figure, namely Barabbas, was released to them, then after a fashion the people themselves become identified with that goat and what it signifies.

(Matt. 27:35; Mark 15:24; Luke 23:34; John 19:23–24). The fourth Gospel gives more space to this event than the others, offering a description of one particular garment. Besides the clothing that they divided into four, the soldiers also took his 'tunic', or in Greek *chitōn*. This item is said to be 'seamless, woven from the top in one piece' (v. 23). Regarding this garment they said, 'Let us not tear it, but let us cast lots for it to see whose it will be' (v. 24). The Gospel-writer does seem to be drawing special attention to this tunic. Perhaps the reason for this is that several elements here point to the levitical high priest, especially in relation to the Day of Atonement.

The making of the high-priestly garments is prescribed in Exodus 28. There the Israelites are commanded to make 'a breastpiece, an ephod, a robe, a woven tunic, a turban, and a sash' (28:4; cf. 29:5). Now according to the LXX translation of these terms, it is the fourth that appears as the *chitōn*, rendering the Hebrew noun *kuttōnet*, 'shirt, tunic, coat'. This type of garment was not in fact unique to the high priest, since the same was to be made for the ordinary priests also (Exod. 28:40). The item preceding this in the list, *mĕ'îl*, 'robe', appearing as *podērēs* in the LXX, was intended exclusively for the high priest (28:35). The word itself implies that it was long, reaching to the feet. It was designed in an unusual fashion:

> Make the robe of the ephod woven wholly of blue cloth, with an opening for the head in the middle of it; it shall have a woven binding around the opening, like the opening in a coat of mail, so that it will not tear.
> (Exod. 28:31–32)

It seems to me that it is this piece of clothing that the special garment of John 19 is alluding to, even though the word *chitōn* is used there. There are good reasons for us to come to this conclusion. First and foremost is the fact that Flavius Josephus, the Jewish historian and a first-century contemporary of the apostle John, gives a description of the high priest's robe in the following terms:

> The high priest is adorned with all of the aforementioned garments, but over these he wears a coat [*chitōn*] made of blue, which is also a robe [*podērēs*]. In our language [Hebrew] it is called *meeir* [i.e. *mĕ'îl*] . . . Now this coat [*chitōn*] was not composed of two pieces, nor was it sewed together upon the shoulders and the sides, but it was one long piece woven so as to have an opening for the neck.
> (*Antiquities of the Jews* 3.161)

Clearly, Josephus is talking about the specifically high-priestly vestment, listed in Exodus 28:4 as *mĕ'îl*. And yet, while he does use the term *podērēs* to describe this, as does the LXX, his actual preferred word for the item is *chitōn*, the word appearing in John 19:23 for Christ's garment. Josephus would have been alive prior to the destruction of the temple by the Romans, and as he himself seems to have been a priest[26] he would have been acquainted with the ministrations of the high priest and the clothes he wore. For him, in the first century, a more suitable Greek term for the unique robe of the high priest was evidently *chitōn*. We further note that the manner in which Josephus describes this coat agrees closely with the description given in John 19:24, namely that it was woven in one piece or, in other words, seamless. From these two facts it could reasonably be argued that John is making deliberate allusion to the robe of the high priest and that this fact would be recognized by readers from a Jewish background.

Lexical terms also connect the two garments. The high priest's robe was said to be 'woven wholly [*hyphanton holon*] of blue cloth' (Exod. 39:22), while that of Jesus is described as 'woven whole [*hyphantos di' holou*] from the top' (John 19:23).

More than this, the particular design of the garment in question is related in each context to the idea of tearing, or to be more precise, *not* tearing. Regarding the high priest's robe, the text states that it was fashioned in this specific way 'so that it will not tear' (Exod. 28:32). And with regard to Jesus' comparable garment, the soldiers say: 'Let us not tear it' (John 19:24), a suggestion that is made as a direct consequence of the description of it as being made of one piece.[27] We will speak further of this.

What is written, therefore, concerning the seamless garment of Jesus seems intended to evoke the robe of the high priest. This sacred minister, we recall, was the principal celebrant on the Day of Atonement and the sole individual who entered the inner chamber of the sanctuary. Jesus, then, is likewise a high-priestly figure, and in this connection we remember the so-called 'high-priestly prayer' that he had offered a short while earlier in John (ch. 17).[28] However, what

---

[26] Cf. the comments in his autobiography, *The Life of Flavius Josephus* 1.5.

[27] John 19:24 connects to the preceding verse by means of the conjunctive particle *oun*, 'therefore, so, accordingly'.

[28] Ratzinger summarizes the matter as follows: 'The reference to the seamless tunic (*chitōn*) is formulated in this precise way because John evidently wanted to highlight something more than a casual detail. Some exegetes make a connection here with a piece of information provided by Flavius Josephus, who points out that the high priest's garment (*chitōn*) was woven from a single thread (cf. *Antiquities Judaicae* III. 7. 4). Thus we may detect in the evangelist's passing reference an allusion to Jesus' high priestly dignity, which John had expounded theologically in the high-priestly prayer of chapter 17. Not only is this dying man Israel's true king: he is also the high priest who accomplishes his high-priestly ministry precisely in this hour of his most extreme dishonor' (Joseph Ratzinger, *Jesus of Nazareth: Holy Week. From the Entrance into Jerusalem to the Resurrection* [San Francisco, CA: Ignatius Press, 2011], 216–217).

relates Jesus in John 19 more specifically to the high priest in the context of the levitical atonement festival is the often-overlooked fact that the latter did not actually wear his highly decorative vestments for the ritual of that event. These garments of glory were set aside for much less ornate items of plain linen (Lev. 16:4),[29] which he wore when he went into the most holy place to accomplish atonement for his people. In the process of attaining the true and once-for-all atonement, as Jesus was about to die as the sacrifice for sin, his own particular clothing was removed. Then, as the consummation of that death, he entered the chamber that would be his tomb, and before doing so he was clothed in the plain linen of his grave clothes. This latter allusion will be dealt with in a subsequent chapter.[30]

Furthermore, we may see the fact that Christ's special robe was not torn as an indication that he was indeed the true high priest. A levitical law stated that 'the high priest . . . shall not tear his clothes' (Lev. 21:10). It is noteworthy that in the trial scene recorded in the Gospels the then-current Jewish high priest, Caiaphas, did precisely this. Two of the accounts tell us that 'the high priest tore his clothes' (Matt. 26:65; Mark 14:63).[31] Caiaphas broke the Torah command. His torn robe intimated that his was not the true high priesthood. Rather, the untorn robe of Jesus made an allusive declaration that he, and not Caiaphas, was the authentic high priest who that day would make a full and acceptable atonement for the people.[32]

Then, lastly, there is the matter of the veil of the temple, or 'curtain', as it is sometimes called. As all the synoptic Gospels record, this was torn asunder, from top to bottom, immediately upon Christ's death (Matt. 27:51; Mark 15:38; Luke 23:45). The veil in question was hung between the outer holy place of the sanctuary and the inner most holy place (Exod. 26:33), forming a barrier between them. The relevance of this to our present discussion is the fact that

---

[29] As John E. Hartley remarks (*Leviticus* [WBC 4; Dallas, TX: Word, 1992], 235): 'For the ceremony the high priest is to put on linen garments . . . These are not the stately garments of majesty and dignity that the high priest normally wears'; cf. Levine (*Leviticus*, 101): 'For the rites described here [Lev. 16], the High Priest donned unadorned white linen vestments'.

[30] See chapter 27.

[31] We note that Mark describes these vestments as *chitōnas*, a plural form of *chitōn*.

[32] Besides what has been discussed here, several other connections between Jesus at the crucifixion and the Jewish high priest have been claimed. These are of a more tenuous nature and have little or no direct bearing on the Day of Atonement. Here we may mention: (1) the fact that Jesus refused to drink wine before he was nailed to the cross (Matt. 27:34; Mark 15:23), which might be taken as relating to the law that the priests were not to drink alcohol before entering the sanctuary (Lev. 10:9); (2) in being appointed high priest, blood was daubed on the extremities of Aaron's body, namely on his right thumb and big toe, as well as on his right ear (Lev. 8:23). This has been likened to the blood that would have been evident on Christ's hands and feet, and also around his head where the crown of thorns was placed; (3) on the high priest's head was a golden plate engraved with the words 'Holiness to the LORD' (Exod. 28:36), while over Christ's head was a plaque inscribed with his name and the title 'King of the Jews' (Matt. 27:37 etc.).

this veil was only to be passed through on the Day of Atonement, and solely by the high priest (Lev. 16:2). Entrance at any other time or by any other person would result in death. The writer to the Hebrews reiterates the situation under the law: 'Only the high priest entered the second chamber, and that only once a year, and not without taking blood, which he offered for himself and for the sins of the people committed in ignorance' (Heb. 9:7). His comment on this is: 'By this the Holy Spirit indicates that the way into the most holy place has not yet been opened up[33] while the first tabernacle is still standing' (v. 8). Under the old covenant, then, there was almost total exclusion from the dwelling-place of God represented by the inner room of the sanctuary. This severely limited approach showed that the covenant at Sinai did not confer upon its covenant community access to God in anything like its proper fullness. The once-a-year ritual of Yom Kippur was both a token and pre-intimation that at some future time, under a new and better covenant, that access would be granted. This was accomplished in Jesus Christ.

The author of Hebrews goes on to explain:

> When Christ came as high priest of the good things to come, he went through the greater and more perfect tabernacle . . . He did not enter by means of the blood of goats and calves, but he entered the most holy place once and for all by his own blood, having obtained eternal redemption. (Heb. 9:11–12)

This all-surpassing truth, here expressed in the epistle through words of theological exposition, is vividly and forcefully portrayed at the crucifixion by means of the tearing of the veil. Once Jesus dies, the ultimate atoning sacrifice has been offered, and the splitting of the veil, from top to bottom, shows both that the sacrifice has been accepted in heaven and that access through Christ's death is now available to those who would approach by faith in him. With the self-offering of Jesus, the essence of what the Day of Atonement enacted in ritualistic form is now fulfilled in actuality.

Plainly, then, the atoning ritual of Israel in Leviticus 16 constitutes a significant allusory background to the trial and crucifixion of Jesus as recorded in the Gospels. On one hand, he suffered indeed as the Passover lamb to bring his people out from bondage, a spiritual bondage, so accomplishing the true Passover. Yet on the other, he suffered as the once-for-all atoning sacrifice,

---

[33] For the verb usually translated 'disclosed' or 'manifested' I have chosen to follow the rendering of the NJB and REB, 'opened up' (cf. ESV, GNT, 'opened'; NLT, 'not . . . open').

according to the terms of Yom Kippur, through which all the iniquities, transgressions and sins of his people are for ever removed, and we who believe in him may

> have confidence to enter the most holy place by the blood of Jesus, by a
> new and living way opened for us through the veil, that is, his flesh,
> and ... may draw near to God with a sincere heart in full assurance
> of faith.
> (Heb. 10:19–22)

24

The trial and crucifixion 2

Matthew 26:57 – 27:56; Mark 14:53 – 15:41; Luke 22:63 – 23:49; John 18:19 – 19:37

Preceding chapters have shown how allusions have been made in the Gospel accounts concerning Christ's birth to the birth of Isaac, the son of Abraham,[1] and also to the offering of Isaac, the Aqedah, in the episode of Gethsemane.[2] This latter event in the garden, we recall, took place on the same calendar day, calculated from sunset to sunset, as that of the trial and crucifixion which we are now examining. In these later daylight hours of that same day, the one particular day that the Gospel narratives have been building up to, the Isaac allusions continue, and indeed reach their momentous finale.

Although the events of Gethsemane took place only a few short hours earlier, the Gospel narratives of the crucifixion reaffirm the Isaac connection through distinct parallels. In order for him to be offered up, Jesus, like Isaac, is brought to a specific place, the place of his execution. Upon the arrival of Jesus and his escort, the Gospel repeats the exact same phrase as occurs in the Greek version of Genesis 22. There we read that 'they came to the place [*ēlthon epi ton topon*] of which God had told him [Abraham] . . . and he bound his son Isaac and laid him on the altar, on top of the wood' (v. 9). In Luke's version of the passion we find: 'When they came to the place [*ēlthon epi ton topon*] that is called The Skull, they crucified Jesus there' (23:33). It is not just the identical phraseology that establishes the linkage; the passages are linked conceptually too,[3] for the immediately following words in each instance relate to an aspect of the manner of death, the victim consigned to die being affixed to items of wood.[4]

---

[1] Chapter 4.

[2] Chapter 21.

[3] Remembering also that the reader has just recently read the account of Gethsemane with its distinct echoes of the Aqedah. The informed mind has therefore already been attuned to the Isaac connections.

[4] We recall that the Greek verb *stauroō*, 'crucify', more literally indicates 'to attach to a stake', 'stake' being *stauros*. In the New Testament the object of crucifixion is also described as a 'tree', or in Greek *xylon* (Acts 5:30; 10:39; 13:29; 1 Pet. 2:24; cf. Gal. 3:13), the word used for the wood on which Isaac is placed (Gen. 22:9).

At this particular juncture in John's narration the correspondence with Isaac is even more apparent, indeed almost obvious. He writes: 'So they took Jesus,[5] and he went out, carrying his own cross, to the place called the Place of the Skull . . . where they crucified him' (19:16–18). The point of contact is that Isaac, as often noted, carried the wood to the appointed place for himself to be sacrificed upon (Gen. 22:6), just as Jesus bore his own wooden cross, or stake, to the place appointed for his execution. Both victims, therefore, carried their own wood which would be used for their respective self-offerings. One other point of interest here is that among the Jews there was a traditional interpretation of the Aqedah in which Isaac, when bearing the wood, was likened to one being led to crucifixion. Isaac carried the wood, they said, 'like one carries his stake [that is, the cross] on his shoulder'.[6]

The foregoing prepares the way for what is to come. Jesus coming to the particular place where he is going to be sacrificed, bearing his own cross of wood, has suitably called to mind the episode concerning Isaac. The series of allusions to that important incident is now set to reach its climax. Christ is affixed to the cross, as Isaac was laid on the wood. Then later, as his death draws nearer, Jesus calls out to God those memorable words: '*Eli, Eli, lema sabachthani?*' (Matt. 27:46; cf. Mark 15:34, '*Elōi, Elōi, lema sabachthani?*'). This cry of Jesus, commonly known as the 'cry of dereliction', is the principal focus of our present concern in relation to what happened at Moriah. To explain this unavoidably entails some technicalities relating to language and letters.

Plainly, the Greek letters of the saying give a transliteration[7] of a Semitic language, a family of languages that includes Hebrew and Aramaic. The verb is *sabachthani*. As a Semitic verbal form, this is composed of the basic verb extended by two separate suffixes. The final -*ni* indicates the direct object, 'me'. The -*tha* element denotes the grammatical subject, here second-person singular, 'you'. These suffixes have been adjoined to the verbal root *sabach*. There can be no doubt that according to the plain surface-level meaning of the text, this verb is meant to represent the Aramaic *šĕbaq*, having the sense of 'abandon, forsake, leave'. This we know for sure from the translation that immediately follows in both Matthew and Mark: 'My God, my God, why have

---

[5] An allusion is seen by Esswein in the repeated use of the verb 'take'. In the Aqedah God instructed Abraham to 'take' his son and offer him up (Gen. 22:2), though ultimately it is the ram that he 'took' (v. 13). In the trial and crucifixion this verb occurs four times with Jesus as the object (John 18:31; 19:1, 6, 16). See Mitchell Alexander Esswein, 'Is He Going to Kill Himself? The Willing Self-Sacrifice of Jesus and the Akedah in the Fourth Gospel', *Sacra Scripta* 11.2 (2013): 258.

[6] Midrash Rabbah 56.3 (on Gen. 22:6); cf. D. A. Carson, *The Gospel According to John* (PNTC; Leicester: Apollos, 1991), 609: 'Even some Jewish scholars thought the Isaac episode evocative of crucifixion.'

[7] That is, the representation of a statement in one language in the letters of another.

you *forsaken* me?'[8] As such, Christ's cry is clearly presenting a rendering of the original Hebrew of Psalm 22:1 into Aramaic.[9] There the Hebrew verb, 'forsake', is *'āzab*, quite distinct from its Aramaic equivalent.

At this level, then, it appears perfectly obvious that Jesus is drawing attention to the twenty-second psalm. Why he should do so is not difficult to ascertain. One just has to read the psalm to discover that the person who is apparently abandoned by God is not in fact left forsaken. After speaking of his crying out to God and receiving no answer (vv. 1–2), the psalmist reminds God of how the ancestors of Israel had similarly cried out to him, and they had been heard and delivered (vv. 3–5). He then describes the details of his terrible suffering (vv. 6–18), a part of Scripture which contains a verse explicitly cited in the crucifixion account,[10] and several implicit references relating to the same event.[11] The psalm, therefore, is certainly to be viewed as prophetic, as a prefiguring of the sufferings of Messiah.[12] The next section contains another appeal for God to come and save him (vv. 19–21). The tone of the psalm then changes dramatically as the psalmist turns to praise (vv. 22–31). He gives his reason for this in verse 24: 'For he [God] has not despised nor detested the affliction of the afflicted; nor has he hidden his face from him, but when he cried to him he heard.'[13] Put simply, although the psalm begins with such a cry of dereliction, it ends with a shout of praise, for the sufferer's prayer is answered and he is delivered. To call out the first verse of the psalm, as Jesus does, would be to elicit the entire psalm,[14] including of course the positive resolution to the supplicant's

---

[8] Why certain of his hearers should wrongly say that Jesus was calling on 'Elijah' is not explained. There was indeed some similarity between the words 'My God' (*'ēlî* in Matthew; *'ĕlāhî* in Mark) and 'Elijah' (*'ēliyyāhû*). Perhaps this, along with the evident agony he was experiencing, and possibly too his Galilean accent, are sufficient to account for the failure to understand. Alternatively, it might be the case that the misunderstanding was deliberate, as a form of mockery. Of these I prefer the latter option, for which see Daniel Fanous, *Taught by God: Making Sense of the Difficult Sayings of Jesus* (Rollinsford, NH: Orthodox Research Institute, 2010), 227.

[9] This may be compared with the standard Targum of the Psalms: 'My God, my God, why have you forsaken me [*šĕbaqtanî*]?' (22:1). The Syriac Peshitta contains the same verb.

[10] Ps. 22:18, concerning the casting of lots for Christ's clothes, is quoted in John 19:24.

[11] For the role of Ps. 22 in the passion narrative, see Raymond E. Brown, *The Death of the Messiah: From Gethsemane to the Grave. A Commentary on the Passion Narratives in the Four Gospels*, vol. 2 (New York, NY: Doubleday, 1994), 1455–1456.

[12] Cf. Bruce K. Waltke and James M. Houston, *The Psalms as Christian Worship: A Historical Commentary* (Grand Rapids, MI: Eerdmans, 2010), 377, 414–415.

[13] For this latter part of the verse the LXX reads: 'when I cried to him, he heard me', introducing first-person singular pronouns.

[14] Cf. Curtis Mitch and Edward Sri, *The Gospel of Matthew* (Catholic Commentary on Sacred Scripture; Grand Rapids, MI: Baker, 2010), 360: 'By quoting the opening line of this psalm, Jesus evokes the whole of Ps 22'; also Richard B. Hays, *Echoes of Scripture in the Gospels* (Waco, TX: Baylor University Press, 2016), 85: 'we cannot stop reading the psalm with its opening cry, "My God, why have you forsaken me?" Mark has signaled his readers that the *whole* psalm is to be read as a prefiguration of Jesus' destiny' (italics original).

initial predicament. It would seem to be this ultimate salvation to which Jesus is directing the minds of those who would hear him. His abandonment is not absolute,[15] for the affliction he is undergoing, leading finally to his death, will not be the end. He will rise again to praise the Lord.[16] So, first, Jesus would appear to be applying the psalm, with its favourable outcome, to himself. He was communicating that the situation he was presently in, although a terrible ordeal,[17] one in which he was seemingly abandoned by God, was far from the end on the matter. Such an ordeal was foretold in the Scriptures and was consequently part and parcel of the overall divine purpose.

Then, second, we may also interpret Christ's words on the cross allusively. Here we propose that in this so-called cry of dereliction there is a further allusion to the offering of Isaac in Genesis 22 – one final and climactic allusion. Returning to the word *sabachthani*, when the manner of transliteration is investigated we find that there could be a completely different underlying Semitic verb. The basic verb form represented as *sabach* could well be something other than the Aramaic *šĕbaq*. Beginning with the first letter of the transliteration, *s*, the Greek letter *sigma*, we note that this is a sibilant. Sibilants are essentially 's' and 'z' sounds. *Sigma* is the only letter with an 's' sound in New Testament Greek.[18] Semitic languages, however, tend to have several such letters in their alphabets. Hebrew and Aramaic, for example, have *s*, called *samech*, *ṣ*, called *tsade*, *ś*, called *sin*, and *š*, called *shin*. In transliteration the Greek *sigma* would be required to do duty for all of these. In understanding *sabach* to be the Aramaic *šĕbaq*, we have taken the *sigma* to represent the consonant *shin*, but it need not be so. It might indicate any of the other 's' sibilants. The second consonant of the verb *sabach* can only be *beit*. There are no other options in this case. But of all the consonants within the verb it is the *ch*,[19] known in Greek as

---

[15] It may indeed be questioned if there is any real abandonment of the sufferer by God at all. The psalmist does declare, after all, that 'he [God] has not hidden his face from him' (22:24). On the cross, following his outcry and immediately before he passes away, Jesus called out to God, 'Father, into your hands I commit my spirit' (Luke 23:46), another echo of a psalm (31:5). How would such words and sentiment be possible if Jesus had in actual fact been deserted? This latter saying evidently expresses continuing relationship. Even after death there would not appear to be a separation. Elsewhere the psalmist says to God: 'Where can I go from your Spirit? . . . If I make my bed in Sheol, you are there' (Ps. 139:7–8). The term 'Sheol' denotes the place of the dead. In the LXX it appears as *hadēs* ('Hades'). In such a place as this, declares the psalmist, God is still present. A helpful discussion concerning how the Son was not in fact abandoned by the Father is to be found in Thomas H. McCall, *Forsaken: The Trinity and the Cross, and Why It Matters* (Downers Grove, IL: InterVarsity Press, 2012).

[16] It is very relevant to notice, in this context, that Heb. 2:12 cites Ps. 22:22 ('I will declare your name to my brothers; in the midst of the assembly I will praise you') as being uttered by Christ.

[17] I would not want in the least to minimize the actual extent of Jesus' physical suffering. Yet despite this, his words from the cross still instruct us.

[18] Greek has a separate consonant for 'z', *zeta*, but this is not relevant to our discussion.

[19] This is a hard, aspirated 'ch' sound, similar to that in 'loch' and 'Bach'.

chi, that is the most interesting. In our surface-level reading we have assumed that this stands for the letter *q*, *qoph*. This is indeed possible. However, a study of the transliteration of Hebrew words into Greek letters in the Septuagint reveals that *chi* is considerably more often used to represent the consonant *k*, *kaph*. This can be demonstrated through an examination of the multitude of names contained in the opening portion of 1 Chronicles. Taking chapters 1 to 9, a simple count shows that *chi* in the Greek text stands in the place of *kaph* in the Hebrew a total of sixty-six times. Yet in these same nine chapters *chi* stands for *qoph* only twice. The consonant *qoph*, we find, is principally represented there by the Greek letter *k*, *kappa*.[20] From this we see that the relative proportions are overwhelmingly in favour of the Greek *chi* being used to indicate the Hebrew consonant *kaph*, and only rarely *qoph*.

Behind the Greek transliteration *sabach*, therefore, we propose that at a deeper level allusion is being made to another verb other than the Aramaic *šĕbaq*, and that another meaning may justifiably be understood apart from 'forsaken'. If we take the initial *s*, *sigma*, to represent the sibilant *samech*, as it often does, and if we take the final *chi* to stand for the consonant *kaph*, as it most frequently does, then we may quite legitimately arrive at a verb derived from the root *s-b-k*. This could either be the Hebrew *sābak* or the Aramaic *sĕbak*, both having the same meaning.[21] As a verb this would signify 'entangle, entwine', as in Nahum 1:10 (ESV, NIV: 'entangle') and Job 8:17 (ESV, NIV: 'entwine'). Cognate nouns indicate something entangled or intertwined. One such noun in fact appears in Genesis 22, making this discussion directly relevant to the account concerning Isaac. When Abraham was prohibited from carrying out the sacrifice of his son, he was shown a ram caught in a thicket (22:13). The Hebrew noun translated 'thicket' here is *sĕbak*, that is, an entanglement, a noun self-evidently from the same root as the verb *sābak*.[22]

In the light of the foregoing, when Jesus uttered those words, '*Eli, Eli, lema sabachthani?*', the last word could quite legitimately be understood as a form of either the Hebrew or the Aramaic verb that means 'entangle'.[23] The saying

---

[20] By way of illustration I will briefly give more precise details from 1 Chr. 1. Here *chi* appears in the place of *kaph* nine times (in the names Enoch, Lamech, Meshech, Ashkenaz, Cush, Canaan, [another] Enoch, Keran, Achbor). The same letter *chi* represents *qoph* just once (in the name Qeturah). Over against this the Greek letter *kappa* is used for *qoph* no fewer than eleven times (in the names Kenan, Isaac, Keder, Kedemah, Ishbak, Korah, Kenaz, Amalek, Jaakan, Masrekah and [another] Kenaz).

[21] Also sometimes spelled with the consonant *ś* (*sin*) in the place of *samech*, but this would make no difference to its Greek transliteration.

[22] The same noun (*sĕbak*) occurs in Isa. 9:18 and 10:34 (both 'thickets of the forest'), and a closely related noun (*sĕbōk*) appears in Ps. 74:5 ('thicket of trees') and Jer. 4:7 ('thicket').

[23] This proposal has previously received a scholarly airing in Berel Dov Lerner, 'Untangling σαβαχθανι (Matt. 27:46 and Mark 15:34)', *NovT* 56.2 (2014): 196–197.

could then be translated, 'My God, my God, why have you *entangled* me?' Here, I would argue, is a highly suggestive allusion to the Genesis episode. As the account there tells us, God had commanded that Isaac should be offered up, but that was not the ultimate divine intention. At the climax of the story, the sacrifice was forestalled and Abraham was shown the ram,[24] evidently provided by God,[25] which he took and 'offered it up as a burnt-offering instead of his son' (v. 13). The Hebrew preposition 'instead of' here is *taḥat*, represented in the LXX by *anti*, which can mean 'in the place of'. This clearly speaks of substitution. At the last moment Isaac was not required to die, but the ram was offered in his place. Not so with Jesus. He, figuratively speaking, *was* the ram caught in the thicket.[26] His fate was determined and unchangeable. In his case, there was to be no divine intervention and no substitution. And this he underscores, for those with minds to receive it, through the verbal allusion to the thicket in which the original ram had become entangled, a circumstance which he now applies to himself. That ram died as a substitute for Isaac. If Christ was that entangled ram, then he was the one provided by God[27] to die as a substitute for someone else. And for whom was he to give his life in sacrificial death? Wonderfully, for us.[28] This death he was about to undergo was for all who put their faith in him, that is, for all the spiritual sons and daughters of Abraham.[29]

---

[24] We note the interchange between the 'ram' and the previously mentioned 'lamb' that God would provide (Gen. 22:7, 8). This earlier Hebrew word, *śeh*, need not specifically indicate a 'lamb', namely a young animal, but could more generally denote 'sheep' (as understood by the LXX, *probaton*, 'sheep'), of which the 'ram' was a male specimen.

[25] Divine agency in the events of the cross is also presupposed in Isa. 53:10.

[26] One might wonder whether the crown of thorns, most likely still in place during the crucifixion, additionally forms part of the Aqedah imagery. In a sense, Christ's head was 'entangled' in this, as was the head of the ram in a thicket, which in all probability was some kind of thornbush. The Hebrew noun *sĕbak* is in fact associated with thorns in Isa. 9:18 and Nah. 1:10 ('entangled among thorns').

[27] Rom. 8:32, speaking of God, 'who did not withhold [*ouk epheisato*] his own Son', seems to be an allusion to Gen. 22:12, concerning Abraham ('you have not withheld [*ouk epheisō*] your son').

[28] Fleming Rutledge here appositely remarks: 'For Isaac a substitute was provided – Abraham saw a ram caught in the underbrush. "God himself will provide the lamb for an offering, my son." When Jesus came to the cross to bear the sin of the world in fathomless darkness, there was no substitute for him. He himself was the Lamb. God did not withhold his son, his only son. The Son himself became the substitute – for us' (*The Crucifixion: Understanding the Death of Jesus Christ* [Grand Rapids, MI: Eerdmans, 2015], 266).

[29] Cf. Rom. 4:16, 'Abraham is the father of us all', that is, of all with faith.

25

The two thieves

Luke 23:39–43

In the flow of the crucifixion narrative, one of the Gospels presents a brief dialogue between Jesus and one of the other characters involved. This is the thief on the cross. As is well known, at the same time as Jesus two criminals are also crucified, mention of whom is included in all four Gospels (Matt. 27:38; Mark 15:27; Luke 23:32–33; John 19:18). These men, even though hanging on crosses and suffering like Jesus, initially join in with the crowd and religious leaders who are reviling him (Matt. 27:44; Mark 15:28). As the hours pass, however, one of them experiences a dramatic change of heart. This is recorded for us solely by Luke.

It is our contention that the situation described here by Luke and the exchange of words between Jesus and the penitent thief make allusion to a specific Old Testament passage. This is found in Genesis 40, the chapter concerning the chief cupbearer and chief baker who were accused of wrongdoing by Pharaoh, king of Egypt, and as a result were thrown into prison where Joseph, son of Jacob, was himself incarcerated. The synoptic Gospels, we remember, have previously alluded to the Joseph narrative in the parable of the wicked tenants.[1] Significantly, Luke himself will again include allusions to Joseph in his account of the resurrection appearances.[2]

The most basic elements of each of the two scenarios are very similar. There is the fact that the principal character in each narrative, namely Joseph and Jesus, is falsely accused (Gen. 39:10–20; 40:15; cf. Matt. 26:60; 27:12, 24; Mark 14:57; 15:3; Luke 23:2) and undergoes punishment as a consequence. In this situation he then finds himself with two other offenders, Joseph with two of Pharaoh's servants who have incurred the displeasure of their master (Gen. 40:2–4), and Jesus with the two thieves. Unlike the other synoptic Gospels, where the word *lēstēs*, 'robber, bandit', is used (Matt. 27:38; Mark 15:27), Luke

---

[1] See chapter 18.
[2] See chapter 26.

prefers to describe the men by the more general term *kakourgos*, 'criminal, malefactor, wrongdoer' (Luke 23:32, 33). In each case, then, we have three men, one of whom is innocent,[3] suffering punishment together, and, it is perhaps needless to point out, these are the only two instances in the whole of Scripture where such circumstances apply.

While in prison with the two men, Joseph interpreted their dreams, and in so doing he was in fact foretelling their respective fates. The butler, Joseph declared, would be restored to Pharaoh's favour and would soon be released (Gen. 40:13). For the baker, however, things would not turn out so well. He would remain under Pharaoh's wrath and was soon to be put to death (v. 19). With regard to the two criminals in the Gospel accounts, it is evident that these are two irreligious men since they hurl abuse at Jesus along with the crowds and the leaders. During the course of time, however, one of them undergoes a radical change and adopts a different attitude with respect to Jesus. He then rebukes his fellow thief, reminding him that the two of them are receiving the just deserts of their crimes, to which he adds, 'But this man has done nothing wrong' (Luke 23:41), referring to Jesus. These words remind us of Joseph who was condemned, though innocent, and who said to one of those imprisoned with him, 'I have done nothing that they should put me in this dungeon' (Gen. 40:15).[4] The thief then entreats Jesus that he might find a place in God's kingdom, for that is the effect of his request. So it is that, like Joseph with the butler, Jesus foretells the future experience of grace of one of those condemned with him; 'you will be with me in Paradise', he promised him (Luke 23:43), assuring him of his future blessedness.

The appeal that the thief makes to Jesus has notable verbal connections with words occurring in the Joseph narrative. His request, 'Remember me when you come into your kingdom' (Luke 23:42), is structured around the Greek phrase *mnēsthēti mou hotan*. Precisely the same phrase is found in the Genesis passage: 'Remember me [*mnēsthēti mou*] when [*hotan*] it goes well with you' (40:14). Nowhere else in either Testament is such an expression found.[5]

We also discover that the chief butler, who remained under condemnation, suffered his ultimate fate by being 'hanged' (Gen. 40:22, *ekremasen*), a verb quite suitable to the act of crucifixion (Acts 5:30; 10:39; Gal. 3:13; cf. Deut. 21:22–23).

---

[3] Pharaoh's butler, although later released, had nevertheless committed some wrongful act (Gen. 41:9–10).

[4] In the whole of Scripture such words only occur in connection with Joseph and Jesus.

[5] Alongside this particular verbal allusion, others have noticed the phrase 'the third day' (Gen. 40:20), on which the butler was set free and reinstated, a time phrase with biblical connotations of resurrection (cf. Luke 24:21, 46).

Interestingly, Luke is the only Gospel-writer to use this particular verb of the execution of the two thieves (23:39, *kremasthentōn*).

While the phraseology appearing in the Gospel may reasonably be taken as echoing that in Genesis, especially once the close conceptual relation is appreciated, we notice a blatant contrast between the two events in question. On the earlier occasion it was Joseph, the righteous protagonist, who asked to be remembered by the prisoner who was to be set free. Joseph requested that he might put in a word for him with Pharaoh so that he too could be released from his punishment. The man, however, did not so remember him: 'Yet the chief butler did not remember Joseph, but forgot him' (Gen. 40:23). In the Gospel the direction of the appeal is reversed. It is the condemned man who entreats Jesus, the innocent sufferer, to remember him. What he asks for is, to all intents and purposes, deliverance from his sin and a place in God's eternal kingdom. And this Jesus freely grants (Luke 23:43). The manner of allusion is, in this instance, a notable case of ironic contrast. In the former instance, the one who is guiltless of the offence for which he has been condemned is forgotten and left imprisoned; in the latter, he who is guilty as charged and deserves his punishment is remembered and promised release. The butler, entreated by Joseph, was freed from his suffering and so might be expected to have acted out of gratitude for the one who foretold his deliverance, yet he did not. Jesus, entreated by the criminal, pledges to remember him in the midst of his own sufferings, and abides by his words. The contrast surely serves to highlight the gracious nature of the Son of God. The released butler forgot the plight of the innocent; the crucified Christ on the other hand remembers the plea of the penitent.

Though only a short Gospel text, it is still able to interact allusively with Israel's Scriptures of old. What is conveyed by the allusions can, I hope, be seen to be very meaningful and significant within the context of what transpires at the time of the crucifixion.

26
Resurrection appearances in the synoptic Gospels
Matthew 28:16–20; Mark 16:9–20; Luke 24:13–39

This chapter will include a treatment of all three of those Gospels that we describe as 'synoptic' together. What John has to record about the resurrection will be dealt with separately in due course. Matthew and Luke, all would agree, contain the accounts of several resurrection appearances of Jesus in their final chapters. In nearly all printed Bibles Mark also concludes with a description of several occasions on which the risen Jesus appeared to his followers, though these final verses have been the subject of some controversy, of which more below. The primary intention of all these texts is to provide reason to believe that Christ had indeed risen, and risen in bodily form. Further to this, we once more discover that all three synoptic Gospel endings make allusive reference to particular passages and themes found in the sacred writings of Israel.

Matthew

Allusions to the Old Testament at the ending of Matthew come chiefly in 28:16–20, that is, the very final paragraph. They are not perhaps as extensive or as detailed as those found in other Gospel texts, but the direction in which they point is quite apparent, especially in the light of how Matthew has portrayed Jesus earlier in his composition.

Matthew 28 speaks of the disciples journeying to a mountain, the place where they would meet Jesus. It is one particular mountain to which he had expressly told them to go (v. 16). Here, at this locality they see Jesus, and some worship him, while others doubt (v. 17).[1] Jesus then speaks to them, and the

---

[1] On this doubting, Huizenga makes this pertinent comment: 'I think the sense here isn't straight-up doubt, but rather a sense of joyous disbelief at something obviously so true – there's Jesus himself in the risen flesh – but also something seemingly so impossible. So St. Matthew here isn't denigrating the disciples, but rather reinforcing the wonder provoked by the power of the resurrection' (Leroy A. Huizenga, *Behold*

remainder of the paragraph presents all the direct words he said (vv. 18–20). This passage is usually known as the 'Great Commission'. But the commission mandate really only comes in the last two verses, and these hang upon Christ's opening statement that all authority in heaven and earth has been given to him (v. 18).

Looking at the commentaries we find that in the matter of literary allusions many scholars cite a text in the book of Daniel as forming an allusive background to Matthew's passage. This appears in Daniel 7 where the prophet records a vision in which he saw a figure, described as 'one like a son of man', come into the presence of the Ancient of Days seated on his throne (v. 13). Concerning this 'son of man', we then read that

> authority was given to him [*edothē autō exousia*] and glory and kingship, that all nations [*panta ta ethnē*], tribes, and languages should serve [or 'worship']² him. His dominion is an everlasting dominion that shall not pass away, and his kingship is one that shall never be destroyed.
> (v. 14)

Some of the language here bears a close resemblance to the words spoken by Jesus in Matthew 28: 'All authority has been given [*edothē . . . pasa exousia*] to me in heaven and on earth. Go therefore and make disciples of all nations [*panta ta ethnē*]' (vv. 18–19). Given the lexical similarity, it is hard to doubt the presence of deliberate allusion here.³ Clearly, then, at this important juncture in his Gospel narrative Matthew is, as one scholar puts it, 'portraying the risen Jesus as the triumphant Son of Man figure . . . who exercises ἐξουσία ["authority"] over all the nations of the world in a kingdom that will not pass away'.⁴

I do not believe, however, that Daniel 7:14 is the principal allusion present in Matthew 28:16–20. Daniel's vision depicts a heavenly throne-room scene, whereas the event recorded in the Matthean passage is set on an earthly

---

the *Christ: Proclaiming the Gospel of Matthew* [Steubenville, OH: Emmaus Road, 2019], 414). Cf. Luke 24:41; even once the risen Jesus had made a definite appearance to them, 'they [the disciples] still did not believe for joy, and marvelled'.

² Cf. NIV; NET footnote.

³ See, among others, Patrick Schreiner, *Matthew, Disciple and Scribe: The First Gospel and Its Portrait of Jesus* (Grand Rapids, MI: Baker Academic, 2019), 187; Grant R. Osborne, *Matthew* (ZECNT 1; Grand Rapids, MI: Zondervan, 2010), 1078; R. T. France, *The Gospel of Matthew* (NICNT; Grand Rapids, MI: Eerdmans, 2007), 1112; W. D. Davies and Dale C. Allison Jr, *Matthew 19–28*, vol. 3 (ICC; London: Bloomsbury, 2004), 688; Craig L. Blomberg, *Matthew: An Exegetical and Theological Exposition of Holy Scripture* (NAC 22; Nashville, TN: Broadman, 1992), 431.

⁴ Richard B. Hays, *Echoes of Scripture in the Gospels* (Waco, TX: Baylor University Press, 2016), 184.

mountain, like several other important occurrences within the Gospel. The linguistic connections are, moreover, all contained in a single Old Testament verse and therefore do not produce the kind of more extensive series of allusions that is our prime concern in this volume. I would conclude, then, that although the evoking of Daniel 7:14 is unquestionably real in this context, it only forms an allusion of a secondary nature.

In my estimation, Matthew 28:16–20 exhibits a literary link first and foremost with Moses and Israel at Mount Sinai as described in the Pentateuch. Primarily, this would be the occasion of the giving of the law at Sinai (Exod. 19 onwards), but would also include the later retelling of the same event in the opening portions of Deuteronomy, plus the record of the earlier appearance of God to Moses at the same mountain (Exod. 3 – 4). We recall Matthew's unique series of allusions to Moses and Mosaic themes in the flight to Egypt and the Mosaic backdrop to the Sermon on the Mount,[5] to which we may add the allusions shared by Matthew with other Gospel-writers in the feeding of the multitudes, the walking on the water, and the transfiguration, all evoking events in which Moses was involved.[6] Doubtless, the crucial role that Moses played in the divine purpose, in the exodus, the giving of the law, and the wilderness wanderings, meant that of all Old Testament characters he is the one alluded to most frequently.

Among the more apparent thematic connections with Moses and the law-giving in Matthew 28:16–20 are the mountain-top location, the reference to commandments, the mandate to teach and the promise of presence.[7] The association of such matters with Moses is plain, yet as we examine the data more precisely we soon realize that the intention in this passage, similar to what has been observed in other Mosaic allusions, is not merely to make the risen Jesus correspond to the Moses of former times.

Back in Exodus we read how Moses himself made the journey 'to the mountain' (Exod. 3:1), identified as Horeb. Some time later he and all Israel came to the same mountain, where Moses and a few leading representatives of the whole community ascended (24:9). In Matthew we read that the disciples went to Galilee, 'to the mountain' (28:16). Matthew then appends the words 'to which he had directed them'. It was to one particular mountain that Jesus had instructed them to come. Although such words do not expressly appear in the exodus narrative, it is obvious that the same holds true with respect to Sinai.

---

[5] See chapters 6 and 8.

[6] See chapters 10, 11 and 13.

[7] Cf. Trent Rogers, 'The Great Commission as the Climax of Matthew's Mountain Scenes', *BBR* 22.3 (2012): 393.

Evidently, the Israelites were to come to 'this mountain' (Exod. 3:12) where God appeared to Moses, namely Horeb, otherwise known as Sinai.[8]

The Hebrews, assembled at the foot of Sinai, were privileged to witness a theophany, a manifestation of God in the midst of fire and cloud on the summit of the mountain (cf. Exod. 19:11, 16–19; 20:18). More specifically, as we have seen in our treatment of the transfiguration, Moses was allowed to ascend the mountain and was able to take Aaron and certain other leading members of the congregation with him (24:1–2, 9). On the mountain we are told that these selected few 'saw the God of Israel' (v. 10; cf. v. 11, 'they saw God'). Likewise in Matthew's ending, when the disciples came to the designated mountain we read that 'they saw him' (28:17; cf. v. 10, 'and there they will see me'),[9] namely Jesus. The response on this latter occasion was that the disciples 'worshipped [*prosekynēsan*] him'.[10] This same activity was, of course, specified for the people of Israel to perform at Sinai, as the Lord told Moses, 'they will worship God on this mountain' (Exod. 3:12). The Hebrew verb here is *'ābad*, which can mean 'serve' but is also frequently used in the sense of 'worship', and is translated as such here in many English versions.[11] More importantly for our purpose, we read that this worship was to be enacted by those leaders of Israel permitted to ascend the mountain: 'they shall worship [*proskynēsousin*] at a distance' (Exod. 24:1).[12]

We see, then, that coming to a specific mountain, the experience of seeing God, and the act of worship are all common elements in the Exodus account and this final section of Matthew's Gospel. But what even more strongly binds this latter passage with Sinai is the matter of keeping commandments. In Matthew, Jesus instructs the Eleven to 'make disciples of all nations . . . teaching them to observe everything which I have commanded you' (28:19–20). This latter phrase in Greek is *panta hosa eneteilamēn*. It consists of the quantifying neuter plural adjective 'all, everything' used absolutely,[13] then a relative

---

[8] See chapter 11, n. 6.

[9] Exod. 24:10 (LXX) and Matt. 28:17 do contain the same Greek verb (*idontes* and *eidon* respectively), though in grammatical forms that are quite different and might not be recognized as the selfsame verb by the non-reader of the language.

[10] I concur with the comment of Peter Leithart: 'This is no ordinary bow; they prostrate themselves in total submission to Jesus, acknowledging that he is God' (*Jesus as Israel: The Gospel of Matthew through New Eyes*, vol. 2 [Monroe, LA: Athanasius Press, 2018], 337). Other factors lend support to such a conclusion, to be discussed presently in this section.

[11] E.g. NRSV, NASB, NIV, NJB, REB, NLT, NJPS, among others. According to the NET footnote, this particular verb (*'ābad*) 'is one of the foremost words for worship in the Torah'.

[12] Here the LXX adds 'the Lord' (*tō kyriō*) as the object of worship, a title frequently applied in the New Testament to Jesus.

[13] By 'absolutely' we mean that the adjective stands alone, without an accompanying noun. In English we use adjectives in this way in phrases such as 'the poor', in which 'people' is understood but not expressed.

pronoun that agrees grammatically with the former, plus a form of *entellomai*, 'command', as the main verb. This specific phrase has a good Old Testament pedigree, and one that specifically points to the law given through Moses at Mount Sinai:

everything which I [the LORD] command [*panta hosa an enteilōmai*] you
(Exod. 23:22)

everything which I [the LORD] have commanded [*panta hosa eneteilamēn*] you
(Exod. 29:35)

everything which I have commanded [*panta hosa egō eneteilamēn*] you
(Exod. 31:11)

everything the LORD had commanded [*panta hosa eneteilato*] him
(Exod. 40:16)

everything which the LORD commanded [*panta hosa eneteilato*] Moses
(Num. 29:40)[14]

everything which the LORD commanded [*panta hosa eneteilato*] him
[Moses]
(Deut. 1:3)

everything which the LORD our God has commanded [*panta hosa eneteilato*] us
(Deut. 1:41)

In view of this particular usage, especially when taken with the mountain setting, the informed reader of Matthew 28 cannot have helped but think of Israel receiving the law on Sinai.

Closely connected with the foregoing phrase is the idea of teaching. Matthew 28:20 includes the words 'teaching them' (*didaskontes autous*), that is, the peoples of the nations to whom the apostles are sent. Again this echoes the Sinai narrative, particularly in its Deuteronomic recounting:

---

[14] The reference is Num. 30:1 in the Hebrew Bible.

Hear the statutes and ordinances that I [Moses] am about to teach you [*didaskō hymas*] to perform.
(Deut. 4:1)

The LORD commanded me [Moses] to teach you [*didaxai hymas*] statutes and ordinances, that you might perform them.
(Deut. 4:14)

Stand here by me and I [God] will tell you [Moses] all the commandments and the statutes and the judgments which you shall teach them [*didaxeis autous*], that they may perform them.
(Deut. 5:31)

Now this is the commandment, the statutes, and the judgments which the LORD your God has commanded me [Moses] to teach you [*didaxai hymas*], that you might perform them.
(Deut. 6:1)

This is another clear indication that we are intended to interpret the Matthean passage in the light of what transpired centuries earlier at Sinai.

Then last, but certainly not least, there is the expression 'I am with you [*meth' hymōn*] always', which concludes the first Gospel (Matt. 28:20). This has its counterpart in the encounter between God and Moses at Sinai: 'I will surely be with you [*meta sou*]' (Exod. 3:12), and later with respect to God's presence with the whole nation (Deut. 2:7 [*meta sou*]; 31:6 [*meth' hymōn*], 8 [*meta sou*]).

In this final scene, therefore, of Jesus' earthly life with his disciples, Matthew is evoking the Sinai narratives involving Moses and Israel. And now, as we come to ponder why this is so, there is one all-important matter not yet touched upon with regard to the above correspondences. This is the matter of identifying the grammatical subjects and objects of the various actions. The perceptive reader will hopefully already appreciate what is happening here, especially since the same feature has been encountered in allusions considered previously. Although there is a distinct Mosaic background to what is recorded in Matthew 28:16–20, it is apparent once more that the Gospel-writer is not merely presenting the risen Christ as a new Moses figure. Looking again at the various clauses and phrases cited above, we find that Jesus is not occupying the place of Moses in Matthew's usage of this language. In Exodus, Moses and Israel came to the designated mountain where they saw God and worshipped him, while in Matthew the disciples come to the pre-appointed mountain where they saw

Jesus and worshipped *him*. At Sinai the 'I' of the phrase 'I command you' was the God of Israel, YHWH himself, whereas in Matthew the 'I' pronoun indicates Jesus. Furthermore, the 'I' in the 'I am with you' promise of Exodus is again God, but at the close of Matthew's Gospel it is Jesus himself who pledges his continuing presence. How can one make such a promise unless one is both omnipresent ('with you') and eternal ('always')?[15] Plainly, and remarkably, in Matthew's closing section Jesus is not to be taken as merely corresponding to Moses, but is rather put in the place of the God of the Sinai narrative. For Matthew the allusions subtly but assuredly convey the message, hinted at back in 1:23 and elsewhere in his Gospel, that the Messiah is a divine as well as a human being.[16]

Over against the foregoing, we observe that it is the disciples who seem to be the ones primarily fulfilling the role of Moses. It is the disciples who ascend the mountain, and it is they who are commissioned with the task of teaching what has been commanded. But the scope of this latter extends far beyond that of Sinai – those to be taught are not of the single Hebrew nation, but all the nations of the world.[17] As God instructed Moses to teach the law to Israel, so Jesus instructs his disciples to teach his commands to the whole world. The apparent exclusivity of the Sinai narrative has now, through the advent of Christ, been transformed into a global inclusivity.

In keeping with the implication of Christ's deity is the triadic formula that also occurs in our Matthean passage. The Sinai narrative had also presented such a three-part formula, in the form of 'the God of Abraham and the God of Isaac and the God of Jacob' (Exod. 3:6, 15, 16; 4:5). Like this, the formula in Matthew concerns God, but with an extraordinary difference. In the tripartite phrase 'the name of the Father and of the Son and of the Holy Spirit' (Matt. 28:19), Jesus has included himself as the 'Son'. What else can this be other than a claim to his essential divinity?[18]

---

[15] Cf. Craig S. Keener, 'Gospel Lesson: Matthew 28:16–20', in Roger Van Harn (ed.), *The Lectionary Commentary. The Third Readings: The Gospels* (Grand Rapids, MI: Eerdmans, 2001), 158: 'The passage further presents Jesus as "with" his people (28:20); this image also portrays Jesus as divine. The Gospel earlier introduced Jesus as "God with us" (1:23) and claimed that where even two of his disciples gathered, he was among them (18:20) – a claim Jesus' contemporaries had traditionally reserved for God's own presence.' Similar comments are made by Kenton L. Sparks, in 'Gospel as Conquest: Mosaic Typology in Matthew 28:16–20', *CBQ* 68 (2006): 662–663. Sparks here claims that the Matthean figure of Christ is 'much closer to John's ἐγώ εἰμι (John 8:58) than is often suspected'.

[16] Cf. Leithart, *Jesus as Israel*, vol. 2, 337: 'Jesus is Yahweh on the mountain, a new Mount Sinai, instructing His disciples to keep and teach His commandments; a new Zion, where the disciples worship.'

[17] There is perhaps a further echo here of the patriarchal promise that 'all the nations' (*panta ta ethnē*) would be blessed (cf. Gen. 18:18; 22:18; 26:4).

[18] Cf. Keener ('Gospel Lesson: Matthew 28:16–20', 158): 'The passage also presents him [Jesus] alongside the Father and the Spirit (28:19), which must have startled the first Jewish disciples to hear: the Father was God, and Judaism also recognized the Holy Spirit as God's divine Spirit. To link Jesus with the Father and

We see then that Matthew 28:16–20 echoes the Old Testament Sinai narratives in many ways. Here is an appearance on a mountain and worship too. Here is the giving of what could justifiably be called a new manner of law, which is to be taught. But the sequence of allusions does not produce a simple one-to-one correspondence between the Gospel and the older Scriptures. For in the new revelation Jesus himself corresponds to the God who issued the law, and not just by virtue of his role, but on account of his essential nature as the divine Son who is worshipped and whose eternal omnipresence enables him to be present always with those who follow him.

Mark

Regarding Mark 16:9–20 the first question that usually concerns the reader is its originality. Modern Bibles inform us, in margins and footnotes, that these verses are not in the 'earliest manuscripts'. This is a controversial issue on which I have written at length elsewhere, and I would refer the interested reader to that work.[19] Suffice it to say that this ending was accepted as part of inspired Scripture by all but a few among the early Church Fathers, all the medievals, and all the Reformers and their successors. We do find, moreover, that it displays Old Testament allusions of a similar nature to the conclusions of the other three canonical Gospels, and a description and interpretation of these features is our main concern in this section. It is therefore included here.

In this ending of Mark we read of three separate resurrection appearances of Christ, in which he is progressively seen by more and more witnesses. First, he appeared to Mary Magdalene alone (vv. 9–11). Second, he was seen by two of his followers as they were walking in the countryside (vv. 12–13). Third, Jesus appeared to the gathered disciples, that is, the Eleven, as they were eating (v. 14). On this occasion he also commissioned them to proclaim the gospel in all the world (vv. 15–18). The passage concludes with the ascension of Jesus, and the disciples going out to perform the evangelistic task given them (vv. 19–20).

---

the Spirit this way was tantamount to calling him divine!' Also on this baptismal formula Athanasius of Alexandria (fourth century) stated that 'if God is Father, surely he is Father of one who is his Son by nature and who is the same as him in substance' (*Letter to Serapion*, 2.6).

[19] Nicholas P. Lunn, *The Original Ending of Mark: A New Case for the Authenticity of Mark 16:9–20* (Eugene, OR: Pickwick, 2014). When the editorial notes in modern printed Bibles speak of the 'earliest manuscripts' in this context, it is somewhat misleading to the uninitiated reader. What it means is that the ending of Mark is missing in the earliest *existing* manuscripts. The notes do not generally provide the more detailed information that there are only two such manuscripts in Greek and that both of these date to the middle of the fourth century. The long ending of Mark, however, was actually known and quoted by Church Fathers in the *second* century (e.g. Justin Martyr and Irenaeus of Lyons), and therefore has by far the earliest attestation.

Upon examination there can be little doubt that these disputed verses, especially those relating to the commissioning of the disciples, make further deliberate allusion to Moses, this time to his commissioning in the book of Exodus (chs. 3–4). This is not unrelated to what we saw above in Matthew, but we notice a different emphasis. The first Gospel has more focus on the later Sinai theophany with the accompanying giving of the law, whereas the second Gospel presents allusions that relate exclusively to the earlier call of Moses.

To begin, both the Exodus and Markan events concern an unexpected act of appearing. In the former passage it is stated in the first instance that 'the angel of the LORD appeared to him [Moses]' (Exod. 3:2), yet this is later described as an appearance of YHWH himself – 'the LORD, the God of their fathers, the God of Abraham, the God of Isaac, and the God of Jacob, has appeared to you' (4:5). Related statements occur in other parts of the narrative (3:16; 4:1). All of these appearances are expressed in Hebrew by the verb *nirâ*, 'appeared', 'was seen'. In these verses the LXX renders this particular Hebrew verb by either *ōphthē* or *ōptai*, two tenses of the same Greek verb. These two, especially the former, are the commonest ways of translating *nirâ* into Greek, since like the Hebrew they are passives of the verb 'to see', and so the translators have generally preserved the correspondence of form. Yet elsewhere (Dan. 1:15) the same Hebrew verb is found translated as *ephanē*, as is used of the appearance of the angel of the Lord in Matthew 1:20. This latter form is that found in Mark 16:9 ('he appeared first to Mary Magdalene'), while the virtually synonymous *ephanerōthē* occurs in verse 12 ('he appeared to two of them in another form') and verse 14 ('Jesus appeared to the Eleven'). As Greek had a much richer vocabulary than Hebrew, the existence of multiple words for the same basic idea is not unusual. The fact is that both acts of commission are initiated by the supernatural appearance of a special being.

Having appeared to Moses, the Lord commissioned him to 'go' to Pharaoh back in Egypt (Exod. 3:10): 'Now go, I will send you to Pharaoh' (cf. 4:12, 'Now go [*poreuou*]', and v. 21 'When you go [*poreuomenou sou*] . . .'). Moses was to go as directed in order to bring the Israelites out of their Egyptian bondage. Upon his appearance to the disciples, Jesus commissioned them likewise to 'go' (Mark 16:15, *poreuthentes*) and take the gospel message to all creation. The commission in each account thus begins with the same fundamental command.

In the Old Testament passage, after Moses had received his instructions, the question arose of belief in his forthcoming message to his fellow Hebrews about the appearance of the Lord to him. This theme is given some prominence in the first part of Exodus 4: 'What if they [the Israelites] will not believe [*pisteusōsin*] me or listen to my voice? For they may say, "The LORD has not appeared to you"' (v. 1); 'that they may believe [*pisteusōsin*] that the LORD, the God of their fathers ... has appeared to you' (v. 5). In Exodus 4:31 we read that when Moses returned to the Israelites in Egypt, 'the people believed [*episteusen*]'.[20] In Mark 16 the verb 'believe' and its cognate noun, 'belief, faith', are equally conspicuous. When Mary Magdalene reported the appearance to herself of the risen Jesus, those who heard this 'did not believe [*ēpistēsan*]' (v. 11). Regarding those who received the testimony of the two disciples to whom Christ appeared in the countryside, the text states: 'neither did they believe [*episteusan*]' (v. 13). When Jesus finally appeared to the main body of disciples 'he rebuked them for their unbelief [*apistian*] ... because they had not believed [*episteusan*] those who had seen him after he had risen' (v. 14). Then, following his mandate for the disciples to go into the world with the gospel, Jesus spoke of the response of belief to the message that is preached: 'Whoever believes [*pisteusas*] and is baptized will be saved, but whoever does not believe [*apistēsas*] will be condemned' (v. 16). Both commissioning episodes can be seen therefore to share a similar concern for the all-important matter of belief.

Within this same context of coming to believe, both passages make mention of 'signs'. Moses was given certain signs (*sēmeia*) to perform as a confirmation of his message (Exod. 4:9, 17, 28, 30). Jesus too spoke of 'signs' (*sēmeia*) that would accompany those who believe (Mark 16:17), so 'confirming the word' (v. 20).

One of the signs given to Moses involved his staff turning into a snake (Exod. 4:2–3), which he was then commanded to pick up (v. 4a). So Moses 'stretched out his hand and took hold of it' (v. 4b), at which it reverted to a staff. Among the signs mentioned by Jesus an unusual one is that 'they will pick up snakes' (Mark 16:18). Both Exodus 4:3 and Mark 16:18 contain the same general term for 'snake', namely *ophis*.[21] Additionally, if the Markan variant reading 'and with their hands' (*kai en tais chersin*) is accepted as genuine, then the allusion to Exodus 4:4 (*tēn cheira* and *en tē cheiri*) is even closer. Since Exodus 4 is the only other passage in Scripture which expressly speaks of picking up a snake, it is reasonable to suppose that the verse in Mark is alluding to this context, especially considering the similar subject matter of commissioning and signs.

---

[20] Exod. 4 accounts for no fewer than five out of the total of seven instances of the verb 'believe' in the book of Exodus (4:1, 5, 8, 9, 31; 14:31; 19:9).

[21] This fact seems to go against the oft-heard claim that the author of the Markan ending is basing this part of his text on the incident in Acts 28:3. There the apostle Paul was putting sticks on a fire when 'a viper came out because of the heat, and fastened on his hand'. The Greek word there is *echidna* ('viper'). We also note that Paul does not actually pick up the snake, but rather it attaches itself to him. Evidently, the Mosaic text forms a much closer parallel.

Following on from the commission, each of the two narratives then tells how Moses and the disciples went in obedience to what they had been commanded, spoke the message and performed the signs (Exod. 4:20, 30–31; Mark 16:19–20).

One other feature appears in the Markan ending which relates closely to the call and mission of Moses and this is the idea of hardness of heart. When Jesus was seen by the eleven disciples, on account of their negative response to earlier witnesses of his resurrection, the text says: 'He reproached them for their unbelief and hardheartedness [*sklērokardia*]' (16:14). The hardening of the heart, especially that of Pharaoh and the Egyptians, is a prominent and recurring theme in the exodus account. The hearts of the Egyptians, we read, were hardened at the signs Moses performed (Exod. 4:21 [*sklērynō . . . kardian*]; cf. 7:13; 8:19; 9:7 etc.). Although the disciples respond initially in such a way, they later come to believe. With them, hardheartedness was not permanent, as would seem to have been the case for the Egyptians.

To my mind, then, the allusions in Mark's ending to the commission of Moses in Exodus 3 – 4 are particularly strong, especially since as individual items of correspondence they occur in precisely the same sequence in both texts. Regarding the significance of the allusions, it is apparent that what was seen with respect to Matthew's ending holds true here also. There we saw that the person of God who was seen and worshipped on top of the mountain, and who from there issued forth his commandments, is assumed by the person of Jesus Christ, the Son, the second Person of the trinitarian formula then uttered. Now in the Markan ending, the place of the God who appeared to Moses in the burning bush, and who commissioned him to go and proclaim liberty to the enslaved accompanied by signs and wonders, is occupied by Jesus himself.[22] Surely this is yet another pointer to the fact of his divine nature.

Luke

The allusions to the Jewish Scriptures that may be detected in Luke 24 principally make reference to the patriarch Joseph, the son of Jacob who was rejected by his brothers. It is he, we recall, who forms the main protagonist in the latter chapters of Genesis. Joseph has already been the subject of Gospel allusions in the parable of the wicked tenants[23] and in Luke's account of the two thieves

---

[22] On the relationship between Jesus and the angel of the Lord see Nicholas P. Lunn, *Jesus in the Jewish Scriptures: How the Old Testament Bears Witness to Christ* (London: Faithbuilders, 2020), ch. 9.
[23] See chapter 18.

crucified with Jesus.[24] Luke again makes an unmistakable series of allusions to the same character in his resurrection accounts. The allusions specifically relate to the portion of the Joseph story in which he is reunited with his family after a prolonged absence, predominantly to Genesis 45.[25]

Back in Genesis, when Joseph was sold as a slave by his brothers, the reader is aware that he did not literally die at this time. Nevertheless, the narrative does portray him, from the standpoint of his own family, as though his life had actually ended. He is described in fact as being 'dead' (Gen. 42:38; 44:20) and as one who 'is no more' (42:13, 32). None of his family ever really expected to see him again, despite the supernatural revelations he had earlier shared with them about his future exaltation to a position of great prominence (37:5–11). Jesus, on the other hand, did literally die, though that was not to be the end of him. He had predicted his resurrection to his followers several times (e.g. Matt. 16:21; 20:19; Mark 8:31; Luke 9:22; 18:33), but we are expressly told that they had not understood what he was talking about (e.g. Matt. 16:22; Mark 9:32; Luke 9:35), and therefore they were not expecting to see him again after his cruci-fixion, as the Gospel narratives make clear. Each setting therefore revolves around a person, one whose great future had been foretold, who is considered dead with no anticipation of being seen by them alive again, and yet in each instance it does in fact happen. This establishes a firm thematic correlation between the two.

Coming to the more detailed conceptual and verbal connections, we first observe the fact that in each account both Joseph and the resurrected Jesus are not at first recognized. When Joseph stood before his brothers on the first occa-sion, we read that 'they did not recognize him [*epegnōsan auton*]' (Gen. 42:8). Similarly, when Jesus appeared to two of the disciples, before his later appear-ance to them all, the Gospel says that 'their eyes were kept from recognizing him [*epignōnai auton*]' (Luke 24:16).

After this initial lack of recognition, the two narratives later state that Joseph and Jesus became known to those same persons. The earlier text says that Joseph 'made himself known [*anegnōrizeto*] to his brothers' (Gen. 45:1), while in the Gospel Jesus 'was made known [*egnōstē*] to them' (Luke 24:35), that is, to the same two disciples from whom his identity had been concealed.

---

[24] See chapter 25.

[25] We note how in the Gospels the three episodes identified as alluding to Joseph – to his rejection, his condemnation with two others, and his reunion with his brothers – do so in the same chronological order as in Genesis. This, I would judge, is further evidence that the allusions are not imaginary, but exist in the Gospel texts by intentional design.

At the second encounter with his brothers, Joseph greeted them with the words 'Peace be to you',[26] and with the reassuring 'Do not be afraid [*mē phobeisthe*]' (Gen. 43:23). When Jesus later appeared to the main group of disciples, Luke's account tells us that 'Jesus himself stood in their midst and said to them, "Peace be with you." They were startled and afraid [*emphoboi*]' (Luke 24:36–37). The greeting is the same as in Genesis, as is the presence of fear.

Once Joseph had made himself known to his brothers, the account says that 'they were troubled [*etarachthēsan*] at his presence' (Gen. 45:3). The disciples were evidently disturbed in the same way when confronted with the risen Christ, for he said to them: 'Why are you troubled [*tetaragmenoi*] . . . ?' (Luke 24:38).

In each narrative the key moment of self-identification is expressed using an almost identical construction. Joseph said to his brothers, 'I am [*egō eimi*] Joseph' (Gen. 45:3, 4), while Jesus declared to his disciples, 'It is I [*egō eimi*] myself' (Luke 24:39).

It seems to me that these connections are altogether definite. Not only is similar language employed, but this is done at the corresponding point in each narrative. I therefore conclude that a deliberate association is being created. But there is more. Going back earlier in Luke 24 we find other pointers to Joseph in connection with the initial report that Christ was risen. The brothers' first visit to Egypt was reported to their father back in Canaan with the words 'they told him all [*apēngeilan autō panta*] that had happened to them' (Gen. 42:29), resembling the report of the women who had visited the tomb before the explicit resurrection narrative: 'they told all these things [*apēngeilan tauta panta*] to the Eleven and to all the rest" (Luke 24:9). We may also compare 'They [the brothers] told him [Jacob], saying [*legontes*] "Joseph is still alive [*zē*] . . ."' (Gen. 45:26) with 'They [the women] told us that they had seen a vision of angels who were saying [*legousin*] that he was alive [*zēn*]' (Luke 24:23). Each of these reports has the accompanying response of unbelief. Jacob, we are next told, 'did not believe [*ou episteusen*] them' (Gen. 45:26), and likewise with respect to what the women reported, the disciples 'did not believe [*ēpistoun*] them' (Luke 24:11). Also the verb 'amazed' (Gen. 45:26, *exestē*; Luke 24:22, *exestēsan*) occurs as a further response to the report in both accounts, this being its only occurrence in the Gospel resurrection narratives.[27]

---

[26] This is the Hebrew phrase *šālôm lākem*, which is obscured in many English translations, as in the LXX (*hileōs humin*, lit. 'mercifully to you'). Cf. also Gen. 43:27, which literally states: 'he [Joseph] asked them their peace [*wayyiš'al lākem šālôm*]'.

[27] There is one other possible connection between Joseph and Jesus in this context that is somewhat curious. It may be purely coincidental, or it may be deliberately contrastive. Following the reunion with the brothers, prominence is given by Joseph to 'my father' (Gen. 45:3, 9, 13). The brothers are to 'ascend to

What purpose, then, is served by these allusions? I would suggest there is more than one truth that they are intended to convey. The connotations of allusions can, of course, be manifold. At the most basic level, what happens to Joseph and Jesus demonstrates that God's revelations are confirmed. In spite of the symbolic 'death' of Joseph, the future shown to him in revelatory dreams eventually comes true. He is exalted to a position of high prominence and his brothers come and bow before him, as foreshown. With regard to Jesus something very similar holds true. All that the prophets had foretold about his glorification and kingdom, as well as his own predictions of his resurrection, were all to be fulfilled and not in the slightest bit thwarted by his execution.[28] What happened to Jesus, therefore, is all the more remarkable than what transpired with Joseph, as the death of Jesus was not merely apparent but actual. One might have thought that his crucifixion put paid to all the prophecies and predictions, but this was far from being the case; in fact the veracity of the divine foretellings was fully corroborated.

Looking at the allusions from a different aspect, we find that they also convey the idea of reunion, with the brothers in one case and with the disciples in the other,[29] none of whom thought they would see the departed one again. But it is more than a happy reuniting with the one they considered lost for good. I believe the allusions to the Joseph narrative also introduce an element of reconciliation into the new encounter. Joseph's brothers had rejected him, and Jesus' disciples had abandoned him. Peter had emphatically denied him, while the others had forsaken him and run away, leaving him to his fate (Matt. 26:31, 56; Mark 14:27, 50). There was, then, the disciples' own personal desertion of their Master for which reconciliation was required. The very fact of Jesus, now risen, coming to these same disciples, speaking words of peace and reassurance as he does, is an indication that he is not holding their rejection of him against them. Yet, deeper than this, I see another manner of reconciliation going on here, one that is not personal, that is, on the part of the disciples themselves individually, but one that is emblematic, in which the disciples are representative. Israel as a nation had rejected Jesus[30] and sought his demise (as intimated in the parable of the

---

my father' (45:9, *anabēte pros ton patera mou*) bearing gifts that Joseph provided (v. 23). Following his resurrection, Jesus makes reference to 'my father' (Luke 24:49), to whom Jesus himself will ascend and from whom a great gift, that of the Holy Spirit, will be sent (cf. Acts 2:38).

[28] Together with this we may see that Christ's response to the thief on the cross, that he should be with him in his kingdom, is also validated. Since for Jesus death was not final, he could offer the repentant thief a place with him in paradise (Luke 23:42–43).

[29] Both eleven in number (see n. 32 below).

[30] Cf. John 1:11, 'He came to his own, but his own did not receive him' (also Acts 4:10–11).

wicked tenants,[31] which also manifests allusions to Joseph and his brothers, as seen earlier), handing him over to the Gentiles to dispose of him. Now in Luke's resurrection scene, he who was rejected is both reunited and reconciled to Israel, this being the new Israel embodied in his disciples, originally a band of twelve,[32] according to the number of the tribes of Jacob. These disciples, then, as they welcome the risen Christ, depict in allusory form the anticipation of the Jewish people's future restoration to union with their Lord, and their ultimate incorporation within the eschatological true Israel of God.

---

[31] This parable, we recall, is closely associated with the prophecy concerning 'the stone that the builders rejected' (Ps. 118:22), which is adjoined to the parable in all three synoptic Gospels (Matt. 21:42; Mark 12:10; Luke 20:17).

[32] After the departure of Judas there were now only eleven of this special group present to witness the resurrection. This is a number that occurs in relation to Joseph. In one of his dreams he beheld eleven stars, representing the other sons of Jacob, his brothers, bowing down to him (Gen. 37:9, *prosekynoun*). This was fulfilled when these eleven later came and bowed before Joseph (43:26, 28). In Luke's Gospel, Jesus made an appearance to, among others, those described as 'the Eleven' (Luke 24:33; cf. v. 9), who 'worshipped him' (v. 52, *proskynēsantes*).

27

The burial and the empty tomb

John 19:38 – 20:12

Here we examine a sequence of text that covers two distinct occasions. The first is that of the burial of Jesus on the evening of the crucifixion (John 19:38–42), the second the visits of Mary Magdalene and two male disciples to the tomb early on the first Easter Sunday (20:1–12). These form one uninterrupted account in John's record.[1] In these passages we will uncover a series of allusions based on the same basic Old Testament themes.

Our first section describes how, with Pilate's permission (19:38), Joseph of Arimathea and Nicodemus perform certain burial customs with the body of Jesus and then place it in the tomb (vv. 39–42). We next read of Mary coming to the tomb to discover that the stone has been rolled away from the entrance (20:1). At this she runs and tells Peter, who was with another disciple, 'the one Jesus loved' (v. 2), traditionally identified as John himself. Together the two men hurry to the tomb to see for themselves. John arrives first and, looking inside, sees the linen cloths that had covered Jesus' body, but he does not enter (vv. 3–5). When Peter gets there, he himself goes inside. He sees the same cloths and the other piece of material that was wrapped around Jesus' head (vv. 6–7). John, presumably the younger of the two, then enters the tomb behind Peter (v. 8). Following their visit to the tomb the two disciples return to their homes (v. 10), but Mary, who has apparently come back to the tomb again, is left there alone crying. When she looks into the tomb she sees two angels clothed in white

---

[1] Understanding that chapter divisions were a much later editorial edition to the text. We note that the same basic happenings appear elsewhere in the Gospels, though recounted from different perspectives and presenting different details. The burial is, of course, recorded in all four Gospels. The passage about Mary and the others going to the tomb in the first part of John 20 has its closest parallel in Luke 24:1–12, though each account presents a slightly different perspective. At first sight it appears that John's record concerns only one woman, Mary Magdalene, while Luke includes other women besides (v. 10). Reading the details of John 20, however, reveals that when speaking Mary uses the first-person plural pronoun 'we' (v. 2), showing that she was not in fact alone. Conversely, Luke would seem to state that only Peter ran to the tomb (24:12), whereas in John he is accompanied by another disciple (20:4). Later in the same chapter of Luke, however, the two journeying to Emmaus reported that 'some of those who were with us went to the tomb and found it just as the women had said' (24:24), making it clear that Peter had not gone to the tomb unaccompanied. Our study here focuses, as far as Old Testament allusions are concerned, exclusively on John's account.

sitting where the body of Jesus had been placed (vv. 11–12). This leads directly into the appearance of Jesus to Mary (vv. 13–18), which will form the topic of our next chapter.[2]

The plain meaning of the text concerns the fact that on the morning of the first Easter the tomb was found to be empty. Of this there were multiple witnesses, both men and women. These, we read, did not instantly come to the conclusion that Jesus had risen. Although he had foretold that this very thing would happen, they initially sought a more rational explanation. The first assumption was that the body had been moved elsewhere (John 20:2; cf. v. 13).

Viewing the text allusively, I would propose that behind the literal details there lies once more the Jewish Day of Atonement, or Yom Kippur, especially as it relates to the ark of the covenant. We will be looking again, therefore, at Leviticus 16, containing the ceremony of atonement in which the ark played a central role, and also at certain passages in Exodus and Numbers where the ark and its function in the sanctuary are described. The important annual festival of Yom Kippur, we saw previously, formed a significant part, by way of literary allusion, of the narrative concerning Christ's prayer in Gethsemane and also his crucifixion.[3] Arguably, this holy day, together with the feast of Passover, comprise the most important elements of the Old Testament background to the Gospels for appreciating the death of Jesus. Now the Day of Atonement takes on further significance with regard to his resurrection also.

Before we examine the details, it needs to be pointed out that the Old Testament allusions in these passages of John are variegated, that is to say, they depict Jesus at one moment as one particular entity in the corresponding Old Testament text and in the next moment as something else in the same text. Thinking for a moment of the letter to the Hebrews, there we discover that the writer, in his unpacking of the levitical ceremonies, relates Jesus to the high priest (4:14), to the sacrifice (10:10), to the veil (10:20) and indeed to the altar (13:10). In interpreting the symbolism involved in the old-covenant ritual, as far as Hebrews is concerned, Jesus clearly cannot be limited to any one element; rather, many things, to some degree or another, indicate differing aspects of his saving work when interpreted figurally. The same applies to the series of allusions we are dealing with here in the fourth Gospel. Jesus is portrayed in terms of varying elements within the basic Day of Atonement ceremony. This should occasion no surprise. In previous chapters we have already seen, in a single

---

[2] We point out here the transitional nature of vv. 10–12. They bring to a close the first episode of the chapter and begin the second. In a sense, therefore, these verses belong to both.

[3] Chapters 20 and 23.

episode, how Jesus represented allusively both Joshua and the ark,[4] and both the high priest and the offering.[5]

To begin, we make the important observation that the tomb in which the body of Jesus was laid was in a garden (John 19:41), so the burial and the visits in question all occurred in a garden setting. As was pointed out earlier in our treatment of Jesus praying in Gethsemane, it is widely recognized by biblical scholars that there is a close association between the Hebrew sanctuary – whether the tabernacle or the later temple – and the garden of Eden. The sanctuary, it was there explained, is adorned with trees and flowers as though it were a kind of garden. On Yom Kippur the garden-like sanctuary, of course, figures prominently in the proceedings, since the entire atoning ceremony that takes place on that day is carried out within that sacred precinct.

As the principal locality of both scenarios, we find a small, enclosed and presumably dark space within the larger 'garden' area. While in Leviticus 16 the ritual centres on the cube-shaped inner sanctum of the tabernacle (cf. v. 12, vv. 16–17), in the Gospel the action revolves around the tomb situated in the garden. These are both, in effect, chambers[6] separated off from what lies outside by means of something that is explicitly identified. In the one case, the separating item takes the form of a veil (Exod. 40:3, 21), in the other a sealed stone (John 20:1). Each of these, we remember, was equally impassable under normal circumstances, the former at the express command of God (cf. Lev. 16:2) and the latter under the authority of the Roman governor (cf. Matt. 27:66).

In the last verses of John 19 we find that the author picks up several elements connected with the ark of the covenant and applies them to Jesus. The preparations for the burial of his body and its placement in the tomb subtly yet purposely echo, I would suggest, the installation of the ark in the inner chamber of the tabernacle. This is the impression received from a number of smaller details within the text, which follow.

In connection with Christ's body John here several times employs the verb 'take, carry' (*airein*). In our Johannine passages this occurs three times in speaking of the moving of the body (19:38 [twice]; 20:2) and twice more in the following section (20:13, 15). In contrast this verb does not appear at all in the parallel passages in the other Gospels. Back in the Greek version of the Old Testament this is the same verb that is used of the transportation of the ark

---

[4] See chapter 17.

[5] See chapter 20.

[6] The resemblance between the tomb and the most holy place has been noticed by Christian expositors since ancient times. See, e.g., Daniel A. Smith, *Revisiting the Empty Tomb: The Early History of Easter* (Minneapolis, MN: Fortress, 2010).

(Exod. 25:15; 37:5; Num. 4:15; Deut. 10:8 etc.). It may be a minor point, but it contributes to the association when viewed together with the other connections. Both the ark and the body of Jesus are conveyed by human hands to the place where they are laid to rest.

Then there is the act of covering the item in question. The ark was covered before it was moved (Num. 4:5), while the body of Jesus was wrapped in cloth before it was taken to its place of burial (John 19:40). There is not, to be sure, an exact similarity between the respective uses of the coverings. The one was for transportation purposes only, while the other was intended to remain once inside the chamber. Yet again we remind ourselves that allusion is not at all a specific reference to an identical item or action. Its effectiveness rather lies in bringing an earlier object or event to mind. The act of covering with material does, I would claim, have this effect once taken in conjunction with other allusory features of the text.

Fragrant spices are involved in connection with both the ark and the body of Jesus. Regarding the former of these, it was anointed with holy oil for the purpose of consecration. This was carried out with respect to both the priests and the sacred objects of the sanctuary (Exod. 30:26). The first-listed ingredient of this anointing oil was myrrh (v. 23, *smyrnēs*). As regards Jesus' body, in the preparatory rites for burial it was anointed with spices, the first-mentioned of which was likewise myrrh (John 19:39, *smyrnēs*).[7]

In John's narratives of Christ's burial and resurrection, as with the verb 'take, carry', the verb 'put, place, lay' (*tithenai*) appears frequently with the 'body' as its direct object. The Gospel says, for example, that 'because the tomb was nearby, they laid [*ethēkan*] Jesus there' (John 19:42; also 19:41; 20:2, 13, 15). The verb is used much less in the other Gospels.[8] Back in Exodus this verb occurs repeatedly for the putting of the ark and other sacred objects within the tabernacle. Moses, for example, is instructed by God: 'Set up the tabernacle . . . and put [*thēseis*] the ark of the testimony in it' (40:2–3; also vv. 5, 6, 22, 24, 26, 29).[9] Therefore, as the ark was placed within the innermost chamber of the sanctuary, so the body of Jesus was placed within the tomb. Immediately after the former action, the sanctum was partitioned off by the veil, and after the latter the tomb was closed off with the stone, as mentioned (40:3; cf. John 20:1).

---

[7]. The measures given for the total quantity of spices in each context are both in multiples of ten – 1,000 in Exod. 30:23 and 100 in John 19:39.

[8] It is found three times in Mark (15:46, 47; 16:6), twice in Luke (23:53, 55) and just once in Matthew (27:60).

[9] Cf. also 2 Chr. 35:3, 'they put [*ethēkan*] the holy ark in the house which Solomon the son of David king of Israel had built'.

In these foregoing instances, I remind the reader of what was stated in the introduction respecting the presence of accumulation. Some of the verbs and ideas here might appear common and insignificant in themselves, but taken together they all in fact point, as instances of allusion, in the same direction. The correspondences we have so far, then, consist of the act of carrying, the covering with a cloth, the application of myrrh, the placement in a specific location, this being a small enclosed chamber, and the shutting off of this space with a particular object serving that purpose. I, for one, already find this sixfold series compelling for establishing the presence of deliberate allusion, yet certain other details remain to discuss, some of which could be regarded as creating an even stronger bond between the two scenarios.

Up until this point, it is Jesus, or his body, that is being associated allusively with the ark of the Old Testament passages. Such a literary relationship is entirely appropriate, and was seen in an earlier chapter.[10] The ark of the covenant was, of course, the most sacred object in the whole of the Israelite sanctuary. It was constructed of both wood and gold, and contained within it were the tablets of the law, the golden pot of incorruptible manna, and Aaron's staff that budded (Heb. 9:4). As a holy item it especially betokened the glory of God (cf. 1 Sam. 4:21–22; Heb. 9:5), and it was further conceived to be the meeting-place between God and his people (Exod. 25:22; 30:6). In short, the ark was nothing less than a representation of the presence of God.[11] In view of who Jesus was, then, it is quite proper that he should be connected with this Old Testament object. It is he who displays the divine glory, and he is the locus in which humankind and God are united. It is he who has God's law laid up in his heart and who dispenses the life-giving manna. And above all else, it is in him that God is present.

As we proceed into John 20, we find now that a switch has occurred with respect to the nature of the allusions. These continue to point to the ark, but now more specifically in relation to the Day of Atonement. The Old Testament ark, located within the most holy place, had the shape of a rectangular box with a flat lid (Exod. 25:10–22). At the ends of the lid rose up the cherubim. We are not entirely sure what these figures looked like, but we do know they possessed wings. They are often understood in both Jewish and Christian sources to be angel-like creatures.[12] The most important thing about this ark in connection

---

[10] Chapter 5.

[11] Cf. Douglas K. Stuart, *Exodus: An Exegetical and Theological Exposition of Holy Scripture* (NAC 2; Nashville, TN: Broadman & Holman, 2006), 569; here Stuart states that '[t]he Ark symbolized God's presence'.

[12] See, e.g., Genesis Rabbah 21.9; Maimonides, *The Guide for the Perplexed* 3.45; cf. also Stuart, *Exodus*, 571: 'The most we can say for certain is that cherubs were some sort of intelligent, powerful angelic being depicted as winged.'

with Yom Kippur is that it served as the primary focus of the entire ceremony, being the very place where atonement was made. Traditionally, the Hebrew term indicating the lid (*kappōret*) has been translated as 'mercy-seat'. However, due to its etymological relation to the verb 'atone' (*kippēr*) and its central role in the levitical atoning ritual, some versions render it as 'atonement cover' (e.g. NIV),[13] which is perhaps better. The LXX similarly relates the lid (*hilastērion*) to the idea of atonement (*hilasmos*). It was on this cover of the ark that the blood of the sin-offering for the people of Israel was applied by the high priest (cf. Lev. 16:15).

In the Gospel passage we are told that when Mary looked into the tomb 'she saw two angels in white, sitting where the body of Jesus had been, one at the head and the other at the foot' (John 20:12). In other words, within the burial chamber Mary beheld a flat surface, most probably a raised rectangular slab, with an angelic figure at each end. It would, it seems to me, be almost impossible for any early Jewish Christian, as well as the biblically informed Gentile believer, in reading or hearing this description not to think of the ark. I do not consider it unreasonable, therefore, to conclude that the picture given here is intentionally designed to be reminiscent of the inner sanctum of the tabernacle with the ark positioned within it.[14] In each instance the place between the two figures was inextricably linked to the notion of sacrifice, specifically an atoning sacrifice. One was sprinkled with the blood of a goat; the other received the body of an infinitely superior offering.

Alongside the foregoing, it should not be overlooked that each of the two aforementioned enclosures containing the ark or an ark-like scene comes to be opened up on the particular occasion in question. Yom Kippur was the only day of the Jewish calendar when the most holy place in the innermost part of the sanctuary was opened up, when the veil was drawn back to allow entrance. Regarding the tomb, which had been closed up and sealed, it was to be reopened, giving access on this Easter morning.

Another noteworthy detail in the scene within the opened tomb is the grave clothes that had been on Christ's body. These were first seen by Peter and the other disciple who came with him, but also no doubt by Mary, who looked into the tomb (John 20:11). What they saw was 'linen cloths' plus 'the cloth that had

---

13 Cf. 'atonement lid' (NET); 'cover – the place of atonement' (NLT).

14 Cf. Robert H. Smith, *Easter Gospels: The Resurrection of Jesus According to the Four Evangelists* (Minneapolis, MN: Augsburg, 1983), 161: 'Ask an audience of ordinary Christians what Old Testament scene comes to mind as they picture two angels in a small dark place stationed one at the head and one at the foot of a shelf or slab, and almost immediately someone will respond, "The ark of the covenant in the Holy of Holies." That response is naive, uncomplicated, and correct.' Cf. also Raymond E. Brown, *The Gospel According to John, XIII–XXI* (AB 29A; New York, NY: Doubleday, 1966), 989.

been upon his head', which was described as (lit.) 'rolled up in one place' (vv. 6–7). A corresponding feature of the Day of Atonement ceremony readily comes to mind. Before the offering of sacrifices commenced, the officiating high priest was to put on linen garments: 'He shall put on the holy linen tunic, and shall have the linen undergarments next to his body, fasten the linen sash, and put on the linen turban' (Lev. 16:4). The commentators tell us that these would have been items of plain white linen.[15] Then later, once the atoning ritual had been enacted, the high priest removed these linen clothes and put on his usual clothing. It is striking that the former were to be left in the most holy place (vv. 23–24). In each case, therefore, items of linen material which previously adorned the one entering, whether the high priest or Jesus, are left behind in the chamber in question.

John's account, then, can be seen to strongly resonate with the Old Testament passages about the ark, and more especially with those concerning the ark on the important religious festival of Yom Kippur. The significance of the allusions is not, generally speaking, difficult to discern. The Day of Atonement, as shown in other chapters,[16] has already played a major part in providing a background for allusions in the passion narrative of the Gospels. In essence the allusions in these post-crucifixion passages of John are telling us that *the* atonement, the actual atonement and not that priestly ritual involving goats that merely foreshadowed the real event, has now been completed. As the ark, or more precisely the flat lid of the ark, provided the place where the figural act of atonement was made, so the dead body of Jesus placed on the slab in the tomb indicated that through his death the true atonement had once and for all been completed.[17] Just as the Greek Old Testament had described the lid of the ark as the *hilastērion*, or 'place of atonement', so Christ had provided the perfect *hilasmos*, 'means of atonement' (cf. 1 John 2:2; 4:10).[18] The completion of the act, understood within the context of the levitical prescriptions, is especially well portrayed through the folded grave clothes. As the high priest on that day

---

[15] E.g. Baruch A. Levine, *Leviticus* (JPS Torah Commentary; Philadelphia, PA: Jewish Publication Society, 1989), 101; Gordon J. Wenham, *The Book of Leviticus* (NICOT; Grand Rapids, MI: Eerdmans, 1979), 230. The Mishnah describes the high priest's garments for this occasion as *bigdê lābān*, 'clothes of white' (*Yoma* 3.6).

[16] See chapters 20 and 23.

[17] Cf. Heb. 9:12, 'He did not enter by means of the blood of goats and calves; but he entered the Most Holy Place once for all by his own blood, having obtained eternal redemption' (NIV).

[18] Ratzinger defines *hilastērion* more precisely in connection with the idea of 'expiation', that is, the removal of sin (rather than the propitiation of God). He nevertheless sees a close association between the mercy-seat and the offering of Christ. He states: 'The meaning of the Day of Atonement is accomplished in him [Jesus]. In his self-offering on the Cross, Jesus, as it were, brings all the sin of the world within the love of God and wipes it away.' See Joseph Ratzinger, *Jesus of Nazareth: Holy Week. From the Entrance into Jerusalem to the Resurrection* (San Francisco, CA: Ignatius Press, 2011), 39–40.

emerged from the holy of holies having left behind the garments he had been wearing, signifying that all was fulfilled for obtaining atonement on behalf of Israel, so Jesus emerged from the tomb leaving behind the cloths that had till then covered his body, showing that what was required to atone for the sins of the world had now been accomplished in full.

More can be said, however, regarding the disciples at the tomb. Further verbal links are to be detected between the actions of the disciples in John 20 and the instructions given to a special group of Levites with respect to the ark in Numbers 4. The Levites, the reader will be aware, were the ministers appointed from among the Israelites to assist the priests in the duties of the sanctuary. The tribe of Levi was therefore the ministerial tribe. As such, we note some interesting language used to describe their relation to both God and the high priest. First, we find it stressed several times that the Levites belonged to God: 'They are mine', he says (Num. 3:12, 13, 45; 8:14).[19] Then, having claimed ownership of the Levites, it is equally affirmed that God was giving them to Aaron and his male descendants the priests:

You shall give [dōseis] the Levites to Aaron and his sons; they are given entirely [doma dedomenoi] to him from among the children of Israel. (Num. 3:9)

I have given [apedōka] the Levites as a gift [apodoma dedomenous] to Aaron and to his sons from among the sons of Israel (Num. 8:19)

Behold, I myself have taken your fellow Levites from among the sons of Israel; they are a gift given [doma dedomenon] to you (Num. 18:6)

In sum, then, the Levites were taken by God and belonged to him, but were then given, or gifted, to Aaron and his sons as their assistants in the holy ministry.

From among the Levites the members of one particular clan, the Kohathites, were entrusted with the important task of bearing the ark itself, along with other sacred objects that furnished the tabernacle and temple (Num. 4:1–20). Although their work brought them into close association with the ark and other items, the Kohathites were nevertheless strictly ordered to maintain a

---

[19] The reason for this particular divine claim to Levi lies in the substitution of this tribe for the firstborn of Israel (cf. Num. 3:12–13; 8:16–17), who were protected through the blood of the Passover lamb in Egypt.

separation, with serious consequences if they failed to do so. We read that 'they shall not touch [*ouch hapsontai*] the holy things, or they will die' (Num. 4:15).[20] With regard to the sanctuary, God further declared that 'they shall not go in [*ou mē eiselthōsin*] to see [*idein*] the holy things, or they will die' (v. 20). Note the verbal sequence, 'go in . . . see'. In short, these men, although ministers, were not permitted to touch or even to look at the ark and other items of the sanctuary. If this was true of the men of Kohath, those specifically charged with transporting the sacred furniture, then how much more would it apply to those not so appointed?

The above details concerning the Levites, and particularly the Kohathites, all have their correspondences in the fourth Gospel with respect to the disciples. As regards the language of belonging and giving, as seen of the Levites, we find similar terms in John 17 speaking not just of the twelve disciples but of all believers. In this prayer to God the Father, Jesus acknowledges 'They are yours' (v. 9; cf. v. 6). At the same time, throughout the prayer he repeatedly describes the disciples as those who had been given to him by the Father:

I have manifested your name to the men you gave [*edōkas*] me out of the world; they were yours and you gave [*edōkas*] them to me.
(John 17:6)

I do not pray for the world but for those you have given [*dedōkas*] me.
(John 17:9)

I desire that they also, whom you have given [*dedōkas*] me, be with me where I am, that they may see my glory.
(John 17:24)

See also verse 2 and verse 12 of the same chapter. The parallels between the gift of the Levites to Aaron and the giving of the disciples to Christ are, I believe, unmistakable. For John, then, the disciples, meaning all followers of Jesus, are made to correspond to the Levites of the Mosaic law code.

However, when we come to the prohibitions placed on the Levites, or more strictly on those of the Kohathite clan of Levi entrusted with the holy items, we discover a radical difference present in our passage under discussion in John. Mary Magdalene, Peter and the other disciple all approach the tomb of Jesus,

---

[20] For this reason metal rings were fitted to these items (e.g. Exod. 25:12) so that the Kohathites could insert poles and lift the holy objects without actually touching them.

depicted in allusory fashion as a kind of inner sanctuary containing something reminiscent of the ark. Yet the restrictions placed on the Kohathites have no place here. While these latter were expressly told not to 'go in . . . and see', this is precisely what Peter did. Coming to the tomb, 'he went in [*eisēlthen*] and saw [*eiden*]' (John 20:6). Likewise, immediately after Peter, the second disciple 'also went in [*eisēlthen*] . . . and saw [*eiden*]' (v. 8). And as regards the Kohathites being forbidden to 'touch' the holy objects, we find that Mary did this very thing. A little later in John 20, once the resurrected Jesus had appeared to her,[21] he said to Mary: 'Do not touch me [*mē mou haptou*] for I have not yet ascended to my Father' (v. 17). The form of the words indicates that she was doing exactly this. The sense is in fact 'Stop clinging to Me' (NASB), for he had something else to do.[22] He was not prohibiting her from touching him at all.[23] Here then is another instance in which the allusion contains a reversal, one that is altogether meaningful. Whereas to enter and see was prohibited to the Levites and punishable by death, the two male disciples who do this very thing suffer no harm, but rather the opening up of the tomb is almost an invitation for them to actually enter and take a look. Similarly, while the levitical ministers were commanded not to touch, Mary's encounter with Jesus and his closeness to her allow her to do just that.

Since the verbal connections to the Torah include Mary as well as Peter and John, the truths that they indicate cannot relate to the respective ministerial roles of the Levites and the apostles. Rather, the application may be taken with reference, not specifically to the Twelve, but to Christian disciples in general, as is also implicit in Christ's use of 'those you have given me', noted above (John 17:9). With respect to the echoes of Numbers 4:15 and 20 in John 20, the intent

---

[21] Since the act of touching requires Jesus to be present in person, this cannot fall within the first portion of John 20 (vv. 1–12), from which Jesus himself is absent. The reference to the touch, therefore, necessarily falls within the next section (vv. 13–18), describing his appearance to Mary.

[22] Commentators differ considerably as to what ascending to the Father might entail. In his commentary Carson remarks that '[t]his verse belongs to a handful of the most difficult passages in the New Testament' (D. A. Carson, *The Gospel According to John* [PNTC; Leicester: Apollos, 1991], 641–642). The words might possibly contain a further allusion to the Day of Atonement ritual. Once the atoning offerings had been performed the high priest's duties of the day concluded with burnt-offerings for himself and his people (Lev. 16:24). What is interesting here is the fact that what we call a 'burnt-offering' in English is actually 'that which *ascends*' ('*ōlâ*) in Hebrew. For further discussion, see Nicholas P. Lunn, 'Jesus, the Ark, and the Day of Atonement: Intertextual Echoes in John 19:38–20:18', *JETS* 52.4 (2009): 731–746.

[23] R. T. France comments: 'There seems to be no reason why Mary should not touch him, and indeed Matthew tells us that when the women first saw the risen Lord they "came to him, clasped his feet and worshiped him" (Matt. 28:9). Probably we should understand the Greek tense here in the strict sense. The present imperative with a negative means "Stop doing something" rather than "Do not start something." Here it will mean "Stop clinging to me" and not, "Do not begin to touch me"' (*The Gospel According to John* [NICNT; Grand Rapids, MI: Eerdmans, 1995], 741–742). Cf. also Maximilian Zerwick, *Biblical Greek* (Rome: Editrice Pontificio Istituto Biblico, 1990), 80. We note too Luke 23:39, 'See my hands and my feet, that it is I myself. *Touch* me and see, for a spirit does not have flesh and bones as you see I have.'

is evidently contrastive, denoting the radical difference of approach to the sacred and divine between the old administration and the new. The Mosaic covenant prevented even those ministers especially appointed for the carrying of the holy vessels from becoming too familiar with the objects in their charge. To enter the sanctuary to catch a glimpse of them or to touch them before they were properly covered issued in death. In stark opposition to this, John portrays the followers of Christ acting contrary to the prohibition that had been in force for many centuries. They are now freely able to enter in, to see and to touch, spiritually speaking, with no danger of death as a result. The old administration was marked by distance and death, the new by access and intimacy. Further still, the former legislation related solely to especially ordained ministers who were exclusively male, while the new order allows for both those appointed apostles and lay disciples, men and women, to freely approach.

In conclusion, we have seen that through allusive reference to Old Testament passages concerning the ark and elements of the tabernacle regulations, John's Gospel is building up a picture of Jesus in terms of Mosaic categories readily appreciated by those from a Judaic background or by others biblically literate. Readers are being directed to the Day of Atonement ceremony, the primary expiatory ritual of ancient Israel. Uniquely on that day of the Jewish calendar, the mercy-seat, or 'atonement cover', of the ark featured in the elaborate ceremony described in Leviticus 16 where it served to receive the blood of the sin-offering. Corresponding to this, the fourth Gospel portrays a symbolic ark which received the bleeding body of Christ. The significance of such an image, though implicit, is apparent – of Jesus, not as a mere foreshadowing, but as the actual means whereby atonement is attained. By creating further echoes of the Torah, John implicitly draws out other wonderful truths of the gospel. No longer is God concealed and unapproachable, but in Christ he is now revealed and made accessible. To draw near to God-made-flesh bore no threat of death, but rather through his own atoning death there is the offer of life. In this way John's words at the beginning of his Gospel are more fully appreciated: 'the law was given through Moses; grace and truth came through Jesus Christ' (1:17).

28
Jesus appears to Mary
John 20:10–18

Our passage is a direct continuation of the text studied in the preceding chapter.[1] After the departure of Peter and the other disciple, Mary remains by the tomb weeping (John 20:10–11). The two angels she views in the tomb ask her why she is crying, to which she replies that the body has been taken away and she does not know where it has been placed (vv. 12–13). Then, turning, she sees a man standing nearby, but does not recognize him as Jesus (v. 14). A brief exchange takes place between them, in which she supposes him to be the gardener (v. 15), but when he calls her by name, 'Mary', she realizes who it is (v. 16). Evidently, she holds on to him in some manner, which he tells her not to do but to go and inform his disciples that he is ascending to the Father (v. 17). The section concludes with Mary going to the disciples, saying that she had seen Jesus and relaying what he had said (v. 18).

At the plain level of meaning, the passage relates the first of a number of resurrection appearances of Jesus on the third day after his execution and burial. It is striking that it should be made to a woman, Mary Magdalene, rather than to a man. Considering the male-dominated culture of the time, such a happening is something that would hardly have been invented. The testimony of women at that period had much less value than that of men in a Jewish court of law.[2] The event therefore shows every indication of being authentic.

In the matter of allusions, there can be little doubt that this passage is intended to evoke Eden and the first human couple in Genesis 2 – 3. The connections, both thematic and linguistic, are particularly compelling, and the description of them need not detain us too long.

An obvious parallel between the two contexts is that both are situated within a garden (Gen. 2:8; John 19:41). In the garden, moreover, there are a man and a woman, Adam and Eve in the one instance, Jesus and Mary in the other.

---

[1] Recalling what was stated in the preceding chapter (n. 2) concerning the transitional function of vv. 10–12.

[2] See Mishnah, *Rosh ha-Shanah* 1.8.

240

Adam had been placed in the garden 'to work it and care for it' (Gen. 2:15). To all intents and purposes, therefore, he was the gardener. Seeing Jesus in the garden where the tomb was located, Mary at first believes him to be the 'gardener' (John 20:15).

The entrance to the garden of Eden was in the 'east' (Gen. 3:24). Conceptually, for obvious reasons, the east is closely associated with the sunrise and the dawning of a new day.[3] One is the place of the sunrise, the other the time of the sunrise. This latter was when Christ arose from the dead.[4] Accordingly, Jesus entered the garden, not necessarily from the east geographically, but as the light of day rose in the east.[5]

At the entrance-way to Eden God posted figures called 'cherubim' in order 'to guard the way to the tree of life' (Gen. 3:24).[6] While we are unable to say with any definiteness what cherubim looked like, they were probably angelic creatures of some kind, as suggested in the preceding chapter.[7] What we do know is that there were more than one, for 'cherubim' transliterates the Hebrew noun *kĕrubîm*, which bears a plural ending.[8] Traditional depictions of the scene show two cherubim, the number made explicit in several Jewish Targums.[9] To enter the garden, therefore, would require one to pass these cherubic figures. Evidently, they were stationed there to prevent this very thing happening, for upon the fall into sin of the first man and woman they were to be barred from the tree of life that stood in the middle of the garden (2:9). Two corresponding figures appear in John 20, already discussed in the preceding chapter. These were the two angels located at the head and foot of the burial slab on which the body of Jesus had been laid (v. 12). Here we earlier stated that the scene is evocative of the ark of the covenant with its two cherubim, one at either end. As Mary looks into the tomb and sees this sight, the body is no longer there. Christ has risen from death to life, emerging from the cold stone slab into the morning sunlight of the garden rising from the east. In so doing, Jesus entered his new life between the two angelic figures, suggestive of a symbolic re-entry into Eden.

---

[3] We may note that in Hebrew the noun *mizrāḥ*, 'east', is cognate to the verb *zāraḥ*, meaning to 'shine forth' (cf. Isa. 58:10).

[4] In English we call this 'Easter', a word which, if taken back to its old Germanic origins, has connotations of both 'dawn' and 'east'.

[5] A fact in itself which is evidently full of symbolism, frequently brought out within the context of Easter services.

[6] Along with the cherubim there was 'a flaming sword that flashed back and forth'.

[7] See chapter 27, n. 12.

[8] The singular form is *kĕrûb*, 'cherub' (e.g. Exod. 25:19).

[9] The Jerusalem Targum reads: 'He [God] cast out Adam, and made the glory of his Shekinah to dwell at the front of the east of the Garden of Eden, above the two Cherubs.' Targum Neofiti and the Fragmentary Targum are almost identical.

Back in Eden the man was created first, and the woman second (Gen. 2:18–22). And it was the former who named the latter. This he did twice in fact, according to the narrative. First he said, 'She will be called Woman [*gynē*]' (2:23), and then later, 'The man called his wife's name Eve' (3:20). One is the more generic term, the other her own personal name. When Jesus encounters Mary in the garden, he first addresses her simply as 'Woman' (John 20:15), being the vocative form *gynai*. A moment later he addresses her again, this time as 'Mary' (v. 16). Christ's forms of address here can be seen to parallel those of Adam with reference to Eve in Eden, that is, a twofold appellation, first the generic term, second the personal name. Not only this, but Mary's response is to call Jesus 'Rabboni' in return. This Aramaic expression, literally meaning 'my master', was a common honorific term for one in the position of a teacher. But more importantly for our purposes, it could also have the sense of 'my husband',[10] which is entirely suitable to our allusory context. In these particular terms of address, therefore, we find yet another reason to suppose that the reader is being deliberately drawn back to that earlier garden narrative.

We may further add that in Eden the man first named his wife after she had been brought into being while he was in a deep sleep:

> The LORD God caused a deep sleep to fall upon the man, and he slept; then he took one of his ribs and closed up the flesh in its place. The LORD God fashioned the rib he had taken from the man into a woman.
> (Gen. 2:21–22)

It was when he awoke that Adam found the woman present with him in the garden. Before our scene in John, Jesus has also been in a deep sleep, metaphorically speaking, this being the sleep of death.[11] While so asleep, a wound was likewise made in his side (John 19:34).[12] When he awakes, a woman is there before him in the garden. Here then is another thematic parallel with what occurred in Eden – each male protagonist recovers consciousness from his 'sleep' and is found in the company of a woman, both in a garden setting.

---

[10] See, e.g., Hos. 2:7 (2:9 in MT), where the Hebrew *'îšî*, 'my husband', is rendered in the Aramaic Targum of the Prophets as *ribbônî*. Sarah also uses the same title for Abraham, her husband, in Gen. 18:12 according to both Targum Onkelos and Targum Jonathan. (The vowel in the first syllable, *rib-*, is how the word appears when Masoretic vocalization was applied to the Aramaic text. This follows a later phonological rule according to which an original *a* vowel in an unstressed syllable is transformed into *i*. The original pronunciation of the word would therefore have been *rabbônî*.)

[11] Elsewhere in John's Gospel, 'sleep' is used figuratively with respect to death (John 11:11–13).

[12] See the comments in Addison Hodges Hart, *The Woman, the Hour, and the Garden: A Study in the Imagery of the Gospel of John* (Grand Rapids, MI: Eerdmans, 2016), 87.

Lastly, we again note the presence of a prohibition to touch. In speaking to the serpent in Genesis 3, the woman informed the creature that God had said with respect to the tree of the knowledge of good and evil that 'you shall not eat from it, nor shall you touch [*hapsēsthe*] it, lest you die' (v. 3).[13] In John 20, we recall, Jesus told Mary not to touch him (v. 17, *mē haptou*). As was discussed in the preceding chapter, he did so not to prohibit the act of touching but rather to have her cease from the touching that she was in fact doing, and this for reasons other than that the touching itself was wrong. So, similar words occur in both contexts, though used in somewhat different ways.[14]

Clearly, then, the account of the resurrection appearance to Mary Magdalene contains a series of thematic and verbal allusions to the Eden narrative. The picture we derive from the presence of these is one of the new Adam coming into the garden and meeting the new Eve. The concept of Jesus as an Adam-like figure is known elsewhere in the New Testament (e.g. Rom. 5:14–19; 1 Cor. 15:45–49). As the original Eve was the wife of the first man Adam, so Mary may be taken as representing the bride of Christ, that is, the church (cf. 2 Cor. 11:2; Eph. 5:31–32; Rev. 21:9). The idea communicated, therefore, is that of a new beginning for the human race. In the first garden man and woman were originally created, but fell into sin and death, and now in this second garden a new man emerges, triumphant over sin and death, and is united with his new partner, one delivered from sin and death. In other words, what is depicted here is the re-creation of humankind through Christ, that is, the emergence of a new creation.[15]

The new-creation aspect is further brought out through the time phrase that introduces John's account. In 20:1 it is stated that what follows took place 'on the first day of the week'. This in itself speaks of a new beginning – the Genesis creation narrative consisting of a sequence of a week of days with the creative activity commencing on the explicitly designated first day.[16] From the perspective of the weekly cycle, the first was also the eighth.[17] It is noteworthy that John

---

[13] As commentators point out, there is no record of God actually saying these particular words ('nor shall you touch it') to Adam and Eve, but that is another issue.

[14] A deliberate connection between the two is advocated in Mariusz Rozik, 'Discovering the Secrets of God's Gardens: Resurrection as New Creation', *Liber Annuus* 58 (2008): 21.

[15] Cf. Rowan Williams, *God with Us: The Meaning of the Cross and Resurrection, Then and Now* (London: SPCK, 2017), 101: 'the bedrock of what is going on in the resurrection of Jesus Christ is the remaking of creation itself . . . It's the start of the world because it's the day of the resurrection'.

[16] I also wonder if the occurrences of 'morning' (John 20:1, where the Greek has *prōi*, 'morning'; cf. NLT, CEV, ISV, CEB) and 'evening' (v. 19) that bracket the first resurrection appearance are a deliberate echo of the 'evening' and 'morning' of each day of creation (Gen. 1:5, 8, 13, 19, 23, 31).

[17] See Mary L. Coloe, 'The Garden as a New Creation in John', *The Bible Today* 53.3 (2015): 162–163; cf. also Williams, *God with Us*, 101. Williams remarks: 'so often in the early Church – and today in the Eastern Church – Sunday is thought of as the "eighth day" of the seven-day week.'

20 records resurrection appearances on the first day and then on the eighth day (cf. v. 26). Also significant perhaps is that in the fourth Gospel, in which a sequence of seven signs is a prominent feature, the resurrection of Jesus is itself an eighth sign.[18] And the very time of day at which Christ appears on this first day, namely 'early in the morning' (v. 1), speaks yet further of newness, marked by the dawning of the light of a new day.[19]

Broadly speaking, the allusions teach us two basic truths. The garden of Eden, or more precisely the bliss, union and life with God that it symbolizes, has been reopened to man and woman. Having been sealed off because of one man's sin, it has now been opened up again due to one man's righteousness (cf. Rom. 5:15–17). As such, the barrier to the allusory garden having been removed, it is now populated by a new humanity, embodied in Jesus and Mary. Unlike the first human couple, the former bears his own righteousness, innate to his essential being, while the latter participates in that righteousness through her relationship with him.[20] By this means, a restoration is brought about of God's original purposes for those created in his image, and human beings may now live according to their intended status within the wider creation.

What the allusions indicate, therefore, is mostly contrastive in nature, since a great reversal has taken place, the final undoing of what human sin had caused. Accordingly, the cherubim once served to block the way back into the garden, but the two angels now mark the passage into the new garden.[21] The first Adam returned to the dust; the second Adam returned to life, life everlasting. In Eden the first couple touched that which brought them death; in the later garden Mary was able to touch the source of new life.[22] We further see that Adam and Eve hid from the presence of the Lord (Gen. 3:8), while Mary actively sought him (John 20:15).[23] The first man and woman were driven from

---

[18] This view of Christ's resurrection, as the eighth sign, has been advocated by a number of scholars, e.g. Daniel A. Smith, *Revisiting the Empty Tomb: The Early History of Easter* (Minneapolis, MN: Fortress, 2010), 149–152; Jeannine K. Brown, 'Creation's Renewal in the Gospel of John', *CBQ* 72 (2010): 287–288.

[19] Rozik ('Discovering the Secrets of God's Gardens', 14) holds the view that the rising of the sun 'symbolises awakening life'. He continues: 'The day's life begins with the coming of the sun from the east, the first people were called to life by God in Eden in the east; and, finally, at sunrise Mary Magdalene discovered Jesus' empty tomb, the sign of his new life.'

[20] The two are, in effect, counted as one flesh, as per the original man–woman union in Gen. 2:24 (cf. Eph. 5:31). In this context we may add that some see the clinging of Mary to Jesus in John 20:17 as another allusion to the Edenic situation, in which it is stated that a man shall 'cling to his wife', and in so doing 'the two shall become one flesh'.

[21] Cf. Rozik ('Discovering the Secrets of God's Gardens', 21). Rozik here avers that the presence of angels in John's account proclaims not only the opening of Jesus' tomb but also the opening of the way that leads to the re-establishment of humankind's lost relation with God.

[22] We observe that in this new-creation setting, Jesus is to be taken not only as the counterpart to Adam but also as the truth ultimately signified by the tree of life. As Jesus himself said, he is 'the resurrection and the life' (John 11:25).

[23] Cf. Hart, *The Woman, the Hour, and the Garden*, 87.

their garden in shame, but Mary, we may well imagine, left her garden with great joy.

The new-creation undertones of our Gospel text bring us to one final important feature occurring in the immediately following passage. During the evening of that same first day of the week on which he rose, the resurrected Jesus appears to the band of disciples gathered together behind locked doors (John 20:19). Having greeted them and shown the wounds in his hands and side, he then performs an unusual act: 'he breathed on them and said "Receive the Holy Spirit"' (v. 22). Since the mind of the informed reader has already been directed back to Eden in the foregoing garden encounter, there ought to be a ready recognition of yet another allusion to the same portion of Genesis at this point. The verb that John uses here, *enephysēsen*, 'he breathed into/upon', is its sole occurrence in the entire New Testament. Not only this, but it is exceedingly rare in the Greek Old Testament also, where it is found just twice. Significantly, one of these places is Genesis 2, when God created the first human being in Eden. The account says, 'Then the LORD God formed the man from the dust of the ground, and breathed [*enephysēsen*] into his nostrils[24] the breath of life; and the man became a living being' (v. 7).[25] In this original creation of humanity it is the 'LORD God' himself who provided the life-giving breath to the fashioned but still inanimate dust. Until that breath was imparted, the man remained completely lifeless. It was an essential component of what made him a living creature.

In view of the preceding allusions to Eden, and in view of the rarity of the above verb and its occurrence in the exact same form, we would be warranted to conclude that John 20:22 is another in the series of allusions appearing in that chapter. This would mean that Jesus is much more than just a new Adam. Seeing he is the Giver of Life, the one who breathes his Spirit into the rest of the new humanity, one might go so far as to say he is the 'Lord God' of the new creation. And indeed, one cannot help but note that both of these divine titles, 'Lord' and 'God', are actually ascribed to Jesus by Thomas just a few verses later in the same chapter (v. 28).[26] Such a conclusion fits well with the traditional 'two natures in one Person' doctrine of the historic Christian faith, of which the fourth Gospel perhaps offers the most explicit presentation out of all the

---

[24] The LXX here reads 'face' instead of 'nostrils'.

[25] The other passage is not totally irrelevant since it depicts the restoration of the dry bones of Israel in the vision of Ezek. 37. There the 'breath' or 'spirit' (Heb. *rûaḥ*) is instructed to breathe (LXX: *emphysēson*) life into the lifeless bones (v. 9). Cf. Michael L. Morales, *Exodus Old and New: A Biblical Theology of Redemption* (Downers Grove, IL: InterVarsity Press, 2020), 177.

[26] More on this will follow in chapter 29.

books in the New Testament. Jesus is both 'God' (1:1) and, being made flesh, is also truly 'man' (1:14; 19:5).

Once again, then, in John we have detected a remarkable set of allusions that point to profound theological truths. With the resurrection, a new way is opened up into Edenic fellowship with God. A renewed human nature has come into being, free from all the imperfections of the old humanity, even from the dominion of death itself. And in this nature he who is himself also divine bestows his Spirit to others so that they too may be incorporated within the new humanity that he is creating.

29

Jesus appears on the eighth day

John 20:24–29

Between his resurrection and ascension Jesus appeared to his followers on a number of different occasions, ten at least according to the information we have in the Gospels and Epistles. A number of these took place on the day that Christ rose, and others happened at certain times afterwards. However, when we consider this whole period of several weeks, there are only three days that are actually specified, by which I mean that in this longer duration events can be pinpointed as having occurred at a particular time only with respect to three of the days involved. These three are the first, the eighth and the fortieth. The first is, obviously, the day of Christ's resurrection itself (cf. Matt. 28:1; John 20:1), on which he appeared several times. The fortieth is the final day of his time on earth, when he made his departure from his disciples and ascended into heaven (Acts 1:3). Between these the only other specifically identified day is the eighth, on which the events took place that are recorded in the passage in John's Gospel that we are shortly going to examine.

Even from the bare facts given so far, a mind steeped in the Old Testament, especially in the Jewish Torah, would in all probability go back to Leviticus 12:1–4, a passage prescribing the ceremonial process of purification following the birth of a son:

> Then the LORD spoke to Moses, saying, 'Speak to the sons of Israel, saying: "When a woman conceives and gives birth to a male child, then she shall be unclean for seven days; as in the days of her menstruation she shall be unclean. On the eighth day the flesh of his foreskin shall be circumcised. Then[1] for thirty-three days she shall remain in the blood of her

---

[1] It is important to connect v. 4 with v. 2. Both of these are speaking of the mother, while the intervening v. 3 relates to the newborn son. So the 'thirty-three days' of v. 4 follow the 'seven days' of v. 2, making a total of forty. This is evident from the fact that the period of ceremonial cleansing for the birth of a girl consisted of 'two weeks' (i.e. fourteen days) plus 'sixty-six days' (v. 5), making a total of eighty days, exactly double that for the birth of a male child.

purification; she shall not touch any consecrated thing, nor come into the sanctuary until the days of her purification are completed."'

Here we have precisely the same total stretch of time, forty days, as in the post-resurrection accounts of Christ, and we have, either explicitly or implicitly, the same three specific times – the first day being the day of the birth, the eighth the day of the child's circumcision and the fortieth marking the end of the whole period. As with the resurrection appearances, no other days are designated apart from these.

Accordingly, both the Gospels and the levitical regulation refer to forty-day periods with something specifically identified as happening on the eighth day. This is not, however, the only correlation. Though at first sight this may not seem so, conceptually there is a much more significant relationship. The Old Testament text concerns childbirth, and more exactly the birth of a male child. The Gospels are speaking of a resurrection from the dead, also of a male. There is an important passage in John's Gospel which presents an analogy to Christ's approaching death and subsequent resurrection. The night before his crucifixion he gave advance warning to his disciples that they were about to experience sorrow:

> Truly, truly, I say to you, that you will weep and mourn, but the world will rejoice. You will grieve, but your grief will be turned into joy. When a woman is in labour she has pain, because her hour has come; but when she gives birth to the child, she no longer remembers the anguish because of the joy that a human being has been born into the world. So you too have grief now; but I will see you again and your heart will rejoice, and no one will take your joy away from you.
> (John 16:20–22)

We note here that the English words 'grief' and 'pain' translate the same Greek term (*lypē*), which includes both these senses, the emotional and the physical. We also draw attention to the preceding context, which speaks of not seeing Jesus and then seeing him again in a 'little while' (vv. 17–19), making it clear that he is here speaking of his coming death and his rising to life afterwards.

In this above-mentioned passage, in the same Gospel incidentally as our principal text, Christ compares the coming time of grief to that of a woman in the state of maternal labour. Labour is a time of pain, which soon, however, gives way to joy when the child is born – 'the joy [*charan*] that a human being [*anthrōpos*] has been born into the world' (v. 21). So too the grief of the disciples at Jesus' death will be replaced by joy when they see him alive again: 'your grief will be turned into joy [*charan*] ... I will see you again and your heart will rejoice [*charēsetai*]' (vv. 20, 22). If the coming grief corresponds to the sorrow that will be experienced at the death of Christ, then the birth that is the cause of such joy is nothing but his resurrection, at which he who is indeed *the* new human being was born into the world. The passage, therefore, gives us warrant for understanding the event of the resurrection as a kind of birth.

In keeping with the foregoing is the fact that the risen Jesus is elsewhere described in the New Testament as the 'first*born* from the dead' (Col. 1:18; Rev. 1:5). That well-known passage from the second psalm, in which God says to the Messiah, 'Today I have begotten you', that is, 'given you birth' (Ps. 2:7),[2] is applied by the apostle Paul, not to Christ's birth from Mary at Bethlehem, but to his resurrection (Acts 13:32–37). Furthermore, in one Old Testament passage the prophet Isaiah similarly likens resurrection to a birth: 'But your dead will live; their corpses will rise. You who dwell in the dust, awake and shout for joy. Your dew is like the dew of the morning; the earth will give birth to her dead' (26:19). Note the presence of joy here also.

Returning, then, to John's Gospel, we have seen that the comparison is explicitly made between the pains of labour and the grief of Christ's death, and between the joy of childbirth and Christ's resurrection. It can be no coincidence, therefore, that on that first day of the week on which he rose, when Jesus appeared to the gathered disciples we read in John that 'the disciples rejoiced [*echarēsan*] when they saw the Lord' (20:20; cf. also Matt. 28:8; Luke 24:41). This is the next mention of joy following the final discourses of Jesus in John chapters 14–17, and it is the joy experienced 'when they [the disciples] saw the Lord', who they thought was dead but was now risen. There can be little doubt that this harks back to the aforementioned 16:17–22 of the same Gospel, since it refers to both the joy and the fact of seeing the Lord (cf. 16:17, 'after a little while you will *see* me'; cf. 19, 22), who had been departed for a 'little while'.

We find, therefore, that the rejoicing of the disciples at seeing Jesus returned from the dead bears an analogy to the joy of a woman who has brought forth a child after a period of pain. This, then, is what happens on that first day of the forty-day period – in Leviticus a male child is born, and in the Gospels Jesus rises to new life.

We next consider the eighth day. According to the same levitical law, this was the day when the male child was to be circumcised: 'On the eighth day the flesh

---

[2] Although many English versions translate the phrase as something like 'I have become your Father', this is in fact quite a free rendering. The Hebrew (along with its Greek translation) says quite plainly, 'I have given you birth.'

of his foreskin shall be circumcised' (12:3). The removal of this piece of flesh was the sign of the covenant, dating back to the time of Abraham (Gen. 17:10–13).

The symbolism involved in the act of circumcision is very striking and quite appropriate for those who were God's own people, a holy nation. It is literally a cutting off of the flesh, relating to an organ of the body particularly associated with carnal desire. As such, it stands as an outward indicator of an inward truth, which is that the people of God are those who have set aside the sinful flesh, in terms of lusts and ungodly passions. The physical, then, points to the spiritual. So it is that later in the Old Testament, as well as in the New, the inspired authors speak of circumcision spiritually, as a circumcision of the heart (e.g. Deut. 10:16; 30:6; Jer. 4:4; cf. Rom. 2:28–29), which is where all such evil desire originates (cf. Mark 7:21).

Now if the first day on which Jesus rose was, in effect, the day of his new birth, then what can we say with regard to the need for a subsequent circumcision, not in its literal practice which he had undergone over thirty years earlier, but in its fuller, spiritual sense? Evidently, the risen Christ had no need for such. For him the crucifixion itself had accomplished once and for all what circumcision represented. His death was, to all intents and purposes, a cutting off of his flesh. In the event of the crucifixion the old Adamic human nature, with which he himself had been born,[3] and which was prone to temptation and subject to death, was utterly destroyed. When Jesus emerged from the tomb he bore the nature of a humanity that was entirely renewed. Any further type of circumcision was totally unrequired.

For the first readers of the Gospels, however, the eighth day after birth had a further significance. Something important for us to know is that with the passing of time the rite of circumcision came to be closely associated with the naming of the male child. Certainly, when we come to the beginning of the Christian era this was undoubtedly the case. In the early part of Luke's Gospel we read:

> Now the time had come for Elizabeth to give birth, and she gave birth to a son. Her neighbours and relatives heard that the Lord had shown his great mercy toward her, and they rejoiced with her. And it happened that on the eighth day they came to circumcise the child, and they were going to call him by the name of his father, Zechariah. But his mother answered and said, 'No; he shall be called John.'
> (1:57–60)

---

[3] Although it is important to stress his own personal sinlessness in that nature (cf. John 8:46; Heb. 4:15).

And when eight days had passed and it was time to circumcise him, his name was called Jesus, the name given by the angel before he was conceived in the womb.
(2:21)

Clearly, then, both John the Baptist and Jesus were given their names on the eighth day after their birth.[4]

Turning now to John 20 we see that verse 26 records a further resurrection appearance that took place literally 'after eight days' (*meth' hēmeras oktō*). Jewish reckoning of time at this period was typically inclusive. We can be quite sure, therefore, that John's phrase is equivalent to meaning 'on the eighth day' after the resurrection, which is to say, the following Sunday.[5] This is why many modern English translations render the phrase as 'a week later' (e.g. NRSV, NIV, REB, CEV, GNT, NCV). Here is John's account of what happened on that eighth day, a week after Christ's first appearance to the disciples at which one of the disciples, Thomas, had not been present, as we read:

Now Thomas (who was called the Twin), one of the Twelve, was not with them when Jesus came. So the other disciples told him, 'We have seen the Lord.' But he said to them, 'Unless I see the mark of the nails in his hands, and put my finger in the mark of the nails, and put my hand in his side, I will not believe.' A week later his disciples were again in the house, and Thomas was with them. Although the doors were locked, Jesus came and stood among them and said, 'Peace be with you.' Then he said to Thomas, 'Put your finger here and see my hands. Reach out your hand and put it into my side. Do not be unbelieving but believe.' Thomas answered him, 'My Lord and my God!' Jesus said to him, 'You believe because you have seen me. Blessed are those who have not seen and yet believe.'
(John 20:24–29)

As on that earlier occasion, the day Jesus was raised, the disciples had experienced joy, in accordance with the analogy of a woman giving birth, so too here

---

[4] We note again the presence of joy at the birth of both John (Luke 1:58) and Jesus (2:10).

[5] See the similar phrases in the Old Testament where 'after *n* days' is equivalent to 'on the *n*th day' (not on the day following the *n*th day), such as: 'she wept before him for seven days while their feast lasted, and on the seventh day he told her' (Judg. 14:17); 'They encamped opposite one another for seven days, and on the seventh day the battle was joined' (1 Kgs 20:29). Cf. also Luke 2:21 cited above, where 'when eight days were passed [lit. "fulfilled"]' indicates the eighth day itself. In agreement with our position here, biblical scholar Don Carson in his comment on John 20:26 states that '*A week later* is an idiomatic rendering of (lit.) "After eight days"; the inclusive reckoning brings the action back to Sunday, one week after Easter' (D. A. Carson, *The Gospel According to John* [PNTC; Leicester: Apollos, 1991], 657).

there is a distinct analogy with what was to take place on the eighth day after the birth. As I said, we are not looking here for circumcision of any kind. Rather, we are looking for something that corresponds to the act of naming. And John demonstrably provides it. Once Thomas was invited to touch the risen Jesus, and once his former unbelief had been transformed into faith, the disciple declared those words: 'My Lord and my God!' (v. 28). Here, at the level of allusion, is the naming of Jesus on the eighth day from his new birth. This is remarkable for at least two reasons. First, the names, or appellations, that are ascribed to Jesus are divine. Thomas is plainly declaring Jesus to be none other than God himself! What John wrote in the prologue to his Gospel (1:1–18), Thomas now expressly believes to be the truth, the fact that Jesus was 'the Word' which 'was God' (v. 1) and which 'became flesh' (v. 14). Second, it is extraordinary that this allusive naming of Christ should be granted specifically to Thomas, a disciple who had previously affirmed his unbelief. In a roundabout way it is teaching us that if even a doubter like Thomas came to see the truth of Christ's essential deity, then it must indeed be true. If it were not, then a person of a sceptical disposition like him would not be convinced. In other words, Thomas is seeing and touching the risen Jesus on behalf of all those coming after him whose natural inclination would be to say, 'Unless I see . . . I will not believe.' The naming act of Thomas, then, is ascribing to Jesus his essential identity, that wondrous truth not only plainly stated in John's prologue but also hinted at elsewhere in the same Gospel (e.g. 5:18; 10:30; 14:9).[6] Even though Christ is truly human, he is nevertheless also, and crucially, truly divine.

Lastly, we think about the period of forty days as a whole. It is apparent from the law in Leviticus 12 that this time related to the condition of the mother, not the child. Evidently, the newborn child remained with his mother throughout the whole of this time, but apart from the ritual of the eighth day everything else was done for the benefit of the woman. What she underwent during this period was to enable her to be purified from the effects of childbirth and to be reinstated as a full worshipping member of the Israelite community. We find that until these forty days were over, she, and presumably her child likewise, were not permitted to 'come into the sanctuary' (Lev. 12:4).

In our Gospel analogy, who is it that could be identified as having the part of the mother? We are not thinking here of the virgin Mary, who bore Jesus in

---

6 Scholars recognize that Thomas's declaration of Jesus as God forms a literary bracketing, or 'inclusio', with the beginning of the Gospel. Note the remark in R. J. Karris (ed.), *The Collegeville Bible Commentary: New Testament* (Collegeville, MN: Liturgical Press, 1992), 1017: 'With this profession, John creates his own literary inclusio to the Gospel, the corresponding covers to his book of good news; for "My Lord and my God" at the conclusion corresponds to the opening ". . . and the Word was God" (1:1). The two statements are intentionally parallel.'

the literal sense. But rather, who was the woman who gave birth to Christ figuratively speaking? Perhaps some would see it as pressing the details of the allusion too far, but it is possible, I believe, to suggest an identification for the mother who gave Jesus birth. The mother-figure is Israel – the true Israel, that is. This is the Israel sometimes spoken of by the prophets as the virgin daughter of Zion (e.g. Isa. 37:22; 62:11), and who represents the faithful Israelite community as a whole. She is the figure that John saw in the vision of the Apocalypse, appearing as 'a woman clothed with the sun, with the moon under her feet, and with a crown of twelve stars on her head' (Rev. 12:1). That woman, John tells us, 'was with child; and she cried out, being in labour and in pain to give birth' (v. 2), and 'she gave birth to a son, a male child, who will rule all the nations with a rod of iron; and her child was caught up to God and to his throne' (v. 5). This woman of the vision is the ideal Israel that gives birth to Messiah.[7] And within the context of John 20 this womanly figure, the community of the true people of God, is that small and frightened band of disciples; these are the then-existing representation of the faithful Israel. And Jesus was the first to be reborn among such through the resurrection of his body.

As far-fetched as this idea may at first seem, it does actually fit well with our analogy. Referring back again to the words of Jesus in John 16:20–22, cited earlier, who is it whose pain is turned into joy when the child is eventually born? It is of course the mother. And who is it, in the comparison, whose grief is transformed into joy at the resurrection of Jesus? We saw earlier that it was in fact the disciples who grieved (John 20:20). As the mother's pain has become joy because of the birth, so the disciples' sorrow has become joy on account of the resurrection. In this analogy it is evidently this small group of the faithful that corresponds to the mother-figure, playing the part of that community in which Messiah had been birthed, so to speak. They constituted the matrix into which the risen Christ came. Following his rebirth, for forty days he remained with them, for their benefit, not his, though they named him, as it were, on the eighth day. During this time, not only did he convince them of his return to newness of life but he also instructed them in the important matters of the kingdom of God and the coming of the Spirit (cf. Acts 1:1–8). Then, finally, when the forty days came to an end he ascended, though in a spiritual sense he never actually left them (cf. Matt. 28:20). What did the disciples do next? It is interesting to note that, after Christ's ascension outside Jerusalem, we are told elsewhere that the disciples went back into the city and 'they stayed continually in the temple,

---

[7] We ought not to forget that it was indeed from Israel that Christ received his human nature (cf. Rom. 9:4–5, 'They are Israelites . . . and from them, according to the flesh, comes the Christ').

praising God' (Luke 24:53). Just as in the levitical law the mother, once the forty-day period with her newborn son was over, was then able to 'come into the sanctuary', so the disciples, when their forty days with the risen Jesus were completed, entered the temple – that is, the Jewish sanctuary in Jerusalem – in order to praise God. And Jesus, of course, at the completion of the same period, entered heaven itself, the true sanctuary, of which the earthly is a mere copy (Heb. 9:24).

In the resurrection appearances of Jesus the presence of allusions to Leviticus 12 is, to my mind, particularly definite, even if one does not care to accept the latter remarks about the mother-figure. The forty-day period with the particular event of the eighth day and the naming of Christ by Thomas are features relating to the Old Testament law that are subtly woven into the Gospel text. To detect the allusions significantly enhances our apprehension of the events that are transpiring. The resurrection of Jesus, the Gospel informs us, is like a new birth, the coming of a new human being into the world. For the first time, a man who is completely free from the effects of the fall, and one who possesses a humanity that is immortal by nature, sets foot on the earth, this being the foundation of our hope and the guarantee that we too will one day share in that same nature. And then, on the eighth day, the man who has been so reborn is expressly identified as being God himself. Jesus is the man, the one who is flesh, who is at the same time Lord and God – Thomas's declaration being the heart of all orthodox Christian confession down through the centuries.

30

Jesus appears by the Sea of Galilee

John 21:1–19

The final chapter of John's Gospel records one of Christ's appearances in Galilee at some unspecified time after his resurrection. Although the passage describes another encounter between the risen Lord and the disciples, a glance at its contents quickly reveals that, apart from the few verses at the end, it largely revolves around the person of Simon Peter. Here we find the dealings between Jesus and Peter that restore, in effect, the relationship threatened on that earlier occasion when the apostle denied his Master three times.[1] Jesus gives Peter three opportunities, one for each denial, to profess his love for him (21:15–17) and to renew his position as a genuine follower (v. 19).

In this account there are, to my mind, readily identifiable allusions to events in the Old Testament concerning the prophet Jonah, who lived some eight centuries before Christ and the apostles. An earlier chapter of this book has suggested that another episode in the Gospels, that of Jesus calming the storm, also alludes to Jonah.[2] It is important to note that the allusions in that earlier context are altogether distinct from those that are to be outlined here. As we saw, the connections between Jesus and the book of Jonah began with Jesus occupying the part of the prophet, but by the time we reached the end of the narrative Jesus had assumed the part of the prophet's God. This was the application of a significant literary device with the purpose of underscoring the divine identity of Christ. Here at the end of the fourth Gospel it is the apostle Peter alone who corresponds to the ancient prophet, and not Jesus in any way.

Thinking of the setting in John 21, the circumstances are in themselves strongly reminiscent of the Jonah narrative. Here is a body of water described as the 'sea' (vv. 1, 7),[3] on which there is a boat. A group of men are said to have 'got into the boat' (v. 3), a phrase which in fact includes the precise Greek term

---

[1] This earlier matter was dealt with in chapter 22.

[2] See chapter 9.

[3] In v. 7, although the NIV, NJB and NLT read 'water', the Greek noun is definitely 'sea' (*thalassa*); cf. NRSV, ESV, NASB, NKJV, REB, NET.

possessing the sense of 'embark' (*embainō*).[4] So, what we are actually reading is: 'they embarked into [*enebēsan eis*] the boat.' The same is said of Jonah where, in the Greek version (LXX), we read that 'he embarked into [*enebē eis*] it [the boat]' (Jon. 1:3).[5]

In each instance one might also say that there is the neglect of a greater calling. In the case of Jonah he was called to proclaim the word of God in Nineveh, but he jumped into a vessel heading in the opposite direction. Peter and the apostles have been called to preach the gospel (as 'fishers of men' [cf. Mark 1:17 AV]), but they revert to their former profession (as fishers of literal fish).[6]

A more significant similarity between the two accounts, and one that surely helps to solidify the connection, is the fact that each of the two central characters ends up going over the side of the boat into the sea. In the case of Jonah we are told that 'they [the sailors] threw him into the sea' (Jon. 1:15; cf. v. 12), while regarding Peter the text literally says: 'he threw himself into the sea' (John 21:7). The closeness in wording makes it difficult to avoid the conclusion that the one is a deliberate echo of the other. In Jonah (LXX) we read *kai exebalon auton eis tēn thalassan*, and in John, *kai ebalen heauton eis tēn thalassan*. If we accept as original the text of the LXX preserved in Codex Sinaiticus, a major Greek manuscript of both Testaments, then the verb form in Jonah should in fact be *ebalon* (that is, the bare verb without a prefix), which would make the two appear even more alike. Needless to say, in the two accounts it is these two alone, Jonah and Peter, who go into the sea.

Having entered the sea, each main character then ends up on the shore. In other words, each passes through the water to come to dry land.

Fish are also prominent in both accounts. In the book of Jonah we read of a 'great fish' (1:17), while in the Gospel we find mention of 'great fish' (21:11), in the plural. It is noteworthy that in the whole of Scripture the adjective 'great' is uniquely found qualifying 'fish' in connection with Jonah and these events of John 21. In the earlier account the fish in a very real sense eats Jonah, since the prophet enters the fish's stomach (Jon. 1:17; 2:1). In John the disciples, by way of reversal, eat the fish (21:13). Also, in contrast, Peter was a fisherman, a catcher of fish, who became a divinely appointed apostle, while Jonah was a divinely appointed prophet who was caught by a fish.

However, what binds the two narratives more closely together than anything else is the name by which Simon Peter was known. The apostle bore the

---

[4] See Henry George Liddell and Robert Scott, *A Greek Lexicon* (Oxford: Clarendon, rev. edn, 1940), 538.

[5] The word for 'boat' (*ploion*) is, of course, also the same in both accounts (Jon. 1:3, 4, 5; cf. John 21:3).

[6] Cf. John 21:3, 'Simon Peter said to them, "I'm going fishing." They said, "We will go with you."'

patronym 'son of Jonah'.[7] Unfortunately, this is obscured in some English versions of John 21, since many modern editors and translators have opted for the variant reading 'son of John' (in vv. 15, 16, 17).[8] The majority of Greek manuscripts here have 'son of Jonah'. At some stage in the copying of the text the two similar names, *Iōna* and *Iōannou*, obviously became confused. Yet, regardless of what certain manuscripts say in John 21, Peter's father was undeniably named 'Jonah', as Matthew informs us when Jesus addresses him as 'Simon bar Jonah' (16:17). Here we are given a transliteration from the Aramaic that permits no ambiguity and where no textual variant exists. Consequently, a good warrant for seeing the apostle Peter as a Jonah-like figure is the simple fact that 'Jonah', uniquely among all New Testament characters, is one of the names used to identify him.

Besides the name, we may also remark that both Jonah and Simon Peter were Galileans. Peter was from Capernaum (Luke 4:31; cf. v. 38), and Jonah from Gath-Hepher in the same northern region designated as Galilee (2 Kgs 14:25; cf. Josh. 19:13).

Finally, there is a resurrection association in each context. In the passage from John this is explicit and obvious. The risen Jesus here appears to Peter and the apostles not long after his resurrection. We are told that this was the third resurrection appearance to the disciples as a group (v. 14).[9] In connection with Jonah, there is the fact that earlier in the Gospels Jesus refers to the 'sign of Jonah', the experience of the prophet being a figure of Christ's own death and resurrection. Jesus had said: 'as Jonah was three days and three nights in the belly of a great fish, so the Son of Man will be three days and three nights in the heart of the earth' (Matt. 12:40). What happened to Jonah, then, was something with definite resurrection overtones.

So why the allusions in John 21? Why bring Jonah to mind at this closing stage in the account of the Gospel? The answer, I would suggest, lies in the fact that Jonah and Peter were both given second chances. Each of the two men received a divine commission, one as a prophet, the other as an apostle. And both failed to be faithful to their calling. Jonah was called to go to Nineveh with a message of judgment and repentance. Instead he fled in the opposite direction. Despite this, following his experience in the watery deep, God granted him

---

[7] Or in Aramaic, *bar yōnâ*.

[8] It should not go unnoticed that the principal Greek manuscripts (codices Sinaiticus, Vaticanus and Ephraemi Rescriptus) which read 'son of John' in John 21 also incorrectly give 'Asaph' (for 'Asa') as the son of Abijah in Matt. 1:7 and 'Amos' (for 'Amon') as the son of Manasseh in 1:10. Although more ancient than many other copies, that does not necessarily make these manuscripts more accurate in every respect.

[9] 'This is now the third time that Jesus was manifested to the disciples, after he was raised from the dead.'

another opportunity to be obedient to his commission. This second time, Jonah went to Nineveh and preached the message as instructed. Peter was called to follow Jesus, with all that that entailed, including the bearing of his own cross (cf. Matt. 10:38; Luke 14:27). Jesus had previously taught: 'If anyone wishes to be my follower, let him deny himself, and take up his cross and follow me' (Matt. 16:24; Mark 8:34; Luke 9:23). But even though Peter had declared his faith in Christ (Matt. 16:16), and despite his protestations of loyalty, even to die if need be (26:35),[10] Peter was unfaithful to his vocation. Rather than deny himself, he denied his Master, as we have seen. Nevertheless, in spite of his failings, he was given the opportunity to be reinstated, and this after he had passed through the water, like Jonah. The entrance into the sea, for both prophet and apostle, may be viewed as a baptism-like experience, indicating the need for a spiritual death and resurrection, or new birth, in order for the original calling to be fulfilled. The new Peter is then recommissioned by his Lord as a chief apostle, each of the three times significantly under the title of 'son of Jonah' (John 21:15, 16, 17), as though Jesus were deliberately drawing attention to the connection.

Also noteworthy, in this context, is the description of the fire on the seashore as an *anthrakia*. This is the very same term as that found in John 18:18, in the passage where Peter originally denied Jesus while standing warming himself at such a fire. Its inclusion here is no doubt intentional to call to mind that earlier occasion, which is here being reversed.

The story of Peter does not end with the last chapter of John's Gospel. It is worthwhile at this point to briefly dip into the Acts of the Apostles, though to do so necessarily entails stepping beyond the bounds of the Gospels. We do this because there we see in fact the Jonah–Peter connection continuing (Acts 10). For once they have turned back from their unfaithfulness, we see that each of the two men ends up going on a particular mission upon divine instruction. And each mission bears some resemblance to the other. Both Jonah and Peter take the word of God to Gentiles, at a time when this would not be expected by the Hebrew nation at large. Moreover, the nationality of those they are sent to is that of the people who were the principal threat to Israel's well-being at the time. In the case of Jonah, he was sent to the Assyrians, soon to rule as the dominant world empire of the age. Regarding Peter, he was sent to Cornelius, representing the empire of Rome which exercised power over much of the known world, including the Jewish homeland. In the former instance, it was the Assyrian king who took the lead, while in the latter it was a Roman military

---

[10] An additional linkage between prophet and apostle is the declared wish to die. Jonah would rather 'die' (*apothanein*) than live if the enemy nation was not to be judged (Jon. 4:3, 8, 9), while Peter declares that he would rather 'die' (*apothanein*) than deny his Lord (Matt. 26:35).

commander, both men of status and power. The one lived at Nineveh (Jon. 3:2), the greatest city and capital of the Assyrian Empire, the other at Caesarea (Acts 10:1), the seat of Roman authority in Judea.[11]

In due course the Assyrians would devastate the northern kingdom of Israel, where Jonah lived, and take captive much of its population. Likewise, after the time of Peter's missionary efforts, the Romans would come and conquer Judea, and similarly take thousands of its inhabitants into captivity.

Certain details in the two narratives confirm the foregoing connection. Joppa (modern-day Jaffa) in Israel features as the point of departure in both accounts, first for the prophet (Jon. 1:3), then much later for the apostle (Acts 9:36–43). The words spoken to them by God to set them on their respective journeys are very similar: 'Arise and go' (Jon. 1:2; 3:2); 'Arise . . . and go' (Acts 10:20).[12] It was at Joppa that Jonah refused to take God's message to the Ninevites, while from exactly the same place Peter obediently took the gospel to Romans.

Each divine emissary was one who 'proclaimed' (Jon. 3:4, *ekēryxen*; Acts 10:42, *kēryxai*) the message from God,[13] and in each case the Gentile audience responded positively. The word was met with faith by the Assyrians who heard Jonah (Jon. 3:5) and evidently also by the Romans who heard Peter (cf. Acts 10:43), and so each group of Gentiles received pardon from God (Jon. 3:10; cf. Acts 11:18).

At the back of both accounts there is also the question of the attitude of the Hebrew people towards Gentiles. Although Jonah was obedient the second time round, it is obvious that he was none too happy about the Assyrians being given the opportunity to repent and avoid God's judgment. Taking the word to non-Jews was also an issue for Peter. This is why he was given a series of visions beforehand, the purpose of which was to teach him that he should not regard any person as unclean (Acts 10:11–16, 28; 11:9). Though both messengers of God are obedient, and both take the word to Gentiles, it is very apparent that with regard to Jonah his basic attitude towards those of other nations remains unchanged, whereas Peter's view of Gentiles is radically altered, though that of certain other Jewish believers was apparently hostile (11:2).

The prophet aside, the book of Jonah itself represents Gentiles who fear God in a favourable light (cf. 1:16, 'the men feared the LORD'), as indeed does the

---

[11] H. H. Ben-Sasson (ed.), *A History of the Jewish People* (Cambridge, MA: Harvard University Press, 1976), 247–248.

[12] 'Arise [*anastēthi*], go [*poreuthēti*] to Nineveh'; cf. 'Arise [*anastas*], go down, and go [*poreuou*] with them.'

[13] The verb 'proclaim' (*kēryssō*) and the noun 'proclamation' (*kērygma*) are standard New Testament terms for the apostolic declaration of the gospel. Such words occur five times altogether in the short book of Jonah (1:2; 3:2, 4, 5, 7), out of forty-four occurrences in total in the whole Greek Old Testament.

passage about Peter's visit to Cornelius (Acts 10:2, 22, 'one who feared God'). Peter's opening words (vv. 34–35) present a good summary of both events: 'I truly understand that God shows no partiality, but in every nation whoever fears him and does what is right is acceptable to him.'[14]

As is well known, according to common tradition the apostle Peter was later to end up preaching the message, not just to an individual Roman household in Caesarea, but at the heart of the empire, in the city of Rome itself. And it was in that place, faithfully fulfilling his commission, that Peter's previously expressed willingness to die for his Lord was ultimately realized.[15]

---

[14] For further discussion of Peter and Jonah in Acts 10, see Robert W. Wall, 'Peter "Son" of Jonah: The Conversion of Cornelius in the Context of Canon', *JSNT* 29 (1987): 79–90.

[15] Cf. John 21:18–19.

31
Conclusion

In this volume over thirty instances[1] of extended allusion in passages throughout the four Gospels have been brought to the reader's attention. While this may well account for most cases of such a feature in the Gospel corpus, there are, I am sure, other occurrences that remain for others to alight upon. One area that might prove fruitful in this regard is, I would suggest, that of the Johannine discourses, which I have touched upon very little. I feel certain that behind these weighty speeches of Jesus lie specific passages of the Jewish Scriptures waiting to be discovered, and once this has been done it will assuredly bestow on the meaning of his words an even greater profundity. There are probably other parables too, such as that of the prodigal son, and other events, such as the cleansing of the temple, which would be more deeply appreciated if their Old Testament background were identified. Then, of course, the scope of investigation may be broadened to include the Acts of the Apostles. The immediately preceding chapter demonstrated how allusions to the prophet Jonah centring on the apostle Peter were not only found in a Gospel passage but also surfaced in Acts. Scholars have already unearthed a number of other extended allusions in that book, as commentaries show.[2]

The kind of literary phenomenon dealt with here reveals the high level of artistry involved in the composition of the Gospels. Often enough, classic works of human literature receive praise for the literary skill of their authors. Even a greater degree of such skill, I would imagine, ought to be expected in the writings of those we believe to have been divinely inspired. The overarching involvement of one essential Author endows Holy Scripture with a unity that allows accounts originating from diverse human authors to be intricately

---

[1] Chapter 26, we recall, looked at distinct resurrection appearances occurring in the three synoptic Gospels, all in a single chapter.

[2] A prime example can be seen in Acts 12, where Peter's deliverance from prison is replete with allusions to the Passover and exodus redemption, Old Testament events often alluded to in the Gospels as we have shown on several occasions. See, e.g., David G. Peterson, *The Acts of the Apostles* (PNTC; Grand Rapids, MI: Eerdmans, 2009), 362; Mikael C. Parsons, *Acts* (Paideia Commentaries on the New Testament; Grand Rapids, MI: Baker, 2008), 175.

interconnected beneath the surface level of the text. Scripture exploits this underlying unity with full effect, as I hope has been amply demonstrated.[3]

What we have been looking at in these chapters, however, is much more than a mere literary device employed for art's sake. The content of the allusions is to a very large extent theological. It contributes greatly to the theology of the Gospel passage under discussion. Further still, the import of the allusions is frequently more specifically Christological, bound up with the all-important question of the nature and identity of Jesus Christ. This latter function of the allusions was something that I had not foreseen when I first undertook the task, at least with regard to its extent and depth. Reviewing now the various passages treated, I would conclude that this component of the allusions is without doubt the most significant element within the present work. Not once, but time and again, we have seen the allusions undergo a conspicuous switch in their object of reference. In a single passage they may in the first instance depict Christ in terms of a particularly prominent Old Testament figure – a lawgiver, leader or prophet. However, as the series of allusions progresses, a transformation occurs, and the allusions proceed to indicate an altogether different object of attention, namely God himself. Consequently, in these Gospel allusions the person of Jesus is found to be recast, as it were, from a solely human character to very Deity, to the 'LORD', YHWH, the 'I AM' of the Old Testament. And this is found to be so regarding the portrayal of Christ in Matthew, Mark and Luke as much as in John. While the latter may exhibit Jesus as God in a more explicit fashion, the same wondrous revelation is equally present in the other three Gospels, a fact that runs counter to much modern theological thought. Our study has undergirded the momentous truth which the creeds of the church have professed for centuries, namely that the person known as Jesus of Nazareth is indeed the God of heaven made flesh on earth.

I close with the hope and prayer that this work has been enlightening, encouraging and edifying to its reader, and that through these studies of the Gospels his or her faith in the incarnate Lord has been strengthened.

---

[3] In this context we should perhaps point out that our demonstration also showed the presence of the same phenomenon in the two most disputed texts in the Gospels, namely Mark 16:9–20 and John 7:53 – 8:11. How this fact touches upon the issue of the canonicity of these passages is a question that will be left for the reader to explore further.

Bibliography

Ahearne-Kroll, Stephen P., 'Genesis in Mark's Gospel', in Maarten J. J. Menken and Steve Moyise (eds.), *Genesis in the New Testament* (LNTS; London: Bloomsbury, 2012), 27–41.

Alexander, T. Desmond, and Brian S. Rosner (eds.), *New Dictionary of Biblical Theology: Exploring the Unity and Diversity of Scripture* (Leicester: Inter-Varsity Press, 2000).

Allen, Leslie C., *Ezekiel 1–19* (WBC 28; Dallas: Word, 1994).

Allen Jr, O. Wesley, *Matthew* (Fortress Biblical Preaching Commentaries; Augsburg, MN: Fortress, 2013).

Allison Jr, Dale C., *The New Moses: A Matthean Typology* (Minneapolis, MN: Fortress, 1993).

Alter, Robert, *The Five Books of Moses: A Translation with Commentary* (New York, NY: W. W. Norton & Co., 2004).

Arndt, William F., Walter Bauer and F. Wilbur Gingrich, *A Greek-English Lexicon of the New Testament and Other Early Christian Literature* (Chicago, IL: University of Chicago Press, 1957).

Ashley, Timothy R., *The Book of Numbers* (NICOT; Grand Rapids, MI: Eerdmans, 1993).

Bamberger, Bernard J., 'Leviticus', in W. Gunther Plaut (ed.), *The Torah: A Modern Commentary* (New York, NY: Union of American Hebrew Congregations, 1981).

Barrett, C. K., *The Gospel According to St. John: An Introduction with Commentary and Notes on the Greek Text* (Philadelphia, PA: Westminster, 1978).

Bauckham, Richard, *Gospel Women: Studies of the Named Women in the Gospels* (London: T&T Clark, 2002).

Beale, Gregory K., 'Adam as the First Priest in Eden as the Garden Temple', *Southern Baptist Journal of Theology* 22.2 (2018): 9–24.

——, *The Book of Revelation* (NIGTC; Grand Rapids, MI: Eerdmans, 1999).

——, *A New Testament Biblical Theology: The Unfolding of the Old Testament in the New* (Grand Rapids, MI: Baker Academic, 2011).

____, *Redemptive Reversals and the Ironic Overturning of Human Wisdom* (Short Studies in Biblical Theology; Wheaton, IL: Crossway, 2019).

____, *The Temple and the Church's Mission: A Biblical Theology of the Dwelling Place of God* (NSBT 17; Leicester: Apollos, 2004).

Beale, G. K., and D. A. Carson (eds.), *Commentary on the New Testament Use of the Old Testament* (Grand Rapids, MI: Baker Academic, 2007).

Beavis, Mary Ann, 'The Resurrection of Jephthah's Daughter: Judges 11:34–40 and Mark 5:21–24, 35–42', *CBQ* 72.1 (2010): 46–62.

Beetham, Christopher A., *Echoes of Scripture in the Letter of Paul to the Colossians* (Leiden: Brill, 2008).

Bellamy, Michelle L., 'The Elijah-Elisha Cycle of Stories: A Ring Composition', PhD dissertation, University of Boston, 2013.

Bellinzoni, Arthur J., *The Building Blocks of the Earliest Gospel: A Roadmap to Early Christian Biography* (Eugene, OR: Wipf & Stock, 2018).

Bengel, John Albert, *Gnomon of the New Testament* (Eugene, OR: Wipf & Stock, 2004 [repr. of 1877 edn]).

Ben-Sasson, H. H. (ed.), *A History of the Jewish People* (Cambridge, MA: Harvard University Press, 1976).

Blomberg, Craig L., 'Matthew', in G. K. Beale and D. A. Carson (eds.), *Commentary on the New Testament Use of the Old Testament* (Grand Rapids, MI: Baker Academic, 2007), 1–110.

____, *Matthew: An Exegetical and Theological Exposition of Holy Scripture* (NAC 22; Nashville, TN: Broadman, 1992).

Blount, Brian K., *Revelation: A Commentary* (NTL; Louisville, KY: Westminster John Knox, 2009).

Bock, Darrell L., *Luke 1:1–9:50* (BECNT 3A; Grand Rapids, MI: Baker, 1994).

Bock, Darrell L., and Mitch Glaser, *Messiah in the Passover* (Grand Rapids, MI: Kregel, 2017).

Boling, Robert G., and G. Ernest Wright, *Joshua: A New Translation with Introduction and Commentary* (AB 6; New York, NY: Doubleday, 1982).

Brown, Francis, S. R. Driver and Charles A. Briggs, *A Hebrew and English Lexicon of the Old Testament* (Oxford: Clarendon, rev. edn, 1953).

Brown, Jeannine K., 'Creation's Renewal in the Gospel of John', *CBQ* 72 (2010): 275–290.

____, 'Genesis in Matthew's Gospel', in Maarten J. J. Menken and Steve Moyise (eds.), *Genesis in the New Testament* (LNTS; London: Bloomsbury, 2012), 42–59.

____, *The Gospels as Stories: A Narrative Approach to Matthew, Mark, Luke, and John* (Grand Rapids, MI: Baker Academic, 2020).

Brown, Raymond E., *The Birth of the Messiah: A Commentary on the Infancy Narratives in the Gospels of Matthew and Luke* (New York, NY: Doubleday, 1993).

_____, *The Death of the Messiah: From Gethsemane to the Grave. A Commentary on the Passion Narratives in the Four Gospels* (New York, NY: Doubleday, 1994).

_____, *The Gospel According to John, XIII–XXI* (AB 29A; New York, NY: Doubleday, 1966).

Burgon, John W., *Plain Commentary on the Four Holy Gospels* (London: John Henry Parker, 1855).

Buttrick, George A. (ed.), *Interpreter's Dictionary of the Bible* (Nashville, TN: Abingdon, 1962).

Calvin, John, *Commentaries*, vol. 8, tr. John King (Grand Rapids, MI: Baker, 1998).

Carson, D. A., *The Gospel According to John* (PNTC; Leicester: Apollos, 1991).

Chalmers, Aaron, *Exploring the Religion of Ancient Israel: Prophet, Priest, Sage and People* (Downers Grove, IL: InterVarsity Press, 2012).

Clines, David J. A., *Job 1–20* (WBC 17; Dallas, TX: Word, 1989).

Coloe, Mary L., 'The Garden as a New Creation in John', *The Bible Today* 53.3 (2015): 159–164.

Compton, Jared M., 'Shared Intentions? Reflections on Inspiration and Interpretation in Light of Scripture's Dual Authorship', *Themelios* 33 (2008): 23–33.

Congar, Yves M. J., *The Mystery of the Temple, Or the Manner of God's Presence to His Creatures from Genesis to the Apocalypse* (London: Burns & Oates, 1962).

Coote, Robert B., 'The Book of Joshua', in Leander E. Keck (ed.), *The New Interpreter's Bible*, vol. 2 (Nashville, TN: Abingdon, 1998).

Cranfield, C. E. B., *The Gospel According to St. Mark: An Introduction and Commentary* (Cambridge: Cambridge University Press, 1959).

Culpepper, R. Alan, 'The Gospel of Luke', in Leander E. Keck (ed.), *The New Interpreter's Bible*, vol. 9 (Nashville, TN: Abingdon, 1995).

Danby, Herbert, *The Mishnah, Translated from the Hebrew with Introduction and Brief Explanatory Notes* (Oxford: Oxford University Press, 1933).

Davies, W. D., and Dale C. Allison Jr, *Matthew 1–7: Volume 1* (ICC; Edinburgh: T&T Clark, 1988).

_____, *Matthew 19–28: Volume 3* (ICC; London: Bloomsbury, 2004).

De Boer, M. C., *Johannine Perspectives on the Death of Jesus* (Kampen: Kok Pharos, 1996).

De Villiers, Pieter G. R., 'The Powerful Transformation of the Young Man in Mark 14:51–52 and 16:5', *HTS Theological Studies* 66.1 (2010), article 893, seven pages.

Doig, Kenneth F., *New Testament Chronology* (Lewiston, NY: Edwin Mellen, 1990).

Douglas, Mary, *In the Wilderness: The Doctrine of Defilement in the Book of Numbers* (Oxford: Oxford University Press, 2001).

Duguid, Iain M., *Numbers: God's Presence in the Wilderness* (Wheaton, IL: Crossway, 2006).

Durham, John I., *Exodus* (WBC 3; Waco, TX: Word, 1987).

Edwards, James R., *The Gospel According to Mark* (PNTC; Grand Rapids, MI: Eerdmans, 2002).

Emadi, Samuel, *From Prisoner to Prince: The Joseph Story in Biblical Theology* (NSBT 59; London: Apollos, 2022).

Erickson, Richard J., 'Joseph and the Birth of Isaac in Matthew 1', *BBR* 10 (2000): 35–51.

Esswein, Mitchell Alexander, 'Is He Going to Kill Himself? The Willing Self-Sacrifice of Jesus and the Akedah in the Fourth Gospel', *Sacra Scripta* 11.2 (2013): 231–261.

Estelle, Bryan D., *Echoes of Exodus: Tracing a Biblical Motif* (Downers Grove, IL: InterVarsity Press, 2018).

Fanous, Daniel, *Taught By God: Making Sense of the Difficult Sayings of Jesus* (Rollinsford, NH: Orthodox Research Institute, 2010).

France, R. T., *The Gospel According to John* (NICNT; Grand Rapids, MI: Eerdmans, 1995).

_____, *The Gospel of Matthew* (NICNT; Grand Rapids, MI: Eerdmans, 2007).

Fretheim, Terence E., *Exodus: A Biblical Commentary for Teaching and Preaching* (Interpretation; Louisville, KY: John Knox, 1991).

Gage, Warren Austin, *The Gospel of Genesis: Studies in Protology and Eschatology* (Eugene, OR: Wipf & Stock, 2001).

Gale, Aaron M., *Redefining Ancient Borders: The Jewish Scribal Framework of Matthew's Gospel* (London: T&T Clark, 2005).

Galvin, Garrett, *Egypt as a Place of Refuge* (Tübingen: Mohr Siebeck, 2011).

Garland, David E., *Luke* (ZECNT 3; Grand Rapids, MI: Zondervan, 2011).

Gaster, Theodor H., 'Demon', in George A. Buttrick (ed.), *Interpreter's Dictionary of the Bible*, vol. 1 (Nashville, TN: Abingdon, 1962): 817–824.

Gertoux, Gerard, 'Dating the Two Censuses of P. Sulpicius Quirinius', viewable at <www.academia.edu/3184175/Dating_the_two_Censuses_of_Quirinius> (accessed 23 Jan. 2023).

Ginzberg, Louis, *Legends of the Jews*, vol. 1 (Philadelphia, PA: Jewish Publication Society of America, 1909).

Green, Joel B., *The Gospel of Luke* (NICNT; Grand Rapids, MI: Eerdmans, 1997).

Greidanus, Sidney, *Preaching Christ from Genesis: Foundations for Expository Sermons* (Grand Rapids, MI: Eerdmans, 2007).

Guardini, Romano, *The Lord* (Washington, DC: Gateway, 1996).

Hamilton Jr, James M., *Psalms, vol. 2: 73–150* (Evangelical Biblical Theological Commentary; Bellingham, WA: Lexham Academic, 2021).

Harrison, Roland K., *Numbers: An Exegetical Commentary* (Grand Rapids, MI: Baker, 1992).

Harstad, Adolph L., *Joshua* (Concordia Commentary; St Louis, MO: Concordia, 2004).

Hart, Addison Hodges, *The Woman, the Hour, and the Garden: A Study in the Imagery of the Gospel of John* (Grand Rapids, MI: Eerdmans, 2016).

Hartley, John E., *The Book of Job* (NICOT; Grand Rapids, MI: Eerdmans, 1988).

_____, *Leviticus* (WBC 4; Dallas, TX: Word, 1992).

Hatina, Thomas R., 'The Focus of Mark 13:24–27: The Parousia, or the Destruction of the Temple?' *BBR* 6.1 (1996): 43–66.

Hauerwas, Stanley, *Matthew* (Brazos Theological Commentary on the Bible; Grand Rapids, MI: Brazos, 2006).

Hays, Richard B., *Echoes of Scripture in the Gospels* (Waco, TX: Baylor University Press, 2016).

_____, *Reading Backwards: Figural Christology and the Fourfold Gospel Witness* (London: SPCK, 2015).

Hayward, C. T. R., 'The Sacrifice of Isaac and Jewish Polemic against Christianity', *CBQ* 52.2 (1990): 292–306.

Heil, John Paul, 'Jesus as the Unique High Priest in the Gospel of John', *CBQ* 57.4 (1995): 729–745.

Hertz, J. H., *The Pentateuch and Haftorahs: Hebrew Text, English Translation, and Commentary* (London: Soncino, 1981).

Hill, Edmund, and Michele Pellegrino (eds.), *The Works of Saint Augustine, Part III, vol. 1: Sermons 1–19* (Brooklyn, NY: New City Press, 1990).

Hoehner, Harold W., *Chronological Aspects of the Life of Christ* (Grand Rapids, MI: Zondervan, 1978).

Huizenga, Leroy A., *Behold the Christ: Proclaiming the Gospel of Matthew* (Steubenville, OH: Emmaus Road, 2019).

_____, *The New Isaac: Tradition and Intertextuality in the Gospel of Matthew* (Leiden: Brill, 2009).

_____, 'Obedience unto Death: The Matthean Gethsemane and Arrest Sequence and the Aqedah', *CBQ* 71.3 (2009): 507–526.

Instone-Brewer, David, *Traditions of the Rabbis from the Era of the New Testament, vol. 1: Prayer and Agriculture* (Grand Rapids, MI: Eerdmans, 2004).

_____, *Traditions of the Rabbis from the Era of the New Testament, vol. 2A: Feasts and Sabbaths: Passover and Atonement* (Grand Rapids, MI: Eerdmans, 2011).

Jastrow, Marcus, *A Dictionary of the Targumim, the Talmud Babli and Yerushalmi, and the Midrashic Literature* (New York, NY: Judaica Press, 2007 [repr. of 1903 edn]).

John, Jeffrey, *The Meaning in the Miracles* (Norwich: Canterbury Press, 2001).

Karris R. J. (ed.), *The Collegeville Bible Commentary: New Testament* (Collegeville, MN: Liturgical Press, 1992).

Kautzsch, E., and A. E. Cowley, *Gesenius' Hebrew Grammar* (Oxford: Clarendon, 2nd English edn, 1910).

Keener, Craig S., 'Gospel Lesson: Matthew 28:16–20', in Roger Van Harn (ed.). *The Lectionary Commentary. The Third Readings: The Gospels* (Grand Rapids, MI: Eerdmans, 2001), 158–161.

Keil, C. F., 'The Pentateuch', in C. F. Keil and F. Delitzsch, *Commentary on the Old Testament* (Peabody, MA: Hendrickson, 1996 [repr. of 1866 edn]), vol. 1.

Keil, C. F., and F. Delitzsch, *Commentary on the Old Testament* (Peabody, MA: Hendrickson, 1996, 10 vols. [repr. of 1866–91 edn]).

Knust, Jennifer, and Tommy Wasserman, 'Earth Accuses Earth: Tracing What Jesus Wrote upon the Ground', *HTR* 103.4 (2010), 407–446.

Kreitzer, Larry J., and Deborah W. Rooke (eds.), *Ciphers in the Sand: Interpretations of the Woman Taken in Adultery (John 7:53–8:11)* (Sheffield: Sheffield Academic Press, 2000).

Lee, Dorothy A., 'Paschal Imagery in the Gospel of John: A Narrative and Symbolic Reading', *Pacifica: Australasian Theological Studies* 24 (2011): 13–26.

Leithart, Peter, *1 & 2 Kings* (Brazos Theological Commentary on the Bible; Grand Rapids, MI: Brazos, 2006).

_____, *Jesus as Israel: The Gospel of Matthew through New Eyes*, vol. 1 (Monroe, LA: Athanasius Press, 2017).

_____, *Jesus as Israel: The Gospel of Matthew through New Eyes*, vol. 2 (Monroe, LA: Athanasius Press, 2018).

Lenski, R. C. H., *Commentary on the New Testament* (Minneapolis, MN: Augsburg, 1961 [repr. of 1943 edn]).

Leonard, Jeffery, 'Identifying Inner-Biblical Allusions: Psalm 78 as a Test Case', *JBL* 127.2 (2008): 241–265.

Lerner, Berel Dov, 'Untangling σαβαχθανι (Matt. 27:46 and Mark 15:34)', *NovT* 56.2 (2014): 196–197.

Levering, Matthew, *Participatory Biblical Exegesis: A Theology of Biblical Interpretation* (Notre Dame, IN: University of Notre Dame Press, 2008).

Levine, Baruch A., *Leviticus* (JPS Torah Commentary; Philadelphia, PA: Jewish Publication Society, 1989).

Liddell, Henry George, and Robert Scott, *A Greek Lexicon* (Oxford: Clarendon, rev. edn, 1940).

Lightfoot, John, *A Commentary on the New Testament from the Talmud and Hebraica*, 4 vols. (Peabody, MA: Hendrickson, 2003 [repr. of 1859 edn]).

Lunn, Nicholas P., *Jesus in the Jewish Scriptures: How the Old Testament Bears Witness to Christ* (London: Faithbuilders, 2020).

_____, 'Jesus, the Ark, and the Day of Atonement: Intertextual Echoes in John 19:38–20:18', *JETS* 52.4 (2009): 731–746.

_____, *The Original Ending of Mark: A New Case for the Authenticity of Mark 16:9–20* (Eugene, OR: Pickwick, 2014).

McCaffrey, U. P., 'Psalm Quotations in the Passion Narratives of the Gospels', *Neotestamentica* 14 (1980): 73–89.

McCall, Thomas H., *Forsaken: The Trinity and the Cross, and Why It Matters* (Downers Grove, IL: InterVarsity Press, 2012).

McCarthy, Carmel (ed. and tr.), *Saint Ephrem's Commentary on Tatian's Diatessaron* (Journal of Semitic Studies Supplement 2; Oxford: Oxford University Press, 2000).

McKeown, James, *Genesis* (Two Horizons Old Testament Commentary; Grand Rapids, MI: Eerdmans, 2008).

Maclean, Jennifer K. Berenson, 'Barabbas, the Scapegoat Ritual, and the Development of the Passion Narrative', *HTR* 100.3 (2007): 309–334.

Menken, Maarten J. J., and Steve Moyise (eds.), *Genesis in the New Testament* (LNTS; London: Bloomsbury, 2012).

Milgrom, Jacob, *Leviticus 1–16: A New Translation with Introduction and Commentary* (AB 3; New York, NY: Doubleday, 1991).

_____, *Numbers* (JPS Torah Commentary; Philadelphia, PA: Jewish Publication Society, 1992).

Mitch, Curtis, and Edward Sri, *The Gospel of Matthew* (Catholic Commentary on Sacred Scripture; Grand Rapids, MI: Baker, 2010).

Moffitt, David M., 'God Attested by Men: Echoes of Jonah and the Identification of Jesus with Israel's God in the Storm-Stilling Stories of Matthew's Gospel', in David M. Moffitt and Isaac Augustine Morales (eds.), *A Scribe Trained for the Kingdom of Heaven: Essays on Christology and Ethics in Honor of Richard B. Hays* (Lanham, MD: Lexington Books, 2021), 25–45.

Morales, Michael L., *Exodus Old and New: A Biblical Theology of Redemption* (Downers Grove, IL: InterVarsity Press, 2020).

____, *Who Shall Ascend the Mountain of the Lord? A Biblical Theology of the Book of Leviticus* (NSBT 37; Nottingham: Apollos, 2015).

Morris, Leon, *The Gospel According to Matthew* (PNTC; Grand Rapids, MI: Eerdmans, 1992).

Moscicke, Hans M., 'Jesus as Goat of the Day of Atonement in Recent Synoptic Gospels Research', *Currents in Biblical Research* 17.1 (2018): 59–85.

____, 'Jesus, Barabbas, and the Crowd as Figures in Matthew's Day of Atonement Typology (Matt 27:15–26)', *JBL* 139.1 (2020): 125–153.

____, *The New Day of Atonement: A Matthean Typology* (Tübingen: Mohr Siebeck, 2020).

Moses, A. D. A., *Matthew's Transfiguration Story and Jewish-Christian Controversy* (Journal for the Study of the New Testament Supplement Series 122; Sheffield: Sheffield Academic Press, 1996).

Motyer, J. Alec, *The Prophecy of Isaiah: An Introduction and Commentary* (Downers Grove, IL: InterVarsity Press, 1993).

Neusner, Jacob, *Introduction to Rabbinic Literature* (New York, NY: Doubleday, 1994).

____, *A Rabbi Talks with Jesus* (Montreal: McGill-Queen's University Press, 2000).

Nolland, John, *The Gospel of Matthew* (NIGTC; Grand Rapids, MI: Eerdmans, 2005).

Noort, Edward, and Eibert J. C. Tigchelaar (eds.), *The Sacrifice of Isaac: The Aqedah (Genesis 22) and Its Interpretations* (Leiden: Brill, 2002).

Oden, Thomas C., *The African Memory of Mark: Reassessing Early Church Tradition* (Downers Grove, IL: InterVarsity Press, 2011).

Orlov, Andrei A., *The Atoning Dyad: The Two Goats of Yom Kippur in the Apocalypse of Abraham* (Leiden: Brill, 2016).

Osborne, Grant R., *Matthew* (ZECNT 1; Grand Rapids, MI: Zondervan, 2010).

_____, *Revelation* (BECNT; Grand Rapids, MI: Baker Academic, 2002).

Oswalt, John N., *The Book of Isaiah: Chapters 40–66* (NICOT; Grand Rapids, MI: Eerdmans, 1998).

Pao, David W., and Eckhard J. Schnabel, 'Luke', in G. K. Beale and D. A. Carson (eds.), *Commentary on the New Testament Use of the Old Testament* (Grand Rapids, MI: Baker Academic, 2007), 251–414.

Parsons, Mikael C., *Acts* (Paideia Commentaries on the New Testament; Grand Rapids, MI: Baker, 2008).

Payne, Philip B., 'The Fallacy of Equating Meaning with the Human Author's Intention', *JETS* 20 (1977): 243–252.

Perrin, Nicholas, *Finding Jesus in the Exodus* (New York, NY: Hachette, 2014).

Peterson, David G., *The Acts of the Apostles* (PNTC; Grand Rapids, MI: Eerdmans, 2009).

Pitre, Brant, 'Jesus, the New Temple, and the New Priesthood', *Letter & Spirit* 4 (2008): 49–86.

Plaut, W. Gunther (ed.), *The Torah: A Modern Commentary* (New York, NY: Union of American Hebrew Congregations, 1981).

Postell, Seth D., *Adam as Israel: Genesis 1–3 as the Introduction to the Torah and Tanakh* (Eugene, OR: Pickwick, 2011).

Poythress, Vern S., 'Dispensing with Merely Human Meaning: Gains and Losses from Focusing on the Human Author, Illustrated by Zephaniah 1:2–3', *JETS* 57 (2014): 481–499.

_____, 'The Presence of God Qualifying Our Notions of Grammatical-Historical Interpretation: Genesis 3:15 as a Test Case', *JETS* 50 (2007): 87–103.

Ratzinger, Joseph (Pope Benedict XVI), *Jesus of Nazareth: From the Baptism in the Jordan to the Transfiguration* (New York, NY: Doubleday, 2007).

_____, *Jesus of Nazareth: Holy Week. From the Entrance into Jerusalem to the Resurrection* (San Francisco, CA: Ignatius Press, 2011).

_____, *Jesus of Nazareth: The Infancy Narratives* (London: Bloomsbury, 2012).

Ridderbos, Herman, *The Gospel of John: A Theological Commentary* (Grand Rapids, MI: Eerdmans, 1997).

Rindge, Matthew S., 'Reconfiguring the Akedah and Recasting God: Lament and Divine Abandonment in Mark', *JBL* 131.4 (2012): 755–774.

Rogers, Trent, 'The Great Commission as the Climax of Matthew's Mountain Scenes', *BBR* 22.3 (2012): 383–398.

Rooke, Deborah W., 'Wayward Women and Broken Promises: Marriage, Adultery and Mercy in Old and New Testaments', in Larry J. Kreitzer and Deborah W. Rooke (eds.), *Ciphers in the Sand: Interpretations of the Woman Taken in Adultery (John 7:53–8:11)* (Sheffield: Sheffield Academic Press, 2000), 17–52.

Rosik, Mariusz, 'Discovering the Secrets of God's Gardens: Resurrection as New Creation', *Liber Annuus* 58 (2008): 9–27.

Rutledge, Fleming, *The Crucifixion: Understanding the Death of Jesus Christ* (Grand Rapids, MI: Eerdmans, 2015).

Sailhamer, John H., *The Pentateuch as Narrative: A Biblical-Theological Commentary* (Grand Rapids, MI: Zondervan, 1992).

Sanlon, Peter, *Simply God: Recovering the Classical Trinity* (Nottingham: Inter-Varsity Press, 2014).

Sarna, Nahum M., *Exodus* (JPS Torah Commentary; Philadelphia, PA: Jewish Publication Society, 1991).

Saward, John, *Redeemer in the Womb: Jesus Living in Mary* (San Francisco, CA: Ignatius Press, 1993).

Schauss, Hayyim, *The Jewish Festivals: A Guide to Their History and Observance* (New York, NY: Schocken Books, 1962).

Schmutzer, Andrew, 'Jesus' Temptation: A Reflection on Matthew's Use of Old Testament Theology and Imagery', *Ashland Theological Journal* 40 (2008): 15–42.

Schreiner, Patrick, *Matthew, Disciple and Scribe: The First Gospel and Its Portrait of Jesus* (Grand Rapids, MI: Baker Academic, 2019).

Smith, Daniel A., *Revisiting the Empty Tomb: The Early History of Easter* (Minneapolis, MN: Fortress, 2010).

Smith, Robert H., *Easter Gospels: The Resurrection of Jesus According to the Four Evangelists* (Minneapolis, MN: Augsburg, 1983).

Sparks, Kenton L. 'Gospel as Conquest: Mosaic Typology in Matthew 28:16–20', *CBQ* 68 (2006): 651–663.

Stade, Christopher (tr.), *The Explanation by Blessed Theophylact Archbishop of Ochrid and Bulgaria of the Holy Gospel According to Saint Matthew* (House Springs, MO: Chrysostom Press, 2006).

Stander, H. F., 'The Greek Church Fathers and Rahab', *Acta Patristica et Byzantina* 17 (2006): 37–49.

Stokes, Ryan E., 'Not over Moses' Dead Body: Jude 9, 22–24 and the *Assumption of Moses* in Their Early Jewish Context', *JSNT* 40.2 (2017): 192–213.

Stuart, Douglas K., *Exodus: An Exegetical and Theological Exposition of Holy Scripture* (NAC 2; Nashville, TN: Broadman & Holman, 2006).

Stubbs, David L., *Numbers* (Brazos Theological Commentary on the Bible; Grand Rapids, MI: Brazos, 2009).

Thackeray, H. St John, *The Septuagint and Jewish Worship: A Study in Origins* (London: Oxford University Press, 1921).

Troost-Cramer, Kathleen, *Jesus as Means and Locus of Worship in the Fourth Gospel: Sacrifice and Worship Space in John* (Eugene, OR: Pickwick, 2017).

Turner, David L., *Matthew* (BECNT; Grand Rapids, MI: Baker, 2008).

Tur-Sinai, N. H., *The Book of Job: A New Commentary* (Jerusalem: Kiryath Sepher, 1967).

Van Harn, Roger E. (ed.), *The Lectionary Commentary. The Third Readings: The Gospels* (Grand Rapids, MI: Eerdmans, 2001).

Van Harn, Roger E., and Brent A. Strawn (eds.), *Psalms for Preaching and Worship: A Lectionary Commentary* (Grand Rapids, MI: Eerdmans, 2009).

Van Ruiten, J. T. A. G. M., 'Abraham, Job and the Book of *Jubilees*: The Intertextual Relationship of Genesis 1:1–19, Job 1–2:13 and *Jubilees* 17:15–18:19', in Edward Noort and Eibert J. C. Tigchelaar (eds.), *The Sacrifice of Isaac: The Aqedah (Genesis 22) and Its Interpretations* (Leiden: Brill, 2002), 58–85.

Wall, Robert W., 'Peter "Son" of Jonah: The Conversion of Cornelius in the Context of Canon', *JSNT* 29 (1987): 79–90.

Waltke, Bruce K., and James M. Houston, *The Psalms as Christian Worship: A Historical Commentary* (Grand Rapids, MI: Eerdmans, 2010).

Webster, John, *The Domain of the Word: Scripture and Theological Reason* (London: Bloomsbury, 2012).

Wenham, Gordon J., *The Book of Leviticus* (NICOT; Grand Rapids, MI: Eerdmans, 1979).

White, Thomas J., *Exodus* (Brazos Theological Commentary on the Bible; Grand Rapids, MI: Brazos, 2016).

Williams, Rowan, *God with Us: The Meaning of the Cross and Resurrection, Then and Now* (London: SPCK, 2017).

Williams, Stephen N., 'The Transfiguration of Jesus Christ', *Themelios* 28.1 (2002): 13–25.

Williamson, H. G. M., *Ezra, Nehemiah* (WBC 16; Nashville, TN: Word, 1985).

Witherington III, Ben, *Matthew* (Smyth & Helwys Bible Commentary; Macon, GA: Smyth & Helwys, 2006).

Wright, N. T., *Jesus and the Victory of God* (London: SPCK, 1996).

Wright IV, William M., *The Bible and Catholic Ressourcement: Essays on Scripture and Theology* (Steubenville, OH: Emmaus Academic, 2019).

Wright IV, William M., and Francis Martin, *Encountering the Living God in Scripture: Theological and Philosophical Principles for Interpretation* (Grand Rapids, MI: Baker Academic, 2019).

Yamauchi, Edwin M., *Persia and the Bible* (Grand Rapids, MI: Baker, 1990).

Young, Brad H., *The Parables: Jewish Tradition and Christian Interpretation* (Grand Rapids, MI: Baker Academic, 2012).

Zerwick, Maximilian, *Biblical Greek* (Rome: Editrice Pontificio Istituto Biblico, 1990).

Scripture acknowledgments

Index of Scripture references

OLD TESTAMENT

Genesis
1:1 *16*
1:5 *243*
1:6–8 *75*
1:8 *243*
1:13 *243*
1:19 *243*
1:20–22 *75*
1:23 *243*
1:28 *58*
1:31 *243*
2 *245*
2 – 3 *240*
2:4 *16*
2:7 *137, 245*
2:8 *240*
2:9 *241*
2:12 *164*
2:15 *164, 241*
2:18–22 *242*
2:21–22 *242*
2:23 *242*
2:24 *244*
3 *243*
3:3 *243*
3:8 *244*
3:14 *138*
3:19 *137*
3:20 *242*
3:24 *164, 241*
5:1 *16*
9:1 *58*

9:25 *98*
10 *73*
10:5 *25*
11:30 *33*
12:3 *34, 58*
14:17–24 *7*
14:24 *180*
15 – 18 *32*
15:1 *32, 33*
15:6 *32*
15:18 *103*
15:19 *103*
16:1 *33*
17:8 *98*
17:10–13 *250*
17:18–21 *34*
17:19 *33*
18:1–15 *16*
18:3 *34*
18:11 *33*
18:12 *242*
18:13 *33*
18:14 *34, 179*
18:18 *58, 220*
19:8 *187*
21 *32*
21:1 *34*
21:1–17 *16*
21:3 *33*
21:8 *34*
21:12 *171*
22 *35, 122, 170, 177, 179, 205, 208, 209*
22:1 *172*

22:2 *122, 171, 172, 177, 206*
22:3 *173, 180*
22:5 *172, 180*
22:6 *173, 206*
22:7 *173, 174, 178, 210*
22:8 *210*
22:9 *170, 173, 175, 205*
22:10 *173, 175, 176, 180*
22:11–12 *174*
22:12 *171, 172, 174, 180, 210*
22:13 *179, 181, 206, 209, 210*
22:16 *171, 172*
22:18 *34, 58, 220*
23:19 *104*
25:5 *142*
26:4 *35, 58, 220*
26:5 *38*
26:30 *159*
28:14 *35, 58*
31:46 *159*
32:28 *153*
35:21 *39*
36:11 *103*
37 *152, 153*
37:3 *152*
37:4 *152*
37:5–11 *225*
37:9 *228*
37:11 *152*

37:13 *152*
37:14 *152*
37:18 *152*
37:20 *152*
37:24 *153*
37:27 *153*
37:28 *154*
37:33–34 *153*
39:5 *142*
39:10–20 *211*
40 *211*
40:2–4 *211*
40:13 *212*
40:14 *212*
40:15 *211, 212*
40:19 *212*
40:20 *212*
40:22 *212*
40:23 *213*
41:9–10 *212*
42:8 *225*
42:13 *153, 225*
42:29 *226*
42:32 *153, 225*
42:38 *225*
43:23 *226*
43:26 *228*
43:27 *226*
43:28 *228*
44:20 *153, 225*
45:1 *225*
45:1–15 *154*
45:3 *226*
45:4 *226*
45:9 *155, 226, 227*

Genesis (cont.)
45:11 *142*
45:13 *226*
45:23 *227*
45:26 *226*
48:4 *98*

Exodus
1 *48*
1:17 *48*
1:18 *48*
1:19 *48, 49*
1:22 *46, 49*
2:15 *46, 47*
3 – 4 *216, 222, 224*
3:1 *216*
3:2 *222*
3:6 *220*
3:10 *46, 49, 222*
3:12 *49, 217, 219*
3:13–14 *90, 167*
3:14 *90*
3:15 *220*
3:16 *220, 222*
4 *222, 223*
4:1 *222, 223*
4:2–3 *223*
4:3 *223*
4:4 *223*
4:5 *220, 222, 223*
4:8 *223*
4:9 *223*
4:12 *222*
4:17 *69, 223*
4:19 *47*
4:20 *48, 69, 224*
4:21 *222, 224*
4:22 *45, 52*
4:23 *45*
4:28 *223*
4:30 *223*

4:30–31 *224*
4:31 *223*
6:23 *110*
7:13 *224*
8:19 *224*
9:7 *224*
12 *7, 156*
12:1–11 *157*
12:3 *146*
12:6 *82, 168*
12:7 *85, 158*
12:8 *48, 82*
12:21–28 *74*
12:22 *158*
12:31 *48*
12:31–42 *48*
12:37 *74, 76*
12:39 *74*
12:42 *48*
12:46 *168, 189*
13:2 *45*
13:4 *78*
13:21 *37*
14 *52, 53*
14 – 15 *88*
14:10 *93*
14:11–12 *93*
14:13 *93, 94*
14:16 *69, 94*
14:19 *166*
14:21 *92, 94*
14:24 *92*
14:26 *94*
14:27 *94*
14:29 *74, 93*
14:30 *94*
14:31 *223*
15:2 *94*
15:4 *94*
15:5 *94*
15:8 *93, 94*

15:12 *94*
15:19 *93*
15:22 *54, 74*
16 *57, 73, 78, 82*
16:1 *74*
16:2 *81*
16:2–3 *55*
16:3 *74*
16:4 *75, 81*
16:7 *81*
16:8 *81*
16:9 *81*
16:12 *75, 81*
16:13 *75*
16:15 *75*
16:16 *75*
16:18 *75*
16:21 *75*
16:33–34 *22*
16:35 *98*
17 *57*
17:2 *56*
17:7 *56*
18:21 *75*
18:25 *74, 75*
19 *216*
19:3 *62*
19:5 *58*
19:9 *112, 223*
19:11 *217*
19:16 *37, 89*
19:16–19 *217*
19:18 *89*
20:1–17 *157*
20:18 *217*
21:1 – 23:19 *157*
23:15 *78*
23:17 *185*
23:22 *218*
23:23 *98*
23:28 *104*

24 *108, 112, 156, 157, 159, 160, 189*
24:1 *217*
24:1–2 *217*
24:3 *64, 157*
24:4 *72, 157*
24:5 *157*
24:6 *158*
24:7 *64, 157*
24:8 *158, 159*
24:9 *110, 216, 217*
24:10 *110, 119, 159, 217*
24:11 *110, 159, 217*
24:13 *89, 121, 160*
24:14 *160*
24:15 *37, 89, 110, 112*
24:16 *109, 112*
24:17 *110*
24:18 *62, 108, 112*
25 *160*
25:3 *164*
25:7 *164*
25:8 *112*
25:10–22 *17, 233*
25:11 *40*
25:12 *237*
25:15 *232*
25:16 *22*
25:18 *40*
25:18–20 *37*
25:19 *241*
25:21 *22*
25:22 *22, 233*
25:24 *40*
25:31–36 *164*
26:1 *112*
26:6 *40*
26:29 *40*
26:31 *164*

26:33 *202*
27:9 *185*
27:13–15 *41, 164*
27:21 *185*
28 *40, 200*
28:4 *20, 200, 201*
28:30 *185*
28:31–32 *200*
28:32 *201*
28:35 *200*
28:36 *202*
28:40 *200*
29:5 *200*
29:35 *218*
29:45–46 *54*
30:6 *233*
30:23 *40, 232*
30:26 *232*
30:34 *40*
31:2–3 *53*
31:11 *218*
32 *109, 133*
32:7 *109*
32:8 *57*
32:10 *57*
32:15 *63*
32:20 *110, 133*
32:24 *110*
32:25 *109*
32:31 *57*
33 *108*
33 – 34 *87*
33:6 *89*
33:7 *18*
33:11 *122*
33:18 *89, 110, 121*
33:19 *89, 110*
33:20 *89, 91, 110, 122*
33:21 *89*
33:23 *89, 122*

34 *109*
34:4 *62*
34:5 *112*
34:5–6 *89*
34:12 *94*
34:14 *57*
34:28 *108*
34:29 *63, 119*
34:29–30 *111*
34:30 *112*
34:35 *111*
35:30–31 *53*
37:5 *232*
38:8 *185*
38:26 *76*
39:14 *72*
39:22 *201*
40:2–3 *232*
40:3 *231, 232*
40:5 *232*
40:6 *232*
40:9 *41*
40:16 *218*
40:21 *231*
40:22 *232*
40:24 *232*
40:26 *232*
40:29 *232*
40:34 *37*
40:34–35 *28, 37*
40:35 *18, 112*

Leviticus
1:4 *165*
1:5 *185*
1:15 *158*
2:1 *40*
2:1–2 *184*
4:7 *158*
4:20 *165*
4:32 *40*

5:6 *165*
6:25 *185*
8:10 *41*
8:15 *158*
8:23 *202*
10:9 *202*
12 *252, 254*
12:1–4 *247*
12:2 *247*
12:3 *250*
12:4 *252*
12:5 *247*
14:11 *185*
15:16–17 *167*
16 *161, 162, 164, 166, 190, 191, 193, 195, 197, 198, 202, 203, 230, 231, 239*
16:2 *21, 166, 169, 203, 231*
16:4 *202, 235*
16:5 *190, 191*
16:7–8 *190*
16:8 *193, 194, 196*
16:9 *190, 193*
16:10 *190, 191, 193, 194*
16:12 *163, 185, 231*
16:13 *163, 169*
16:13–15 *164*
16:14 *163, 165*
16:15 *163, 234*
16:15–16 *191, 193*
16:16–17 *231*
16:21 *193, 194*
16:22 *193*
16:23–24 *235*
16:24 *238*
16:26 *194*

16:29 *168*
17:11 *158, 165*
19:18 *157*
21:10 *202*
21:21 *40*
22:4 *167*
23:3 *82*
23:5 *82*
23:10–11 *78*
23:14 *40*
23:27 *161*
23:28 *165*
24:7 *40*
26:14 *64*
26:40 *132*

Numbers
1:3 *76*
1:4–16 *74*
1:46 *76*
3:4 *185*
3:7 *38*
3:7–8 *164*
3:9 *236*
3:12 *236*
3:12–13 *236*
3:13 *236*
3:38 *38*
3:45 *236*
4 *236*
4:1–20 *236*
4:5 *232*
4:15 *232, 237, 238*
4:20 *42, 237, 238*
4:32 *185*
5 *131, 133, 134, 135, 136, 137, 184, 185, 186, 187, 188*

Numbers (*cont.*)
5:11–31 *128, 132, 133, 184*
5:12 *132, 137, 184*
5:12–13 *128*
5:12–31 *133*
5:13 *129, 132, 184*
5:14 *132*
5:15 *129, 132, 138, 184*
5:16 *129, 185*
5:17 *128, 129, 130, 135, 136, 185*
5:18 *129, 130, 132, 134, 187*
5:19 *130, 132, 134, 186, 187*
5:19–21 *128*
5:20 *132*
5:20–22 *186*
5:21 *129, 133, 134*
5:21–22 *135*
5:22 *128, 134*
5:23 *128, 130, 134, 135, 187*
5:24 *128, 130, 134, 187*
5:25 *129, 132, 184*
5:26 *184*
5:27 *129, 130, 132, 133, 134*
5:28 *132*
5:29 *132*
5:30 *129, 132*
5:31 *130*
6:1–21 *133*
7:89 *18*
8:14 *236*
8:16–17 *236*
8:19 *236*
8:25–26 *164*

8:26 *38*
9:3 *82*
9:7 *40*
9:12 *168, 189*
9:15 *37*
11 *73, 78*
11:1 *81*
11:13 *74*
11:17 *54*
11:21 *74*
12:6–8 *107*
12:8 *122*
13:6 *102*
14 *103*
14:6–9 *102*
14:30 *102*
14:33–34 *54*
14:38 *102*
16:40 *185*
17:8 *22*
17:10 *22*
18:6 *236*
21:4–9 *7*
21:32 *104*
27:17 *74*
29:40 *218*
30:1 *218*
31:16 *132*
32:7 *94*
32:12 *103*
34:19 *102*
35:51–52 *98*

Deuteronomy
1:3 *218*
1:6 *89*
1:31 *52*
1:41 *218*
2:7 *54, 219*
3:20 *25*
4:1 *63, 64, 219*

4:5 *63*
4:10 *89*
4:12 *89*
4:14 *219*
4:15 *89*
4:38 *98*
5:1 *64*
5:4 *122*
5:27 *64*
5:31 *63, 219*
6 – 8 *58*
6:1 *63, 219*
6:3 *64*
6:5 *157*
6:13 *56, 57*
6:15 *57, 132*
6:16 *56*
7:2 *99*
7:12 *64*
8:2–3 *54*
8:3 *55*
9:9 *62*
10:2 *22*
10:8 *232*
10:10 *62*
10:16 *250*
11:23 *104*
12:28 *64*
13:18 *64*
15:5 *64*
17:6 *108*
18 *108, 117*
18:15 *64, 107, 108, 117*
18:18 *64, 107*
18:20 *65*
19:15 *108*
21:22–23 *212*
22:22–24 *131*
23:10–11 *167*
28:1 *64*

28:15 *64*
28:21 *94*
28:37 *133*
30:6 *250*
31:1 *62*
31:6 *219*
31:8 *219*
31:16 *132*
31:24 *62*
32:5 *52, 109*
32:6 *52*
32:16 *132*
32:18–20 *52*
32:20 *109*
32:45 *62*
32:51 *132*
33:8 *56*
34:1 *107, 146*
34:3 *146*
34:5–6 *107*
34:10 *107*

Joshua
1 – 6 *144, 145*
1:15 *145*
2 *140*
2:1 *140, 141, 143, 146*
2:1–21 *100*
2:2 *100*
2:2–3 *100*
2:3 *141*
2:4 *100*
2:10 *100, 145*
2:11 *100*
2:13 *142*
2:15 *141*
2:18 *141*
2:19 *141*
2:26 *141*
3:12 *140, 146*

3:15 *145*
3:16 *146*
4:2 *146*
4:4 *146*
4:8 *72, 140*
4:19 *146*
5:1 *98*
5:10 *141*
5:10–11 *146*
5:12 *98*
6 *140*
6:3–5 *147*
6:5 *147*
6:6–8 *149*
6:7 *147, 149*
6:9 *149*
6:11 *147*
6:13 *147, 149*
6:14 *147*
6:14–15 *147*
6:16 *147*
6:18 *147*
6:20 *147*
6:22 *141*
6:22–25 *100*
6:23 *141*
6:24 *41*
6:25 *142, 143*
6:26 *147*
7:6 *149*
7:24 *142*
9:3 *101*
9:3–4 *101*
9:5 *101*
9:7 *101*
9:9 *101*
9:12 *101, 102*
9:14 *102*
9:15–21 *101*
9:21 *101*
9:26 *101*

10:6 *101*
14 – 15 *102, 104*
14:6 *102, 103*
14:6–15 *104*
14:13 *104*
19:13 *257*
19:49–50 *104*
24:12 *104*

Judges
1:16 *146*
7:8 *25*
7:10 *180*
11:34 *171*
13 *16*
14:17 *251*
21:12 *187*

Ruth
4:21–22 *100*

1 Samuel
1 *16*
2:22 *185*
4:21–22 *233*
25 *124, 126*
25:1–38 *123*
25:2 *124*
25:7 *124*
25:8 *124*
25:11 *124*
25:13 *124*
25:16 *124*
25:25 *124*
25:37 *125*
25:38 *125*

2 Samuel
2:21 *180*
6 *19*
6:2 *19, 21*

6:3 *19*
6:9 *20*
6:11 *21*
6:12 *20*
6:14 *20*
6:15 *20*
6:16 *20*
7 *17–18, 19*
7:1–2 *19*
7:5–6 *19*
7:13 *17*
7:14 *17*
7:16 *17*
11:3 – 12:20 *103*
23:39 *103*

1 Kings
1:49 *25*
6 *41*
6:18 *164*
6:19 *41*
6:20 *40*
6:21 *40*
6:22 *40*
6:28 *40*
6:29 *164*
6:30 *40*
6:32 *164*
7:51 *41*
8:10–11 *28*
8:11 *37*
14:22 *132*
18:42–45 *69*
19 *87*
19:1–3 *89*
19:8 *89, 108*
19:11–12 *90*
20:29 *251*

2 Kings
2:5 *107*

2:11 *107*
2:13 *79*
2:15 *79, 107*
2:18 *107*
4 *82*
4:41 *77*
4:42 *76, 77*
4:42–44 *73,*
76–77
4:43 *77*
4:43–44 *80*
4:44 *77*
14:25 *257*

1 Chronicles
1 – 9 *209*
2:18 *102*
3:19 *27*
4:15 *103*
5:25 *132*
9:26 *41*
15 – 17 *19*
15:17–18 *19*
15:21 *19*
15:24 *19*
15:27 *20*
15:28 *20*
16:4 *20*
16:5 *20*
16:7–36 *21*
16:13 *21*
16:13–17 *21*
16:15 *21*
16:17 *21*
16:42 *20*
17 *17*
23:32 *38*

2 Chronicles
3:1 *182*
5:13 *20*

2 Chronicles (cont.)
7:3 *41*
8:15 *41*
12:2 *132*
35:3 *232*

Ezra
1 *28*
1 – 2 *25, 26*
1:1 *25*
1:1–3 *24*
1:2 *25*
1:3 *25*
1:5 *25, 26*
1:11 *25*
2 *26, 27*
2:1 *25*
2:2 *26, 27*
2:6 *27*
2:21 *26*
2:21–35 *26*
2:36 *26, 27*
2:40 *27*
2:59 *25, 26*
2:62 *26, 29*
2:68 *26*
3:2 *27*
3:8 *27*
4:3 *27*
5:2 *27*
6:16–18 *28*
9:9 *28*
10:2 *132*

Nehemiah
7:5 *26*
7:26 *26*
9:11 *93*
9:15 *81*
9:20 *53*
9:36 *28*

13:5 *40*
13:9 *40*

Esther
3:7 *78*
3:9 *25*

Job
3:8 *195*
8:17 *209*
9 *87, 90*
9:4–11 *88*
9:5–13 *89*
9:8 *95*
9:11 *88, 89, 91*
17:16 *137*
26:5 *95*

Psalms
2 *114, 117*
2:2 *114*
2:7 *108, 114*
2:8 *114*
2:9 *114*
2:11–12 *114*
18:4 *95*
22 *207*
22:1 *189*
22:1–2 *207*
22:3–5 *207*
22:6–18 *207*
22:18 *189, 207*
22:19–21 *207*
22:20 *171*
22:22 *208*
22:22–31 *207*
22:24 *207, 208*
22:29 *137*

30 *137*
30:9 *137*
31:5 *189, 208*
33:6 *69*
33:9 *69*
35:19 *189*
40:8 *22*
41:9 *189*
69:4 *189*
69:21 *189*
74:5 *209*
74:13–14 *95*
74:14 *195*
78 *73*
78:24–25 *75*
78:29 *75*
78:52 *74*
80:1 *21*
80:8–19 *152*
81:7 *56*
89:8–9 *70*
89:27 *45*
91:4 *18*
91:11 *56*
91:12 *56*
99:1 *21*
105 *21, 73*
105:40 *81*
106 *73*
106:19 *89*
106:39 *132*
107:23–29 *71*
110:1 *154*
114 *73*
114:3 *52*
114:5 *52*
118:22 *228*
118:22–23 *153*
139:7–8 *208*
139:8 *18*
141:2 *164*

Proverbs
6:22 *111*
9:1–5 *55*
17:8 *94*

Ecclesiastes
3:20 *137*
12:7 *137*

Song of Songs
1:8 *39*

Isaiah
5:1–7 *152*
6:6 *185*
7:6 *111*
7:14 *31*
9:1 *19*
9:18 *209, 210*
10:34 *209*
26:19 *249*
27:1 *195*
37:22 *253*
41:4 *90*
42:1 *108, 114*
42:1–4 *115*
43:10 *90*
43:25 *90*
46:4 *90*
48:12 *90*
51:12 *90*
52:6 *90*
52:13 – 53:12 *115*
53:10 *173, 210*
53:12 *189*
58:10 *241*
62:11 *253*
63:9 *53*
63:11 *53, 54*

63:14 *53*
65:15 *133*

Jeremiah
3:6 *132*
4:4 *250*
4:7 *209*
11:21 *65*
18:20 *111*
24:9 *133*
26:6 *133*
26:20 *65*
29:18 *133*
31:9 *52*
42:18 *133*
44:8 *133*
44:12 *133*

Ezekiel
8:3 *132*
16:38 *132*
20:27 *132*
34:17 *39*
37 *245*
37:9 *245*
40:6 *41*
43:5 *37*
44:8 *38*
44:11 *185*

Daniel
1:15 *222*
6:12 *25*
7 *116, 215*
7:13 *189, 215*
7:13–14 *116*
7:14 *215, 216*
9:6 *65*

Hosea
2:7 *242*

11:1 *44, 45, 46, 48,*
 52, 58

Jonah
1:2 *259*
1:3 *68, 256, 259*
1:4 *68, 256*
1:5 *68, 256*
1:6 *68*
1:8 *70*
1:12 *68, 256*
1:15 *68, 256*
1:16 *68, 69, 259*
1:17 *256*
2:1 *256*
2:2–6 *95*
3:2 *259*
3:4 *259*
3:5 *259*
3:7 *259*
3:10 *259*
4:3 *258*
4:5–8 *112*
4:8 *258*
4:9 *258*

Micah
5:2 *26*
7:15 *183*

Nahum
1:10 *209, 210*

Haggai
1:1 *27*
2:5 *54*

Zechariah
6:11 *27*
8:13 *133*
9:9 *144*

12:10 *189*
13:3 *65*
13:7 *189*

Malachi
4 *108*
4:4–6 *107*

NEW TESTAMENT

Matthew
1 – 2 *61*
1:1 *31, 65*
1:1–17 *16, 30–31*
1:2 *31*
1:5 *100, 143*
1:6 *31*
1:7 *257*
1:10 *257*
1:13 *29*
1:16 *31*
1:17 *31*
1:18 *31, 33, 65*
1:18–19 *30*
1:18–25 *30–32, 171*
1:19 *32*
1:20 *32, 33, 222*
1:20–21 *30*
1:21 *33, 46, 49*
1:22–23 *30*
1:23 *31, 33, 36, 58,*
 66, 220
1:24–25 *30*
1:25 *31, 33*
2 *6, 48*
2:1 *41*
2:2 *44, 48*
2:7 *48*
2:9 *37*
2:11 *40, 41, 42*
2:12 *48*

2:13 *44*
2:13–23 *44*
2:14 *47, 48*
2:14–15 *46*
2:15 *44, 52, 58*
2:16 *44, 46, 49*
2:18–25 *35, 36*
2:19 *47*
2:20 *47, 48*
2:20–21 *46*
2:21 *48*
3 – 4 *61*
3:13 – 4:11 *51*
3:16 *51, 53*
3:17 *58, 106, 171*
4 *54*
4:1 *51, 53, 54*
4:1–11 *58*
4:2 *54*
4:3 *52, 55, 58*
4:3–10 *51*
4:4 *55*
4:6 *52, 56, 58*
4:7 *56*
4:9 *56*
4:10 *56*
5:1 *62*
5:1–2 *62*
5:1 – 8:1 *61, 62*
5:6 *73*
5:17 *118*
5:17–20 *63*
5:20 *134*
5:21–48 *63*
5:22 *65*
5:27–28 *65*
5:32 *65*
5:34 *65*
5:39 *65*
5:44 *65*
5:46–47 *142*

Matthew (cont.)
6:1 *63*
7:21 *65*
7:22 *65*
7:24 *63, 64, 100*
7:24–27 *63*
7:26 *63, 64, 104*
7:27–28 *62*
7:28 *62*
7:28–29 *65*
8:1 *62*
8:5–13 *99*
8:16 *83*
8:23–27 *67*
8:24 *67, 68*
8:25 *68*
8:25–26 *67*
8:26 *68*
8:27 *67, 68, 70*
8:28 *68*
9:10–11 *142*
9:25 *118*
10:2 *110*
10:4 *98*
10:38 *258*
11:19 *142*
12:38 *134*
12:40 *257*
12:41 *70*
14 *84*
14:13 *73, 74, 91*
14:13–16 *72*
14:13–21 *72, 91*
14:14 *73, 74*
14:15 *74, 83, 84*
14:17–20 *72*
14:18 *77*
14:19 *75, 78, 85*
14:20 *75, 77*
14:21 *76*
14:22 *87*

14:22–27 *87*
14:23 *83, 84, 87, 92*
14:24 *87, 94*
14:25 *88, 92*
14:25–26 *87*
14:26 *93*
14:27 *87, 90, 93*
14:28–31 *87*
14:30 *94*
14:30–31 *94*
14:31 *94*
14:32 *87, 94*
14:33 *87, 91*
15:9 *12*
15:21 *97*
15:21–28 *97*
15:22 *98, 99, 100*
15:23 *97, 99*
15:24 *99*
15:25 *99, 101*
15:26 *97, 99*
15:27 *97, 99, 103*
15:28 *97, 99*
15:32 *73, 74*
15:32–39 *72*
15:36 *75, 78*
15:37 *72, 75, 77*
15:38 *76*
16:2 *83*
16:13 *106*
16:13–14 *113*
16:15–16 *113*
16:16 *258*
16:17 *96, 257*
16:18 *110*
16:21 *113, 115, 225*
16:22 *225*
16:22–23 *115, 176*
16:23 *115*
16:24 *258*
16:24–26 *113*

16:25 *115*
16:27–28 *113, 115*
17:1 *106, 109, 118*
17:1–8 *80*
17:1–9 *106, 114*
17:2 *107, 111, 121*
17:3 *107, 111*
17:4 *107, 112*
17:5 *18, 107, 108,*
    112, 114, 122, 171
17:6 *107, 113*
17:7–8 *107*
17:8 *118*
17:9 *111*
17:10–13 *113, 118*
17:14–21 *109, 118*
17:15 *110*
17:17 *109*
17:22–23 *113, 118*
18:6 *94*
18:16 *108*
18:17 *142*
18:20 *220*
20:8 *83*
20:19 *225*
20:19–34 *145*
21:1–2 *146*
21:1–10 *144*
21:2 *146*
21:5 *144*
21:6 *146*
21:8 *147*
21:9 *147, 149*
21:23–27 *151*
21:28–32 *151*
21:33 *151*
21:33–46 *151*
21:34 *151*
21:35–36 *151*
21:37 *151, 152*
21:38 *152*

21:38–39 *151*
21:39 *153*
21:40 *151*
21:41 *151, 154*
21:42 *153, 228*
21:44 *154*
21:46 *151*
22:37–40 *157*
22:41–46 *154*
23:2 *134*
23:34 *152*
24 *116*
24:16 *149*
26:4 *173*
26:17–30 *156*
26:19 *84, 157*
26:20 *83*
26:26 *85*
26:26–28 *84, 156*
26:27 *158*
26:28 *159*
26:30 *171*
26:31 *189, 227*
26:35 *186, 258*
26:36 *162, 172*
26:36–46 *161, 170*
26:37 *162, 172, 175*
26:39 *162, 165, 174*
26:40 *167*
26:41 *172*
26:42 *165, 174, 181*
26:43 *167*
26:44 *163, 165*
26:45 *167*
26:47 *173, 177*
26:50 *174*
26:51 *176*
26:51–52 *176*
26:53 *175, 176*
26:54 *176*
26:55 *173*

26:56 *227*
26:57 – 27:56 *189,*
  205
26:59 *173*
26:60 *211*
26:63 *154*
26:64 *116, 189*
26:65 *202*
26:69–75 *184*
26:72 *187*
26:74 *186, 187*
26:75 *187*
27:1 *173*
27:2 *154, 175*
27:12 *211*
27:15 *190, 193*
27:16 *190, 192*
27:17 *192*
27:18 *154, 190*
27:20 *173, 190*
27:21 *190, 193, 197*
27:24 *199, 211*
27:25 *199*
27:26 *190, 197*
27:34 *189, 202*
27:35 *200*
27:37 *202*
27:38 *211*
27:40 *106*
27:44 *211*
27:46 *189, 206, 209*
27:51 *202*
27:57 *83*
27:60 *232*
27:66 *231*
28 *214, 215, 218*
28:1 *247*
28:8 *249*
28:9 *238*
28:10 *217*
28:16 *214, 216*

28:16-20 *214, 215,*
  216, 219, 221
28:17 *214, 217*
28:18 *215*
28:18–19 *215*
28:18–20 *215*
28:19 *220*
28:19–20 *217*
28:20 *218, 219,*
  220, 253

Mark
1:9-13 *51*
1:10 *51, 53*
1:11 *58, 106, 171*
1:12 *51, 54*
1:13 *54*
1:19 *110*
1:21 *83*
2:16 *134*
3:16 *110*
4:35–36 *67*
4:35–41 *67*
4:37 *67, 68*
4:38 *68*
4:38–39 *67*
4:39 *68, 69*
4:41 *67, 68, 70*
5:1 *68*
5:6 *118*
5:35 *118*
5:37 *118, 162*
5:39 *118*
5:41 *118*
5:42 *118*
6 *90*
6:30–37 *72*
6:30–44 *72, 91*
6:31 *74*
6:32 *73, 74, 91*
6:33 *74*

6:34 *74*
6:35 *73, 74*
6:37 *77*
6:38–42 *72*
6:39–40 *75*
6:40 *77*
6:41 *75*
6:42 *75*
6:43 *72*
6:44 *76*
6:45 *87*
6:45–52 *87*
6:46 *87*
6:47 *92, 93*
6:48 *88, 89, 92, 94*
6:48–49 *87*
6:49 *93*
6:50 *87, 90, 93*
6:51 *87, 94*
7:1 *134*
7:11 *12*
7:21 *250*
7:24 *100*
7:24–30 *97*
7:25 *97, 100, 101*
7:26 *97, 104*
7:27 *97*
7:28 *97*
7:29 *97*
7:29–30 *97*
8:1–10 *72*
8:6 *77*
8:8 *72, 75, 77*
8:9 *76*
8:27 *106*
8:27–28 *113*
8:28 *117*
8:29 *113*
8:31 *113, 225*
8:34 *258*
8:34–37 *113*

8:38 *113, 115*
9:2 *106, 109, 162*
9:2–10 *106*
9:3 *107, 111*
9:4 *107, 111*
9:5 *107, 112*
9:7 *18, 107, 112,*
  114, 122, 171
9:8 *107, 118*
9:11–13 *118*
9:14–29 *109, 118*
9:19 *109*
9:20 *109*
9:21 *118*
9:22 *110*
9:23–24 *118*
9:26 *118*
9:27 *118*
9:31–32 *113, 118*
9:32 *225*
10:46–52 *145*
11:1 *145*
11:1–11 *144*
11:2 *146*
11:8 *147*
11:9 *147, 149*
11:12–14 *147*
11:20–21 *147*
11:27–33 *151*
12:1 *151*
12:1–12 *151*
12:2 *151*
12:3–5 *151*
12:6 *151, 152*
12:7 *152*
12:7–8 *151*
12:8 *153*
12:9 *151*
12:10 *153, 228*
12:12 *151*
13 *116*

Mark (cont.)
14:1 146, 173
14:12–26 156
14:15 156
14:22–24 156
14:27 189, 227
14:32 162
14:32–42 161, 170
14:33 162, 173
14:35 162, 165
14:36 174, 177, 181
14:37 167
14:38 172
14:39 165
14:40 167
14:41 163
14:43 173, 177
14:46 174
14:48 173
14:50 227
14:51–52 9
14:53 – 15:41 205
14:55 173
14:57 211
14:63 189, 202
14:66–72 184
14:71 186, 187
15:1 175
15:3 211
15:6 190
15:7 190
15:10 154, 190
15:11 190, 193, 198
15:15 190, 193
15:23 202
15:24 200
15:27 211
15:28 189, 211
15:34 189, 206, 209
15:38 202
15:39 106

15:42 84
15:46 232
15:47 232
16 223
16:5 9
16:6 232
16:9 222
16:9–11 221
16:9–20 214, 221, 262
16:11 223
16:12 222
16:12–13 221
16:13 223
16:14 221, 222, 223, 224
16:15 222
16:15–18 221
16:16 223
16:17 223
16:18 223
16:19–20 221, 224
16:20 223

Luke
1:5 19
1:5–25 16
1:10 164
1:26–38 16–17, 30, 171
1:26–56 16
1:27 17, 31
1:28–30 17
1:28–38 35
1:30 34
1:31–35 17
1:32 17, 27, 31
1:32–33 17, 29
1:33 32
1:34 17, 18, 31, 34
1:35 18

1:36 19
1:36–37 17
1:37 17, 34, 179
1:38 17
1:39 17, 19
1:39–56 16–17
1:41 20
1:41–44 17
1:42 20
1:43 20
1:44 20
1:45 17
1:46–55 17, 21
1:54 21
1:54–55 21
1:55 32
1:56 17, 21
1:57–60 250
1:58 251
1:68 34
1:69 31
1:73 32
1:78 34
2 27, 29, 39
2:1 24, 26
2:1–5 24, 25
2:2 26
2:3 25
2:4 25, 26, 27, 29, 31
2:4–5 17, 24
2:8 37
2:8–20 35
2:9 37
2:10 251
2:11 27, 31
2:16 36
2:17 42
2:21 251
2:40 34
3:21–22 51

3:22 51, 53, 58, 106
3:23 51
3:27 27, 29
3:31–32 100
4 54
4:1 51, 53, 54
4:1–12 51
4:2 54
4:3 52, 55, 58
4:3–12 51
4:4 55
4:6–7 56
4:8 56
4:9 52, 58
4:9–11 56
4:12 56
4:31 257
4:36 111
4:38 257
5:21 134
6:14 110
7:34 142
7:39 143
8:22 67
8:22–25 67
8:23 67, 68
8:24 67, 68
8:25 67
8:26 68
8:42 118
8:52 118
8:53 118
8:54 118
8:56 118
9:10–12 72
9:10–17 72
9:12 74
9:13 77
9:13–17 72
9:14 75, 76
9:16 77

9:17 *75, 77*
9:18–19 *113*
9:20 *113*
9:22 *113, 225*
9:23 *258*
9:23–25 *113*
9:26 *113, 115*
9:27 *172*
9:28 *106, 110*
9:28–36 *106*
9:29 *107, 111*
9:30 *111*
9:30–31 *107, 111*
9:31 *111, 115*
9:32 *111*
9:33 *107, 112*
9:34 *18, 112, 113*
9:34–35 *107*
9:35 *112, 114, 225*
9:36 *107, 118*
9:37–43 *109, 118*
9:38 *118*
9:41 *109*
9:43 *118*
9:44–45 *113, 118*
11:32 *70*
11:53 *134*
12:13 *123*
12:14 *123*
12:15 *123*
12:16–21 *123*
12:18 *123*
12:19 *123*
12:20 *123, 125*
12:21 *123*
14:27 *258*
15:1 *142*
18:22 *125*
18:31 *140*
18:33 *225*
19:1 *140*

19:1–10 *140, 145*
19:2 *142, 146*
19:3–4 *140*
19:5 *141*
19:6 *141*
19:7 *141, 143*
19:8 *140, 142, 143*
19:9 *140, 142, 143*
19:11–27 *9*
19:28–44 *144*
19:37 *147*
19:41 *147*
19:43 *147*
19:43–44 *148*
19:44 *147*
20:1–8 *151*
20:9 *151*
20:9–19 *151*
20:10 *151*
20:10–12 *151*
20:13 *151, 152*
20:14 *152*
20:14–15 *151*
20:15 *151, 153*
20:17 *153, 228*
20:19 *151, 152*
21 *116*
22:1 *141*
22:4 *111*
22:7–20 *156*
22:17–20 *156*
22:19 *84*
22:20 *159*
22:31–33 *184*
22:33 *186*
22:37 *189*
22:39–46 *161, 170*
22:40 *172*
22:41 *162, 165*
22:42 *181*
22:43 *166, 175*

22:44 *165, 166, 173*
22:45–46 *167*
22:46 *172*
22:47 *177*
22:52 *173*
22:53 *177*
22:54–62 *184*
22:57 *185*
22:61 *188*
22:62 *187*
22:63 – 23:49 *205*
23:2 *211*
23:18 *193, 198*
23:19 *190*
23:25 *190*
23:30 *150*
23:32 *212*
23:32–33 *211*
23:33 *205, 212*
23:34 *200*
23:39 *213, 238*
23:39–43 *211*
23:41 *212*
23:42 *212*
23:42–43 *227*
23:43 *212, 213*
23:45 *202*
23:46 *189, 208*
23:53 *232*
23:54 *84*
23:55 *232*
24 *224, 226*
24:1–12 *229*
24:9 *226, 228*
24:10 *229*
24:11 *226*
24:12 *229*
24:13–39 *214*
24:16 *225*
24:21 *212*
24:22 *226*

24:23 *226*
24:24 *229*
24:33 *228*
24:35 *225*
24:36–37 *226*
24:38 *226*
24:39 *226*
24:41 *215, 249*
24:46 *212*
24:49 *227*
24:52 *228*
24:53 *254*

John
1:1 *16, 246, 252*
1:1–18 *252*
1:11 *227*
1:14 *120, 160, 171, 246, 252*
1:17 *239*
1:21 *117*
1:25 *117*
1:28 *145*
1:29 *82, 158, 168*
1:29–34 *51*
1:32 *51, 53*
1:36 *82*
1:42 *94*
2:19 *72*
2:21 *121*
3:14–15 *7*
3:16 *171*
3:29 *188*
4:10 *136*
4:11 *136*
5:14 *127*
5:18 *252*
6 *80, 81, 82, 85*
6:1 *92*
6:1–7 *72*
6:1–15 *72, 91*

John (cont.)
6:4 *74, 82, 85, 91*
6:5 *74*
6:6 *79, 127*
6:8–12 *72*
6:9 *77*
6:10 *76*
6:11 *75*
6:12 *75, 76*
6:13 *72, 76, 77*
6:14 *117*
6:16–17 *87*
6:16–21 *87*
6:18 *87, 94*
6:19 *87, 93*
6:20 *87, 90, 93*
6:21 *87, 94*
6:24 *80*
6:25–59 *80*
6:26 *75, 80*
6:31 *81, 91*
6:32 *78, 81*
6:33 *81*
6:35 *81*
6:40 *81*
6:41 *22, 81*
6:42 *81*
6:43 *81*
6:48 *22, 81*
6:49 *81, 91*
6:50 *81*
6:51 *22, 81*
6:51–56 *82*
6:52 *81*
6:54 *158*
6:54–56 *85*
6:55 *81*
6:58 *81, 91*
6:59 *80*
6:61 *81*
7 *138*

7:38 *136*
7:40 *117*
7:45–52 *128, 134*
7:48 *134*
7:49 *134, 138*
7:53 – 8:1 *128*
7:53 – 8:11 *127,
   134, 262*
8 *131, 133, 136,
   137, 138*
8:2 *129*
8:3 *127, 128, 129*
8:4 *129*
8:4–5 *128*
8:5 *131*
8:5–8 *136*
8:6 *127, 128, 130,
   136*
8:7 *128*
8:8 *128, 130, 136*
8:9 *128, 129, 130,
   138*
8:10–11 *128*
8:11 *127, 129, 130,
   135*
8:46 *250*
8:58 *220*
8:59 *91*
9:13 *127*
10:17–18 *72*
10:30 *252*
11:11–13 *242*
11:25 *244*
11:53 *173*
12:1 *146*
12:12–19 *144*
12:13 *147*
12:14 *2*
12:15 *144*
12:33 *127*
13 *156*

13:1 – 14:31 *156*
13:2 *156*
13:18 *189*
13:26 *156*
13:30 *159*
13:33 *160*
13:34 *157*
13:36 *160*
14 *156*
14 – 17 *249*
14:2–3 *160*
14:3 *160*
14:7 *160*
14:8 *159*
14:9 *160, 252*
14:10 *160*
14:28 *160*
14:31 *156*
15:25 *189*
16:8 *136*
16:17 *249*
16:17–19 *248*
16:17–22 *249*
16:19 *249*
16:20 *249*
16:20–22 *248*
16:21 *248*
16:22 *249*
17 *161, 201, 237,
   238*
17:2 *237*
17:5 *120*
17:6 *237*
17:9 *237, 238*
17:12 *237*
17:24 *237*
18 *167*
18:1 *145, 161, 163*
18:2–3 *177*
18:3 *173*
18:3–12 *161, 170*

18:4 *167*
18:5 *167*
18:6 *167*
18:7–8 *186*
18:8 *167*
18:10 *176*
18:12 *175*
18:13 *184*
18:15 *184*
18:15–18 *184*
18:16 *184*
18:18 *184, 185,
   258*
18:19 *184*
18:19 – 19:37 *205*
18:24 *175, 184*
18:25–27 *184*
18:26 *163*
18:28 *127*
18:31 *206*
18:39 *190, 193*
19 *200, 202, 231*
19:1 *206*
19:5 *246*
19:6 *206*
19:16 *206*
19:16–18 *206*
19:18 *211*
19:23 *201*
19:23–24 *200*
19:24 *189, 201, 207*
19:27 *186*
19:31 *84*
19:34 *242*
19:36 *7, 168, 189*
19:37 *189*
19:38 *229, 231*
19:38–42 *229*
19:38 – 20:12 *229*
19:39 *232*
19:39–42 *229*

19:40 *232*
19:41 *231, 232, 240*
19:42 *232*
20 *229, 233, 236,*
 238, 241, 243,
 244, 251, 253
20:1 *229, 231, 232,*
 243, 244, 247
20:1–12 *229, 238*
20:2 *229, 230, 231,*
 232
20:3–5 *229*
20:4 *229*
20:6 *238*
20:6–7 *229, 235*
20:8 *229*
20:10 *229*
20:10–11 *240*
20:10–12 *230,*
 240
20:10–18 *240*
20:11 *234*
20:11–12 *230*
20:12 *234, 241*
20:12–13 *240*
20:13 *230, 231,*
 232
20:13–18 *230,*
 238
20:14 *240*
20:15 *231, 232,*
 240, 241, 242,
 244
20:16 *240, 242,*
 243
20:17 *240, 243,*
 244
20:18 *240*
20:19 *245*
20:20 *249, 253*
20:22 *245*

20:24–29 *247, 251*
20:26 *244, 251*
20:28 *245, 252*
21 *255, 257*
21:1 *255*
21:1–19 *255*
21:3 *255, 256*
21:7 *255, 256*
21:11 *256*
21:13 *256*
21:14 *257*
21:15 *257, 258*
21:15–17 *255*
21:16 *257, 258*
21:17 *257, 258*
21:18–19 *260*
21:19 *127, 255*

Acts
1:1–8 *253*
1:3 *247*
1:13 *110*
1:16 *177*
1:18 *177*
2:23 *173*
2:36 *155*
2:38 *227*
3:22–23 *117*
4:4 *149*
4:6 *184*
4:10–11 *227*
4:11 *153*
4:25–26 *114*
5:30 *205, 212*
7:31 *111*
7:45 *27*
7:46 *34*
9:36–43 *259*
10 *111, 258*
10:1 *259*
10:2 *260*

10:11–16 *259*
10:17 *111*
10:20 *259*
10:22 *260*
10:28 *259*
10:34–35 *260*
10:39 *205, 212*
10:42 *259*
10:43 *259*
11:2 *259*
11:9 *259*
11:18 *259*
12 *261*
13:29 *205*
13:32–37 *249*
13:33 *114*
18:19 *172*
21:4 *172*
25:12 *111*
28:3 *223*

Romans
1:3 *17*
1:4 *116*
2:28–29 *250*
3:21 *108, 158*
4:16 *210*
5:14–19 *243*
5:15–17 *244*
8:15 *174*
8:32 *170, 210*
9:4–5 *253*
9:7 *171*
9:27 *154*
9:29 *2*
11:5 *154*
11:26 *154*

1 Corinthians
5:7 *82, 168*
10:1–2 *95*

10:2 *52*
11:25 *159*
15:27 *2*
15:43 *116*
15:45–49 *243*

2 Corinthians
11:2 *188, 243*
13:1 *108*

Galatians
1:14 *12*
2:9 *157*
3:11 *2*
3:13 *205, 212*
4:6 *174*
4:29 *33*

Ephesians
5:31 *244*
5:31–32 *243*

Philippians
3:21 *116*

Colossians
1:18 *249*
2:9 *42, 121*

1 Timothy
3:16 *116*
5:19 *108*

2 Timothy
2:8 *17*
3:15 *187*

Hebrews
1:1–2 *118*
1:5 *114*
2:12 *208*

Hebrews (cont.)
3:1–3 *121*
3:5–6 *121*
4:8 *27*
4:14 *22, 230*
4:15 *250*
5:1 *40*
5:5 *114*
5:10 *169*
6:20 *169*
7:1–22 *7*
7:16 *22*
7:26 *22, 169*
8:1 *169*
8:6 *157*
9:4 *22, 233*
9:5 *233*
9:7 *203*
9:8 *203*

9:11–12 *168, 203*
9:12 *235*
9:15 *22, 157*
9:22 *193*
9:24 *254*
10:4 *165*
10:5–7 *22*
10:10 *230*
10:19–22 *204*
10:20 *230*
11:17 *170, 172*
11:18 *171*
11:31 *100, 141, 143*
12:24 *157*
13:10 *230*

James
2 *143*
2:21 *170*

2:25 *143*
5:10 *65*
5:17 *69*

1 Peter
1:18–19 *7*
1:19 *82*
2:7 *153*
2:24 *205*

2 Peter
1:15 *115*
1:16 *108*
1:21 *7*

1 John
2:2 *235*
4:9 *171*
4:10 *235*

Jude
9 *107*
22–24 *107*

Revelation
1:5 *249*
2:27 *114*
5:6 *7, 82*
5:8 *164*
5:9 *7*
5:12 *82*
6:16 *150*
8:3–4 *164*
12:1 *253*
12:2 *253*
12:5 *114, 253*
19:15 *114*
21:9 *188, 243*
22:16 *17*